Beautiful Visualization

Edited by Julie Steele and Noah Iliinsky

O'REILLY®

Köln · Sebastopol · Tokyo

Beautiful Visualization

Edited by Julie Steele and Noah Iliinsky

Published by O'Reilly Media, Inc., 1005 Gravenstein Highway North, Sebastopol, CA 95472.

O'Reilly books may be purchased for educational, business, or sales promotional use. Online editions are also available for most titles (*http://my.safaribooksonline.com*). For more information, contact our corporate/institutional sales department: (800) 998-9938 or *corporate@oreilly.com*.

Editor: Julie Steele
Production Editor: Rachel Monaghan
Copyeditor: Rachel Head
Proofreader: Rachel Monaghan

Indexer: Julie Hawks
Cover Designer: Karen Montgomery
Interior Designer: Ron Bilodeau
Illustrator: Robert Romano

Printing History:

June 2010:   First Edition.

ISBN: 978-1-449-37986-5
[LSI]   [2013-07-19]

All author royalties from this book will be donated to Architecture for Humanity.

CONTENTS

Preface

THIS BOOK FOUND ITS BEGINNINGS as a natural outgrowth of Toby Segaran and Jeff Hammerbacher's *Beautiful Data* (O'Reilly), which explores everything from data gathering to data storage and organization and data analysis. While working on that project, it became clear to us that visualization—the practice of presenting information for consumption as art—was a topic deep and wide enough to warrant a separate examination. When done beautifully, successful visualizations are deceptive in their simplicity, offering the viewer insight and new understanding at a glance. We hoped to help those new to this growing field uncover the methods and decision-making processes experts use to achieve this end.

Particularly intriguing when assembling a list of potential contributors was how many ways the word *beautiful* can be interpreted. The book that founded this series, Andy Oram and Greg Wilson's *Beautiful Code* (O'Reilly), defined beauty as a simple and elegant solution to some kind of problem. But visualization—as a combination of information and art—naturally combines both problem solving and aesthetics, allowing us to consider beauty in both the intellectual and classic senses.

We hope you will be as delighted as we are by the diversity of backgrounds, projects, and approaches represented in this book. Different as they are, the chapters do offer some themes to the thoughtful and observant. Look for ideas about storytelling, color use, levels of granularity in the data, and user exploration woven throughout the book. Tug on these threads, and see where they take you in your own work.

The royalties for this book are being donated to Architecture for Humanity (*http://www. architectureforhumanity.org*), an organization dedicated to making the world better by bringing design, construction, and development services to the places where they are most critically needed. We hope you'll consider how your own design processes shape the world.

How This Book Is Organized

Here's a preview of what you'll find in this book:

Chapter 1, *On Beauty*, by Noah Iliinsky, offers an examination of what we mean by beauty in the context of visualization, why it's a worthy goal to pursue, and how to get there.

Chapter 2, *Once Upon a Stacked Time Series: The Importance of Storytelling in Information Visualization*, by Matthias Shapiro, explains the importance of storytelling to visualization and walks readers through the creation of a simple visualization project they can do on their own.

Chapter 3, *Wordle*, by Jonathan Feinberg, explains the inner workings of his popular method for visualizing a body of text, discussing both the technical and aesthetic choices the author made along the way.

Chapter 4, *Color: The Cinderella of Data Visualization*, by Michael Driscoll, shows how color can be used effectively to convey additional dimensions of data that our brains are able to recognize before we're aware of it.

Chapter 5, *Mapping Information: Redesigning the New York City Subway Map*, by Eddie Jabbour, explores the humble subway map as a basic visualization tool for understanding complex systems.

Chapter 6, *Flight Patterns: A Deep Dive*, by Aaron Koblin with Valdean Klump, visualizes civilian air traffic in the United States and Canada to reveal a method to the madness of air travel.

Chapter 7, *Your Choices Reveal Who You Are: Mining and Visualizing Social Patterns*, by Valdis Krebs, digs into behavioral data to show how the books we buy and the people we associate with reveal clues about our deeper selves.

Chapter 8, *Visualizing the U.S. Senate Social Graph (1991–2009)*, by Andrew Odewahn, uses quantitative evidence to evaluate a qualitative story about voting coalitions in the United States Senate.

Chapter 9, *The Big Picture: Search and Discovery*, by Todd Holloway, uses a proximity graphing technique to explore the dynamics of search and discovery as they apply to YELLOWPAGES.COM and the Netflix Prize.

Chapter 10, *Finding Beautiful Insights in the Chaos of Social Network Visualizations*, by Adam Perer, empowers users to dig into chaotic social network visualizations with interactive techniques that integrate visualization and statistics.

Chapter 11, *Beautiful History: Visualizing Wikipedia*, by Martin Wattenberg and Fernanda Viégas, takes readers through the process of exploring an unknown phenomenon through visualization, from initial sketches to published scientific papers.

Chapter 12, *Turning a Table into a Tree: Growing Parallel Sets into a Purposeful Project*, by Robert Kosara, emphasizes the relationship between the visual representation of data and the underlying data structure or database design.

Chapter 13, *The Design of "X by Y": An Information-Aesthetic Exploration of the Ars Electronica Archives*, by Moritz Stefaner, describes the process of striving to find a representation of information that is not only useable and informative but also sensual and evocative.

Chapter 14, *Revealing Matrices*, by Maximilian Schich, uncovers nonintuitive structures in curated databases arising from local activity by the curators and the heterogeneity of the source data.

Chapter 15, *This Was 1994: Data Exploration with the NYTimes Article Search API*, by Jer Thorp, guides readers through using the API to explore and visualize data from the *New York Times* archives.

Chapter 16, *A Day in the Life of the New York Times*, by Michael Young and Nick Bilton, relates how the *New York Times* R&D group is using Python and Map/Reduce to examine web and mobile site traffic data across the country and around the world.

Chapter 17, *Immersed in Unfolding Complex Systems*, by Lance Putnam, Graham Wakefield, Haru Ji, Basak Alper, Dennis Adderton, and Professor JoAnn Kuchera-Morin, describes the remarkable scientific exploration made possible by cutting-edge visualization and sonification techniques at the AlloSphere.

Chapter 18, *Postmortem Visualization: The Real Gold Standard*, by Anders Persson, examines new imaging technologies being used to collect and analyze data on human and animal cadavers.

Chapter 19, *Animation for Visualization: Opportunities and Drawbacks*, by Danyel Fisher, attempts to work out a framework for designing animated visualizations.

Chapter 20, *Visualization: Indexed.*, by Jessica Hagy, provides insight into various aspects of the "elephant" we call visualization such that we come away with a better idea of the big picture.

Conventions Used in This Book

The following typographical conventions are used in this book:

Italic

> Indicates new terms, URLs, email addresses, filenames, and file extensions. Also used for emphasis in the text.

`Constant width`

> Used for program listings, as well as within paragraphs to refer to program elements such as variable or function names, databases, data types, environment variables, statements, and keywords.

`Constant width bold`

> Used for emphasis within code listings.

`Constant width italic`

> Shows text that should be replaced with user-supplied values or by values determined by context.

Using Code Examples

This book is here to help you get your job done. In general, you may use the code in this book in your programs and documentation. You do not need to contact us for permission unless you're reproducing a significant portion of the code. For example, writing a program that uses several chunks of code from this book does not require permission. Selling or distributing a CD-ROM of examples from O'Reilly books does require permission. Answering a question by citing this book and quoting example code does not require permission. Incorporating a significant amount of example code from this book into your product's documentation does require permission.

We appreciate, but do not require, attribution. An attribution usually includes the title, author, publisher, and ISBN. For example: "*Beautiful Visualization*, edited by Julie Steele and Noah Iliinsky. Copyright 2010 O'Reilly Media, Inc., 978-1-449-37986-5."

If you feel your use of code examples falls outside fair use or the permission given above, feel free to contact us at *permissions@oreilly.com*.

How to Contact Us

Please address comments and questions concerning this book to the publisher:

O'Reilly Media, Inc.
1005 Gravenstein Highway North
Sebastopol, CA 95472
800-998-9938 (in the United States or Canada)
707-829-0515 (international or local)
707-829-0104 (fax)

We have a web page for this book, where we list errata, examples, and any additional information. You can access this page at:

http://www.oreilly.com/catalog/0636920000617

To comment or ask technical questions about this book, send email to:

bookquestions@oreilly.com

For more information about our books, conferences, Resource Centers, and the O'Reilly Network, see our website at:

http://www.oreilly.com

Safari® Books Online

 Safari Books Online is an on-demand digital library that lets you easily search over 7,500 technology and creative reference books and videos to find the answers you need quickly.

With a subscription, you can read any page and watch any video from our library online. Read books on your cell phone and mobile devices. Access new titles before they are available for print, and get exclusive access to manuscripts in development and post feedback for the authors. Copy and paste code samples, organize your favorites, download chapters, bookmark key sections, create notes, print out pages, and benefit from tons of other time-saving features.

O'Reilly Media has uploaded this book to the Safari Books Online service. To have full digital access to this book and others on similar topics from O'Reilly and other publishers, sign up for free at *http://my.safaribooksonline.com*.

Acknowledgments

First and foremost, we both wish to thank the contributors who gave of their time and expertise to share their wisdom with us. Their collective vision and experience is impressive, and has been an inspiration in our own work.

From Julie: Thanks to my family—Guy, Barbara, Pete, and Matt—for your constant support, and for being the first encouragers of my curiosity about the world. And Martin, for your companionship and never-ending flow of ideas; you inspire me.

From Noah: Thanks to everyone who has supported me in this particular line of inquiry over the years, especially my teachers, colleagues, and family, and everyone who has asked good questions and made me think.

## CHAPTER ONE

On Beauty

Noah Iliinsky

THIS CHAPTER IS AN EXAMINATION OF WHAT WE MEAN BY BEAUTY in the context of visualization, why it's a worthy goal to pursue, and how to get there. We'll start with a discussion of the elements of beauty, look at some examples and counterexamples, and then focus on the critical steps to realize a beautiful visualization.*

What Is Beauty?

What do we mean when we say a visual is beautiful? Is it an aesthetic judgment, in the traditional sense of the word? It can be, but when we're discussing visuals in this context, beauty can be considered to have four key elements, of which aesthetic judgment is only one. For a visual to qualify as beautiful, it must be aesthetically pleasing, yes, but it must also be *novel*, *informative*, and *efficient*.

Novel

For a visual to truly be beautiful, it must go beyond merely being a conduit for information and offer some novelty: a fresh look at the data or a format that gives readers a spark of excitement and results in a new level of understanding. Well-understood formats (e.g., scatterplots) may be accessible and effective, but for the most part they no longer have the ability to surprise or delight us. Most often, designs that delight us do

---

* I use the words *visualization* and *visual* interchangeably in this chapter, to refer to all types of structured representation of information. This encompasses graphs, charts, diagrams, maps, storyboards, and less formally structured illustrations.

so not because they were designed to be novel, but because they were designed to be effective; their novelty is a byproduct of effectively revealing some new insight about the world.

Informative

The key to the success of any visual, beautiful or not, is providing access to information so that the user may gain knowledge. A visual that does not achieve this goal has failed. Because it is the most important factor in determining overall success, the ability to convey information must be the primary driver of the design of a visual.

There are dozens of contextual, perceptive, and cognitive considerations that come into play in making an effective visual. Though many of these are largely outside the scope of this chapter, we can focus on two particulars: the *intended message* and the *context of use*. Keen attention to these two factors, in addition to the data itself, will go far toward making a data visualization effective, successful, and beautiful; we will look at them more closely a little later.

Efficient

A beautiful visualization has a clear goal, a message, or a particular perspective on the information that it is designed to convey. Access to this information should be as straightforward as possible, without sacrificing any necessary, relevant complexity.

A visual must not include too much off-topic content or information. Putting more information on the page may (or may not) result in conveying more information to the reader. However, presenting more information *necessarily* means that it will take the reader longer to find any desired *subset* of that information. Irrelevant data is the same thing as noise. If it's not helping, it's probably getting in the way.

Aesthetic

The graphical construction—consisting of axes and layout, shape, colors, lines, and typography—is a necessary, but not solely sufficient, ingredient in achieving beauty. Appropriate usage of these elements is essential for guiding the reader, communicating meaning, revealing relationships, and highlighting conclusions, as well as for visual appeal.

The graphical aspects of design must primarily serve the goal of presenting information. Any facet of the graphical treatment that does not aid in the presentation of information is a potential obstacle: it may reduce the efficiency and inhibit the success of a visualization. As with the data presented, less is usually more in the graphics department. If it's not helping, it's probably getting in the way.

Often, novel visual treatments are presented as innovative solutions. However, when the goal of a unique design is simply to be different, and the novelty can't be specifically linked to the goal of making the data more accessible, the resulting visual is almost certain to be more difficult to use. In the worst cases, novel design is nothing more than the product of ego and the desire to create something visually impressive, regardless of the intended audience, use, or function. Such designs aren't useful to anyone.

Learning from the Classics

The vast majority of mundane information visualization is done in completely standard formats. Basic presentation styles, such as bar, line, scatter, and pie graphs, organizational and flow charts, and a few other formats are easy to generate with all sorts of software. These formats are ubiquitous and provide convenient and conventional starting points. Their theory and use are reasonably well understood by both visual creators and consumers. For these reasons, they are good, strong solutions to common visualization problems. However, their optimal use is limited to some very specific data types, and their standardization and familiarity means they will rarely achieve novelty.

Beautiful visualizations that go on to fame and fortune are a different breed. They don't necessarily originate with conventions that are known to their creators or consumers (though they may leverage some familiar visual elements or treatments), and they usually deviate from the expected formats. These images are not constrained by the limits of conventional visual protocols: they have the freedom to effectively adapt to unconventional data types, and plenty of room to surprise and delight.

Most importantly, beautiful visualizations reflect the qualities of the data that they represent, explicitly revealing properties and relationships inherent and implicit in the source data. As these properties and relationships become available to the reader, they bring new knowledge, insight, and enjoyment. To illustrate, let's look at two very well-known beautiful visualizations and how they embrace the structure of their source data.

The Periodic Table of the Elements

The first example we'll consider is Mendeleev's periodic table of the elements, a masterful visualization that encodes at least four, and often nine or more, different types of data in a tidy table (see Figure 1-1). The elements have properties that recur periodically, and the elements are organized into rows and columns in the table to reflect the periodicity of these properties. That is the key point, so I'll say it again: the genius of the periodic table is that it is arranged to reveal the related, repeating physical properties of the elements. The structure of the table is directly dictated by the data that it represents. Consequently, the table allows quick access to an understanding of the properties of a given element at a glance. Beyond that, the table also allows very accurate predictions of undiscovered elements, based on the gaps it contains.

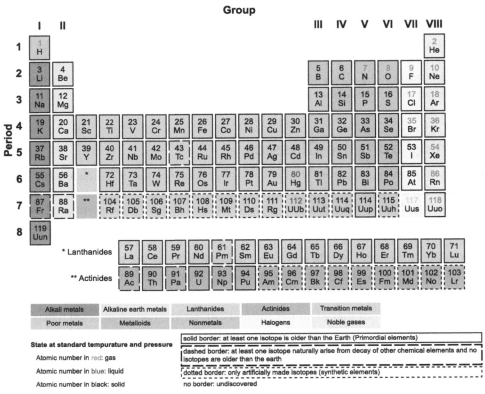

Figure 1-1. *A basic example of Mendeleev's periodic table of the elements*

The periodic table of the elements is absolutely informative, arguably efficient, and was a completely new approach to a problem that previously hadn't had a successful visual solution. For all of these reasons, it may be considered one of the earlier beautiful visualizations of complex data.

It should be noted that the efficacy and success of the periodic table were achieved with the absolute minimum of graphical treatment; in fact, the earliest versions were text-only and could be generated on a typewriter. Strong graphic design treatment isn't a requirement for beauty.

The London Underground Map

The second classic beautiful visualization we'll consider is Harry Beck's map of the London Underground (aka the Tube map—see Figure 1-2). The Tube map was influenced by conventions and standards for visuals, but not by those of cartography. Beck's background was in drafting electrical circuits: he was used to drawing circuit layout lines at 45° and 90° angles, and he brought those conventions to the Tube map.

That freed the map of any attachment to accurate representation of geography and led to an abstracted visual style that more simply reflected the realities of subway travel: once you're in the system, what matters most is your logical relationship to the rest of the subway system. Other maps that accurately show the geography can help you figure out what to do on the surface, but while you're underground the only surface features that are accessible are the subway stations.

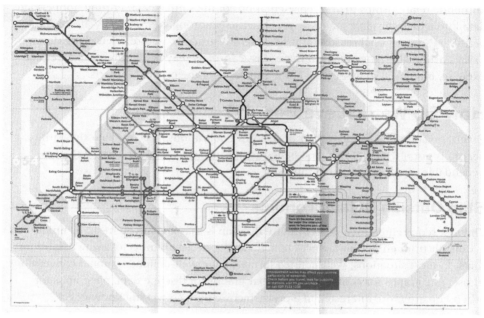

Figure 1-2. The London Underground ("Tube") map; 2007 London Tube Map © TfL from the London Transport Museum collection. Used with permission.

The London Underground map highlighted the most relevant information and stripped away much of the irrelevant information, making the pertinent data more easily accessible. It was executed with a distinctive and unique graphical style that has become iconic. It is widely recognized as a masterpiece and is undoubtedly a beautiful visualization.

Other Subway Maps and Periodic Tables Are Weak Imitations

Due to the success of the periodic table and the London Underground map, their formats are often mimicked for representations of other data. There are periodic tables of just about everything you can imagine: foods, drinks, animals, hobbies, and, sadly, visualization methods.* These all miss the point. Similarly, Underground-style

* See *http://www.visual-literacy.org/periodic_table/periodic_table.html.*

maps have been used to represent movies of different genres,* relationships among technology companies,† corporate acquisition timelines,‡ and the subway systems of cities other than London.

Of these examples, the only reasonable alternate use of the latter format is to represent subways in other cities (many of these—Tokyo, Moscow, etc.—are quite well done). All the other uses of these formats fail to understand what makes them special: their authentic relationships to and representations of the source data. Putting nonperiodic data into a periodic table makes as much sense as sorting your socks by atomic number; there's no rational reason for it because the structure you're referencing doesn't exist. Casting alternate data into these classic formats may be an interesting creative exercise, but doing so misses the point and value of the original formats.

How Do We Achieve Beauty?

Given the abundance of less-than-beautiful visualizations, it's clear that the path to beauty is not obvious. However, I believe there are ways to get to beauty that are dependable, if not entirely deterministic.

Step Outside Default Formats

The first requirement of a beautiful visualization is that it is novel, fresh, or unique. It is difficult (though not impossible) to achieve the necessary novelty using default formats. In most situations, well-defined formats have well-defined, rational conventions of use: line graphs for continuous data, bar graphs for discrete data, pie graphs for when you are more interested in a pretty picture than conveying knowledge.

Standard formats and conventions do have their benefits: they are easy to create, familiar to most readers, and usually don't need to be explained. Most of the time, these conventions should be respected and leveraged. However, the necessary spark of novelty is difficult to achieve when using utilitarian formats in typical ways; defaults are useful, but they are also limiting. Defaults should be set aside for a better, more powerful solution only with informed intent, rather than merely to provide variety for the sake of variety.

Default presentations can also have hidden pitfalls when used in ways that don't suit the situation. One example that I encountered was on a manufacturer's website, where its retailers were listed alphabetically in one column, with their cities and states in a second column. This system surely made perfect sense to whoever designed it, but the design didn't take into account how that list would be used. Had I already known the names of the retailers in my area, an alphabetical list of them would have been useful.

---

* See *http://blog.vodkaster.com/2009/06/25/the-top-250-best-movies-of-all-time-map/*.

† See *http://informationarchitects.jp/wtm4/*.

‡ See *http://www.meettheboss.com/google-acquisitions-and-investments.html*.

Unfortunately, I knew my location but not the retailer names. In this case, a list sorted by the most easily accessible information (location) would have made more sense than a default alphabetic sort on the retailer name.

Make It Informative

As I mentioned earlier, a visualization must be informative and useful to be successful. There are two main areas to consider to ensure that what is created is useful: the intended message and the context of use. Considering and integrating insight from these areas is usually an iterative process, involving going back and forth between them as the design evolves. Conventions should also be taken into consideration, to support the accessibility of the design (careful use of certain conventions allows users to assume some things about the data—such as the use of the colors red and blue in visuals about American politics).

Intended message

The first area to consider is what knowledge you're trying to convey, what question you're trying to answer, or what story you're trying to tell. This phase is all about planning the function of the visual in the abstract; it's too early to begin thinking about specific formats or implementation details. This is a critical step, and it is worth a significant time investment.

Once the message or goal has been determined, the next consideration is how the visualization is going to be used. The readers and their needs, jargon, and biases must all be considered. It's enormously helpful in this phase to be specific about the tasks the users need to achieve or the knowledge they need to take away from the visualization. The readers' specific knowledge needs may not be well understood initially, but this is still a critical factor to bear in mind during the design process.

If you cannot, eventually, express your goal concisely in terms of your readers and their needs, you don't have a target to aim for and have no way to gauge your success. Examples of goal statements might be "Our goal is to provide a view of the London subway system that allows riders to easily determine routes between stations," or "My goal is to display the elements in such a way that their physical properties are apparent and predictions about their behaviors can be made."

Once you have a clear understanding of your message and the needs and goals of your audience, you can begin to consider your data. Understanding the goals of the visualization will allow you to effectively select which facets of the data to include and which are not useful or, worse, are distracting.

Context of use. It's also important to recognize the distinction between visuals designed to reveal what the designer already knows, and visuals intended to aid research into the previously unknown (though the designer may suspect the outcome in advance). The former are tools for presentation; the latter are tools for examination. Both may take standard or unconventional formats, and both benefit from the same process and treatments. However, it is important to be clear about which type of visual is being designed, as that distinction affects all subsequent design choices.

Visualizations designed to reveal what is already known are ubiquitous, appearing wherever one party has information to convey to another using more than just text. Most graphs and charts that we encounter are meant to communicate a particular insight, message, or knowledge that is evident in the underlying data: how a team is performing, how a budget is divided, how a company is organized, how a given input affects a result, how different products compare to each other, and so on. The data might reveal other knowledge or insights as well, but if they aren't important for the purpose at hand, the design need not focus on revealing these other messages or trends. The process of designing these visualizations is therefore aided by having a well-defined goal.

Visualizations designed to facilitate discovery are commonly found in more specific, research-oriented contexts in science, business, and other areas. In these cases, the goal is typically to validate a hypothesis, answer a specific question, or identify any trends, behaviors, or relationships of note. Designing these visualizations can be more challenging if it's unclear what insights the data may reveal. In contexts where the shape of the answer is unknown, designing several different visualizations may be useful.

The periodic table is an interesting hybrid of these purposes, in that it was used to visualize both known and unknown information. The structure of the table was defined by the properties of the elements known at the time, so in that way it was a reference to existing knowledge, as it is used today. However, this structure resulted in gaps in the table, which were then used to predict the existence and behavior of undiscovered elements. In this latter mode, the table was a tool of research and discovery.

Make It Efficient

After ensuring that a visualization will be informative, the next step is to ensure that it will be efficient. The most important consideration when designing for efficiency is that every bit of visual content will make it take longer to find any particular element in the visualization. The less data and visual noise there is on the page, the easier it will be for readers to find what they're looking for. If your clearly stated goal can't justify the existence of some of your content, try to live without it.

Visually emphasize what matters

When you've identified the critically necessary content, consider whether some portion of it—a particular relationship or data point—is especially relevant or useful. Such content can be visually emphasized in a number of ways. It can be made bigger, bolder, brighter, or more detailed, or called out with circles, arrows, or labels. Alternately, the less-relevant content can be de-emphasized with less intense colors, lighter line weight, or lack of detail. The zones in the Tube map, for example, are visually deemphasized: they exist, but clearly aren't as relevant as the Tube lines and stations.

Note that this strategy of emphasizing relevance typically applies to presentation data, not research data: by changing the emphasis, the designer is intentionally changing the message. However, highlighting different facets or subsets of unknown data is a valid way to discover relationships that might otherwise be lost in the overall noise.

Use axes to convey meaning and give free information

One excellent method for reducing visual noise and the quantity of text while retaining sufficient information is to define axes, and then use them to guide the placement of the other components of the visualization. The beauty of defining an axis is that every node in a visualization can then assume the value implied by the axis, with no extra labeling required. For example, the periodic table is made up of clearly defined rows (periods) and columns (groups). A lot of information can be learned about an element by looking at what period and group it occupies. As a result, that information doesn't have to be explicitly presented in the element's table cell. Axes can also be used to locate a portion or member of the dataset, such as looking for an element in a particular period, southern states, or a Tube station that is known to be in the northwest part of London.

Well-defined axes can be effective for qualitative as well as quantitative data. In qualitative contexts, axes can define (unranked or unordered) areas or groupings. As with quantitative axes, they can provide information and support the search for relevant values.

Slice along relevant divisions

One last way to reduce visual clutter and make information more accessible is to divide larger datasets into multiple similar or related visualizations. This works well if the information available can be used independently and gains little (or infrequent) value from being shown in conjunction with the other data in the set. The risk here is that there may be relevant, unsuspected correlations among seemingly unrelated datasets that will only become evident when all the data is displayed together.

Use conventions thoughtfully

After the influences of the intended message, context of use, and data have been taken into consideration for your unique situation, it's worth looking into applying standard representations and conventions. Intentional and appropriate use of conventions will speed learning and facilitate retention on the part of your readers. In situations where a convention does exist, and doesn't conflict with one of the aforementioned considerations, applying it can be extremely powerful and useful. The examples we've examined have used default, conventional representations for element symbols, subway line colors, and compass directions. Most of these seem too obvious to mention or notice, and that's the point. They are easily understood and convey accurate information that is integrated extremely rapidly, while requiring almost no cognitive effort from the user and almost no creative effort from the designer. Ideally, this is how defaults and conventions should work.

Leverage the Aesthetics

Once the requirements for being informative and efficient have been met, the aesthetic aspects of the visual design can finally be considered. Aesthetic elements can be purely decorative, or they can be another opportunity to increase the utility of the visualization. In some cases visual treatments can redundantly encode information, so a given value or classification may be represented by both placement and color, by both label and size, or by other such attribute pairings. Redundant encodings help the reader differentiate, perceive, and learn more quickly and easily than single encodings.

There are other ways in which aesthetic choices can aid understanding: familiar color palettes, icons, layouts, and overall styles can reference related documents or the intended context of use. A familiar look and feel can make it easier or more comfortable for readers to accept the information being presented. (Care should be taken to avoid using familiar formats for their own sake, though, and falling into the same traps as the designers of the unfortunate periodic tables and Tube-style maps.)

At times, designers may want to make choices that could interfere with the usability of some or all of the visualization. This might be to emphasize one particular message at the cost of others, to make an artistic statement, to make the visualization fit into a limited space, or simply to make the visualization more pleasing or interesting to look at. These are all legitimate choices, as long as they are done with intention and understanding of their impact on the overall utility.

Putting It Into Practice

Let's look at one more example of a successful, data-driven visualization that puts these principles to work: a map of the 2008 presidential election results from the *New York Times*.* Figure 1-3 is a standard map of the United States, with each state color-coded to represent which candidate won that state (red states were won by the Republican candidate, blue states by the Democratic candidate). This seems like a perfectly reasonable visualization making use of a default framework: a geographic map of the country. However, this is actually a situation in which an accurate depiction of the geography is irrelevant at best and terribly misleading at worst.

Figure 1-3. *A geographically accurate electoral vote results map of the United States*

New Jersey (that peanut-shaped state east of Pennsylvania and south of New York that's too small for a label) has an area of a little more than 8,700 square miles. The total combined areas of the states of Idaho, Montana, Wyoming, North Dakota, and South Dakota is a bit more than 476,000 square miles, about 55 times the area of New Jersey, as shown in Figure 1-4. If we were interested in accurate geography and the shape, size, and position of the states, this would be a fine map indeed. However, in the context of a presidential election, what we care about is relative influence based on the electoral vote counts of each state. In fact, the combined total of those five states is just 16 electoral votes, only one more than New Jersey's 15 votes. The geographically accurate map is actually a very inaccurate map of electoral influence.

* Source: *http://elections.nytimes.com/2008/president/whos-ahead/key-states/map.html*.

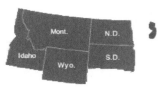

Figure 1-4. *Relative size of five states versus New Jersey*

The surface area of a state has nothing to do with its electoral influence; in this context, an entirely different sort of visualization is needed to accurately represent the relevant data and meet the goal of the visualization. To this end, the *Times* also created an alternate view of the map (Figure 1-5), in which each state is made up of a number of squares equivalent to its electoral vote value. This electorally proportionate view has lost all geographic accuracy regarding state size, and almost all of it regarding shape. The relative positions of the states are largely retained, though, allowing readers to find particular states in which they may have interest and to examine regional trends. The benefit of sacrificing geography here is that this visualization is perfectly accurate when it comes to showing the electoral votes won by each party and each state's relative influence. For example, when we look at this new map, a comparison of the size of the five states previously mentioned versus New Jersey now accurately depicts their 16 to 15 electoral vote tallies, as shown in Figure 1-6.

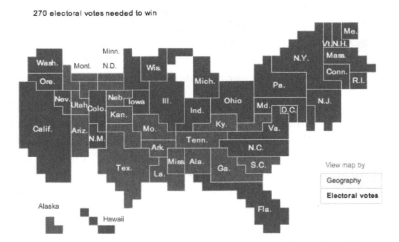

Figure 1-5. *A proportionally weighted electoral vote results map of the United States*

Figure 1-6. *Relative electoral vote influence of five states versus New Jersey*

You may have noticed that another trade-off was made here: because readers can't see the outlines of each individual square, they can't easily count the 15 or 16 squares in each of the areas we're comparing. Also, because a decision was made to retain the shape of each state to the extent possible, the aggregated red and blue blocks in Figure 1-6 are shaped very differently from each other, making it difficult to compare their relative areas at a glance. So, this is a great example of the necessary balancing act between making use of conventions (in this case, the shape of the states) and presenting data efficiently and without decoration.

The success of this visualization is due to the fact that the designers were willing to move away from a standard, default map and instead create a visual representation based primarily on the relevant source data. The result is a highly specialized image that is much more accurate and useful for its intended purpose, even if it's not very well suited for typical map tasks such as navigation. (In that way, it is similar to the Tube map, which is optimized for a very particular style of information finding, at the expense of general-purpose geographical accuracy.)

Conclusion

While this has been a brief treatment of some of the strategies and considerations that go into designing a successful visualization, it is a solid foundation. The keys to achieving beauty are focusing on keeping the visualization useful, relevant, and efficient, and using defaults and aesthetic treatments with intention. Following these suggestions will help ensure that your final product is novel, informative, and beautiful.

CHAPTER TWO

Once Upon a Stacked Time Series

The Importance of Storytelling in Information Visualization

Matthias Shapiro

THE ART OF INFORMATION VISUALIZATION is something of a strange beast. Very few disciplines require such a range of skills from their practitioners. The best visualizations not only require several talents, but may require their creators to move between these different talents quickly. Furthermore, during the process of creating the final visual, the creators may realize that certain information that was discarded early on is vital to a full understanding, or that a calculation made early in the process did not produce an accurate result.

In his exceptional book *Visualizing Data* (O'Reilly), Ben Fry identifies seven stages of creating an information visualization: acquire, parse, filter, mine, represent, refine, and interact. Each stage requires a certain level of technical or artistic talent, and information visualization necessitates the close integration of these talents. When acquiring and parsing the data, the information visualization artist may be imagining how to interact with it. As he refines the representation, he may recall a step in the filtering process that excluded data that turns out to be relevant. The best visualizations tend to be dreamed up and executed by either single individuals with abilities across a wide range of disciplines, or small teams working very closely together. In these small, agile environments, the full range of talents can intersect and produce a stunning image or interactive product that can communicate a concept in a way that is more natural to human comprehension than a string of digits.

While many of the talents required for creating good information visualizations are widely recognized, there is one that is commonly overlooked in more formal settings—probably because nearly every visualization author engages in it subconsciously and because it is such a natural part of the process that is hardly seems worth mentioning. This talent is the art of storytelling.

Stories have a marvelous way of focusing our attention and helping us to discern why the data presented is important or relevant to some part of our lives. It is only inside of a context that data is meaningful, and using the data as part of a story is an excellent way of allowing the data to make a lasting impact. The most effective information visualizations will make themselves a pivotal point in a story or narrative within the viewers' (or users') minds.

Not every information visualization requires a story. Some are simply beautiful to look at and can exist merely as fine works of art. However, most visualizations have a goal or purpose and present their data in a meaningful way, in the context of some kind of story.

Question + Visual Data + Context = Story

Most visualization stories begin with some kind of question that orients the viewer to the topic and context within which the data is most meaningful. This can be done explicitly or implicitly, but the context must be clear. The question contains the premise and introduction to the story, and leads us up to the point at which the data can take over the storyline.

Many of the key parts of a story are related as part of the process of placing the visualization in a context. We frequently find the visualization context as part of an introductory text to an infographic or visualization. The context provides information that answers questions such as:

- What data are we looking at?

- In what time frame does this data exist?

- What notable events or variables influenced the data?

Consider the visualization in Figure 2-1. Assuming the user is coming to this from a place of relative ignorance, we can be confident only that he will understand that the data is mapped along a timeline and that the timeline is in some way relevant to an election. Outside of that, there is almost no valuable context to guide the user in making sense of this visualization.

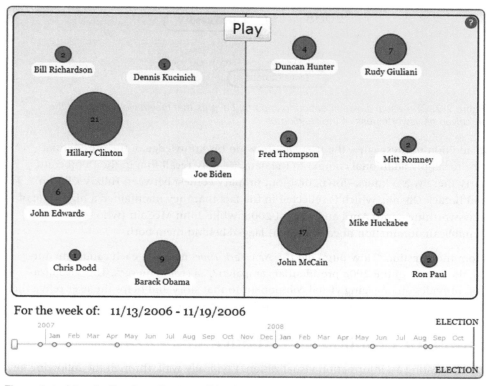

Figure 2-1. *Visualization from Designer Silverlight**

If we take a step forward and assume that our user is familiar with some of the more famous names on the visualization, we can assume he will know that this visualization measures some metric related to presidential candidates in the two years preceding the 2008 U.S. presidential election.

The full context is only revealed if the user clicks on the question mark in the upper-right corner, at which point he is informed that the visualization maps the number of times each presidential candidate was mentioned in the *New York Times* in a given week. Once this information is revealed, the user can see that this is a rough map of newsworthiness as determined by the *New York Times* writers.

Returning to the questions listed previously, we now know what data we're looking at and what the time frame is. This visualization is interactive: if the user presses the "Play" button at the top, dots along the timeline pop out to reveal important events that may have influenced the data one way or another (Figure 2-2).

* See *http://tr.im/I2Gb*.

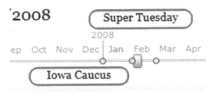

Figure 2-2. The visual draws attention to important events that may have influenced the perceived newsworthiness of the candidates

In addition to these cues, the user can draw on his knowledge of the presidential race to supply additional context to the data. He may recall that in the Democratic party there was a knock-down, drag-out primary contest between Hillary Clinton and Barack Obama, which is reflected in the fact that they maintained a high level of newsworthiness into April and May of 2008, while John McCain (who secured the Republican nomination in early March) lagged behind them both.

From the question "How often did the *New York Times* mention each candidate during the course of the 2008 presidential campaign?," a story emerges. This visualization provides an engaging visual component to that story and helps the user relive the drama of the two-year presidential campaign in the space of a minute.

Steps for Creating an Effective Visualization

When creating an information visualization, I typically walk through the following key steps:

1. Formulate the question.

2. Gather the data.

3. Apply a visual representation.

Formulate the Question

Asking the question that drives the story you're trying to tell is not necessarily a task that must be done at the beginning of the visualization journey. Don't feel bad if you start digging into the data before you have a finalized question in your head. Often, it is not until we have a good understanding of the data that we know how to ask a good question about it. However, asking a question (or at least keeping a question or set of questions in mind) can be useful when gathering and filtering the necessary data.

You may want to start with a topic to focus your data search and refine your question as you gather more data. For example, let's say we want to communicate that carrying out the U.S. Census is an enormous task. This is a good topic to start us out in our data search because it is broad enough that there are many pieces of data that can help give context to this idea. We could find the relevant data and create a visualization based on:

- The number of surveys filled out

- The number of pencils used

- The number of miles census workers walked

My favorite U.S. Census–related data to watch is the number of federal employees over time. Statistics show a spike of 200,000–300,000 federal employees between March and July of a census year. These employment figures then drop off as the census process completes.

The specific question that we ultimately ask will have a heavy impact on the final representation of the visual. For example, we might ask "How much paper does it take to record all the information necessary for a census?" and show sheets of paper covering a small city as a representation of the surveys, or we might ask "How many people does it take to count everyone in the country?" and use icons of people to represent the spike in federal employment figures at census time. These questions both relate to the original topic of the scope of the U.S. Census, but they draw from different sets of data and result in drastically different visuals.

When asking a question for the purposes of creating an information visualization, we should focus on questions that are as data-centric as possible. Questions that begin with "where," "when," "how much," or "how often" are generally good starting points: they allow us to focus our search for data within a specific set of parameters, so we're more likely to find data that lends itself to being mapped visually.

Be especially careful if you find your question starts with "why." This is a good sign that you are moving from a more formal portrayal of data into data analysis.

Gather the Data

Finding exactly the data you want can be a difficult task. Often, instead of trying to gather your own data, you're better off taking data that is already available and trying to find a way to portray it. That is, it may be better to start (as mentioned earlier) with a dataset and construct a question as you find patterns in the data. If you're creating a data visualization for a purpose other than as a hobby or out of pure curiosity, it is likely that you already have a dataset to work from. However, there are still several datasets available that may inspire or inform some aspect of your work.

There are many good places to start looking at data. One of the largest and most diverse repositories can be found at Data.gov (*http://www.data.gov*). This site houses an enormous collection of data, from migratory patterns of birds to patent bibliographies to Treasury rate statistics and federal budget data.

Other excellent sources of data include:

- The Census Bureau (*http://www.census.gov*) for a wide variety of demographic and geographic data

- The Bureau of Labor Statistics (*http://www.bls.gov*) for extensive data on employment in the United States (click on the "Databases and Tables" tab and scroll down to the Historical News Release Tables for the easiest access to the data)

- The New York Times APIs (*http://developer.nytimes.com*) for easy API access to huge sets of data including congressional votes, bestseller lists, article searches, movie reviews, real estate listings and sales in New York City, and more

Once you have the raw data, you may want parse it, organize it, group it, or otherwise alter it so that you can identify patterns or extract the specific information you wish to portray. This process is known as "data munging" and is usually an ad hoc attempt to "play around" with the data until interesting patterns emerge. If this process sounds a little opaque or nonspecific, don't worry; we'll walk through an example of data munging in the hands-on tutorial in the next section.

Apply a Visual Representation

Now that we have the data, we come to the task of deciding how to portray it. This means making decisions about what kind of visual representation of the data will aid viewers in understanding it.

A visual representation is some kind of visual dimension that can change in correspondence to the data. For example: an *XY* graph is a simple visual presentation that maps an *x, y* data point in a two-dimensional plane. Map enough points, and an obvious visual pattern may emerge even if there is no immediately identifiable pattern in the raw data itself.

Let's take a look at the most commonly used visual representations.

Size

Size is probably the most commonly used visual representation, and for good reason. When differentiating between two objects, we can judge very quickly between sizes. Moreover, using size helps cut through the fog of comparing two unfamiliar numbers. It is one thing to hear or read that methadone is the most lethal recreational drug in the UK and quite another to see that information in the context of deaths caused by other dangerous drugs, as shown in Figure 2-3.

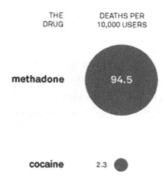

THE
DRUG

DEATHS PER
10,000 USERS

methadone   94.5

cocaine   2.3

Figure 2-3. *From David McCandless's information visualization "World's Deadliest Drugs"*

While size is an extremely useful and intuitive representation, it is also often overused. Many poorly constructed graphs misinform and confuse simply because their creators wanted to visualize some data, but knew of only one way to visually present it.

Color

Color is a fantastic representation method for enormous sets of data. We can identify many gradations and shades of color and can see differences in a high resolution. This makes color a natural choice for representing big-picture trends, like what we might see in weather maps. For this reason, it is commonly used for identifying patterns and anomalies in large datasets.

Figure 2-4 is a zoomed-out view of a set of data about stocks over the course of just over three months.

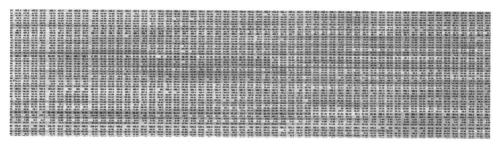

Figure 2-4. *The 30 most watched Motley Fool CAPS stocks tracked over several months and visualized using a red-to-green color scale*

Even though the type is far too small to read, we can easily recognize rows that show positive or negative growth. We can also make an overall assessment of the trends in the data with very little intellectual effort expended.

Color is less useful for smaller datasets or data that is differentiated by small ranges. If there are not stark ranges in the data, it can be difficult for even a trained eye to spot important differences.

As an example, let's assume a dataset with a range between 1 and 100 and a color scheme that ranges from red (representing 1) to yellow (50) to green (100). In such a scheme, consider the 10-point difference in Figure 2-5. As you can see, the difference is subtle and may not be easily distinguishable to many viewers.

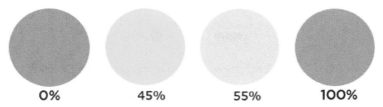

Figure 2-5. *Color image representing the difference between 45% and 55% in a color visualization*

If you're creating a visualization in which it is important for viewers to be able to distinguish between data points at 45% and 55%, you may need to alter the points at which the colors change or steer away from using color as your primary representation method.

A word should also be put in for those who suffer from colorblindness, which affects nearly 1 out of 10 individuals. If you need your visualization to reach the largest possible audience, you may want to consider using ranges like black-to-white instead of green-to-red. For more information about design and colorblindness, consider visiting We Are Colorblind (*http://wearecolorblind.com*), a website devoted to designing in a way that is accessible to the colorblind.

Location

A location representation method attaches data to some kind of map or visual element corresponding to a real or virtual place. An everyday example of a locative visualization is when we are presented with a simple outline of an airplane or a theater in order to choose a seat.

In Figure 2-6, we see the county-by-county crime rates for 1996 and 2008 rendered onto a map of Florida.

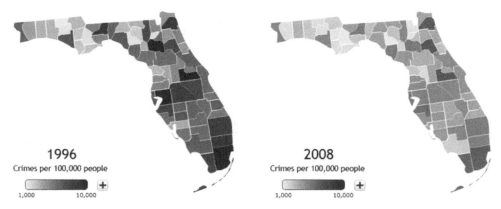

1996
Crimes per 100,000 people

1,000   10,000

2008
Crimes per 100,000 people

1,000   10,000

Figure 2-6. *Florida county map shaded to indicate crime rate by county*

Location presentation methods are especially valuable when the audience has some familiarity with the location being portrayed. Such familiarity allows the audience members to project their personal contexts onto the visualization and draw conclusions based on their personal experience with the area.

Networks

A network presentation shows binary connections between data points and can be helpful in viewing the relationships between those data points. A number of online network visualizations have sprung up that allow people to see maps of their friends on Facebook or their followers on Twitter.

Figure 2-7 shows a network visualization of my Facebook friends and how many of them have "friended" one another.

Through this network mapping, we can perceive at a glance the different social networks to which I belong (or belonged). Furthermore, the density of the groups corresponds fairly well to the social intimacy of those groups.

One thing to keep in mind with network visualizations is that if they are not carefully constructed, the thousands of data points may just turn into a visually messy glob of connections that isn't helpful in increasing our understanding of how those connections are meaningful.

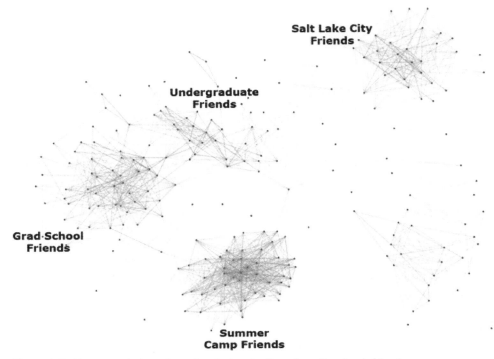

Salt Lake City Friends

Undergraduate Friends

Grad-School Friends

Summer Camp Friends

Figure 2-7. *Nexus rendering of a network visualization of my Facebook friends*

Time

Data that changes over time (stock quotes, poll results, etc.) is traditionally portrayed along a timeline. In recent years, though, software with animation capabilities has allowed us to portray such data in a different manner. Animations like the *New York Times*'s "Twitter Chatter During the Super Bowl"* (shown in Figure 2-8) compress a longer period of time so that we can watch the data change in an accelerated environment.

Pressing the "Play" button in the top-left corner starts the animation, and the most popular words used in Super Bowl–related tweets across the country grow and shrink according to their frequency of use through the course of the game.

This visualization gives users a series of helpful contextual clues along the timeline indicating when major events happened in the game. By doing this, the authors provide valuable context and relieve the users from the task of remembering how the game played out. Instead, they can focus on the words being used in tweets across the country and let the application alert them when a key event is driving the data.

* See *http://www.nytimes.com/interactive/2009/02/02/sports/20090202_superbowl_twitter.html.*

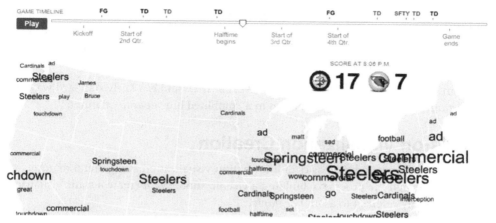

Figure 2-8. *New York Times visualization of commonly used words in 2009 Super Bowl–related tweets*

Using multiple visual presentation methods

Many excellent information visualizations use more than one of these visual presentation methods to give a full picture of the data. In the online application *NameVoyager* (*http://www.babynamewizard.com/voyager*), users can type in the first few letters of a name and see a history of how many people have given their child a name beginning with those letters (Figure 2-9).

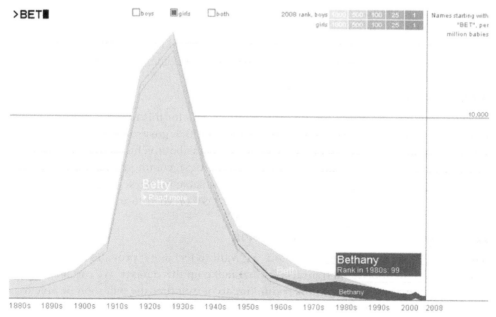

Figure 2-9. *The NameVoyager baby name explorer charts name frequency by year*

Here, two visual dimensions are presented. The first is time: we see the frequency with which names beginning with the entered letters were used represented along a timeline. The second is size: shaded areas on the graph indicate how many children were given certain names in certain years.

This particular type of graph is called a *stacked time series* and is a fairly standard way of visualizing several pieces of information in a combined but separate manner.

Hands-on Visualization Creation

Now that we've covered the basics of information visualization in a general manner, let's walk through the process of building a visualization. We'll create a static visualization, commonly referred to as an *infographic*.

To do this walkthrough, we will need the following tools:

- Microsoft Excel (or Google Documents in a pinch)
- Adobe Photoshop (GIMP, a free image-manipulation program, will also work)

In order to replicate the process as closely as possible, I'll walk through the discovery process in the order in which it actually happened rather than following the "Question-Data-Presentation" method described earlier.

Data Tasks

When constructing this tutorial visualization, I started out messing around with the data and formulated the question as the shape of the information became clear. Because the process of sifting through data is often very ad hoc, I'll simply describe my discovery in general terms. We'll walk through the details later in this section.

Gathering the data

I decided to use easily accessible, publicly available data for this tutorial, so I started looking at a number of pieces of data collected by the U.S. government and placed online in the interest of transparency. I settled on data about vehicles traded in and purchased via the Car Allowance Rebate System (CARS), commonly referred to as the "Cash for Clunkers" program. The data I used is available in two separate Excel files at *http://www.cars.gov/carsreport*. It is also available in CSV or MDB format.

Sorting the data: The discovery version

When we're done with this visualization, we want to feel like it provides some kind of insight into the individual transactions that make up this dataset. We can imagine someone driving in a beat-up clunker thinking to herself that she will soon be able to rid herself of her old, inefficient vehicle and replace it with a beautiful new one.

What kind of vehicle is she driving? Is she looking to replace it with something similar but newer and more efficient (an "old sedan to new sedan" trade)? Or does she want to swap her vehicle for something totally different (a trade more along the lines of "SUV for two-door coupe")?

The data we're looking at is the result of over 650,000 individual stories that each required motivation, drive, time, and effort to report. We won't be able to tease out those individual stories from the data, but our visualization will help tell a larger story about those people's choices. Our goal is to find a way to tell a story that is interesting and new to our users/viewers.

Here are the steps I took in sorting and filtering through the data as I was trying to discover that story.

After downloading the dataset, I started looking at the trade-in data and tried to group it in many different ways. Grouping it by car model seemed interesting at first, but this was somewhat tedious because the vehicles are grouped by engine and transmission type, so the same model might have several different entries.

However, in the process of looking at the vehicles by model, I was struck by the fact that several makes had a fairly high number of trade-ins. I became curious to see if people were more eager to trade one make of vehicle over another, so I began sorting the vehicles by make.

Warning: Asking questions like "are people eager to trade in one make over another?" is a dangerous thing to do when creating a visualization. The data can tell us a large number of things, but it is rare that data will give us good information on things that are as complex as human motivation. It is one thing to portray the data as it is and another thing to interpret what the data means. It would be a mistake to state as a part of your visualization that, because more Ford vehicles were traded in than any other make, people were eager to get rid of Fords. Such a statement would dismiss dozens of important variables, including things like market share, type of vehicles sold, Ford's position in large vehicle sales, age of the vehicles, etc. It is a good rule of thumb to restrict a visualization to stating things that can be seen from the data alone and allow the users or viewers to draw their own conclusions.

With all of that said, asking these kinds of questions internally can be an effective driver for discovery, so don't shy away from asking them at this early stage—just shy away from answering them in the final visual.

I began sorting vehicles by make and tallying up the sums for the trade-in vehicles, and I thought it would be interesting to see a comparison of the makes of the trade-ins (Honda, Toyota, GM, Ford, Chrysler) versus the makes of the new vehicles purchased. As I started collecting that data, it became clear that there were so many vehicle makes, it would be difficult to clearly portray that many separate data points. As a result, I started trying to group by "parent make"—i.e., grouping together vehicle makes by the companies that owned those makes. For example, Lexus is a division of Toyota, so I grouped Lexus and Toyota trade-ins together under the parent company, Toyota.

Eventually, I decided that the most compelling portrayal of the information would be to group the makes together under the parent *country*. This approach has the benefit of reducing the number of data points to about a dozen, as well as grouping the information in a way that isn't immediately apparent in the data. By doing this, we're able to get a new and fresh look at the data.

Sorting the data: The technical version

Now that we've walked through the thought process, let's walk through replicating that process in the files.

If you download the Excel files, you can open them up and see that the data is arranged first by vehicle category (with trucks first and cars second) and then alphabetically by vehicle make (Acura, Audi, BMW, and so on). In order to sort the data for our purposes, the easiest thing to do will be to categorize the data by vehicle make. Later, we will determine which makes correspond to the various countries in which the parent companies are based.

To sort the data in Excel, simply select the New_Vehicle_Make column in the *new-vehicles* file or the Trade_in_make column in the *trade-in-vehicles* file and select "Sort & Filter->Sort A to Z." If Excel asks you if you want to expand the selection, accept that option.

You can add together all the cars purchased or traded for a particular make by entering =SUM(and using the mouse to select all the cells in the Count column for a particular make. As a method of checking your first attempt, add up all the Acura purchases. The result should be 991. Gather sums for all the makes and, if it helps you to look at the data, move the results to another page.

This is the perfect time to play around with the data if you're so inclined. Try to figure out which cars sold the best, or which year's models were traded in the most frequently. Even in a dataset as small as this one, there are dozens of interesting questions to ask. One of them might pop out at you and inspire a new and compelling visualization. At the very least, this is an excellent opportunity to practice looking at data.

There are many ways to sort this kind of data. It might be more efficient (and would certainly be impressive) to write a script or small program that walks through the CSV file and pulls the data into a summary file that is easy to look at. The reason for using Excel in this example was to try to help people who are not familiar with programming engage with the data and participate in creating visualizations.

Formulating the Question

At this point in the process, we should have a firm enough grasp of what we want to do that we can formulate a solid question for this visualization. Our question is, "In the 'Cash for Clunkers' program, what proportion of vehicles were purchased from manufacturers based in which countries?"

Within the context of this question, we can choose to establish a number of relevant pieces of information as an appropriate setup for the visualization, keeping in mind that our target audience may not be intimately familiar with the topic. Here are a few items that will help contextualize the data:

- The program cost $2,850,162,500 and provided money for 677,081 vehicle purchases.

- For each vehicle that was purchased, a vehicle was traded in and scrapped.

- The program ran from July 1, 2009 until August 24, 2009.

- Vehicles eligible for trade-in had to get less than 18 miles per gallon (MPG).

- Vehicles eligible for purchase had to get more than 22 MPG.

For the purposes of this visualization, we're most interested in the fact that there was a correspondence between vehicles purchased and vehicles scrapped. This creates an interesting balance (and hence a certain kind of drama) between the kinds of vehicles people wanted to get rid of and the vehicles they wanted to purchase. As we put together the data and visualization, we'll keep this balance in mind and orient the visuals accordingly.

With the question in hand, we have a solid basis for manipulating the data further by grouping and sorting it as guided by our question.

Grouping the data

This step takes a little bit of research. In order to group the makes by country, we need to find out which vehicle makes correspond to which companies. There are over 50 makes represented in these two files, so the research could take some time. In this task, Wikipedia is your friend since it will provide quick answers regarding the ownership of various vehicle makes (for example, Chrysler owns or owned six makes that are represented in this dataset) as well as the countries in which they are headquartered.

I've provided a helpful table containing this data, to save you time (Table 2-1).

Table 2-1. *Vehicles grouped by make, company, and country*

Make	Owned by	Country	Make	Owned by	Country
Jaguar	Tata	England	Hyundai	Hyundai	South Korea
Land Rover	Tata	England	Kia	Hyundai	South Korea
BMW	BMW	Germany	Volvo	Volvo	Sweden
MINI	BMW	Germany	Saab		Sweden
Mercedes-Benz	Daimler	Germany	American Motor	Chrysler	U.S.
smart	Daimler	Germany	Chrysler	Chrysler	U.S.
Audi	Volkswagen	Germany	Dodge	Chrysler	U.S.
Porsche	Volkswagen	Germany	Eagle	Chrysler	U.S.
Volkswagen	Volkswagen	Germany	Jeep	Chrysler	U.S.
Acura	Honda	Japan	Plymouth	Chrysler	U.S.
Honda	Honda	Japan	Ford	Ford	U.S.
Isuzu	Isuzu	Japan	Lincoln	Ford	U.S.
Mazda	Mazda	Japan	Mercury	Ford	U.S.
Mitsubishi	Mitsubishi	Japan	Merkur	Ford	U.S.
Infiniti	Nissan	Japan	Buick	GM	U.S.
Nissan	Nissan	Japan	Cadillac	GM	U.S.
Subaru	Subaru	Japan	Chevrolet	GM	U.S.
Suzuki	Suzuki	Japan	GMC	GM	U.S.
Lexus	Toyota	Japan	Hummer	GM	U.S.
Scion	Toyota	Japan	Oldsmobile	GM	U.S.
Toyota	Toyota	Japan	Pontiac	GM	U.S.
			Saturn	GM	U.S.

Keep in mind, however, that grouping the makes this way raises some questions about the data that we'll need to answer before we continue. For example, Jaguar is a quint-essentially British company with its headquarters in England. Nevertheless, it is owned by the Indian company Tata Motors. Should we categorize Jaguar as an English car or an Indian one?

The "correct" method of dealing with these kinds of questions is largely a matter of personal preference. The important thing to remember is to maintain consistency in the representation of this decision and to indicate to the viewer that you have made the decision one way or another. Usually, a footnote at the corner of the visualization is sufficient.

Applying the Visual Presentation

At this point, we should have all of our data in exactly the format we want: vehicles traded or purchased, organized by country. It's time to choose our visual presentation of the data.

We'll be representing two dimensions of information in this visualization. The first is the quantity of cars organized by country, and the second is a visual differentiation between cars purchased and cars traded in. The differentiation between purchased vehicles and "clunked" vehicles is an "either-or" differentiation, so there won't be any gradations in the information, which will simplify the presentation. To differentiate between vehicles purchased and traded, we can use a simple color method: red to represent "traded" and green to represent "purchased."

Since we're dealing with a few points of data with enormous variation, it makes the most sense to use size to represent the information. This presentation choice will call attention to the scope of this variation in an intuitive and compelling way. The easiest implementation will be to use circles or bars of varying sizes to represent the numbers of trades and purchases.

A note about area and circles

If we're using circles to represent the data, we need to remember that we're going to be varying the area, not the radius or diameter, of the circle. If we take the number of U.S. vehicles purchased (575,073) and choose to represent it with a radius of 50 pixels, we will use the following equation in Excel to determine the size of each of the other circles:

$$SQRT((US\_Baseline\_Radius^2 * Target\_Vehicles)/US\_Vehicles)$$

I'm taking the time to point this out because this is probably one of the most common mistakes when creating information visualizations with circles or with area in general. Scaling a circle by linearly increasing the radius or diameter will result in quadratic increases and decreases of the area of the circle, as shown in Figure 2-11; the correct relationship is shown in Figure 2-10.

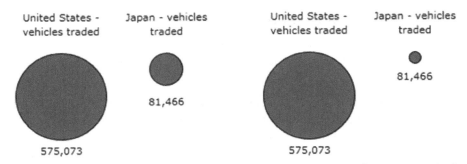

United States -
vehicles traded

Japan - vehicles
traded

81,466

575,073

Figure 2-10. *Correct (scaling the area)*

United States -
vehicles traded

Japan - vehicles
traded

81,466

575,073

Figure 2-11. *Incorrect (scaling the radius)*

Having said all of that, we're not going to use circles. Don't worry, I have a good reason.

Presenting the data with country maps

Since our information story centers on countries, we're going to use shape maps of the various countries and size those maps appropriately. This provides a couple of valuable additions to our visualization.

First, using the shapes of the countries will give this project a *visual hook*. If their home countries are on the list, the viewers will be able to pick them out immediately and it will draw their attention. Along these same lines, we will be able to hook into any emotions our users may have concerning their home countries or any other countries with which they are familiar. A hook like this makes it more likely that the audience will remember or recommend the visualization.

Second, using country shapes instead of circles will enable the visualization to communicate at a number of different sizes. Even at thumbnail size, the shape of a country is so recognizable that the users will know that the visualization has something to do with different countries. A set of circles reduced down to thumbnail size just looks like a set of circles.

Third, if we used only circles or bars, we would be reliant on text to convey the names of the countries in the visualization. This isn't necessarily bad, but comprehension time would be increased, as the users would have to read the text before they could understand the visualization. This would increase the risk of reducing the immediate impact of the visualization.

Finally, the audience is accustomed to seeing these different countries in the context of a world map where the relative sizes are always the same. Taking these familiar shapes out of that context and placing them in a context where South Korea is larger than Germany or the United States is smaller than Japan creates interest by violating expectations. Think of it as a "twist" in the plot of the story.

Having decided that we should use countries instead of circles, we need to find visual representations of the countries on our list. Our best bet on that count is to search for a country name along with the *.svg* file extension. SVG stands for scalable vector graphics and is an open standard for vector images maintained by the World Wide Web Consortium (W3C). It is a popular vector image standard, particularly for free images and maps, and many vector manipulation applications support it.

Wikimedia Commons (*http://commons.wikimedia.org*) has a number of free, high-quality maps in vector format. These maps scale very well and are excellent for this kind of project. Some of the countries that are hard to find can also be pulled from vector maps of the world that are available on Wikimedia Commons. These files can be opened as editable vector files in Adobe Illustrator or Inkscape (*http://www.inkscape.org*) or as bitmaps in GIMP. From Illustrator, the vector objects can be copied and pasted directly into Photoshop.

In the interest of simplicity, we'll display only countries responsible for a certain minimum (1,000+ vehicles) of either the traded-in or purchased cars. This means we should have maps for the United States, Japan, South Korea, Germany, Sweden, and the United Kingdom.

Once we have images of the countries we want, we're ready to size them for the final visualization.

Building the Visual

Having moved the visuals into an image-manipulation program, we need to size them so that they appropriately represent the proportions of vehicles traded in and purchased.

My methodology for this is to take the largest piece of data (in this case, it is the number of U.S.-made vehicles that were traded in: 575,073) and scale it to a size that fits comfortably on the canvas of the infographic. This kind of anchor shape is just a practical way of making sure that none of the graphic elements becomes too large for elegant display. This piece of data becomes the anchor against which we will scale all the other elements.

Once we have the size of the anchor shape, we need to calculate how many pixels are in it. There is a trick available in Photoshop and GIMP that lets us easily count the pixels we have selected in a particular layer. Both applications have a window called "Histogram" that displays the number of pixels that are currently selected. Using this tool, we can determine the number of pixels in the anchor shape and calculate how many pixels our other shapes need to be using the following formula:

Target_Size = Target_Number * Anchor_ Size / Anchor_Number

For example, 81,466 Japanese vehicles were traded in. If we size the U.S. map so that it comprises 25,000 pixels, the equation for determining how large to make the map of Japan would be:

Japan_Size = 81,466 * 25,000 / 575,073 = 3,542 pixels

I generally use Excel to make these calculations so that they are easy to save, double-check, and replicate.

Using the Histogram trick, we can resize the irregular shapes of the target countries and scale them until they contain the number of pixels appropriate for the corresponding data point visualization.

I decided to arrange the countries along a vertical axis in order to accommodate the medium in which this visualization will be viewed (a page in this book). This approach also gives symmetry to the color elements and reinforces the green/red, bought/clunked dichotomy of the data.

We now have the core of our visualization done. Providing some context in an introductory blurb and adding a footnote about our decision regarding the country of origin for Jaguars and Land Rovers gives us the result shown in Figure 2-12.

This visualization now meets our criteria. It sets up the story with an introduction at the top, it provides a compelling layout that draws the viewers' attention, and it is instantly understandable. We've set up the "bought/clunked" dichotomy with color-coding and reinforced it with symmetrical physical placement (important if we want individuals who are colorblind to be able to understand our infographic). Our visualization tells what we hope is a compelling story in the minds of our viewers.

WINNERS & CLUNKERS

Between July 1 and August 24, 2009, the federal goverment provided 677,081 rebates to individuals who traded in an older, inefficient vehicle for a new fuel efficient one.

This is a visual of the countries from which vehicles were "clunked" and the countires that built the cars for which they were traded.

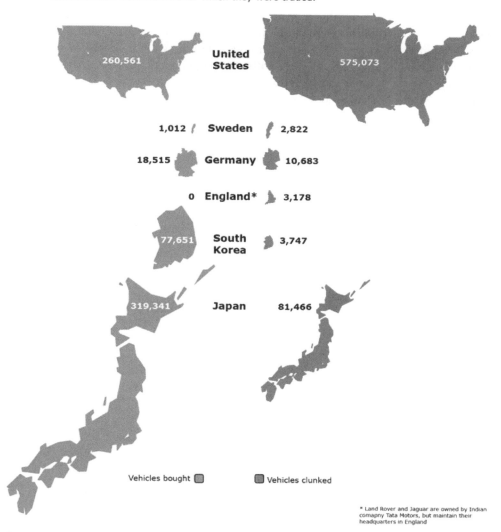

Figure 2-12. *Final visualization*

Conclusion

This tutorial has touched on only a small subset of the skills that can be used to create effective visualizations. A deeper foundation in fields like color theory, typography, computational data mining, and programming, as well as a background in the data subject, will all be valuable aids in creating compelling visualizations.

Despite the variety of fields that inform the visualization creation process, they are unified by the fact that every visualization is part of some kind of story. Even the simplest bar graph displaying a company's earnings data is drawing from information that is more memorable and more valuable within the larger context (perhaps a change in management style). It is these contexts and the stories that we associate with them that give visualizations their long-lasting impact and power.

## CHAPTER THREE

Wordle

Jonathan Feinberg

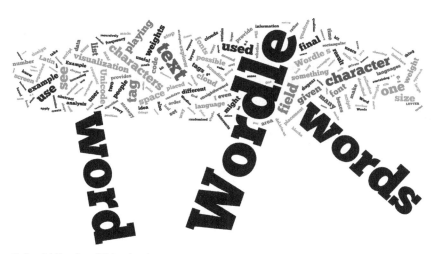

Figure 3-1. *A Wordle of this chapter*

BY NOW, EVEN PEOPLE who have never heard of "information visualization" are familiar with the colorful word collage known as *Wordle*, "the gateway drug to textual analysis."* Like any such drug, Wordle was designed for pleasure, although its roots lie in the utilitarian tag clouds popularized by such sites as del.icio.us and Flickr.

---

* See *http://www.profhacker.com/2009/10/21/wordles-or-the-gateway-drug-to-textual-analysis/*.

Wordle's Origins

In 2004, my colleague Bernard Kerr and I made a social bookmarking application, which Bernard named "dogear" (Millen, Feinberg, and Kerr, 2006). Any application that lets users tag content is bound to provide a *tag cloud*, a vaguely rectangular collection of clickable keywords. So, when we designed dogear, we made sure to feature a prominent tag cloud on every page (see Figure 3-2).

Figure 3-2. *The author's tags as they appeared in dogear*

I never found tag clouds to be particularly interesting or satisfying, visually. There's not much evidence that they're all that useful for navigation or for other interaction tasks, either.[*] But when blogger Matt Jones[†] posted his del.icio.us tags as a beautiful, typographically lively image (see Figure 3-3), I was thrilled. I thought that there was no reason why a computer program couldn't create something similar. At the very least, I wanted to end up with something that could—like Jones's cloud—put the dot of an "i" into the lower counter of a "g", something well beyond what tag clouds could do at the time.

---

[*] See *http://doi.acm.org/10.1145/1240624.1240775*.
[†] See *http://magicalnihilism.com/2004/07/04/my-delicious-tags-july-2004/*.

Figure 3-3. *Matt Jones's typographically aware tag cloud*

I spent a week or so creating the code for what I called the "tag explorer" (see Figure 3-4), a Java applet that permitted users to navigate through dogear by clicking on tags related to the current context.

Tags for Koranteng A. Ofosu-Amaah's politics bookmarks

Figure 3-4. *The dogear tag explorer**

---

* See *http://www.flickr.com/photos/koranteng/526642309/in/set-72157600300569893.*

It was immediately clear that the tag explorer was useful as a *portrait* of a person's interests, as when a number of my fellow IBMers used screenshots of the tag explorer to illustrate their résumés and email signatures (see Figure 3-5).

 Jonathan Feinberg
Senior Software Engineer
Collaborative User Experience
IBM Research
Cambridge, MA

Figure 3-5. *The author's 2006 work email signature*

When dogear became an IBM product,* the tag explorer did not go with it, and I forgot all about it. When I found the tag explorer code by chance a couple of years later, I thought it was worth developing.

The original tag explorer was intimately tied to dogear, and to the idea of tag clouds in general. I wanted to find a way to decouple the word-cloud effect from the whole idea of "tags," since the pleasing and amusing qualities of the word cloud seemed generally accessible, while "tags" were familiar only to a technologically sophisticated crowd. This led to the idea of simply counting words. Once I had decided to build a system for viewing *text*, rather than *tags*, it seemed superfluous to have the words *do* anything other than merely exist on the page. I decided that I would design something primarily for pleasure, in the spirit of Charles Eames's remark, "Who would say that pleasure is not useful?" This decision, in turn, made it easy to decide which features to keep, which features to reject, and how to design the interface (shown in Figure 3-6).

Paste in a bunch of text:

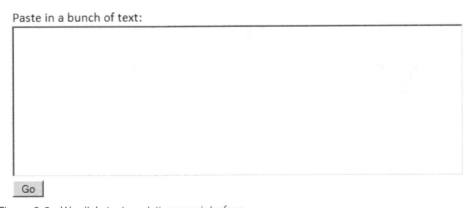

Go

Figure 3-6. *Wordle's text-analytics user interface*

Since Wordle (as it was now called) was meant to be pleasing, I had to give some thought to the expressive qualities of fonts and color palettes (see Figure 3-7).

---

* See *http://www-01.ibm.com/software/lotus/products/connections/bookmarks.html*.

Figure 3-7. *Wordle provides varied palettes, fonts, and layouts*

I believe that my efforts to simplify Wordle, and to emphasize pleasure over business, have been paid for many times over. Wordle has been used in ways I'd never anticipated, by far more people than I'd dared to expect. Some of Wordle's success is due to the design of the web application itself, with its one-paste/one-click instant gratification. However, to the extent that the design of the Wordle visualization itself has contributed to its ubiquity, it might be worth looking at what Wordle is *not* before we examine in detail what it is and how it works.

Anatomy of a Tag Cloud

The typical tag cloud is organized around lines of text.[*] If one word on a line is larger than another, the smaller word will have a disproportionate amount of whitespace overhead, which can look awkward. For example, see Figure 3-8, where "everett hey" has an enormous expanse of white above, because the line height is determined by its neighbor "everett everett".

lmar damn delmar delmar delmar everett delmar gopher delmar huh delr pping dropping dusty road dynamite nelson eckard pappy eighty-four years everett av verett everett everett hey everett hisses everett hm everett hold t rett sir everett snaps everett stares everett wears exchange glances faded stripes family farm fe eorge nelson gettin married gonna paddle gonna save gooc

Figure 3-8. *Lost in White Space[†]*

One way to mitigate the ragged whitespace caused by such extreme contrasts in size is to squash different word weights into a small number of bins, as del.icio.us does. In Figure 3-9, the "programming" tag has been used 55 times and "scripting" only once, but the font for the more frequently used word is only 50% larger. Notice also the use of font weight (boldness) to enhance the contrast between different word weights.

---

[*] For a thorough survey of tag cloud designs, with thoughtful commentary, see *http://www.smashingmagazine.com/2007/11/07/tag-clouds-gallery-examples-and-good-practices/*.

[†] See *http://manyeyes.alphaworks.ibm.com/manyeyes/page/Tag_Cloud.html*.

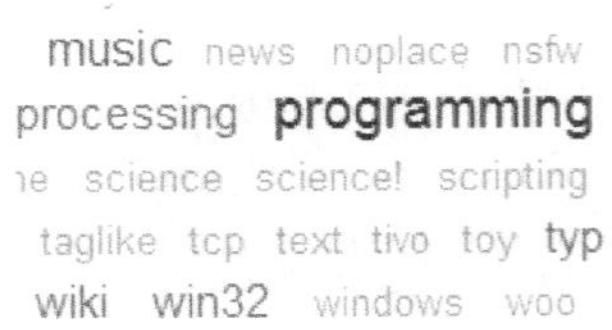

music news noplace nsfw
processing programming
science science! scripting
taglike tcp text tivo toy typ
wiki win32 windows woo

Figure 3-9. *Squashing the scale of differences between word weights*

In effect, del.icio.us is scaling the word weights—roughly—by logarithm. It's sensible to scale weights using logarithms or square roots when the source data follows a power-law distribution, as tags seem to do.*

Somewhere between these earnest, useful designs and the fanciful world that Wordle inhabits, there are other, more experimental interfaces. The WP-Cumulus† blog plug-in, for example, provides a rotating, three-dimensional sphere of tags (see Figure 3-10).

plugin
netbook
wifi
fix
Microsoft
Asus
themes
update
Software

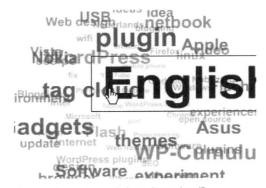

Figure 3-10. *WP-Cumulus: can't...quite...click on "tag cloud"...*

The desire to combine navigation with visualization imposes certain constraints on the design of a word cloud. But once we are liberated from any pretense of "utility"—once we're no longer providing navigation—we can start to *play* with space.

Filling a Two-Dimensional Space

There are lots of computer science PhDs to be garnered in finding incremental improvements to so-called *bin-packing* problems.‡ Luckily, the easy way has a respectable name: a randomized greedy algorithm. It's *randomized* in that you throw stuff on the screen somewhere near where you want it to be, and if that stuff intersects with other stuff, you try again. It's *greedy* in that big words get first pick.

* See *http://www.citeulike.org/user/andreacapocci/article/1326856*.

† See *http://wordpress.org/extend/plugins/wp-cumulus/*.

‡ See *http://en.wikipedia.org/wiki/Bin_packing_problem*.

Wordle's specific character depends on a couple of constraints. First, we are given a list of words, with associated (presumably meaningful) weights. We can't show any word more than once, and we don't want to distort the shape of the word beyond choosing its font size. If we remove those constraints, though, many other interesting and beautiful effects are possible.

For example, you can use a randomized greedy strategy to fill almost any region (not just a rectangle) as long as you have a set of words as a palette, from which you can arbitrarily choose any word, at any size, any number of times (see Figure 3-11).

Figure 3-11. *Do not underestimate the power of the randomized greedy algorithm*

Consider Jared Tarbell's exquisite Emotion Fractal[*] (see Figure 3-12), which recursively subdivides a space into ever-smaller random rectangles, filling the space with ever-smaller words. This effect depends on a large set of candidate words, chosen at random, with arbitrary weights.

---

[*] See *http://levitated.net/daily/levEmotionFractal.html*.

Figure 3-12. *Jared Tarbell's Emotion Fractal*

If you don't mind distorting your fonts by elongating or squashing the words as needed, other effects are possible. For example, Figure 3-13 shows a variation on the venerable treemap,* which uses text, rather than rectangles, to fill space. Each word fills an area proportional to its frequency; each rectangular area contains words strongly associated with each other in the source text.

Figure 3-13. *Word treemap of an Obama speech*

* See *http://www.cs.umd.edu/hcil/treemap-history/*.

It must be said that long before there were Processing sketches and Flash applets, people were exploring these sorts of typographical constructions in mass media and in fine art (Figure 3-14); we have been probing the boundary between letters as forms and letters as signs for a long time (Figure 3-15). The goal of these algorithmic explorations is to allow the wit and elegance of such examples to *influence* the representation of textual data.

Given this rather brief tour of the technical and aesthetic environment in which Wordle evolved, we're now ready to look at Wordle's technical and aesthetic choices in a bit more detail.

Figure 3-14. *Herb Lubalin and Lou Dorfsman's Typographicalassemblage (courtesy of the Center for Design Study)*

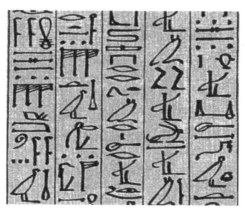

Figure 3-15. *Before we made pictures with words, we made words with pictures*

How Wordle Works

Wordle is implemented as a Java applet. Some of the technical details I provide here will be in terms of Java-specific features. Nothing described here is impossible in other languages, using other libraries and frameworks, but Java's strong support for Unicode text processing and 2D graphics (via the Java2D API) makes these things pretty straightforward.

Text Analysis

We'll now take a step back and consider some of the fundamental assumptions that determine Wordle's character. In particular, we have to examine what "text" is, as far as Wordle is concerned.

While this kind of text analysis is crude compared to what's required for some natural-language processing, it can still be tedious to implement. If you work in Java, you might find my cue.language library[*] useful for the kinds of tasks described in this section. It's small enough, it's fast enough, and thousands use it each day as part of Wordle.

Remember that natural-language analysis is as much craft as science,[†] and even given state-of-the-art computational tools, you have to apply judgment and taste.

Finding words

Wordle is in the business of drawing pictures of *words*, each having some *weight*, which determines its size. What does Wordle consider to be a "word"?

Wordle builds a regular expression (regex) that recognizes what it considers to be words in a variety of scripts, and then iteratively applies that regex to the given text, as illustrated in Example 3-1. The result is a list of words.

Example 3-1. *How to recognize "words"*

```
private static final String LETTER = "[@+\\p{javaLetter}\\p{javaDigit}]";
private static final String JOINER = "[-.:/''\\p{M}\\u2032\\u00A0\\u200C\\u200D~]";
/*
A word is:
    one or more "letters" followed by
    zero or more sections of
        one or more "joiners" followed by one or more "letters"
*/
private static final Pattern WORD =
    Pattern.compile(LETTER + "+(" + JOINER + "+" + LETTER + "+)*");
```

---

[*] See *http://github.com/vcl/cue.language*.

[†] For an illuminating demonstration of this craft, see Peter Norvig's chapter on natural-language processing in the sister O'Reilly book *Beautiful Data*.

A *letter* is any character that the Java `Character` class considers to be either a "letter" or a "digit," along with @ (at sign) and + (plus sign). *Joiners* include the Unicode M class, which matches a variety of nonspacing and combining marks, other pieces of punctuation commonly found in URLs (since Wordle users expect to see URLs preserved as "words"), the apostrophe, and several characters used as apostrophes in the wild (such as U+2032, the PRIME character). Wordle accepts the tilde (~) as a word joiner but replaces it with a space in the output, thereby giving users an easy way to say "keep these words together" without having to find the magical key combination for a real nonbreaking space character.

Determining the script

Having extracted a list of words (whatever we take "word" to mean), we need to know how to display those words to the viewer. We first need to know what characters we'll be expected to display, so that we can choose a font that supports those characters.

Wordle's collection of fonts is organized in terms of what *scripts* each can support, where a *script* is what you might think of as an alphabet: a collection of *glyphs* that can be used to visually represent sequences of *characters* in one or more languages. A given script, in Unicode, is organized into one or more *blocks*. So, the task now is to determine which fonts the user might want to use by sniffing out which blocks are represented in the given text.

Java provides the static method `UnicodeBlock.of(int codePoint)` to determine which block a given code point belongs to. Wordle takes the most frequent words in a text and looks at the first character in each of those words. In the rather common case that the character is in the Latin block, we further check the rest of the word to see if it contains any Latin-1 Supplement characters (which would remove certain fonts from consideration) or any of the Latin Extended blocks (which would bar even more fonts). The most frequently seen block is the winner.

To keep it responsive and limit its use of network resources, Wordle is designed to permit the use of only one font at a time. A more full-featured word cloud might choose different fonts for different words; this could provide another visual dimension to represent, for example, different source texts.

As of this writing, Wordle supports the Latin, Cyrillic, Devanagari, Hebrew, Arabic, and Greek scripts. By design, Wordle does not support the so-called CJKV scripts, the scripts containing Chinese, Japanese, Korean, and Vietnamese ideographs. CJKV fonts are quite large and would take too long for the average Wordle user to download (and would cost a great deal in bandwidth charges). Also, determining word breaks for ideographic languages requires sophisticated machine-learning algorithms and large runtime data structures, which Wordle cannot afford.

Unicode in a Nutshell

Since Wordle understands text in Unicode terms, here's what you have to know in order to understand some of the terms and notations you'll see here.

The Unicode* standard provides a universal coded character set and a few specifications for representing its characters in computers (as sequences of bytes).

A *character* is an abstract concept, meant to serve as an atom of written language. It is not the same thing as a "letter"—for example, some Unicode characters (accents, umlauts, zero-width joiners) are only meaningful in combination with other characters. Each character has a name (such as GREEK CAPITAL LETTER ALPHA) and a number of properties, such as whether it is a digit, whether it is an uppercase letter, whether it is rendered right-to-left, whether it is a diacritic, and so on.

A *character set* or *character repertoire* is another abstraction: it is an unordered collection of characters. A given character is either in, or not in, a given character set. Unicode attempts to provide a universal character set—one that contains every character from every written language in current and historical use—and the standard is constantly revised to bring it closer to that ideal.

A *coded character set* uniquely assigns an integer—a *code point*—to each character. Once you've assigned code points to the characters, you may then refer to those characters by their numbers. The convention used is an uppercase U, a plus sign, and a hexadecimal number. For example, the PRIME character mentioned earlier in this chapter has the code point U+2032.

Coded characters are organized according to the *scripts* in which they appear, and scripts are further organized into *blocks* of strongly related characters. For example, the Latin script (in which most European languages are written) is given in such blocks as Basic Latin (containing sufficient characters to represent Latin and English), Latin-1 Supplement (containing certain diacritics and combining controls), Latin Extended A, Latin Extended B, and so on.

When it comes time to actually put pixels onto a screen, a computer program interprets a sequence of characters and uses a *font* to generate *glyphs* in the order and location demanded by the context.

* See *http://unicode.org*.

Guessing the language and removing stop words

It would be neither interesting nor surprising to see that your text consists mostly of the words "the," "it," and "to." To avoid a universe of boring Wordles, all alike, such *stop words* need to be removed for each recognized language. To know which list of stop words to remove for a given text, though, we have to guess what language that text is in.

Knowing the script is not the same as knowing the language, since many languages might use the same script (e.g., French and Italian, which share the Latin script).

Wordle takes a straightforward approach to guessing a text's language: it selects the 50 most frequent words from the text and counts how many of them appear in each language's list of stop words. Whichever stop word list has the highest hit count is considered to be the text's language.

How do you create a list of stop words? As with the definition of a "word," described earlier, this kind of thing is a matter of taste, not science. You typically start by counting all of the words in a large corpus and selecting the most frequently used words. However, you might find that certain high-frequency words add a desirable flavor to the output while other, lower-frequency words just seem to add noise, so you may want to tweak the list a bit.

Many of Wordle's stop word lists came from users who wanted better support for their own languages. Those kind folks are credited on the Wordle website.

By default Wordle strips the chosen language's stop words from the word list before proceeding to the next steps, but Wordle users can override this setting via a menu checkbox.

Assigning weights to words

Wordle takes the straight path in assigning a numeric *weight* to each word. The formula is: weight = word count.

Layout

Once you've analyzed your text, you're left with a list of words, each of which has some numeric *weight* based on its frequency in the text. Wordle normalizes the weights to an arbitrary scale, which determines the magnitude of various constants that affect the resulting image (such as the minimum size of a hierarchical bounding box leaf, as described later in this chapter). You're now ready to turn words into graphical objects and to position those objects in space.

Weighted words into shapes

For each word, Wordle constructs a font with a point size equal to the word's scaled weight, then uses the font to generate a Java2D Shape (see Example 3-2).

Example 3-2. *How to turn a String into a Shape*

```
private static final FontRenderContext FRC
    = new FontRenderContext(null, true, true);

public Shape generate(final Font font, final double weight, final String word,
        final double orientation) {
    final Font sizedFont = font.deriveFont((float) weight);
    final char[] chars = word.toCharArray();
    final int direction = Bidi.requiresBidi(chars, 0, chars.length) ?
        Font.LAYOUT_RIGHT_TO_LEFT : Font.LAYOUT_LEFT_TO_RIGHT;
    final GlyphVector gv =
        sizedFont.layoutGlyphVector(FRC, chars, 0, chars.length, direction);
    Shape result = gv.getOutline();
    if (orientation != 0.0){
        result = AffineTransform.getRotateInstance(orientation)
                .createTransformedShape(result);
    }
    return result;
}
```

The playing field

Wordle estimates the total area to be covered by the finished word cloud by examining the bounding box for each word, summing the areas, and adjusting the sum to account for the close packing of smaller words in and near larger words. The resulting area is proportioned to match the target aspect ratio (which is, in turn, given by the dimensions of the Wordle applet at the moment of layout).

The constants used to adjust the size of the *playing field*, the area in which Wordles are laid out, were determined by the time-honored tradition of futzing around with different numbers until things looked "good" and worked "well." As it happens, the precise size of the playing field is rather important, because the field boundaries are used as constraints during layout. If your playing field is too small, your placement will run slowly and most words will fall outside the field, leaving you with a circle (because once a word can't be placed on the field, Wordle relaxes that constraint and you wind up with everything randomly distributed around some initial position). If it's too large, you'll get an incoherent blob (because every nonintersecting position is acceptable).

One "gotcha" to look out for is an especially long word, which could have a dimension far larger than the calculated width or height based on area. You must make sure that your playing field is big enough to contain the largest word, at least.

Remember that the playing field is an abstract space, a coordinate system not corresponding to pixels, inches, or any other unit of measurement. In this abstract space, you can lay out the word shapes and check for intersections. When it comes time to actually put pixels on the screen, you can do some scaling into screen units.

Placement

Having created a place to put words, it's time to position the words in that space. The overall placement strategy is a randomized greedy algorithm in which words are placed, one at a time, on the playing field. Once a word is placed, its position does not change.

Wordle offers the user a choice of placement strategies. These strategies influence the shape and texture of the completed Wordle, by determining where each word "wants" to go. On the Wordle website, the choices are center-line and alphabetical center-line. Both strategies place words near the horizontal center-line of the playing field (not necessarily upon it, but scattered away from it by a random distribution). The alphabetical strategy sorts the words alphabetically and then distributes their preferred x coordinates across the playing field.

Interesting effects are possible through the use of smarter placement strategies. For example, given clustering data—information about which words tend to be used near each other—the placement strategy can make sure that each word tries to appear near the last word from its cluster that was placed on the field (see Figure 3-16).

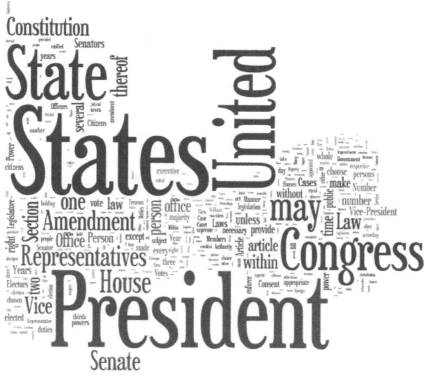

Figure 3-16. *The result of a clustering placement strategy*

The word shapes are sorted by their respective weights, in descending order. Layout proceeds as in Example 3-3, with the result as illustrated in Figure 3-17.

Example 3-3. *The secret Wordle algorithm revealed at last!*

```
For each word w in sorted words:
    placementStrategy.place(w)
    while w intersects any previously placed words:
        move w a little bit along a spiral path
```

Figure 3-17. *The path taken by the word "Denmark"*

To make matters a bit more complicated, Wordle optionally tries to get the words to fit entirely within the rectangular boundaries of the playing field—this is why it's important to guess how big the whole thing is going to be. If the rectangular constraint is turned on, the intersection-handling routine looks like Example 3-4.

Example 3-4. *Constraining words to the playing field*

```
while w intersects any previously placed words:
    do {
        move w a little bit along a spiral path
    } while any part of w is outside the playing field and
            the spiral radius is still smallish
```

Intersection testing

The pseudocode in Example 3-4 breezily suggests that you move a word while it intersects other words, but it does not suggest how you'd go about determining such a thing. Testing spline-based shapes for intersection is expensive, and a naïve approach to choosing pairs for comparison is completely unaffordable. Here are the techniques that Wordle currently uses to make things fast enough:

Hierarchical bounding boxes

> The first step is to reduce the cost of testing two words for intersection. A simple method for detecting misses is to compare the bounding boxes of two words, but it's not uncommon for two such boxes to intersect when the word glyphs do not. Wordle exploits the cheapness of rectangle comparisons by recursively dividing a word's bounding box into ever-smaller boxes, creating a tree of rectangles whose leaf nodes contain chunks of the word shape (see Figure 3-18). Although it's expensive to construct these hierarchical bounding boxes, the cost is recovered by an order of magnitude during the layout. To test for collision, you recursively descend into mutually intersecting boxes, terminating either when two leaf nodes intersect (a hit) or when all possible intersecting branches are excluded (a miss). By taking care with the minimum size of leaf rectangles and by "swelling" the leaf boxes a bit, the layout gets a pleasing distance between words "for free."

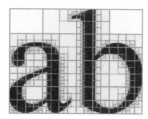

Figure 3-18. *Hierarchical bounding boxes*

Broadphase collision detection

> In choosing pairs of words to test for intersection, the simplest approach is to test the current candidate word against all of the already-placed words. This approach results in a hit test count around the order of N^2, which is far too slow once you get up to 100 words or so. Therefore, Wordle does some extra work to avoid as much collision testing as possible.

Caching

> One very simple improvement stems from the observation that if a word A intersects some other word B, it's very likely that A will still intersect B if A is moved slightly. Therefore, Wordle caches a candidate word's most recently intersected word and tests it first.

Spatial indexing

To further reduce the number of hit tests, Wordle borrows from computational geometry the *region quadtree*, which recursively divides a two-dimensional space (in this case, the Wordle playing field) into four rectangular regions. Here, a quadtree serves as a *spatial index* to efficiently cull shapes from the list of words to be compared to some candidate shape. Once a word is placed on the playing field, Wordle searches for the smallest quadtree node that entirely contains the word, and adds the word to that node. Then, when placing the next word, many already-placed words can be *culled* from collision testing by querying the quadtree.

There's an entire research field around efficient collision detection, much of which is very well summarized in Christer Ericson's (2005) book *Real-Time Collision Detection*. I recommend that book to anyone who wants to play with randomized graphics algorithms like Wordle's; my own quadtree implementation is based on my understanding of its discussion.

Is Wordle Good Information Visualization?

If you consider Wordle strictly as an information visualization tool, certain aspects of its design could be criticized for their potential to mislead or distract its users. Here are some of my own Wordle caveats.

Word Sizing Is Naïve

Wordle does not take into account the length of a word, or the glyphs with which it's drawn, when calculating its font size. The result is that, given two words used the same number of times, the word with more letters will take up more space on the screen, which *may* lead to the impression of the longer word being more frequent.

On the other hand, I don't know of any studies on how relative word size corresponds to perceived relative weight. What's more, the commonly used trick of scaling by the square root of the word's weight (to compensate for the fact that words have *area*, and not mere length) simply makes a Wordle look boring.

Color Is Meaningless

In a medium—your computer screen—that provides precious few dimensions, Wordle is shockingly free with its use of color. Color means absolutely nothing in Wordle; it is used merely to provide contrast between word boundaries and for aesthetic appeal.

Color could be used to code various dimensions, such as clustering (indicating which words tend to be used near each other) or statistical significance (as in the inaugural address word clouds—see Figure 3-19). Wordle could also use color to let two or more different texts be represented in the same space.

Figure 3-19. *"Government" was used a lot in this speech, but not much more than in the other speeches; "pleasing" was used only a couple of times but is an unusual word in the corpus; "people" was used a lot and is unusually frequent*

It should also be mentioned that Wordle makes no provision for colorblind users, although one can always create a custom palette via the applet's Color menu.

Fonts Are Fanciful

Many of Wordle's fonts strongly favor aesthetics and expressiveness over legibility. This has to do, partly, with the design of the Wordle website—the gallery pages would be monotonous without fairly broad letter-form diversity. Most importantly, a font has to look good *in a Wordle*, which may mean that it wouldn't necessarily work well for body text.

For applications where legibility is paramount, Wordle provides Ray Larabie's Expressway font, which is modeled on the U.S. Department of Transportation's Standard Alphabets.

Word Count Is Not Specific Enough

I have seen Wordle used to summarize each book of the New Testament, leading to one page after another of "Lord," which tells you nothing about how the chapters are *distinct* from one another. Merely counting words does not permit meaningful comparisons of like texts. Consider, for example, a blog post. It might be most revealing to emphasize how the post differs from other blog posts by the same author, or to show how it differs from posts on the same topic by other bloggers, or even to show how it differs from the language of newspaper reporting.

There are plenty of statistical measures that one may apply to a "specimen" text versus some "normative" body of text to reveal the specific character of the specimen, with proper attention paid to whether some word use is statistically significant. Given a more nuanced idea of word weight, beyond mere frequency, one could then apply the Wordle layout algorithm to display the results.

I explored this idea in an analysis of every presidential inaugural address,* in which each speech was compared to the 5 speeches nearest to it in time, the 10 nearest speeches, and all other inaugural addresses. Such an analysis has the advantage of revealing the unexpected *absence* of certain words. For example, Figure 3-20 is a visualization of Harry Truman's 1948 inaugural address. On the left is a Wordle-like representation of the words he used, and on the right are the words that his contemporaries used more than he did. This visualization reveals Truman's emphasis on foreign policy.

Figure 3-20. *Harry Truman's 1948 inaugural address: the words in red were conspicuously absent from Harry Truman's speech, relative to those of his contemporaries*

* See *http://researchweb.watson.ibm.com/visual/inaugurals/*.

How Wordle Is Actually Used

Wordle was not designed for visualization experts, text analysis experts, or even experienced computer users. I tried to make Wordle as appliance-like as possible.

As of this writing, people have created and saved over 1,400,000 word clouds in the Wordle gallery. They have been used to summarize and decorate business presentations and PhD theses, to illustrate news articles and television news broadcasts, and to distill and abstract personal and painful memories for victims of abuse. Wordle has also found an enthusiastic community in teachers of all stripes, who use Wordles to present spelling lists, to summarize topics, and to engage preliterate youngsters in the enjoyment of text.

As the survey results in Table 3-1 (Viégas, Wattenberg, and Feinberg, 2009) illustrate, when people use Wordle they feel *creative*, as though they're making something.

Table 3-1. *How people feel when they make a Wordle*

	Agree %	Neutral %	Disagree %
I felt creative	**88**	9	4
I felt an emotional reaction	**66**	22	12
I learned something new about the text	**63**	24	13
It confirmed my understanding of the text	**57**	33	10
It jogged my memory	**50**	35	15
The Wordle confused me	5	9	**86**

So, by one traditional academic measure of a visualization's efficacy—"I learned something new about the text"—Wordle can at least be considered moderately successful. But where Wordle shines is in the creation of *communicative artifacts*. People who use Wordle feel as though they have created something, that the created thing succeeds in representing something meaningful, and that it accurately reflects or intensifies the source text. This sense of meaningfulness seems to be mostly intuitive, in that many people do not realize that word size is related to word frequency (guessing, instead, that the size indicates "emotional importance" or even "word meaning").

The special qualities of Wordle are due to the special qualities of text. Simply putting a single word on the screen, in some font that either complements or contrasts with the sense of the word, immediately resonates with the viewer (indeed, there have been many thousands of single-word Wordles saved to the public gallery). When you juxtapose two or more words, you begin to exploit the tendency of a literate person to make sense of words in sequence. Wordle's serendipitous word combinations create delight, surprise, and perhaps some of the same sense of recognition and insight that poetry evokes intentionally.

Using Wordle for Traditional Infovis

Notwithstanding Wordle's special emotional and communicative properties, the analytic uses of information visualization are certainly available to the expert user. To serve those who want to use Wordle as a visualization for their own weighted text, where the weights are not necessarily based on word frequency, the Wordle website provides an "advanced" interface, where one can enter tabular data containing arbitrarily weighted words or phrases, with (optional) colors.

Still more advanced use is possible through the "Word Cloud Generator" console application, available through IBM's alphaWorks website.[*]

The ManyEyes collaborative data visualization site also provides Wordle as a text-visualization option beside its innovative Phrase Net and Word Tree visualizations (and a more traditional tag cloud).[†]

Conclusion

People often want to preserve and share the Wordles they make; they use Wordles to *communicate*. A beautiful visualization gives pleasure as it reveals something essential.

Acknowledgments

I would like to thank Martin Wattenberg and Irene Greif at IBM CUE for making possible my participation in this book. I am very grateful to Ben Fry, Katherine McVety, Fernanda Viégas, and Martin Wattenberg, who each read this chapter with great care and suggested many improvements. Please see *http://www.wordle.net/credits* for information about the many people who have helped me create and improve Wordle.

References

Ericson, Christer. 2005. *Real-Time Collision Detection*. San Francisco, CA: Morgan Kaufmann.

Millen, D. R., J. Feinberg, and B. Kerr. 2006. "Dogear: Social bookmarking in the enterprise." *Proceedings of the SIGCHI Conference on Human Factors in Computing Systems* (Montréal, Québec, Canada, April 22–27, 2006). *http://doi.acm.org/10.1145/1124772.1124792*.

Viégas, Fernanda B., Martin Wattenberg, and Jonathan Feinberg. 2009. "Participatory visualization with Wordle." *IEEE Transactions on Visualization and Computer Graphics* 15, no. 6 (Nov/Dec 2009): 1137–1144. doi:10.1109/TVCG.2009.171.

---

* See *http://www.alphaworks.ibm.com/tech/wordcloud*.
† See *http://manyeyes.alphaworks.ibm.com/manyeyes/page/Visualization_Options.html*.

## CHAPTER FOUR

Color: The Cinderella of Data Visualization

Michael Driscoll

Avoiding catastrophe becomes the first principle in bringing color to information: Above all, do no harm.

—Edward Tufte, Envisioning Information (Graphics

COLOR IS ONE OF THE MOST ABUSED AND NEGLECTED tools in data visualization: we abuse it when we make poor color choices, and we neglect it when we rely on poor software defaults. Yet despite its historically poor treatment at the hands of engineers and end users alike, if used wisely, color is unrivaled as a visualization tool.

Most of us would think twice before walking outside in fluorescent red Underoos®. If only we were as cautious in choosing colors for infographics! The difference is that few of us design our own clothes, while we must all be our own infographics tailors in order to get colors that fit our purposes (at least until good palettes—like ColorBrewer—become commonplace).

While obsessing about how to implement color on the Dataspora Labs PitchFX viewer, I began with a basic motivating question: why use color in data graphics? We'll consider that question next.

Why Use Color in Data Graphics?

For a simple dataset, a single color is sufficient (even preferable). For example, Figure 4-1 shows a scatterplot of 287 pitches thrown by Major League pitcher Oscar Villarreal in 2008. With just two dimensions of data to describe—the x and y locations in the strike zone—black and white is sufficient. In fact, this scatterplot is a perfectly lossless representation of the dataset (assuming no data points overlap perfectly).

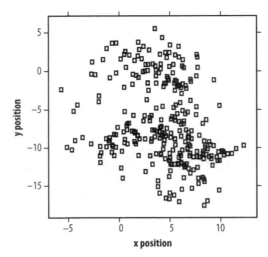

Figure 4-1. *Location of pitches indicated in an x/y plane*

But what if we'd like to know more? For instance, what kinds of pitches (curveballs, fastballs) landed where? Or what was their speed? Visualizations occupy two dimensions, but the world they describe is rarely so confined.

The defining challenge of data visualization is projecting high-dimensional data onto a low-dimensional canvas. As a rule, one should never do the reverse (visualize more dimensions than already exist in the data).

Getting back to our pitching example, if we want to layer another dimension of data—pitch type—into our plot, we have several methods at our disposal:

1. *Plotting symbols.* We can vary the glyphs that we use (circles, triangles, etc.).

2. *Small multiples.* We can vary extra dimensions in space, creating a series of smaller plots.

3. *Color.* We can color our data, encoding extra dimensions inside a color space.

Which technique you employ in a visualization should depend on the nature of the data and the media of your canvas. I will describe these three by way of example.

1. Vary Your Plotting Symbols

In Figure 4-2, I've layered the categorical dimension of pitch type into our plot by using four different plotting symbols.

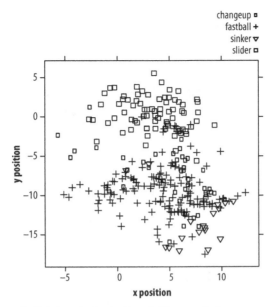

Figure 4-2. *Location and pitch type indicated by plotting symbols*

I consider this visualization an abject failure. There are two reasons why graphs like this one make our heads hurt: because distinguishing glyphs demands extra attention (versus what academics call "preattentively processed" cues like color), and because even after we've visually decoded the symbols, we must map those symbols to their semantic categories. (Admittedly, this can be mitigated with Chernoff faces or other iconic symbols, where the categorical mapping is self-evident).

2. Use Small Multiples on a Canvas

While Edward Tufte has done much to promote the use of small multiples in information graphics, folding additional dimensions into a partitioned canvas has a distinguished pedigree. This technique has been employed everywhere from Galileo's sunspot illustrations to William Cleveland's trellis plots. And as Scott McCloud's unexpected *tour de force* on comics makes clear, panels of pictures possess a narrative power that a single, undivided canvas lacks.

In Figure 4-3, plots of the four types of pitches that Oscar throws are arranged horizontally. By reducing our plot sizes, we've given up some resolution in positional information. But in return, patterns that were invisible in our first plot and obscured in our second (by varied symbols) are now made clear (Oscar throws his fastballs low, but his sliders high).

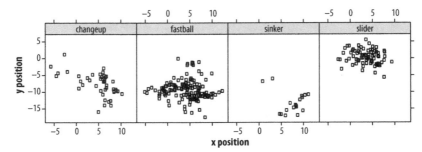

Figure 4-3. *Location and pitch type indicated by facets*

Multiplying plots in space works especially well on printed media, which can display more than 10 times as many dots per square inch as a screen. Additional plots can be arranged in both columns and rows, with the result being a matrix of scatterplots (in R, see the splom function).

3. Add Color to Your Data

In Figure 4-4, I've used color as a means of encoding a fourth dimension of our pitching data: the speed of pitches thrown. The palette I've chosen is a divergent palette that moves along one dimension (think of it as the "redness-blueness" dimension) in the *Lab* color space,* while maintaining a constant level of luminosity.

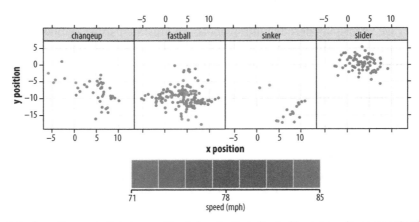

Figure 4-4. *Location and pitch type, with pitch velocity indicated by a one-dimensional color palette*

---

* See *http://en.wikipedia.org/wiki/CIELUV_color_space*.

On the one hand, holding luminosity constant has advantages, because luminosity (similar to brightness) determines a color's visual impact. Bright colors pop, and dark colors recede. A color ramp that varies luminosity along with hue will highlight data points as an artifact of color choice.

On the other hand, luminosity—unlike hue—possesses an inherent order that hue lacks, making it suitable for mapping to quantitative (and not categorical) dimensions of data.

Because I am going to use luminosity to encode yet another dimension later, I decided to use hue for encoding speed here; it suits our purposes well enough. I chose only seven gradations of color, so I'm downsampling (in a lossy way) our speed data. Segmentation of our color ramp into many more colors would make it difficult to distinguish them.

I've also chosen to use filled circles as the plotting symbol in this version, as opposed to the open circles used in all the previous plots. This improves the perception of each pitch's speed via its color: small patches of color are less perceptible. However, a consequence of this choice—compounded by the decision to work with a series of smaller plots—is that more points overlap. Hence, we've further degraded some of the positional information. (We'll attempt to recover some of this information in just a moment.)

So Why Bother with Color?

As compared to most print media, computer displays have fewer units of space but a broader color gamut. So, color is a compensatory strength.

For multidimensional data, color can convey additional dimensions inside a unit of space, and can do so instantly. Color differences can be detected within 200 milliseconds, before you're even conscious of paying attention (the "preattentive" concept I mentioned earlier).

But the most important reason to use color in multivariate graphics is that color is itself multidimensional. Our perceptual color space—however you slice it—is three-dimensioned.

We've now brought color to bear on our visualization, but we've only encoded a single dimension: speed. This leads us to another question.

If Color Is Three-Dimensional, Can I Encode Three Dimensions with It?

In theory, yes—Colin Ware (2000) researched this exact question using red, blue, and green as the three axes. (There are other useful ways of dividing the color spectrum, as we will soon see.) In practice, though, it's difficult. It turns out that asking observers to assess the *amount* of "redness," "blueness," and "greenness" of points is possible, but doing so is not intuitive.

Another complicating factor is that a nontrivial fraction of the population has some form of colorblindness (also known as *dichromacy*, in contrast to normal *trichromacy*). This effectively reduces color perception to two dimensions.

And finally, the truth is that our sensation of color is not equal along all dimensions: there are fewer perceptible shades of yellow than there are "blues." It's thought that the closely related "red" and "green" receptors emerged via duplication of the single long wavelength receptor (useful for detecting ripe from unripe fruits, according to one just-so story).

Because of the high level of colorblindness in the population, and because of the challenge of encoding three dimensions in color, I believe color is best used to encode no more than two dimensions of data.

Luminosity As a Means of Recovering Local Density

For the last iteration of our pitching plot data visualization, shown in Figure 4-5, I will introduce luminosity as a means of encoding the local density of points. This allows us to recover some of the data lost by increasing the sizes of our plotting symbols.

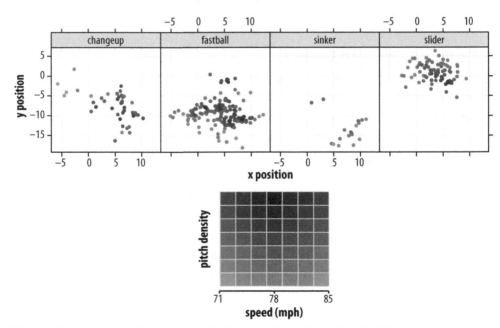

Figure 4-5. *Location and pitch type, with pitch velocity and local density indicated by a two-dimensional color palette (see inset for details)*

Here we have effectively employed a two-dimensional color palette, with blueness-redness varying along one axis to denote speed, luminosity varying along the other to denote local density. As detailed in the "Methods" section, these plots were created using the color space package in R, which provides the ability to specify colors in any of the major color spaces (RGB, HSV, *Lab*). Because the *Lab* color space varies chromaticity independently from luminosity, I chose it for creating this particular two-dimensional palette.

One final point about using luminosity is that observing colors in a data visualization involves overloading, in the programming sense. That is, we rely on cognitive functions that were developed for one purpose (seeing lions) and use them for another (seeing lines).

We can overload color any way we want, but whenever possible we should choose mappings that are natural. Mapping pitch density to luminosity feels right because the darker shadows in our pitch plots imply depth. Likewise, when sampling from the color space, we might as well choose colors found in nature. These are the palettes our eyes were gazing at for millions of years before the RGB color space showed up.

Looking Forward: What About Animation?

This discussion has focused on using static graphics in general, and color in particular, as a means of visualizing multivariate data. I've purposely neglected one very powerful dimension: time. The ability to animate graphics multiplies by several orders of magnitude the amount of information that can be packed into a visualization (a stunning example is Aaron Koblin's visualizations of U.S. and Canadian flight patterns, explored in Chapter 6). But packing that information into a time-varying data structure involves considerable effort, and animating data in a way that is informative, not simply aesthetically pleasing, remains challenging. Canonical forms of animated visualizations (equivalent to the histograms, box plots, and scatterplots of the static world) are still a ways off, but frameworks like Processing* are a promising start toward their development.

Methods

All of the visualizations here were developed using the R programming language and the Lattice graphics package. The R code for building a two-dimensional color palette follows:

```
## colorPalette.R
## builds an (m x n) 2D palette
## by mixing 2 hues (col1, col2)
## and across two luminosities (lum1,lum2)
## returns a matrix of the hex RGB values
makePalette <- function(col1,col2,lum1,lum2,m,n,...) {
    C <- matrix(data=NA,ncol=m,nrow=n)
```

* See *http://processing.org.*

```
        alpha <- seq(0,1,length.out=m)
        ## for each luminosity level (rows)
        lum <- seq(lum1,lum2,length.out = n)
        for (i in 1:n) {
            c1 <- LAB(lum[i], coords(col1)[2], coords(col1)[3])
            c2 <- LAB(lum[i], coords(col2)[2], coords(col2)[3])
            ## for each mixture level (columns)
            for (j in 1:m) {
                c <- mixcolor(alpha[j],c1,c2)
                hexc <- hex(c,fixup=TRUE)
                C[i,j] <- hexc
            }
        }
        return(C)
}


## plot a vector or matrix of RGB colors
plotPalette <- function(C,...) {
    if (!is.matrix(C)) {
        n <- 1
        C <- t(matrix(data=C))
    } else {
        n <- dim(C)[1]
    }
    plot(0, 0, type="n", xlim = c(0, 1), ylim = c(0, n), axes = FALSE,
            mar=c(0,0,0,0),...)

    ## helper function for plotting rectangles
    plotRectangle <- function(col, ybot=0, ytop=1, border = "light gray") {
        n <- length(col)
        rect(0:(n-1)/n, ybot, 1:n/n, ytop, col=col, border=border, mar=c(0,0,0,0))
    }

    for (i in 1:n) {
        plotRectangle(C[i,], ybot=i-1, ytop=i)
    }
}

## Let's put it all together.
## We make two colors in the LAB space, and then plot a 2D palette
## going from 60 to 25 luminosity values.
library(colorspace)
lightRed <- LAB(50,48,48)
lightBlue <- LAB(50,-48,-48)
C <- makePalette(col1=lightBlue, col2=lightRed, lum1=60, lum2=25, m=7, n=7)
plotPalette(C, xlab='speed', ylab='density')
```

Conclusion

As this example has demonstrated, color—used thoughtfully and responsibly—can be an incredibly valuable tool in visualizing high-dimensional data. The final product—five-dimensional pitch plots for all available data for the 2008 season—can be explored via the PitchFX Django-driven web tool at Dataspora labs (*http://labs.dataspora.com/gameday/*).

References and Further Reading

Few, Stephen. 2006. *Information Dashboard Design*, Chapter 4. Sebastopol, CA: O'Reilly Media.

Ihaka, Ross. Lectures 12–14 on Information Visualization. Department of Statistics, University of Auckland. *http://www.stat.auckland.ac.nz/~ihaka/120/lectures.html*.

Sarkar, Deepayan. 2008. *Lattice: Multivariate Data Visualization with R*. New York: Springer-Verlag.

Tufte, Edward. 2001. *Envisioning Information*, Chapter 4. Cheshire, CT: Graphics Press.

Ware, Colin. 2000. *Information Visualization*, Chapter 4. San Francisco, CA: Morgan Kaufmann.

## CHAPTER FIVE

Mapping Information: Redesigning the New York City Subway Map

Eddie Jabbour, as told to Julie Steele

MAPS ARE ONE OF THE MOST BASIC DATA VISUALIZATIONS THAT WE HAVE; we've been making them for millennia. But we still haven't perfected them as a tool for understanding complex systems—and with 26 lines and 468 stations across five boroughs, the New York City subway system certainly is complex. The KickMap™ is the result of my quest to design a more effective subway map, and ultimately to encourage increased ridership.

The Need for a Better Tool

I was born in Queens and raised in Brooklyn. The first subway map I saw was my father's, circa 1960. It made a vivid impression on me because it intimidated me. I saw a gray New York with red, green, and black lines running all over it like a grid (see Figure 5-1), and hundreds of station names attached.* It reminded me of a complex electrical diagram that I couldn't understand; it looked very "adult-serious" and even a little scary. I hoped I'd never have to deal with it.

---

* I now know that map was an early version of the Salomon map. Years later, when I was doing research for the creation of the KickMap, I got to appreciate the beauty of the design of this map.

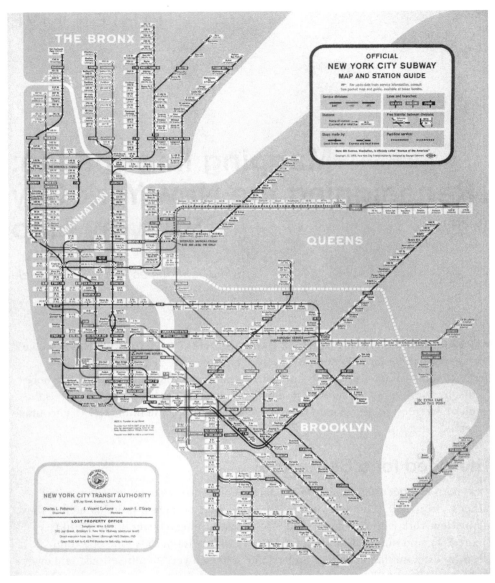

Figure 5-1. *The 1958 New York City Subway map designed by George Salomon. 1958 New York City Subway Map © MTA New York City Transit. Used with permission.*

London Calling

In college I majored in design, and I spent half a year studying at the University of London. I was all on my own in a huge city I had never been to before. I quickly learned that the London Underground was the way to get around and that the "Tube map" was the key to understanding it. That map (which of course is the acclaimed Beck map seen in Figure 5-2) was brilliantly friendly: simple, bright, functionally colorful, designed to help users easily understand connections between lines, and physically tiny. Folded, it fit easily into my pocket, to be whipped out at a second's notice for immediate reference (which I did often!).

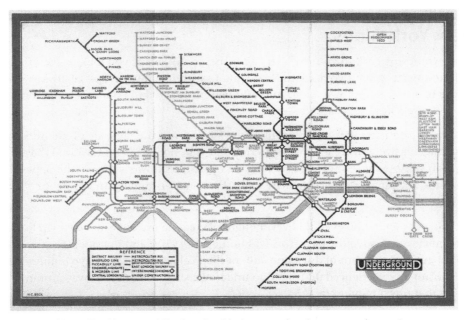

Figure 5-2. *Harry Beck's map of the London Underground makes a complex system appear simple and elegant. 1933 London Tube Map © TfL from the London Transport Museum collection. Used with permission.*

London was a medieval city, and therefore its street pattern is random. You cross a crooked intersection and the name of the street you're on changes. There's no numbered grid to provide a frame of reference (like in New York), and moving through the city can be a disorienting experience. The genius of the Beck map is that it makes order out of this random complexity, with the River Thames as the only visual (and geographic) point of reference to the aboveground world. And for that reason, the map's layout is iconic: when you think of London, you probably think of that Tube map. But even as a design student, I didn't think much about the form of it at the time—it was just so simple and easy to use that travel felt effortless.

The combination of that effective little map and my unlimited monthly "Go As You Please" pass allowed me to use the Underground daily to explore London. I went anywhere and everywhere with ease and got the most that I could out of that great city. The Tube map imparted information so quickly and clearly that it became an indispensible tool and an integral part of my experience. It made me feel that London was "mine" after only a couple of weeks of living there. What a fantastic and empowering feeling!

In fact, I formed such a warm attachment to that valuable tool that at the end of my stay, just before I left the city, I went to my local Underground station and got a brand new Tube map, and when I returned home to New York I had it framed.

New York Blues

When you come back to your own city after six months away, you look at everything with new eyes. When I got back to New York, I saw our subway map—really saw it—for the first time since I was a kid. And I thought, compared to London's, *our subway map is poorly designed*.

I remember thinking that the New York subway map was the opposite of the Beck map: huge in size, unruly in look, cluttered, and very nonintuitive. I realized that this map was in many ways a *barrier* to using our great subway system—the opposite of the Tube map, whose simplicity was a *key* to understanding and using the Underground.

Even as a designer, however, if I ever thought of creating my own subway map I must have quickly dismissed the idea. This was in the late 1970s, and I'm not a T-square kind of guy. The amount of discipline and mechanical time it would have required for anyone but an experienced draftsman to undertake such an endeavor was unthinkable in that precomputer era.

The map's deficiencies left my mind as I pursued my design career. Like most New Yorkers, I used the subway map rarely and never carried it. This was in part because of its size: it was as large as a foldout road map. If I needed the map's information to get to a new location, I would tear out the relevant six-inch square portion from a free map in the station and throw the rest of it in the trash! I often saw tourists struggling with the physical map and felt bad for them, remembering my great experience as a student in London.

Better Tools Allow for Better Tools

Now, fast-forward to one night years later when I was taking an out-of-town client to dinner at a downtown restaurant. As we waited for the train, he confided to me that New York's subway intimidated him. I was surprised: the crime and grime of the 1970s–1990s were virtually gone from the system, and I was proud of our shiny new air-conditioned cars and clean stations. But in our conversation on the way downtown, I realized that his fear lay in not being able to decipher the *complexity* of the system: all the lines and connections. That's when I realized that the problem for him, too, was the map. My client was very well traveled and urbane; if *he* found the system intimidating, then there really was something wrong with the communicator of that system—the map.

At that moment the subway map re-entered my consciousness, and it hasn't left since.

At that point, it was 2002. I had my own design agency and my own staff, each of us with our own computer loaded with a copy of the greatest and most elegant graphic design tool available. I realized that now, just *one person* using a graphic design program like Adobe Illustrator had the power to create his own subway map! And I challenged myself to do something about the map.

Size Is Only One Factor

When I decided to try making a new map as a weekend project (ha!), the first thing I considered was the size. Since the New York City subway system has about twice as many stations as London's, I decided to give myself twice as much space as the Tube map takes. (Even doubling the size of the Tube map, the result was about one-fifth the size of the existing New York subway map.)

First, I took a paper version of the official Metropolitan Transit Authority (MTA) map (a version of which is shown in Figure 5-3), cut it up with scissors, and put it back together in a more efficient way (literally with Scotch® tape), just to see the possibilities. I was encouraged as I managed to reduce the area by more then half. Gone were the 56 bus pop-up boxes and other nonsubway information! Then came the laborious task of creating an actual map. I entered all the station names and lines into an Illustrator document, and in two months, voilà! I had my very own smaller map! I folded it and easily put it in my wallet, and I carried it around and showed it to all my friends. They liked its size, but of course nobody wanted to actually use it, because it still had many of the major design issues that made the MTA map difficult to use.

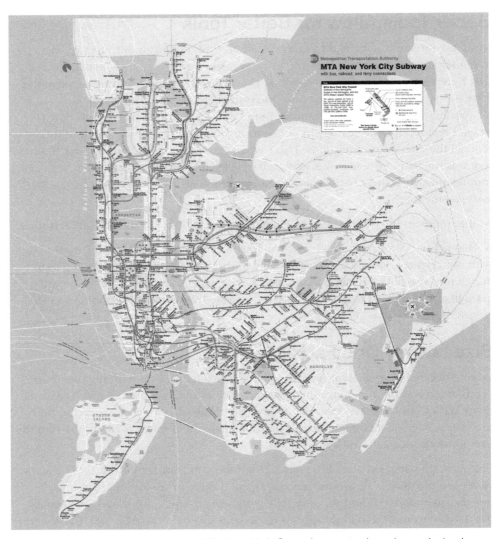

Figure 5-3. *The 2004 version of the MTA New York City subway map, based on a design by Michael Hertz. Besides its visual complexity, incomplete information missing on the map itself forces the the user to rely on the complex charts in the lower right section—right where sitting people block its view in the subway cars—and in the stations where this information, displayed on large posters, is also difficult to read since it is often less than 18 inches off the ground. New York City Subway Map © Metropolitan Transportation Authority. Used with permission.*

It was one thing to reduce the size, but another thing to realize that the way the data was presented was not the best way to present it. So I asked myself: *how would I present all this data?*

To answer this question, I had to ask a few more:

- What maps came before this map?

- Were there any previous conceptions that were discarded but perhaps still relevant?

- What was it about New York City and its subway that historically made it so difficult to map clearly and efficiently?

Looking Back to Look Forward

I did a research dive, and I started buying old transit maps on eBay. I studied subway maps, New York City street maps, and transit maps from all over the world that I had collected on my travels. I filtered through all the design approaches and eclectically took as much as I could from ideas that had already been implemented (some brilliantly).

Of course, in addition to the map designed by George Salomon that had been my father's subway map, I studied carefully the map designed by Massimo Vignelli (see Figure 5-4), which the MTA used from 1972 until 1979, when it was replaced by the Tauranac-Hertz MTA map (which, 30 years later, still prevails). Vignelli's map appealed to me immediately because, although big, it took obvious inspiration from Beck's Tube map, with its 90- and 45-degree angles, explicit station connections, and the use of color to denote individual lines. There were also some smart aspects of the current MTA map that I wanted to keep, despite finding it on the whole unwieldy because there is so much information crammed onto it. In addition, I borrowed liberally from other past efforts that had been discarded or forgotten.

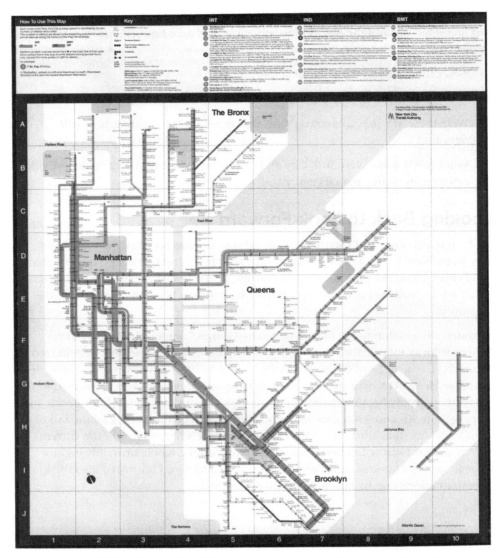

Figure 5-4. *The 1972 MTA New York City subway map designed by Massimo Vignelli. Confusingly distorted geography for style's sake—yet a stunning design icon. 1972 New York City Subway Map © MTA New York City Transit. Used with permission.*

New York's Unique Complexity

As I conducted my research, I started to realize that New York City had its own unique set of challenges that made its subway system impossible to accurately and clearly map using just a diagrammatic method, as other cities like London, Paris, and Tokyo had done. It was also clear that a pure topographic mapping approach wouldn't work, either; New York's unique geography and its gridiron street system both have an impact on mapping its subway system.

There are four significant and conflicting aspects of the New York City subway system that make it impossible to successfully map with either a strict diagrammatic or topographic format:

- The narrow geography of the principal thoroughfare, Manhattan Island, which has 17 separate subway lines running up and down Midtown alone in a width of six city blocks.

- The "cut and cover" method used to construct subway tunnels and elevated lines that follow the city's gridiron street patterns. Because New York City's subway generally follows its gridded street routes, there is a strong psychological link between the subway and the aboveground topography that is not found in a medieval city like London.

- The unique system of many of the subway lines running local, then express, then local again along their routes.

- Its formative history, with the current system evolving from three separate and competing subway systems (the IRT, BMT, and IND) that were poorly coordinated to work as a whole system. (The chaotic tangle of these three competing routes, as they meander and fight their way through the dense street plans of lower Manhattan, downtown Brooklyn, and Long Island City, is the most difficult part of the system to map clearly and accurately.)

The KickMap, shown in Figure 5-5, is based on a combination of ideas I selectively borrowed from many earlier maps (some dating back to the 19th century) and my own innovations. I believe that this unique combination makes my map easier to use than most of the preceding efforts. In the following sections, I'll discuss my inspirations and innovations in more detail.

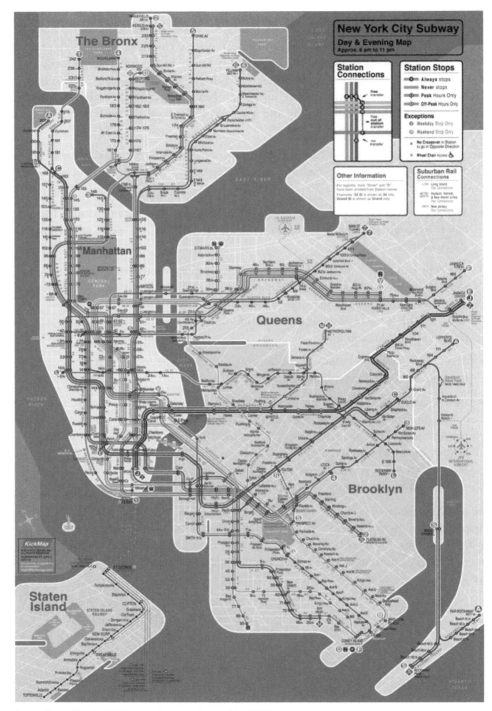

Figure 5-5. *The KickMap as it was released in 2007.*

Geography Is About Relationships

Most of the boroughs—Queens, Brooklyn, Manhattan, and to some extent, the Bronx—already have a grid on top of the subway system because of the way the streets were planned. This makes the aboveground geography not only an intuitive starting point, but also an integral part of the user's experience. Knowing your location—take 42nd Street and 7th Avenue as an example—places you in the grid, which makes it easy to judge distances and locations. This is why the numerous geographical errors that appear in New York City subway maps (like the Vignelli map infamously placing the 50th Street and Broadway stop west of 8th Avenue instead of east) are so glaring and easy to spot.

One of the issues I have with some previous versions of the New York subway map is that I have a hard time believing that the designers ever actually rode the subway as an integral part of their lives in the city. There's a disconnect between many of the decisions they made and the reality of the subway. As part of my design process, I rode the lines and exited the stations at every major intersection with which I was unfamiliar. There is a *strong relationship in New York* between the aboveground and the belowground, and since subway riders don't cease to exist when they leave the subway, it's important for the map to express this relationship as clearly as possible. Otherwise, the result is an uncomfortable feeling of disorientation.

Include the Essentials

Consider the L line in Brooklyn. As a passenger on the train, you're jostled around as you travel and you don't really notice that the line is curving or turning corners along major streets and intersections. But when you get out at the Graham Avenue station, for instance, it's obvious that Metropolitan Avenue and Bushwick Avenue are two major thoroughfares that intersect each other at a right angle. Why wouldn't that show up on the map? If you didn't know how the streets intersected and you just saw a sign for one or the other as you came out of the subway, it would be very difficult to figure out what was going on.

On the Vignelli map, this portion of the L is depicted as a straight line (see Figure 5-6[a]). The Hertz map (Figure 5-6[c]) shows both Metropolitan and Bushwick Avenues, but the line resembles nothing so much as a wet noodle as it half-heartedly depicts the route. I chose to carefully draw a stylized but accurate line describing the path as it runs along each major avenue there, believing this to be the best approach because it is the most helpful to riders (Figure 5-6[b]).

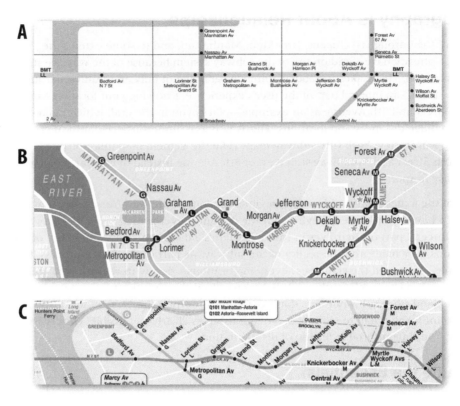

Figure 5-6. *A portion of the L line in Brooklyn as depicted by (a) the Vignelli map, (b) the KickMap, and (c) the Tauranac-Hertz map.*

Conversely, I sometimes made stylistic simplifications to the geography in order to help riders. For example, Queens Boulevard, a major thoroughfare in Queens, was originally five different farm roads, and as a result it jigs and jogs a bit as it makes its way from the Queensboro Bridge east across the borough. Recent maps didn't capture its relationship to the subway because they either ignored it entirely (as in the Vignelli map, shown in Figure 5-7[a]) or obscured it (as in the current MTA map, shown in Figure 5-7[c]). On my map, I styled Queens Boulevard as a straight line; see Figure 5-7(b). I chose to do this so that users could easily see its path and identify the "trade-off" subway lines that travel along it—where one subway line runs along the road and then veers off and another line takes its place. In this case, the 7 line runs along Queens Boulevard until it veers off along Roosevelt Avenue, and the R/V/G/E/F lines come down from Broadway and pick up its path east. My stylized approach uses logic to better convey the subway's relationship to the streets of Queens, which is not clearly apparent on either the Vignelli map or the current MTA map.

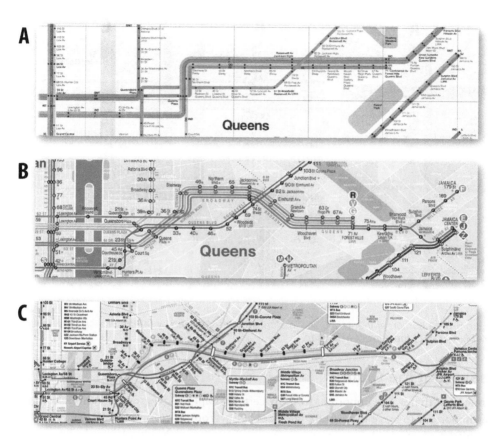

Figure 5-7. *The trade-off along Queens Boulevard as depicted by (a) the Vignelli map, (b) the KickMap, and (c) the current MTA map.*

Another "trade-off" I felt it was important to show clearly is at 42nd Street in Midtown Manhattan, where the 4/5/6 line jogs over from Park Avenue to Lexington Avenue (see Figure 5-8). A would-be rider walking along in Midtown or Murray Hill needs to know which street to go to for a subway entrance. The Vignelli map obscures the shift by treating it as a straight line, relying on text to convey the road switch, and once again the current MTA map is at best vague and noodley. In my map, it's clear which way the user should go.

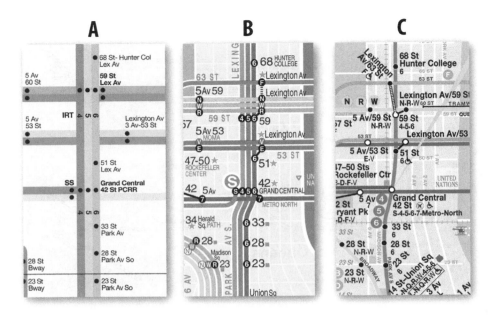

Figure 5-8. *A portion of the 4/5/6 line in Manhattan as depicted by (a) the Vignelli map, (b) the KickMap, and (c) the current MTA map.*

Leave Out the Clutter

While I felt that it was important to show certain shapes aboveground, I also felt that it was important to leave out certain pieces of belowground information. There are several places where the subway tunnels cross and overlap each other beneath the surface. This may be important information for city workers or utility companies trying to make repairs, but for the average commuter, showing these interactions just creates visual noise. I tried to reduce that noise by cleanly separating the lines on the map so they don't overlap. Consider the different depictions of the 4 line and the 5 line in the Bronx (Figure 5-9); sure, the MTA's paths may be accurate, but they're also confusing, and riders don't really need to see those particular details to understand where they're going.

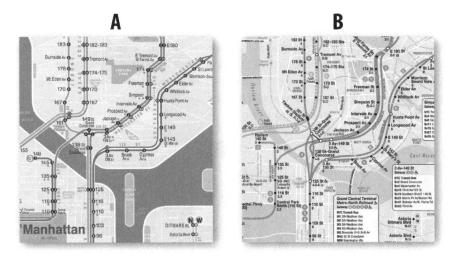

A

B

Figure 5-9. *The 4 line and the 5 line as depicted by (a) the KickMap and (b) the current MTA map.*

Coloring Inside the Lines

The belowground geography is important, but it's more vital for the users to understand which belowground lines will take them where they want to go.

In 1967, the MTA moved past the tricolor theme used on the Salomon and earlier maps and began to use individual colors to illustrate individual lines. However, this shift didn't help simplify the system. It essentially had 26 lines assigned 26 random colors, which didn't really *tell* the user anything beyond illustrating the continuity of a given route. Vignelli's map (Figure 5-10[a]) continued with this color system.

The Tauranac-Hertz (current MTA) map attempted to simplify things by collapsing multiple subway lines onto one graphic line, but this actually made understanding the subway system more complicated, as now you had to read the text next to each and every station to learn whether a specific line stopped there or not; see Figure 5-10(c). What it did get right was that it color-coded sets of subway lines that use the same track—for example, the A/C/E lines are all blue, and the 4/5/6 lines are all green. If you look at the "trunk" lines that run north and south through Manhattan, the colors move from blue to red to orange to yellow to green, creating a spectrum effect. These colors are memorable and help riders discern which lines will take them in the general direction they want to go.

In my map, I preserved the best elements of both approaches; see Figure 5-10(b). I reused the spectral colors on the trunk lines, highlighting an elegance and reality inherent in the system that Tauranac-Hertz understood, but kept it clear by representing each route with its own graphic line. Technically, I did what Vignelli did in that I used 26 distinct colors, but I grouped them in six or seven *families of color* and used different shades for each line in a given family: the A/C/E lines use shades of blue, the 4/5/6 lines use shades of green, and so on.

A   B   C

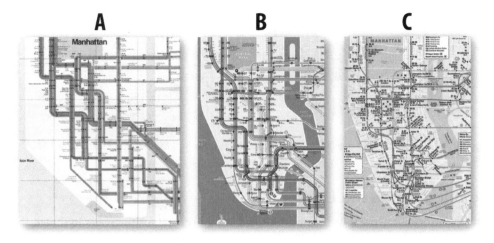

Figure 5-10. *The Manhattan "trunk" lines as depicted by (a) the Vignelli map, (b) the KickMap, and (c) the current MTA map.*

I also made use of line IDs and colors for the station dots.* The crucial idea here was that the map should be quickly *scannable*, rather than just *readable*. At each station where a line stops, I placed the name of that line inside a dot: this way, users can easily see exactly which trains stop at which stations without having to read a list of lines next to each station name. Use of different colored dots enables users to tell *at a glance* whether the train always stops there or has special conditions, such as weekday/weekend or peak hour/off-peak hour restrictions.

Finally, there are about 80 stations in the city where, if you've missed your stop, you can't just get out and conveniently switch direction. I highlighted these locations by placing a small red square next to the station name, indicating to riders who need to turn around which stations to avoid if they don't want to have to leave the station, cross the street, and re-enter the station on the opposite side. The current MTA map shows all the heliports in the city but doesn't provide users with this simple but important piece of *subway* information—a perfect example of its confused priorities.

I believe that taken together, these decisions highlight the innovations that make the KickMap more useable than those that came before it.

---

* This was a big *aha* moment in my process.

Sweat the Small Stuff

Those decisions were easy for me, but other choices were more difficult. Which geographic features did I really need to keep? What angles should I use? How much bus and ferry information should I include?

So, after creating my first comprehensive map that met my initial challenges (Figure 5-5), I decided to refine it and incorporate all of my learning. I was excited.

Try It On

In the car industry, it is common to build what is called a *test mule*, which is a prototype or preproduction car into which every possible experimental feature is crammed; that prototype then undergoes a series of drivability tests to determine what should be removed (because it's not essential or doesn't work quite right). I did the same thing with my map: I created a version (shown in Figure 5-11) into which I put every feature that I might possibly want. Illustrator's layers feature really came in handy here; I put a lot in this map that I ultimately turned off or toned down.

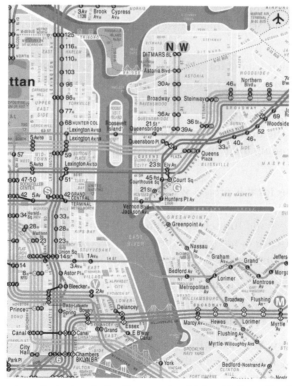

Figure 5-11. *My version of a test mule for the map: I put lots of information in and then edited it down.*

The mule map allowed me to evaluate a variety of trade-offs, such as:

The street grid

> I wanted to present the structure of the streets without interfering with the subway info wherever I could. You'll notice that the mule map includes a lot more streets and street names than the final design.

Beaches

> I thought green spaces were important, and that New Yorkers should be able to find their way to beaches by subway rather than by car. My mule map included municipal swimming pools as well, but ultimately I decided to remove them.

Coastline features

> It was important that real people—like, say, my mom—could easily use this map, and she couldn't care less about certain geographic details (like Steinway Creek or Wallabout Bay) that I included in the mule map. That was a reason to simplify and stylize. But I also wanted to make something any map geek or lover of New York City (like me!) could appreciate. So, there were instances where I let my passion take over. I decided to pay homage to certain subway feats, so I included features like the Gowanus Canal, which the Smith/9th Street station crosses and has to clear (at 91 feet, it's the highest elevated station in the system).

Angular design

> In the final design I standardized a lot of the angles, but I broke that standardization if I had to for clarity's sake. I wasn't a slave to the angles. Stylization is fine, but my goal was to take the stylization and make it work so that riders can always understand what's going on aboveground. I also decided to consistently place station names on the horizontal for easier reading, like on the London Tube map, instead of cramming them in at arbitrary angles.

Bridges and tunnels

> One of my goals for this project was to come up with a tool that would encourage people to take the subway instead of a car. For this reason, I decided to leave out all the car bridges and tunnels (except for the iconic Brooklyn Bridge). I wanted to keep the experience of navigating the subway as clean and easy as possible, without the temptation of using a car, to encourage users to keep riding.

Many of these choices were influenced by the following principle.

Users Are Only Human

There are certain New York icons that help orient the rider and are reassuring. To the extent that they represent something familiar, maps can be quite emotional. So, I saw preserving such icons as a way to build *friendliness* into this tool. I did not design a geographically precise topographical map; I designed a map that is emotionally and geographically *accurate* in a relational sense—Manhattan looks like Manhattan, Central

Park is green, the Hudson River is blue, and the subway stations are positionally accurate in relation to one another and the streets (Delancey Street is shown east of the Bowery, etc.).

For the same humanistic reason, I included certain celebrated landmarks—the Statue of Liberty, Ellis Island, and the Brooklyn Bridge. And I didn't just include them with nametags; I actually included their familiar *shapes*, as was done on subway maps back in the 1930s.*

A City of Neighborhoods

When I travel on the subway to see my mom, I'm not going to see her at the 95th Street subway station; I'm going to see her at her home, which is in Bay Ridge, Brooklyn. This is an important aspect of New York: it is a city made up of neighborhoods, and native New Yorkers think of the city in those terms. That's our frame of reference: we travel from, say, Washington Heights to Bay Ridge.

The current MTA subway map includes some neighborhood names, but they are just dark blue words that compete with the station names and do little to describe the areas. There's no *hierarchy of information*. By color-coding the neighborhoods—which has been done on maps of the city since at least the 1840s—in an unobtrusive way (using pastel tones) and writing their labels in white text so they wouldn't visually interfere with the black text of the station names, I was able to provide layers of information without compromising the clarity and functionality of the subway map.

Again, these elements were literally created in separate digital layers in Illustrator. This allowed me to turn the neighborhoods on and off to determine what really needed to be there and to make several variations of the subway map with and without them.

One Size Does Not Fit All

I believe that separating functions is an important key to any useful visualization or tool.

Another benefit of the layered approach was that it allowed me to custom-tailor the map to the user interface later. The KickMap is available as iPhone and iPad applications, and in that context, the map's detail automatically changes as the user zooms in or out. Besides the apps, commuters still read subway maps in many different contexts: there is the foldout printed version, the huge ones they hang in the stations, the ones they post in the train cars (right behind the seats so that you have to peer past someone's ear to read them), and the one that is posted online. Currently, you get basically the same map in each place, but that shouldn't be the case: in each context, a slightly different version, optimized just for that specific environment, should be available.

---

* I wanted to put the Empire State Building in there, but it would have cluttered up Midtown, and my goal all along was that it really had to be a simple and functional *subway* map!

Each version should have its own design, tailored to the context in which it appears. The big maps that hang in the stations, for instance, should show you the neighborhoods, but the one in the subway car that riders reference to make quick decisions, like whether to get off at the next station, need not. And why does the map in the subway car have to give you all that *bus* information?

Contexts aren't just physical, either. After 11:00 pm in New York, 26 routes reduce to 19. So, in addition to the main day/evening KickMap, I made the night map shown in Figure 5-12. Instead of relying on a text-heavy, hard-to-read chart at the bottom of a one-size-fits-all map to determine when a certain route is available, a night map should be available to riders (not only on their iPhones, but also in the subway cars).

Figure 5-12. *The night version of the KickMap shows only the lines that run between 11:00 p.m. and 6:30 a.m.*

When it came to making a night map, I simplified the day/evening version and took out most of the street and neighborhood information, as it seemed redundant.

Also, I do love the simple and elegant aesthetic of Beck's Underground map, and keeping the night map's form simple pays homage to it!

Conclusion

Ultimately, I do think the KickMap accomplished most of my goals: to make the subway lines and their connections as clear as possible for easier navigation, and to provide users with a clear representation of where they are once they exit a station so that the subway feels familiar and welcoming to all.

My main goal, however, was to get my map out there into the hands of subway riders. After the MTA rejected my design, I found an alternative way to distribute it, via Apple's iTunes—two apps, one free and one paid, for the iPhone, iPod Touch, and iPad.

All of the choices I made were aimed at trying to make the user experience as seamless and pleasant as possible. Clearly I'm striking a chord, as over 250,000 people (and counting) have now downloaded copies of the KickMap from iTunes. That's really great but I still want the KickMap—or something superior—to replace the current one in the subway system. I want people to be comfortable and even happy when using our unbeatable 24-hour subway system. It is a complex system, but if people know how easy it can be—if the map becomes a friend* instead of an obstacle—ridership will increase. Ultimately, that benefits not only the system itself, but also all of us who live, work, visit, and breathe here.

---

* I think many people are passionate about the subway map as a great symbol of New York. The map shows the subway as kind of a dynamic capillary system nourishing the city. This is true not only conceptually but also historically: the subway was built to "nourish" new residential areas with cheap transportation to and from the central business districts so the City could continue to grow and thrive.

## CHAPTER SIX

Flight Patterns: A Deep Dive

Aaron Koblin with Valdean Klump

THERE ARE ROADS IN THE SKY. We can't see them, but they are there: distinct, sharply defined avenues, traversed by thousands of airplanes every day. As individual observers we might never guess this was the case, but plotting the raw flight data shows us otherwise (Figure 6-1).

Flight Patterns is a project I started in 2005 that visualizes civilian air traffic in the United States and Canada. It exists in two mediums: still imagery, which traces aircraft arriving and departing from U.S. and Canadian airports over a 24-hour period, and video imagery, which depicts the same data in motion. In this chapter, I'll show you some of these images and talk about the techniques I used to render them. I'll also share some thoughts on why I find this project so compelling, and why I hope you will as well.*

---

* All of the images in this chapter are available in high resolution online, so if you find them intriguing, I recommend that you visit my website to get a better look at them: *http://www.aaronkoblin. com/work/flightpatterns/*. On the site, you may zoom in to the visualizations as well as view them in colors indicating aircraft altitude, model, and manufacturer. You may also view videos of the flight data in motion.

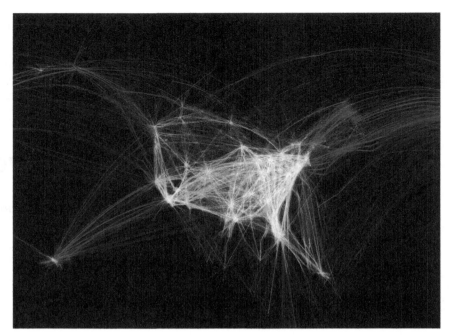

Figure 6-1. *Flight Patterns, a visualization of aircraft location data for airplanes arriving at and departing from U.S. and Canadian airports*

To begin with, I want to draw your attention to what I believe are the two most striking features of the visualization. The first is the tendency of airplanes to follow the exact same flight paths as other planes. When I originally rendered the data, I expected to see tight groupings of planes close to airports and a vast dispersion between them. Instead, I found the opposite: flight paths between airports tend to cluster, and then, as the planes get closer to landing or departing, their flight paths tend to disperse (Figures 6-2 and 6-3).

When you think about it, this is quite interesting. The sky is wide open, without any natural restrictions whatsoever, so planes can travel by any route they choose. And yet when looking at Flight Patterns, it almost appears as if there's a map to the sky, a kind of aerial highway system, with designated routes between various destinations. You can even make out the roads.

Why is this happening? To be honest, I don't know for sure. The routes may simply be the most efficient flight paths, or—more likely, I think—they may be determined by a combination of many factors: the airplanes' autopilot systems, government-mandated flight paths, directions from the carriers, air traffic control systems, rules meant to limit traffic over areas with large populations, and meteorological factors such as wind direction and air pressure. Regardless, I think this tendency is striking, because it shows the logical organization of a completely open space. It's for this reason that I chose the word "patterns" for the name of the project.

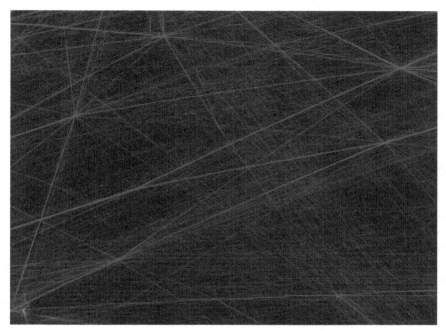

Figure 6-2. *Closeup of a section of Figure 6-1 that reflects what I expected to find throughout the data: flight paths going in every direction*

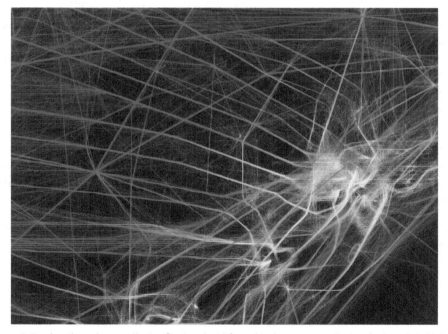

Figure 6-3. *Another closeup that reflects what I found to be common instead: clear, bright lines that indicate flight paths followed closely by high volumes of planes*

The second striking feature of Flight Patterns is that it allows us to visualize the vastness of the U.S. and Canadian air transportation system. To me, this is what makes data visualization so valuable. We cannot grasp the totality of flight traffic in the U.S. and Canada by looking up at the sky or by seeing the raw numbers, but we can understand it through visualization. Viewed together, the flight paths show us more than the sum of their parts: they show us a system—and the system, I believe, is beautiful. It reveals something not just about flight paths, but about the geography of human populations, and more broadly, of our species's clear desire to travel.

Techniques and Data

Flight Patterns was created with Processing,* a programming language that is particularly suited for data visualization. Once the flight data was procured (always a critical step), I wrote a simple Processing program to translate each data point's latitude and longitude into a 2D map on my computer screen. Concurrently, I added selective color to each point to indicate information such as altitude and aircraft model. I then exported all of these images as TGA files.

The videos were a little trickier. Showing the airplanes as moving dots failed to reveal the progress of each flight. So instead I drew lines between each data point, and, after a set time interval (3 minutes or 5 minutes, depending on the dataset), I added a 4% black opacity layer over the entire map. This meant that older flight paths would fade into the background over time, which helped to show the planes' progress.

The data used in Flight Patterns is a processed version of the Aircraft Situation Display to Industry (ASDI) feed, a record of all civilian flight paths that is published by the FAA.† The feed is available only to companies with ties to the aviation industry. Thanks to my colleague Scott Hessels, I received 28 hours' worth of this flight data in 2005. My initial visualization was a contribution to the Celestial Mechanics project completed along with Gabriel Dunne at UCLA's Design | Media Arts program.

The initial dataset I worked with was from March 19–20, 2005, and includes 141,029 flights, sampled every 3 minutes, for a total of 6,871,383 data points. Three years later, in 2008, I worked with *Wired* magazine to obtain another dataset. This data came from August 12–13, 2008, and includes 205,514 flights, sampled every minute, for a total of 26,552,304 data points.

The data I received that was derived from the ASDI feed included the following information for each data point:

---

* See *http://processing.org*.
† "Civilian" means all nonmilitary commercial and private flights tracked by the FAA.

- Latitude

- Longitude

- Altitude

- Aircraft manufacturer

- Aircraft model

- Timestamp

- Flight number

If you are interested in seeing some of the data yourself, the FAA presently provides a sample of the ASDI feed in XML format at *http://www.fly.faa.gov/ASDI/asdi.html*.

Color

Flight Patterns does not use any complex mapmaking techniques: simply plotting the data speaks for itself. However, color plays an important role in telling different stories using the same flight paths. Figures 6-4 through 6-9 show some examples.

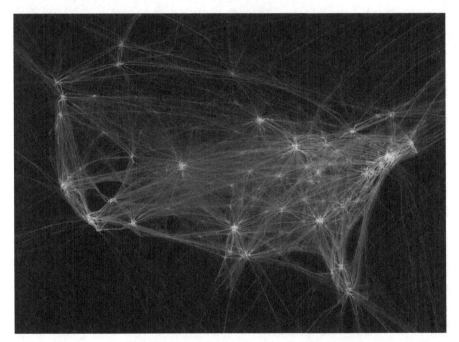

Figure 6-4. *In this map, color indicates altitude, with pure white meaning the plane is at ground level*

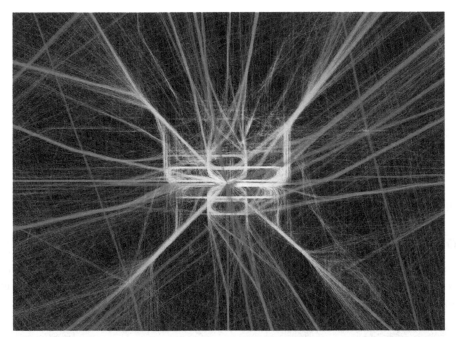

Figure 6-5. *A closeup on the Atlanta airport, clearly showing the layout of the runways (again, color indicates altitude)*

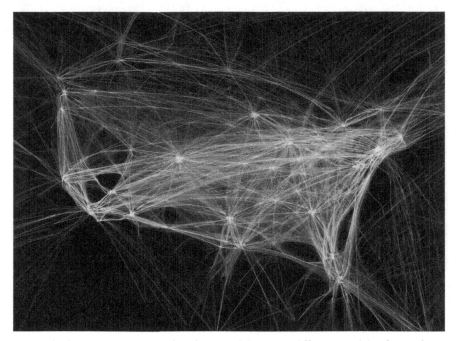

Figure 6-6. *In this map, color is used to distinguish between different models of aircraft*

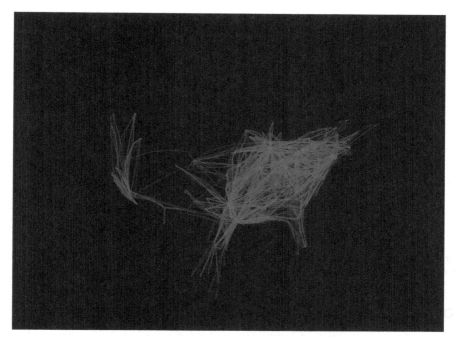

Figure 6-7. *A map of a single aircraft model, showing only flights on Embraer ERJ 145 regional jets*

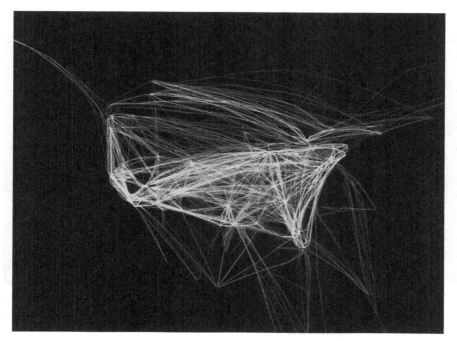

Figure 6-8. *Another map of a single aircraft model, showing only flights on Boeing 737 jets*

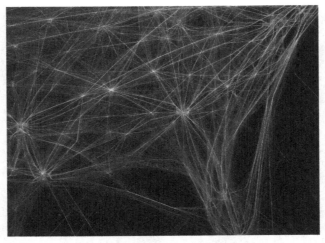

Figure 6-9. *In this map, separate colors show takeoffs and landings: orange indicates a descending plane and blue indicates an ascending plane*

Motion

In motion, Flight Patterns reveals new pieces of information, including aircraft direction and volume over time. The visualization tracks flights from one evening to the next in order to show the country falling asleep and waking up the following day (Figures 6-10 and 6-11).

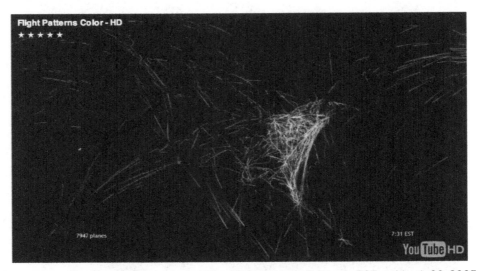

Figure 6-10. *The East Coast wakes up: this still image, from 7:31 a.m. EST on March 20, 2005, shows high activity on the East Coast and virtual stillness on the West Coast (except for a few redeye flights flying northeast from Hawaii)*

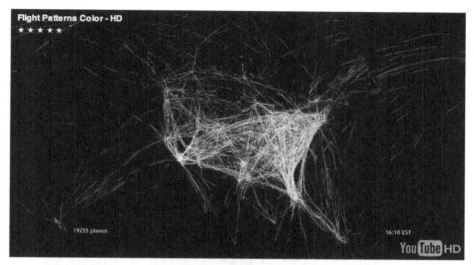

Figure 6-11. *At 4:10 p.m. EST, we see a very different story: at this moment, air traffic peaks with 19,255 planes in the air*

On my website, I've also included a video of a 3D visualization that plots altitude along the *z*-axis in a 3D projection. In order for this axis to be discernible versus the lateral scale of the continent, I've exaggerated the altitude considerably, and it makes for a dense but interesting visualization. It doesn't print well, however. I recommend you take a look online if you're interested.

Anomalies and Errors

Like many datasets, the data I used in Flight Patterns contained a number of errors and anomalies, some of which I removed. For example, while trying to find the fastest flight in the dataset, I identified one flight that crossed the entire country in 6 minutes—clearly an error. Another flight zigzagged dramatically (and impossibly) north and south while crossing the country—another clear error. I removed both of these flights.

There were other anomalies, however, that I kept. For example, the flight paths over the north Atlantic appear jagged (Figure 6-12). I opted to keep this data in the visualization because it was important to show the flights coming from Europe. I don't know why those errors are there. They could indicate problems with the planes' instruments, the processing of the ASDI, or an error by the data supplier. After fretting about it for a long time, I decided to simply leave the data as it was. Also, when looking for the shortest flight, I found that over 3,000 aircraft had reported their locations without ever departing the airport; I kept these anomalies, too.

Figure 6-12. *Flight paths over the north Atlantic show some anomalies in the data*

If you look carefully at the visualization, you will notice some interesting features. One obvious example is the restricted no-fly zones over Nevada (Figure 6-13). It doesn't appear as if these no-fly zones are completely restricted, though: a tiny number of flights crossing this dark space are just discernable.

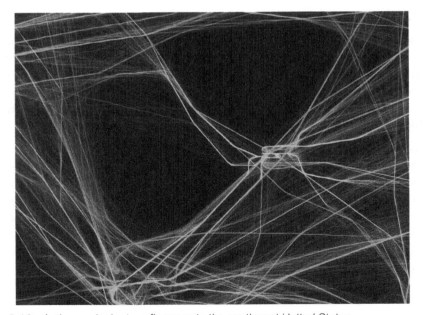

Figure 6-13. *A closeup look at no-fly zones in the southwest United States*

Every time you work with large, organic datasets, you will find errors and anomalies, and I think it's important to consider how to handle them. For each case, I ask myself, will I harm the integrity of the data by manipulating it? If the answer is yes, it's best to simply leave the data as it is or, in the case of obvious errors, remove them entirely. If anything, you should celebrate anomalies rather than removing them (and be sure to investigate them for the interesting stories).

Conclusion

Flight Patterns is a simple data visualization, and this simplicity makes it compelling for several reasons. For one thing, the project reveals a map of our air transit system, which is something that has never before been visualized publicly, as far as I'm aware. Secondly, the visualization is easy to understand, even though it is made entirely from data—the airports in the visualization create nodes that conform to our geographical conception of North America (Figure 6-14). Likewise, the densest flight paths fall over areas of high population, just as we'd expect.

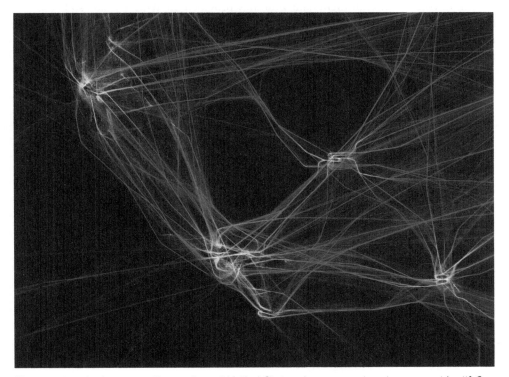

Figure 6-14. *A closeup on the southwest United States—how many airports can you identify?*

Finally, I find Flight Patterns compelling because it is comforting. This is perhaps a strange emotion to associate with a map, but by showing the orderliness of air transport and by uncovering the mystery of how planes get from place to place, Flight Patterns reveals a logical system that we are only a tiny part of when sitting in seat 16A at 34,000 feet. It's comforting, I think, to see a system that works so well, at such a high volume. With over 200,000 flights in one day in the U.S. and Canada alone, we truly have created roads in the sky, every one of them guiding thousands of people from origin to destination, and with a remarkable safety record. In this sense, Flight Patterns is more than a data visualization: it is a showcase for the miracle of modern air travel.

Acknowledgments

I owe the idea and inspiration for Flight Patterns to two colleagues at UCLA, Gabriel Dunne and Scott Hessels. In 2005, we started an art project called Celestial Mechanics (*http://cmlab.com*) that depicts air and space systems in motion. A small part of the project was devoted to aircraft flight data, and they provided me with the data so I could build what became Flight Patterns. Thanks also to Mark Hansen, of UCLA, and *Wired* magazine (especially Carl DeTorres) for further assistance in procuring the data for these images.

## CHAPTER SEVEN

Your Choices Reveal Who You Are: Mining and Visualizing Social Patterns

Valdis Krebs

DATA MINING AND DATA VISUALIZATION GO HAND IN HAND. Finding complex patterns in data and making them visible for further interpretation utilizes the power of computers, along with the power of the human mind. Used properly, this is a great combination, enabling efficient and sophisticated data crunching and pattern recognition.

In this chapter, we will explore several datasets that reveal interesting insights into the human behaviors behind them. Patterns formed by event attendance and object selection will give us clues into the thinking and behavior of the humans attending the events and choosing the objects. Often, our simple behaviors and choices can reveal who we are, and whom we are like.

Early Social Graphs

In the 1930s, a group of sociologists and ethnographers did a small "data mining" experiment. They wanted to derive the social structure of a group of women in a small town in the southern United States. They used public data that appeared in the local newspaper. Their dataset was small: 18 women attending 14 different social events.

They wondered: could we figure out the social structure (today we call it a *social graph*) of this group of women? To this end, they posed the following questions:

- Who is a friend of whom?
- Which social circles are they all in?
- Who plays a key role in the social structure?

Identifying network structures normally involves invasive interviews and surveys. Would it be possible to derive network structures by just examining public behaviors? The real question was: *do public choices reveal who you are* and whom you are like?

Being able to see actual connections inside any human system, organization, or community is critical to understanding how groups work and how their members behave. Social network analysis (SNA) is a currently popular set of social science methods used for marketing, improving organizational effectiveness, building economic networks, tracking disease outbreaks, uncovering fraud and corruption, analyzing patterns found in online social networks, and disrupting terrorist networks. SNA techniques can also reveal underlying network structures in the Southern Women dataset, as we will see in a bit.

SNA started as *sociometry* in the early 20th century. Jacob Moreno's drawings of friendship links (or *sociograms*) between students in his school are very popular amongst social science historians, and business scholars point to the famous Hawthorne factory worker studies from earlier in the century and the sketches of work interactions between the "Bank Wiring Room" employees. Friendship ties amongst the Wiring Room employees are illustrated in Figure 7-1.

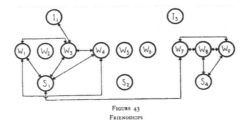

FIGURE 43
FRIENDSHIPS

Figure 7-1. *Early 20th-century social graph used in studying workflows amongst employees*

SNA maps a human system as nodes and links. The nodes are usually people, and the links are either relationships between people or flows between people. The links can be directional. When the nodes are of only one type—for example, people, as in the Moreno and Hawthorne studies—it is called *one-mode analysis*.

However, the Southern Women study began as a slightly more complex form of social analysis: two-mode. There were two sets of nodes—people and events—and the links showed which people attended which events. The social graph for the two data modes are shown in Figure 7-2. The women are the blue nodes on the left, while the events that each attended are the green nodes on the right. People are represented by circles, while events are represented by squares.

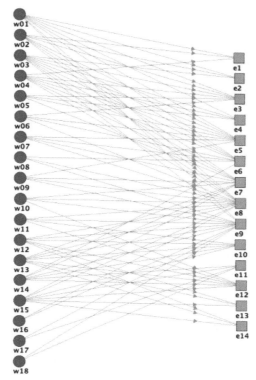

Figure 7-2. *Two-mode view of the Southern Women social event dataset*

This diagram reveals various types of conclusions, such as:

- Woman #3 attended more events than woman #18.

- Event #8 had the most attendees.

Other than these simple observations, the two-mode view does not reveal any obvious patterns, such as the women's social structure or the relationships among the events. To see these deeper insights, we can transform the two-mode data into one-mode data by using a popular social network analysis technique: *transforming nodes to links*. In the first transformation, we'll take the event nodes and view them as links instead:

> Woman X is connected to woman Y as they both attended Event Z.

The more events the women attended together, the stronger their tie is. We can also shift the focus to look at the network of events:

> Event A is connected to event B if they were both attended by the same woman, C.

The more women who attended the same two events, the stronger the connection is between the two events. There are many methods to calculate the link strength when transforming a two-mode network to a one-mode network. In this example, we use the simplest method: adding up the co-occurrences.

The network of events is shown in Figure 7-3. A thicker line reveals a stronger relationship between two events—i.e., that more women attended both events. The SNA software organizes the network according to who is connected to whom using an advanced graph layout algorithm: a node's place in the network is determined by its connections *and* the connections of those connections.

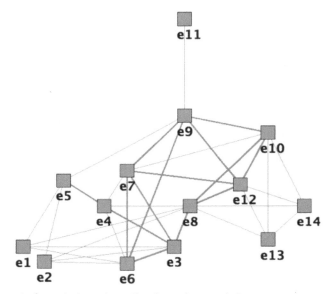

Figure 7-3. *Layout of events based on attendance by people in common*

The center of the graph attracts the better-connected nodes, while the less-connected nodes are pushed toward the periphery. Thus, it is obvious at a glance which events were most important in this social calendar. However, we still do not have a picture of what interests us the most: the emergent social network of the women in this small town. To begin to reveal that network, I used my *gradual inclusion* method, which focuses initially on the strongest ties in the structure and then gradually lowers the membership threshold to reveal weaker ties in the network, allowing more people to connect to whoever is there already. This method usually ignores the very weak ties in the data, dismissing them as *social noise*. In this case, with the small dataset, the dismissal of light connectivity must be done carefully. In a dataset with millions of nodes and millions of choices, adjusting the bar for social noise is usually a less delicate operation.

Using a five-point scale, with 5 indicating the strongest tie between two nodes and 1 indicating the weakest, I started using my gradual inclusion method with *strength = 5* links—in other words, identifying those women who had attended the most events in common. Figure 7-4 reveals the strongest ties based on event attendance.

I immediately saw two clusters form: one with women #1, #2, #3, and #4, and the other with women #12, #13, and #15. I colored the nodes using two different colors to distinguish the membership in each group.

Next, I included the next lower level of ties: *strength = 4* links. This resulted in new members being included in each cluster, but did not reveal any connection between the two clusters. As you can see in Figure 7-5, we still have two distinct groups.

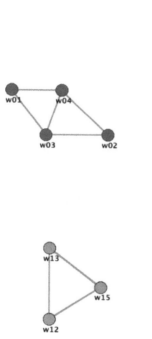

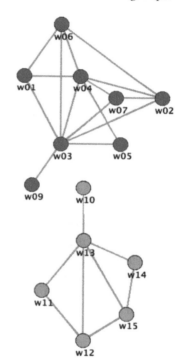

Figure 7-4. *Strongest ties amongst women based on common event attendance*

Figure 7-5. *The two strongest link levels between women attending common social events*

Including the *strength = 3* ties revealed bridging between the groups, as Figure 7-6 illustrates. This is common in most social structures: the strongest ties occur *within* a group, while the weaker, less frequent ties occur *between* groups. There were also some weaker ties within each group, indicating that not everyone within a given group has a strong tie to all members of that group.

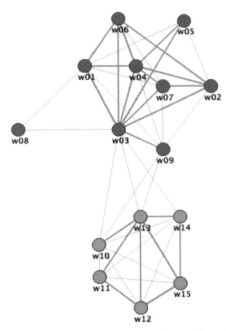

Figure 7-6. *The two groups are bridged with gradual inclusion of weaker ties*

Our social structure is still missing a few nodes: women #16, #17, and #18. They have not met the criteria for attachment in any of the previous waves of inclusion using the gradual inclusion method. Perhaps they are new in town, or are just less social and have attended fewer events, making it more difficult to determine their membership. These three women attach to the network when I lower the threshold to *strength = 2* links. Now all women are attached to the network, while the original two-cluster structure remains. Woman #16 is the only one that does not obviously belong to one cluster or the other; she has equal infrequent ties to both clusters. I therefore classify her as a member of *neither* cluster (not both clusters!) and color her purple. The final emergent social graph is shown in Figure 7-7.

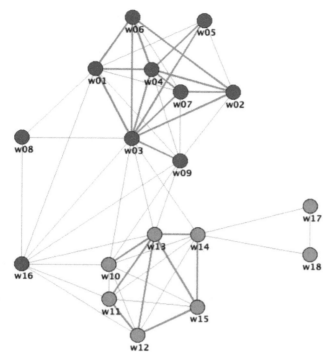

Figure 7-7. *Emergent social graph of women based on common attendance at social events*

All 18 women have now been placed in the social network based on their attendance of local social events. This social network reveals a few interesting things about this small town's social structure:

- Two distinct social clusters exist.

- The clusters are connected. This social overlap reveals some possible commonality in interests and relations between the two clusters.

- Various network roles emerge. Some women are connectors, bridging the two clusters, while others act as internal core members, connecting only to their own groups.

Social graphs like that in Figure 7-7 can be used for marketing purposes or word-of-mouth campaigns. More information can usually be gathered than this simple example provides, but some deductions can nonetheless be drawn from this data:

- Woman #6 will probably not be influenced by what woman #12 does or says.

- Woman #4 probably has the highest internal influence within the blue cluster. She may be the one that reinforces the status quo with everyone in her group.

- Woman #9 in the blue cluster is the *boundary spanner*—the person bridging the two clusters—and probably brings new ideas and opinions into the group. It is good that she has at least one strong tie within the group, to woman #3, who is well connected within the group. People who bring new ideas into a group often need at least one strong, internally well-connected ally.

- Women #16, #17, and #18 may be new in town or may not be "joiners." They have some access to what is happening in the groups, but they may not have access to the real private information in either group because of their weaker connections.

Different data-mining algorithms often produce different results, even with a small dataset such as this one. Over the years, various sociologists and network scientists have re-examined this interesting little dataset, applying their fresh new algorithms to see what patterns emerge. Figure 7-8 shows the results from 21 of the most popular studies. Our results match those of study #13, by Linton Freeman (Freeman 2003): women #1–9 are in one group, women #10–15 and #17–18 are in the other group, and woman #16 belongs to both groups. Freeman was a key player in establishing the field of social network analysis (Freeman 2004) and was especially important in establishing some early network metrics that are still popular today (Freeman 1979).

		1	2	3	4	5	6	7	8	9	10	11	12	13	14	15	16	17	18
1	DGG41	W	W	W	W	W	W	W	W	WW	W	W	W	W	W	W	W	W	W
2	HOM50	W	W	W	W	W	W	W	WW			W	W	W	W	W		W	W
3	P&C72	W	W	W	W	W	W	W	W	W		W	W	W	W	W	W	W	W
4	BGR74	W	W	W	W	W	W	W		W	W	W	W	W	WW	WW		W	W
5	BBA75	W	W	W	W	W	W	W	W	W	W	W	W	W	W	W	W	W	W
6	BCH78	W	W	W	W	W	W			W	W	W	W	W					
7	DOR79	W	W	W	W	W	W			W	W	W	W	W	W				
8	BCH91	W	W	W	W	W	W	W	W	W	W	W	W	W	W	W	W	W	W
9	FRE92	W	W	W	W	W	W	W		W	W	W	W	W	W	W	W		
10	E&B93	W	W	W	W	W	W	W		W	W	W	W	W	W	W			
11	FRI93	W	W	W	W	W	W	W	W	W	W	W	W	W	W	W	W	W	W
12	FR293	W	W	W	W	W	W	W	W	W	W	W	W	W	W	W	W	W	W
13	FW193	W	W	W	W	W	W	W	W	W	W	W	W	W	W	WW		W	W
14	FW293	W	W	W	W	W	W	W	W	W	W	W	W	W	W	W		W	W
15	BE197	W	W	W	W	W	W			W	W	W	W	W	W				
16	BE297	W	W	W	W	W	W	W	W	W	W	W	W	W	W	W		W	W
17	BE397	W	W	W	W	W	W	W	W	W	W	W	W	W	W	W	W	W	W
18	S&F99	W	W	W	W	W	W	W	W	W	W	W	W	W	W	W		W	W
19	ROB00	W	W	W	W	W	W	W	W	W	W	W	W	W	W	W	W	W	W
20	OSB00	W	W	W	W	W	W	W	W	W	W	W	W	W	W	W	W	W	W
21	NEW01	W	W	W	W	W	W	W	**W**	W	W	W	W	W	W	W	W	W	W

Figure 7-8. *Results of 21 studies of the Southern Women social event dataset by network scientists (Freeman 2003)*

Look at the various membership groupings in Table 7-1. Most of the studies came to highly similar conclusions, and all found two distinct clusters in the data. However, there is not total agreement about who is in each cluster, especially for women #8–18.

This table illustrates membership groupings well, but it does not reveal network roles and social distances. The network map in Figure 7-7 does reveal the nuances of the social structure and shows the *points of failure* in the network—that is, where it is most likely to break down. For instance, if woman #3 were to move away, the network would be disrupted the most. It would be interesting to see how both woman #4 and woman #9 would respond to the exit of woman #3.

Social Graphs of Amazon Book Purchasing Data

Amazon.com allows easy access to summary purchase data (transaction data is aggregated to prevent individual identification). The book purchasing data Amazon provides forms a similar network dataset to the event network in Figure 7-3. Instead of attending the same social events, on Amazon, people are connected to one another by purchasing the same books. In both cases, connections are made because certain people make the same choices as others.

On each item's page, Amazon provides the following information:

Customers Who Bought This Item Also Bought

When people buy two items, an association is formed between those items. The more people purchase both items, the stronger the association is and the higher on the list the *also bought* item appears. Although usually people are represented by nodes, in this case Amazon's customers are the links in the network, and the items they purchase are the nodes. Consequently, Amazon is able to generate a network that provides significant information about its customers' choices and preferences, without revealing any personal data about the individual customers. Patterns are revealed, while privacy is maintained. With a little data mining and some data visualization, we can get great insights into the habits and choices of Amazon's customers—that is, we can come to understand groups of people without knowing about their individual choices.

Determining the Network Around a Particular Book

One of the cardinal rules of human networks is "birds of a feather flock together." Friends of friends become friends, and coworkers of coworkers become colleagues. Dense clusters of connections emerge throughout the social space. In the social networks we visualize, we see those birds of a feather near each other on the map.

Let's take a look at a popular computer book available via Amazon: Toby Segaran and Jeff Hammerbacher's *Beautiful Data* (O'Reilly). Among other information, the book's Amazon page provides a product description, publication details, and a brief list of "also bought" books. What does this list tell us about the book we are viewing? Being a student of networks, my inquiry about this book did not stop at the *also bought* books listed on this web page (one step in the network). I wanted to know what would happen if I followed the links to each of those books and joined the lists I found there into a network (one and two steps in the network).

Key to understanding the dynamics of networks is the ability to perceive the *emergent patterns of connections* that surround an individual node, or that are present within and around a community of interest. I wanted to see the network in which my book of interest was embedded. Seeing those connections can provide insight into the *network* neighborhood—the network surrounding this book—which can help a consumer make a smarter purchase.

Tracing the network out two steps from the focus node is a common procedure in social network analysis when studying *ego networks*. An ego network allows us to see *who* is in one's network neighborhood, *how* they are interconnected, and *how* this structure may influence the ego—the focus node.

As I collected the *also bought* books around *Beautiful Data*, I wondered:

- What themes would I see in the books and in their connections?

- What other topics interest the readers of *Beautiful Data*?

- Will *Beautiful Data* end up in the center of one large, massively interconnected cluster or be a part of one distinct community of interest amongst several?

Figure 7-9 shows the book network surrounding *Beautiful Data*. Each node represents a book purchased on Amazon. A gray line links books that were purchased together, with the arrowhead pointing in the direction of the *also bought* book. The red nodes represent other books published by O'Reilly Media, while the yellow nodes represent books from other publishers.

In networks, it is not the number of connections one has, but where those connections lead, that creates advantage. The golden rule in networks is the same as in real estate: *location, location, location*. In real estate, what matters is physical location: geography. In networks, it is virtual location, determined by the pattern of connections surrounding a node.

The nodes in Figure 7-9 self-organize, in the graph space, by their ties to *also bought* books. This allows similar books to self-organize together to form clusters of like topics, which reveal the human communities of interest behind the book clusters. In Figure 7-9, two obvious groupings cling together by topic:

- The bottom-right grouping is all about programmers and programming.

- The grouping at the top of the graph is all about the Semantic Web.

Although clusters emerge in Figure 7-9, they are not as obvious as some others that we will see later; these clusters are intermixed and overlap, especially around other books about modern programming methods and processes.

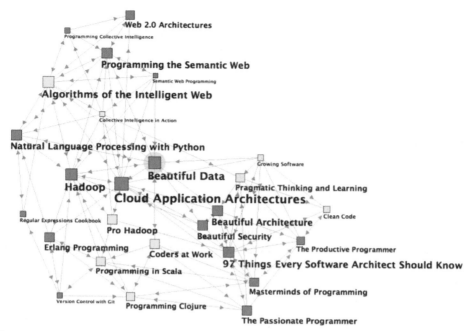

Figure 7-9. *The network neighborhood of books surrounding Beautiful Data*

In addition to clusters of like topics, in Figure 7-9 there are clusters around the publishers, designated by the node colors: red books connect to other red books and yellows connect to other yellows. This indicates that people who like O'Reilly books tend to buy other O'Reilly books. Node size also appears to form a weak pattern of connectivity across similarly sized nodes. Large nodes, the nonlocal influence across the graph, connect to other large nodes, while medium and small nodes often connect to one another. This is a pattern we often see in human networks—again, birds of a feather flock together. It is not a pattern we see with the physical structure of the Internet, though, where many small nodes connect to a few very large nodes, creating an obvious hub-and-spoke pattern. That is often referred to as a *scale-free network.*

Next, I examined the network measures of each node/book, to see which nodes were well positioned in the web of connections. Since this is a directed network, much like the World Wide Web, I calculated influence metrics similar to Google's PageRank. These metrics were calculated using both direct and indirect links around each node. Like on the Web, a better-connected node transfers more influence. These metrics do not reflect sales volumes or the popularity that quantity conveys; rather, they reveal what thousands of Amazon purchasers feel belong together—what the "birds of a feather" books are. The larger nodes have greater influence in this community of interest based on the pattern of *also bought* purchases.

Another common network measure is *structural equivalence*. This measure reveals which nodes play a similar role in a network. Equivalent nodes may be substitutable for one another in the network. As an author, I would *not* like my book to be substitutable with many other books! As a reader, however, I would like equivalent choices. In Figure 7-9, the two books with the most similar link pattern to *Beautiful Data* are *Cloud Application Architectures* and *Programming the Semantic Web*.

Another value-added service that Amazon provides is reader-submitted book reviews. A person considering the purchase of a particular book may be aided by the many reviews that accumulate. Unfortunately, the reviews can be skewed: an author with a large personal network can quickly get a dozen or more glowing reviews of his latest book posted to Amazon, and a reader with a grudge can do the opposite. Doing comparison shopping based on reader reviews alone may, therefore, be misleading.

The book network map may be a better indicator than individual reviews of which other books to buy. Books linked from many other similar books reflect critical choices made by purchasers, who spent money on those books. Surely this behavior is not random; it is executed on the basis of thought and comparisons. A purchase decision is the best review of all, even if it is never written.

The book network maps I've shown are designed to eliminate the *peripheral nodes* in the network (i.e., those with very few connections). The network map in Figure 7-9 shows a *3-core network*—a network in which each node has a minimum of three connections to other nodes. To achieve this, all nodes with only one or two incoming links were removed. These were nodes that led to other communities of interest, that represented new or very old books, or that had very few *also bought* links from this community.

Putting the Results to Work

These community-of-interest maps can also work in a similar capacity with other consumer items. If I am not familiar with a product, an author, an artist, a vintage, a brand, a movie, or a song, I would like to be able to judge it by the company it keeps— its network neighborhood. Here are the relevant questions to ask:

- What nodes point to this item?
- What communities is it a member of?
- Is it central in the community?
- Does it bridge communities?
- Are there equivalent alternatives?

It appears that as a customer of Amazon, I can make smarter decisions by viewing the *embeddedness*—the context within the network—of various items Amazon sells in different communities of interest. Other vendors, such as Netflix and Apple's iTunes, probably do similar analysis before recommending a movie or a new song or artist. By gathering information on thousands of customers and what they choose and organize together, a vendor can form a product-to-product network like that in Figure 7-9, or even a person-to-person network like that in Figure 7-7. Both maps will indicate likely influence patterns and what it makes sense for customers to purchase/rent/download together.

Here are some network rules of thumb that we can distill from the Amazon analysis:

- If you have read one nonfiction book of a structurally equivalent pair, you may not be in a rush to read the second, since the second book probably covers the same information as the first book. On the other hand, you may wish to read a large number of structurally equivalent fiction titles (can't get enough of those cyber-thrillers!).

- If you liked books A, B, and C and want to read something similar, find which books are linked to A and B as well as C. You can only see this in the network diagram; you cannot see these linkages in Amazon's individual lists unless you open three browser windows and compare the lists yourself.

- If you want to read just one book about topic X, find the book with the highest network influence score in the cluster of topic-X books. This follows the Google PageRank approach and may reveal a book with excellent "word of mouth" appeal.

- If the book you are looking for is not in stock, find which other books are structurally equivalent to that book. These will provide similar content and may be available.

A book author and/or publicist could use her knowledge of existing book networks to position a book where there is a *hole*, or gap in the network. A publisher could review evolving book networks, which may change weekly, to adapt its marketing efforts. Amazon, of course, is still the big winner: it has all the data, and a rich upside of hitherto untapped possibilities for analyzing the data and applying the findings.

Social Networks of Political Books

Visualizing book networks on Amazon not only helps us choose which books to purchase, but also gives us insights into larger trends and patterns in a particular sphere of interest. One area that is ripe for exploration is politics. Purchase patterns on Amazon often reflect the results of countrywide surveys of political beliefs and choices.

Two books are connected in the book network if Amazon reports that they were frequently bought together by the same consumer. I don't arrange or color the nodes before feeding the *also bought* data through my social network analysis software,

InFlow 3.1.* The software has an algorithm that arranges the layout of the nodes based on each node's connections. Once the software finds the emergent pattern and identifies any clusters, I review the books in each cluster and then see whether they naturally cluster as blue, red, or purple (my coloring scheme follows the conservative-as-red and liberal-as-blue convention that became popular in the United States during the 2000 presidential election; purple is a combination of red and blue and is used to describe books that fall between the two popular political camps).

I have been doing a social network analysis of the purchase patterns of political books since 2003. Unsurprisingly, from my very first mapping I saw two distinct political clusters: a red one designating those who read right-leaning books and a blue one designating those who read left-leaning books. In my 2003 network analysis, I saw just one book holding the red and blue clusters together. Ironically, that book was named *What Went Wrong*. This map is shown in Figure 7-10.

Figure 7-10. *Divide of political books in 2003*

In the 2004 map (Figure 7-11), constructed several months before the 2004 U.S. presidential election, several books held the two clusters together. Again, at least with the better-selling books, there was very little crossover between the right and left camps: people on each side appeared to be reading more and more books that supported their existing frames of mind. This is not to say that no readers were reading both red and blue books, but they appeared to be in the minority. I looked only at Amazon's best-selling books and at the most common *also boughts* for each book, focusing on the most frequent and intense interactions (as when examining the strong ties in a human network). A deeper look into the Amazon data (if Amazon permitted it) might reveal

* See *http://orgnet.com/inflow3.html.*

these weaker, less frequent, connections amongst blue and red books. I would expect to see a small minority reading books on both sides—many might be in academia, teaching or taking courses where both sides of an issue are presented and debated.

Figure 7-11. *Divide of political books in 2004*

I continued to create these political book maps using Amazon data from 2005 through 2007, and I kept getting the same strong red/blue divide. *The books changed over time, but the overall network pattern remained the same.* How strong was this pattern? To test it, I experimented with my data collection approaches—were the strong patterns an artifact of my methods? No! Regardless of the data collection method, as long as I followed accepted practices—such as "snowball sampling" (Heckathorn 1997)— the results showed strong red and blue clustering. Occasionally a different collection method would result in a few new books sneaking into the mix, but the overall pattern remained stable. The emergent political book network pattern was *not* sensitive to data collection methods and cutoffs, indicating that the pattern was strong and persistent.

In 2008, with the U.S. presidential election approaching, I decided to take several snapshots of the political network. How would it change as we moved closer to Election Day? I captured the network at three critical junctures:

- At the end of the primary season

- After the last convention

- Right before Election Day in November

I expected the red/blue divide to persist, but wondered if any interesting patterns would appear as the presidential election process moved through its phases.

In June 2008, after the major party candidates had been chosen via the primary process, I turned again to the predictive patterns of partisan political polemics. At the Iowa caucus in January of that year, Obama had said, "we are not a collection of red states and blue states, we are the United States of America," and McCain proclaimed his purple "maverick" roots. But what did the book data tell us?

Figure 7-12 was created during June 2008. As a little experiment, I added a new color: light blue. According to the Amazon sales data, these books cluster with the other blues. But looking at the titles and authors, they do not fit in with the common blue themes and the supporters of previous iterations of blue nodes. At this point in time, popular conservatives, independents, and libertarians were all finding more connection with the blue readers than with the red readers. The reds had only George Will bridging them to the rest of the U.S. political world, and a split on the right between the "old conservatives" and the "neo-cons" emerged, with the old conservatives more aligned with the progressives than with the neo-cons in the summer of 2008.

Figure 7-12. *Political book purchase patterns during June 2008*

In August 2008, several anti-Obama books appeared. A new pro-Obama book, with a foreword written by Obama himself, was also in prerelease and being sold on Amazon. Figure 7-13 reveals who was reading these books. The pro-Obama book, *Change We Can Believe In*, is solidly in the blue cluster, indicating that people who had already purchased pro-Obama books were also purchasing this positive book. Similarly, the anti-Obama books—*The Obama Nation* and *The Case Against Barack Obama*—were primarily being purchased by people who had already purchased other anti-Obama books. One of the anti-Obama books, though, is connected to one of the purple books, *The Late Great USA*. Could some undecided voters, not happy with the state of the country, have been reading this book to make up their minds about Obama?

Figure 7-13. *Political book purchase patterns during August 2008*

No books on McCain, either pro or con, were amongst Amazon's best-selling political polemics. Did people already know enough about him at this point in the election cycle, or were they not interested in him? The pattern of connections between the books in the map in Figure 7-13 indicate that the most influential political books at the end of the summer of 2008 were *What Happened* and *The Post American World*—neither addressed the current election! *What Happened* was written by the former press secretary for George W. Bush, but it was being purchased by the blue readers only.

Social network analysis and data mining/visualization provide us with two categories of outcomes:

- Expected versus unexpected results and insights

- Positive versus negative results and insights

These categories intersect, as illustrated in Figure 7-14. In the hundreds of social network analysis projects I have participated in, I have found that clients typically most enjoy seeing what they did not anticipate—the unexpected (and especially *negative unexpected*) patterns that can lead to problems.

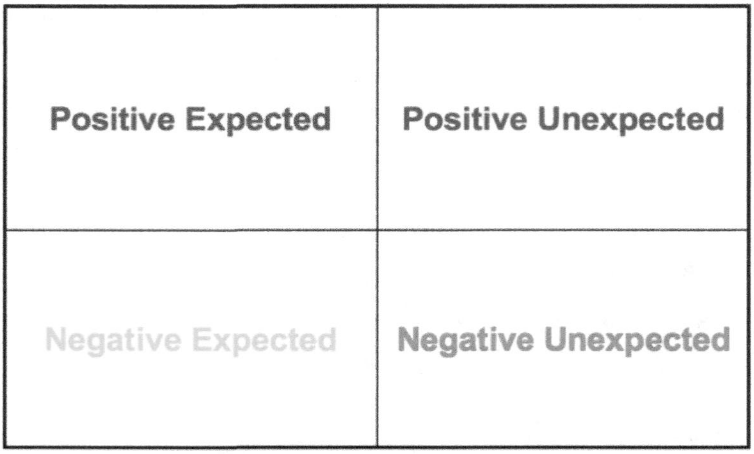

Positive Expected	**Positive Unexpected**
Negative Expected	**Negative Unexpected**

Figure 7-14. *Discovery matrix for social network analysis*

Let's examine our last graph using the discovery matrix in Figure 7-14. In late October 2008, as both presidential campaigns sprinted toward the finish line, I took one more look at the political books being purchased and the patterns they created. The pre-election network map is shown in Figure 7-15. A few unexpected patterns emerge in this map, along with one expected pattern.

Figure 7-15. *Political book purchase patterns a few weeks before the November 2008 election*

Unlike in all the previous maps, there are *no* bridging books between the red and blue clusters—the two sides are totally separate! Red and blue have nothing in common! This pattern reflects the immense polarization and animosity evidenced in the campaign rallies in the run up to the election. Political issues and the great economic problems of the time were not being discussed. This pattern can be classified as a *negative expected* based on the daily actions of each campaign.

Another revelation of the visualization in Figure 7-15 was that right-leaning readers had been buying the key book of community organizers, *Rules for Radicals*. This same group had mocked community organizing! Why were right-of-center readers buying this book, which was normally popular with a left-of-center audience? Was the right trying to figure out why Obama's campaign, based on community organizing principles, had been so successful? This was an *unexpected* pattern, but whether you think it should be classed as positive or negative probably depends on which side you are on.

A final unexpected pattern was that those buying positive books about Obama were not buying other political books. The "about Obama" cluster is disconnected from the other clusters that contain political polemics. This pattern may indicate that these readers are interested only in Obama and this election, not in politics in general.

An *expected* pattern also jumps out from this pre-election political book network map. Since 2004, there have been more registered Democrats than Republicans, so it makes intuitive sense that there are more blue books. In contrast, the right focuses on fewer books to get its message across (the book network map does *not* reflect volume of books sold, so it is possible that readers on the right actually buy a greater volume of fewer books—we don't know, as Amazon does not reveal this data). This is probably viewed as a *positive expected* pattern by both sides, but for different reasons. The right is likely to view its approach as more focused, while the left interprets it as the opposition lacking a variety of opinions. Conversely, the left is likely to view the larger number of books on its side positively, as representing a diversity of opinions, while the right may view it as indicating a scattered and unfocused message.

Conclusion

As the visualizations presented in this chapter have illustrated, *our choices reveal who we are, and whom we are like*. The decisions we make identify not only certain aspects of ourselves, but also what groups we belong to. Since "birds of a feather flock together," our choices provide many insights into the behaviors of others in our groups. In the future (on the Web, for example), many of our choices may not be conscious: our smartphones will communicate with other nearby smart devices looking for ways to connect with their owners. These devices may be programmed to look for the patterns we have examined here. A few brave souls may program their devices to selectively break the typical patterns in which they are embedded—for instance, a red-book reader could strike up a conversation with a blue-book reader after their devices reveal the opportunity to exchange viewpoints.

The Amazon data illustrated that we can gain deep insights into the political choices and behaviors of different groups without knowing anything about the individuals belonging to those groups. Private data does not need to be revealed for us to understand large-scale political patterns based on book purchases. Even more amazing, this data, along with the simple visualizations created to display it, matched the findings of expensive nationwide surveys of potential voters. An hour collecting and mapping

Amazon data gave some of the same insights as thousands of hours spent collecting and analyzing voter survey and interview data. The Pareto 80/20 rule works well here: we get 80% of the insight for much less than 20% of the time invested—an excellent payoff when properly matching data mining with data visualization!

References

Davis, Allison, B.B. Gardner, and M.R. Gardner. 1941. *Deep South: An Anthropological Study of Caste and Class.* Chicago: University of Chicago Press.

Freeman, Linton C. 1979. "Centrality in social networks: I. Conceptual clarification." *Social Networks* 1: 215–239. *http://moreno.ss.uci.edu/27.pdf.*

Freeman, Linton C. 2003. "Finding social groups: A meta-analysis of the southern women data." In *Dynamic Social Network Modeling and Analysis*, eds. Ronald Breiger, Kathleen Carley, and Philippa Pattison. Washington, DC: The National Academies Press. *http://moreno.ss.uci.edu/85.pdf.*

Freeman, Linton C. 2004. *The Development of Social Network Analysis: A Study in the Sociology of Science.* Vancouver, Canada: Empirical Press. *http://aris.ss.uci.edu/~lin/book.pdf.*

Heckathorn, D.D. 1997. "Respondent-driven sampling: A new approach to the study of hidden populations." *Social Problems* 44: 174–199.

Mayo, Elton. 1933. *The Human Problems of an Industrial Civilization.* New York: MacMillan.

Moreno, Jacob L. 1934. *Who Shall Survive? A New Approach to the Problem of Human Interrelations.* Foreword by Dr. W.A. White. Washington, DC: Nervous and Mental Disease Publishing Company.

## CHAPTER EIGHT

Visualizing the U.S. Senate Social Graph (1991–2009)

Andrew Odewahn

IN EARLY 2009, MANY NEWS STORIES emphasized the collapse of bipartisanship. Although much of this reporting was of the typical "he said, she said" variety, one article in particular caught my attention. Chris Wilson, an associate editor at *Slate*, wrote a great piece in which he used voting affinity data and graph visualization to help explain Senator Arlen Specter's party switch (Wilson 2009). The graph showed two large party clusters (Democrats in blue, Republicans in red), connected by a few tenuous threads of senators who consistently voted across party lines.* One of these was Specter.

The piece got me thinking on several dimensions. First, it was really cool to see quantitative evidence making the case for what was an essentially qualitative story. With one glance, you could see that something interesting was happening with Specter that presaged his break with his party. It made me wonder if there was similar evidence about other stories in the news. For example, a lot of reporting fixated on various Senate coalitions—the "Gang of Fourteen," the "New England Moderates," and the "Southern Republicans"—and how they were aiding or thwarting some initiative or another.

Basic civics would have you believe that the Senate, unlike the House, was designed by the Founders to dampen coalitions like these. It's a simple body: there are 100 senators, two from each state, who stand for election every six years. Elections are staggered so that roughly a third of the Senate is up for reelection every two years,

---

* I should note here that in this context, "graph" means a collection of nodes and edges, not an *x, y* data plot.

which implies that Senate coalitions can change, but not drastically. While senators can switch parties, retire, or even die mid-term, these events don't happen that often. Finally, incumbency itself conveys huge advantages. Once in office, senators simply aren't voted out very often.

I was curious about whether I could use graph visualization to paint a broad picture that revealed the structural dynamism in the Senate over time. If the high school story is really true—that the Senate is an inherently conservative body, in the literal sense of tending to oppose change—then the graphs should remain relatively stable. If it's not, then perhaps a visual representation might provide some insights into the incredibly important events that were shaping America in 2009, and the way reporters were covering them.

In this chapter, I'll describe how I used voting data to explore these questions visually. I'll begin by walking you through the steps required to actually produce the visualization. Next, I'll show you the results, discuss how the graphs change over the 18-year period I examined, provide a bit of historical context, and draw some general conclusions about the merits of the "high school civics" view of the Senate. After that, I'll discuss why this is a beautiful (and not merely interesting) visualization, as well as explore the many warts it picked up along the way. Finally, I'll share some general insights I've gleaned through this process that I hope you can put to use in your own work.

Building the Visualization

I started with the basic guidelines suggested in Wilson's article:

- Nodes represent senators; each node has a numerical label that corresponds to an alphabetical list of senators.

- Nodes are colored based on party affiliation. They follow the standard convention of blue for Democrats and red for Republicans. (I also used green for Independents and yellow when a party affiliation wasn't included in the data source.)

- Nodes are connected with an edge if those two senators voted together more than 65% of the time over the course of the selected timeframe.

In addition, I decided to orient the graphs so that the Democrats were on the left and the Republicans were on the right. And, because I wanted to understand how the Senate had evolved, I chunked the data into meaningful timeframes and created a plot for each one.

I settled on the legislative session as my basic unit of time. A legislative session lasts two years, begins and ends on January 3, and is often referred to as "Congress." Each Congress is numbered consecutively. For example, the 104th Congress covers the period from January 3, 1995 to January 3, 1997; the 105th Congress covers the period from January 3, 1997 to January 3, 1999; and so on. (At the time of this writing, the 111th Congress is in session.)

The session was an attractive unit for two reasons. First, it's the shortest consistent time span. The Senate is a dynamic body whose membership can change at any time, particularly during election years, so using a period longer than two years would have risked muddying the relationships by introducing new senators partway through the voting record. Second, and more prosaically, it's the level at which the data was reported, so it was a very convenient choice.

With these preliminary choices out of the way, there were three steps involved in building the visualization: gathering the raw data about senators and their votes, computing an affinity matrix that described how tightly the senators were aligned, and then putting the information into GraphViz (a toolkit for graph visualization) to turn the relationships into a picture. The following sections describe each of these steps in depth.

Gathering the Raw Data

My visualization required two main types of data: metadata about individual senators (name, party affiliation, etc.), and a record of their votes over an extended time. Initially, as many of the big government data sites (*data.gov*, *thomas.com*, etc.) publish information via feeds, the lack of history appeared to be a major obstacle. A particular vote in a session of Congress will be published as it happens, but it is difficult to go back in time to retrieve a full voting record.

Fortunately, I discovered the site GovTrack (*http://govtrack.us*), which bills itself as "a civic project to track Congress." While it largely provides the same data as the other big government sites, it also performs (among other things) the very valuable function of aggregating the feeds into XML files going back to 1991, with partial records available for sessions predating that one. My project therefore included full records of everything from the 102nd session going forward, but the pre-1991 data was incomplete. You can download any and all of the data I used for free from the site's "Source Data" page.* The site has great documentation that clearly describes how to download the data and how it is structured.

On GovTrack, senator metadata is kept in a file called *people.xml*. There are two versions of this file: a *current* file, which contains data on just the people serving in Congress now, and an *historical* file, which contains data on everyone who has ever served in Congress. I used the historical version for this project.

---

* See *http://bit.ly/4iZib*.

In both of these files, information about individual senators (or representatives) appears in a <person> element; each person had a unique ID that is used consistently for that person across the GovTrack datasets. Information about party affiliation is in a child element called <role>. For example, here is the entry for John Kennedy, who was both a representative and a senator (and president, of course):

```
<person id='406274'
    lastname='Kennedy' firstname='John' middlename='Fitzgerald'
    birthday='1917-05-29' ... >
    <role type='rep'
        startdate='1947-01-01' enddate='1948-12-31'
        party='Democrat' state='MA' district='11' />
    <role type='rep'
        startdate='1949-01-01' enddate='1950-12-31'
        party='Democrat' state='MA' district='11' />
    ...
    <role type='sen'
        startdate='1959-01-01' enddate='1960-12-31'
        party='Democrat' state='MA' district='' />
</person>
```

Voting data in GovTrack is organized by two-year legislative sessions. The votes are recorded by *roll call*, which is when the senators come together to vote "Yea" or "Nay" on an issue before them. There are typically several hundred roll calls over the course of a session.

GovTrack records each roll call as an XML file. The next listing, for example, is an excerpt of the roll call file *s1995-247.xml*, which was a vote taken in the 104th Congress on whether to permit the Bell operating companies to provide interLATA commercial mobile services. (Some of these votes are pretty dull.) Note that each <voter> element has an id that links back to the *people.xml* file:

```
<roll
    where="senate" session="104" year="1995" roll="247"
    when="802710180" datetime="1995-06-09T11:03:00-04:00"
    updated="2008-12-30T13:34:55-05:00"
    aye="83" nay="4" nv="13" present="0">
    ...
    <voter id="400566" vote="+" value="Yea" state="MN"/>
    <voter id="300016" vote="-" value="Nay" state="WV"/>
    <voter id="400559" vote="-" value="Nay" state="WA"/>
    <voter id="300011" vote="0" value="Not Voting" state="CA"/>
    <voter id="400558" vote="0" value="Not Voting" state="GA"/>
    ...
</roll>
```

These files—the historical people file and all of the various roll call files—contained all the data I wanted. However, with over 6 MB of data in the *people.xml* file and several thousand roll call votes across the full GovTrack dataset, I wanted this data in a more convenient format. So, I wrote some scripts to extract only the part of the data I needed for my visualization and stored it in a SQLite database. The schema is shown in Figure 8-1. In the interests of simplicity, I assigned a party based on only the most recent <role>, a decision that would come back to haunt me.

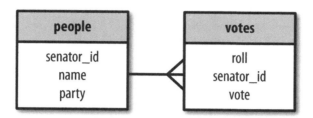

Figure 8-1. *Simple database schema for representing the raw data required for the visualization*

Computing the Voting Affinity Matrix

With the raw data munged into a more pliant format, I was ready to tackle the problem of computing the affinities that would represent the edges in the graph. This entailed building an affinity matrix (Figure 8-2) that tallied the number of times different senators voted the same way on the same bills. I could use this matrix to back out the edge conditions.

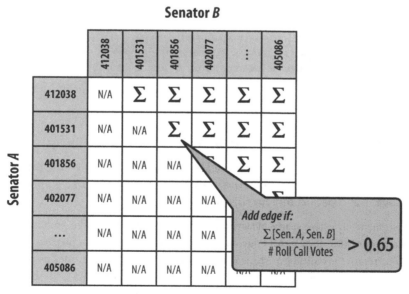

Figure 8-2. *An affinity matrix*

The following pseudocode illustrates the basic logic:

```
# Select all distinct roll calls from the vote table
roll_list =
    select
        distinct roll
    from
        votes
# Process each roll call vote in roll_list
for roll_idx in roll_list:
    # Process "Yea" votes, then "Nay" votes
    for vote_idx in ["Yea", "Nay"]:
        # Find the senators that cast this vote on this roll call
        same_vote_list =
            select
                senator_id
            from
                votes
            where
                roll = roll_idx and
                vote = vote_idx
        # Now tally all the pairs of senators in the list
        for senator_a in same_vote_list:
            for senator_b in same_vote_list:
                affinity_matrix [senator_a, senator_b] += 1
                affinity_matrix [senator_b, senator_a] += 1
# Translate the raw matrix into edges
N = length(roll_list)  # Represents the number of votes in the session
for senator_a in affinity_matrix.rows:
    for senator_b in affinity_matrix.columns:
        if (affinity_matrix[senator_a,senator_b] / N) > 0.65 then:
            add an edge between Senator A and Senator B
```

Because this is a fairly intensive set of computations, I saved the results in another table in my database.

Visualizing the Data with GraphViz

The final step was to turn all this data—the senator metadata and voting records—into a series of images. GraphViz (*http://www.graphviz.org*), an open source graph visualization package, was a perfect tool for this job.

Graph visualization is the study of various *layout algorithms* that take an abstract representation of the nodes and edges in a graph and turn it into a picture. I used GraphViz's "neato" layout algorithm, which works by simulating nodes as positively charged particles and edges as springs. Nodes push each other apart, and the edges pull related nodes together. Initially, everything is plopped down randomly on a plane, and then the algorithm simulates the push and pull of these counterbalancing forces to compute final *x, y* coordinates for each node that represent the "best" overall layout. (For this reason, algorithms like this are called "force-directed layout" algorithms.) Figure 8-3 illustrates the concept.

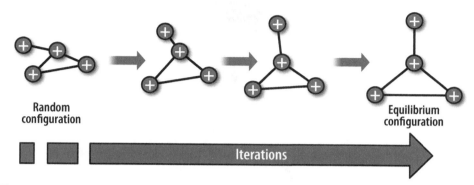

Figure 8-3. *Neato, a force-directed layout algorithm included in GraphViz, simulates nodes as charged particles and edges as springs*

The structures that emerge from this process are proportional to the density of connections within the underlying data. So, a tightly connected group of senators should create a subcluster that repels other subclusters. It's also worth noting that, because it controls the presence or absence of edges, the cutoff value for assigning an edge based on voting affinity determines the degree of clustering observed in the graph. A very low value (say, 20%) would result in relatively few substructures, because many of the votes within a session are routine procedural matters on which most senators agree. Conversely, a very high value (say, 95%) would result in a very fragmented graph, because only the most strongly connected pairs would emerge; this graph would simply look like a collection of random dots that were occasionally connected. The 65% cutoff seemed to be the point that best balanced these competing tensions.

A language called DOT describes the nodes and edges to GraphViz. DOT is straightforward: nodes are declared using unique labels, and edges are declared by connecting two (or more) of these node labels together with a -> symbol. Various other attributes (color, label, etc.) are defined by placing them in square brackets next to the object they modify.

Here is an example DOT file (Gansner, Koutsofios, and North 2006):

```
digraph G{
    a[shape=polygon,sides=5,peripheries=3,color=lightblue,style=filled];
    c[shape=polygon,sides=4,skew=.4,label="helloworld"]
    d[shape=invtriangle];
    e[shape=polygon,sides=4,distortion=.7];
    a -> b -> c;
    b -> d;
}
```

Figure 8-4 shows the corresponding image generated in GraphViz.

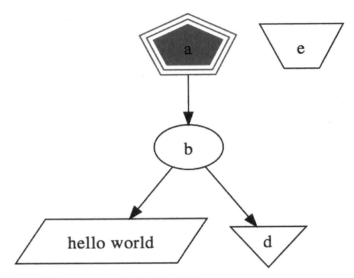

Figure 8-4. *A sample image generated by GraphViz*

So, to create the Senate visualization, I just had to create a DOT file and feed it into GraphViz. This required another script that packaged all the information saved in the database in the preceding steps—the senator's IDs, the labels in an alphabetical list, node colors based on party affiliation, and the edges from the affinity matrix—and fed them into a templating engine that would produce a DOT representation. Here's the template:

```
1  Digraph {
2
3  #for $senator in $vote_data.nodes:
4      $senator['id'] [
5          shape="circle",
6          style="filled",
7          color = $senator['color'],
8          label = "$senator['label']"
9          fontsize = "128",
10         fontname = "Arial",
11     ];
12 #end for
13
14 #for $e in $vote_data.edges:
15     "$e['senator_a']" -> "$e['senator_b']" [arrowhead = none];
16 #end for
17 }
```

Note that the for loops on lines 3 and 14 are used to loop through the nodes and edges, respectively. The items in bold are variables that are replaced on each iteration.

The Story That Emerged

Once I'd pieced together all the scripts I needed and turned them into images, a remarkably coherent story emerged.

Figure 8-5 shows the structure of the 102nd Senate session, which ran from January 3, 1991 to January 3, 1993. During this session, President George H.W. Bush served as president for a year, the first Gulf War was fought, and Bill Clinton was elected president (in 1992, midway through the session). Although two distinct voting blocks emerge, a considerable degree of overlap in the center is apparent, both in terms of the number of senators (i.e., nodes in the middle region) and the edges (i.e., number of cross connections).

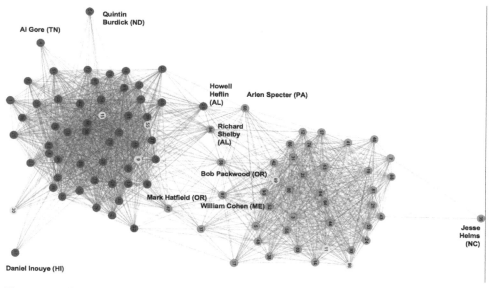

Figure 8-5. *Structure of the 102nd Senate session (January 3, 1991 to January 3, 1993)*

Figure 8-6 shows the structure of the 104th session, just two years later. This (and the preceding two years) represents the "Republican Revolution," in which the Republicans retook both the House and the Senate for the first time in almost 40 years. It was a period marked by intense partisanship, and it saw such events as the government shutdown, voting on the Republicans' "Contract with America," and (on the national scene) the bombing of the Murrah federal building in Oklahoma City. The Senate graph reflects the deep divisions, with both parties locked into separate, tight little balls.

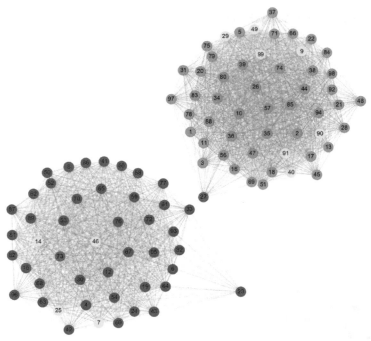

Figure 8-6. *Structure of the 104th Senate session (January 3, 1995 to January 3, 1997)*

Figure 8-7 is a composite of the next six sessions.

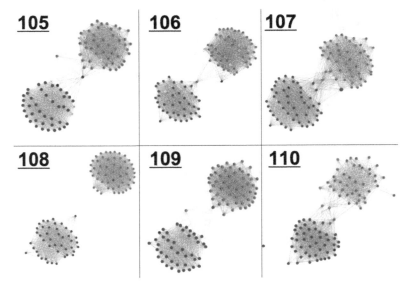

Figure 8-7. *Structures of the 105th through the 110th Senate sessions (January 3, 1997 to January 3, 2009)*

Some of the events and notable structures that occurred over these sessions include:

- 105th session (January 3, 1997 – January 3, 1999). The Republican-controlled House votes to impeach President Clinton during this session. Note the distinct split in the Democratic block, which occurs regularly with the Democrats over the sample period.

- 106th session (January 3, 1999 – January 3, 2001). The impeachment trial of President Clinton is held in the Senate over this term. Although the Senate, like the House, is held by the Republicans, it votes to acquit. It's interesting that the Republican block shows a clearly defined and significant split in this session; this is one of the few times this happens so clearly with the Republicans over the entire 18-year period surveyed.

- 107th session (January 3, 2001 – January 3, 2003). The attacks of September 11th (and the later anthrax attacks directed against the Senate itself) occur during this session; the Iraq war is also authorized. Although there is a small split in the Democratic block that consists mostly of a few senators thought of as more liberal, it's a period of renewed strength in the center, as more connections are made across party lines than at any time since 1991.

- 108th session (January 3, 2003 – January 3, 2005). The Iraq war begins in this session. This session is almost a return to the 104th Congress, with the exception of Ben Nelson (D, NE), who votes with a small group of moderate Republicans consisting of Olympia Snowe (ME), Susan Collins (ME), and Norm Coleman (MN). While the remaining Republicans stay fairly cohesive, the small Democratic fracture remains.

- 109th session (January 3, 2005 – January 3, 2007). The annus horribilis for the Republican party—the Tom Delay and Jack Abramoff scandals, a deeply divisive vote on the Terry Schiavo case, and the disastrous response to Hurricane Katrina ("You're doin' a heckuva job, Brownie!") all occur during this session. Despite this, the Republican senatorial block remains remarkably close-knit. The Democratic block, on the other hand, continues to fracture, with a larger group of senators shifting toward the small, more liberal block.

- 110th session (January 3, 2007 – January 3, 2009). The Democrats take control of both the House and the Senate in this session. Unlike in previous sessions, the Democratic block looks remarkably unified, while the Republican block is fragmented and diffuse.

Although none of the sessions depicted in Figure 8-7 shows as dramatic a break as the one between the 102nd and the 104th, there is a consistent pattern of a fracture in one (or both) of the main blocks over the six sessions. The first six months of the 111th Congress (the session in progress at the time this was written) continues this pattern even more distinctly. As shown in Figure 8-8, the Democratic unity from the 110th session has given way to an almost even split in the block. The Republican Party shows a conservative core surrounded by a fragmented periphery of moderates.

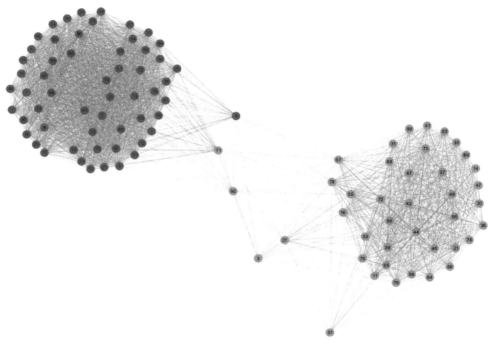

Figure 8-8. *Structure of the first six months of the 111th Senate session (January 3, 2009 – around July 1, 2009)*

So, it does appear that the coalition story that was the talk of the summer of 2009 is backed up in the data. In fact, the Senate has been a dynamic place since at least 1991, with alternating coalitions, parties, and even individuals shaping the directions of key decisions.

Of course, in retrospect, this is hardly news. This pattern of alternating coalitions probably goes back to the very founding of the United States, as George Washington warned in his Farewell Address of 1796 (Figure 8-9).

Figure 8-9. *George Washington's Farewell Address of 1796, from the Rare Book and Special Collections division of the Library of Congress*[*]

Here's what our first president had to say about the tendency of political parties to form factions:[†]

> This spirit, unfortunately, is inseparable from our nature, having its root in the strongest passions of the human mind. It exists under different shapes in all governments, more or less stifled, controlled, or repressed; but, in those of the popular form, it is seen in its greatest rankness, and is truly their worst enemy.
>
> The alternate domination of one faction over another, sharpened by the spirit of revenge, natural to party dissension, which in different ages and countries has perpetrated the most horrid enormities, is itself a frightful despotism.

Washington's warning, directed as it is toward "different ages and countries," strikes me as being as true today as it was back then. So, while the coalition story of 2009 might be news, the fundamental pattern is actually quite old. The characters come and go, but the story stays the same.

* See *http://en.wikipedia.org/wiki/George_Washingtons_Farewell_Address*.
† See *http://avalon.law.yale.edu/18th_century/washing.asp*.

What Makes It Beautiful?

When I was asked to contribute to this book, one of my first thoughts was "But my graphs are so ugly!" The labels are inconsistent across time and somewhat askew, and there are a few glaring inaccuracies in the way I assigned political parties. (I'll describe these flubs in detail shortly.) But as I thought about it further, I decided that the work gets one fundamental thing right, and this makes the warts forgivable.

The choice of a network of related senators as the visual framework was the key element in making this a beautiful visualization. Perhaps the best way to see why is to compare it with another depiction that shows pretty much the same thing, but in a different way. Consider Figure 8-10, which is a time-series chart of a partisanship index that appeared in McCarty, Poole, and Rosenthal (2008).

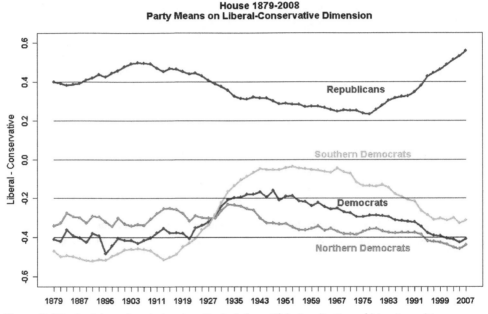

Figure 8-10. *An interesting, but not particularly beautiful, visualization of bipartisanship*

Now, there is absolutely nothing wrong with this chart, and it does a fantastic job of showing that conservatism took off among Republicans in the mid-1970s. It gets even more interesting when you consider how well it reflects the impact of Nixon's "Southern Strategy," which cynically exploited fears about civil rights to turn the once solidly Democratic South into a Republican stronghold. However, while it accurately makes its point, it doesn't provide additional elements that resonate with the viewer, and it takes some studying to see the story.

This is not the case with the social graph approach. For example, knowing that each dot represents a senator, you're naturally drawn in to wonder, "Who is *that* person so far off from the main group?" and then delighted to discover that it's John McCain being all "mavericky." It's also interesting to see the rise in partisanship not as a simple line on a chart, but as two opposing camps pitted against each other, connected by only a few people across the middle; or to see the complete breakdown of bipartisanship in the 104th Congress, when both parties balled up into a hedgehog defense; or to see the internal conflicts within each block as they responded to the broader events of the times.

The possibility for such resonances is what makes my graphs beautiful, rather than just interesting. A line graph can illustrate a fact, and can do so very clearly, but it rarely incites you to probe further and engage with the information. Like a good story, a beautiful visualization should draw you in, provoke questions, and offer a sense of exploration and discovery.

If you can get this element right, viewers will overlook some warts. And my project had several of these.

And What Makes It Ugly?

Although I'm pretty happy with what my graphs ended up showing, there are a few things I would have changed, in hindsight. Most of the problems resulted from me making too many assumptions about the data, as I'll discuss in the next sections.

Labels

A key goal of the visualization was to reveal the global structures among the senators, rather than to reveal details about particular individuals. Occasionally, though, it can be useful to know whom a particular node represents—for example, when a node appears as a central "bridge" or connector between the parties (like Olympia Snowe or Ben Nelson), or off by itself (like John McCain). I wanted it to be possible to quickly identify these "interesting" nodes, while still keeping the focus on the overall pattern. My solution was to assign each senator a label based on alphabetical order, and then use these labels on the corresponding nodes.

While this worked well for an individual session, it failed miserably to preserve any sense of continuity across the sessions. To see why, consider Table 8-1, which shows the senators who were assigned to the labels 1, 50, and 100 across the 11 sessions.

Table 8-1. *Senators occupying the labels 1, 50, and 100 over the 11 sessions in the visualization*

Session	Label 1	Label 50	Label 100
101	Alan Cranston	Pete Domenici	Wyche Fowler
102	Alan Cranston	Paul Simon	Wyche Fowler
103	Alan Simpson	Paul Wellstone	William Roth
104	Alan Simpson	Sam Nunn	William Roth
105	Alfonse D'Amato	Daniel Akaka	William Roth
106	Ben Campbell	Evan Bayh	William Roth
107	Ben Campbell	Evan Bayh	Zell Miller
108	Ben Campbell	Jeff Bingaman	Zell Miller
109	Barack Obama	John Ensign	William Frist
110	Charles Hagel	John Thune	Wayne Allard
111	Kirsten Gillibrand	Joseph Lieberman	Tom Udall

Ideally, each senator should have the same label across all the graphs in which he or she appears. However, a quick look at the table shows just how poorly my method reflects this. For example, consider Joseph Lieberman, who has been Connecticut's senator since 1988. Based on my simple alphabetical ordering process, he appeared as labels 50, 54, 59, 65, 66, 73, 76, and 77 across the 11 graphs. The story was the same for many of the other senators: with the exception of Barack Obama, most of them spent multiple terms in the Senate, but in my system the labels assigned to them were wildly inconsistent.

A better system would have been to create a single list that represented all the senators over the 11 sessions, and then to assign a unique label to each senator based on that list. The trade-off, of course, is that I would have had more than 100 labels, but this would seem to be an acceptable downside, especially if such a list were arranged chronologically based on the year of each senator's first election rather than alphabetically. Another solution would have been to make a dynamic, interactive visualization where the user could (for example) hover over each node and see a pop-up window presenting additional metadata. However, as I designed the visualization for print, this wasn't a viable option for me.

Orientation

In addition to labeling the senators, I wanted my visualization oriented so that Democrats would appear on the left and Republicans on the right. As well as following the established conventions, the idea was that this consistent placement would create some continuity across the various charts. However, this strategy proved difficult to implement because of the nature of the Neato layout algorithm.

The force-directed process described earlier is a great way to reveal the complex structures hidden inside abstract graph data. However, because it depends on a certain amount of randomness, it doesn't produce the same results every time: while the general structure is the same, the orientation will vary considerably. For example, Figure 8-11 shows three different, yet equally valid, layouts for a simple graph.

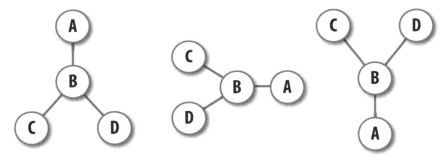

Figure 8-11. *Three equivalent force-directed layouts for the same graph*

In the end, I resorted to opening the image files and rotating them manually. While this workaround achieved the desired orientation, it had the unfortunate side effect of rotating the label text as well, leaving the whole thing looking a bit odd. The schematic in Figure 8-12 illustrates why.

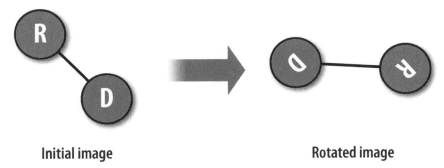

Initial image   Rotated image

Figure 8-12. *Rotating the raw image from the graph layout algorithm so that the Democrats were on the left and the Republicans were on the right had some unexpected side effects on the labels*

In retrospect, it would have been better to invest the time in fixing the orientation programmatically. For example, I could have added an intermediate step to calculate the centroids of the two clusters, and then calculated a rotational angle around the centroid of the entire graph that would produce the orientation I wanted. This extra step would have saved considerable effort in the long run, but it seemed like overkill at the time.

Party Affiliation

The last major wart was the result of a foolish assumption: since senators change parties so infrequently, it seemed safe to assume that each senator's most recent party affiliation could be used for all the graphs. In my visualization, this mistake stood out like a sore thumb.

For instance, consider Joseph Lieberman (again!), who became an Independent in 2006 after losing the Democratic primary to insurgent candidate Ned Lamont. Here's a sample of his entry in the *people.xml* file:

```
<person id='300067' lastname='Lieberman' firstname='Joseph' ... >
    <role startdate='1989-01-01' enddate='1994-12-31' party='Democrat' .../>
    <role startdate='1995-01-01' enddate='2000-12-31' party='Democrat' .../>
    <role startdate='2001-01-01' enddate='2006-12-31' party='Democrat' .../>
    <role startdate='2007-01-01' enddate='2012-12-31' party='Independent' .../>
    ...
</person>
```

As you can see, Lieberman spent 18 years as a Democratic senator before changing his affiliation. However, the last entry in this file lists him as an Independent, so that's the party I assigned him in my ETL (extract, transform, and load) process. As a result, he appears (incorrectly) as a consistent green dot in a sea of Democratic blue in the graphs visualizing the 102nd through 109th Congresses.

To avoid this problem, I should have designed my ETL process to check party affiliation based on the date ranges provided in the <role> element from GovTrack. As with the orientation issue, this didn't seem worth the trouble at the time. In retrospect, it serves as a cautionary tale on making "simplifying assumptions" about unfamiliar data.

Conclusion

I'll end this piece with a few observations I made while working through this project that I hope you might find useful in your own work:

Be prepared to spend a lot of time data munging

When I discovered GovTrack, I thought it would make this project a snap. After all, the data was all right there, neatly packaged up in clear XML. However, actually getting this raw data into a form I was able to use for the project required a considerable amount of time. I'd estimate that 80% of the time I spent on this project was taken up by simply transforming the data—extracting the pieces I wanted, writing database loaders and schemas, and writing the scripts to calculate the affinity data all took much more time than creating the DOT templates. This is apparently a very common phenomenon, so if you find yourself struggling with the data portion of your project, don't get frustrated. It just seems to be part of the territory.

Automate what you can

When you're first getting a handle on the data, it's tempting to bang out a quick and dirty solution. So you string together a series of shell scripts, SQL statements, and maybe some work in Excel to get the data how you want it. This is fine if you're really, really, *really* only going to use your dataset *one time*. But chances are, if your work is at all successful or interesting, you're going to want to go back and change it, reproduce it, or enhance it. And when that time comes, you'll find yourself scratching your head and asking yourself, "Now, which script did I run to calculate that?" So, even if you may just think you're slapping together a one-time hack for a quick project, take the time to develop automated scripts and do some minimal documentation. Your future self will thank you.

Think carefully about how you'll represent time

Because people are often interested in how things have changed from the past or what they may look like in the future, be sure to think about how you'll represent time in your visualization. Sometimes time is revealed explicitly, as in the time series example in Figure 8-10. Sometimes, though, it's in the background. For example, in my project, the sense of movement through time is conveyed cinematically through a progression of images. In any case, just as it does in a movie, a clear sense of pacing and moving through time will help make your work more engaging.

Decide when "good" is "good enough"

Although it's important to spend some time up front working through your data so that you're not bitten by embarrassing problems later, it's also good to know when enough is enough. Unless you're working on a system that truly requires complete accuracy (a heads-up display for a jet aircraft, for example), it's often better to "release early, release often." Show your work to people, get their reactions, see if it's generating the types of responses you'd hoped for, and then iterate.

Approach the problem like a journalist

A lot of other chapters in this book have made the point that a great visualization should tell a story, and I generally agree. However, inherent in this framing is the idea that the people who create visualizations are storytellers. To me, this can have a ring of someone inventing a story, complete with characters and situations to fit a plot. Rather than "storyteller," I think "journalist" is a more accurate metaphor. A journalist tells a story, but it's (ideally) an objective story—the journalist's goal is to uncover the facts piece by piece, untangle messy complexities, and try to weave them into a coherent picture. Ultimately, the fidelity of your visualization's story to the underlying facts in the data is what will truly determine its beauty.

References

Gansner, Emden, Eleftherios Koutsofios, and Stephen North. 2009. "Drawing graphs with DOT." *http://bit.ly/4GlYAp*.

McCarty, Nolan, Keith T. Poole, and Howard Rosenthal. 2008. *Polarized America: The Dance of Ideology and Unequal Riches*. Cambridge, MA: MIT Press. *http://polarizedamerica.com*.

Wilson, Chris. 2009. "The Senate Social Network: Slate presents a Facebook-style visualization of the Senate." *http://bit.ly/FD5QY*.

## CHAPTER NINE

The Big Picture:
Search and Discovery

Todd Holloway

SEARCH AND DISCOVERY ARE TWO STYLES OF INFORMATION RETRIEVAL. Search is
a familiar modality, well exemplified by Google and other web search engines. While
there is a discovery aspect to search engines, there are more straightforward examples
of discovery systems, such as product recommendations on Amazon and movie recommendations on Netflix.

These two types of retrieval systems have in common that they can be incredibly complex under the hood. The results they provide may depend not only on the content
of the query and the items being retrieved, but also on the collective behavior of the
system's users. For example, how and what movies you rate on Netflix will influence
what movies are recommended to other users, and on Amazon, reviewing a book,
buying a book, or even adding a book to your cart but later removing it can affect the
recommendations given to others. Similarly, with Google, when you click on a result—
or, for that matter, don't click on a result—that behavior impacts future search results.

One consequence of this complexity is difficulty in explaining system behavior. We
primarily rely on performance metrics to quantify the success or failure of retrieval
results, or to tell us which variations of a system work better than others. Such metrics
allow the system to be continuously improved upon.

A supplementary approach to understanding the behavior of these systems is to use
information visualization. With visualization, we can sometimes gain insights not
available from metrics alone. In this chapter, I'll show how one particular visualization technique can provide large-scale views of certain system dynamics. The first system we'll look at is a search engine, YELLOWPAGES.COM. The goal will be to get a

big-picture view of user query activity on the site—activity that can in turn be used to improve the design of the system itself. The second system we will look at is a movie recommender built from the dataset of the Netflix Prize, a million-dollar predictive modeling competition that ended recently. That visualization can help us understand the issues inherent in a discovery model based on user preferences.

The Visualization Technique

The technique described in this chapter is all about comparing items of the same type—queries in our first example, and movies in the second. The premise is simple: *we will place items on the page so that similar items are close to one another and dissimilar items are far apart.* This premise is rooted in the Gestalt principle of proximity, which claims that when items are placed close together, people tend to perceive them as belonging to a group.

The first step in creating these visualizations is therefore to define what makes items similar and dissimilar. This can be anything. In our Netflix Prize example, we'll define the similarity of movies as being evidenced by like user ratings. There are very good reasons to use user ratings, but we could alternatively have used movie attributes like genre or actors to define similarity.

Once similarity is defined, an ordination process is needed to convert those similarity values into either 2D or 3D coordinates. There are two main ways of doing ordination. The first is to use a formula that converts a higher-dimensional space into a lower 2D or 3D one. The alternative approach is to view the items as being nodes in a graph, with similar nodes connected by an edge. Then, the ordination is an attempt to place connected nodes near one another and disconnected nodes far apart. In this chapter, we'll use the latter graph-based approach, and we'll discuss the specific tools and algorithms required of it.

After the ordination—that is, after the items are given coordinates—representations of those items (simple circles in these two examples) are placed at those coordinates. The final steps required to create the visualizations include placing labels (which can be quite challenging) and overlaying any additional analytics.

YELLOWPAGES.COM

Until recently, it was quite common to use printed phone books to find people and services. The section for services was known as the Yellow Pages. Within those pages, businesses were grouped by category, and the categories were then sorted alphabetically. It was simple stuff.

YELLOWPAGES.COM (Figure 9-1), a website owned by my employer, AT&T, is a modern local business search engine with the same basic goal as its print ancestor. Obviously, though, being online, it's not limited to organizing its millions of businesses by category and alphabet in the same way the print version was.

Figure 9-1. *YELLOWPAGES.COM: a local business search engine*

Indeed, part of designing or refining such a search engine involves understanding how to organize the business listings given a query, and what features of businesses to involve in that organization. To that end, it can be helpful to take a look at the behavior of users, because that behavior can either validate or undermine our intuitions.

Query Logs

YELLOWPAGES.COM keeps a log of every query executed on the site, so it can use that data to improve its service. Here are the top five queries from the log for December 2008:

1. Restaurants

2. Movie theaters

3. Pizza

4. Walmart [sic]

5. Animal shelters

The top five are a mix of "browse" queries, where people are browsing within categories (e.g., Restaurants), and "search" queries, where people are searching for specific businesses (e.g., Wal-Mart). We will use the log queries as the "items" in our visualization, and we'll ordinate them based on the similarity of the behavior of the users executing those queries. In that way, we can hope to get a big picture of query activity on the system.

The query logs for YELLOWPAGES.COM are currently the property of AT&T. If you would like to look at the contents of a major search engine's query log, AOL has placed a log from 2006 in the public domain. Just Google "AOL query log" to find a current mirror from which to download the 500 MB file.

Categorical Similarity

As stated earlier, we would like our visualization to be based on actual user behavior. For example, we might like two queries to appear near each other if, when a user enters one query, she is likely to click on the same set of businesses she would have if she had entered the other query. However, the data is too sparse to achieve this in practice—the overlapping sets of businesses are very small on average. To handle this sparsity, we'll back off a little and say that two queries are similar if, when a user enters one query, she is likely to click on the same *category* of businesses as she would have if she had entered the other query. It is from this definition of similarity that we will do the ordination.

Visualization As a Substrate for Analytics

At AT&T Applied Research, we have built a number of tools for analyzing queries. One such tool is a predictive model that attempts to determine whether a query is intended to reference a specific business (e.g., Walgreens) or for browsing among a type of business (e.g., drug stores). We can overlay these predictions on top of our visualization to get a big-picture sense of the breakdown between these "search" vs. "browse" queries.

There are many visual encodings we could use to show which of these two classes a query belongs to. The most obvious one, and the approach we have adopted, is coloring the nodes: in our visualization *the green nodes are queries that are predicted to be searches for a specific business*, and *other queries are left black*. There may be some incorrect colorings, reflecting errors in this particular predictive model.

Figure 9-2 shows the queries "Goodwill" and "Salvation Army" in green, meaning they have been (correctly) predicted to be queries for specific businesses.

Figure 9-2. *"Search" queries are colored green in our visualization*

The Visualization

The final visualization is presented in Figure 9-3. It shows the top 4,600 queries from December 2008. When looking at this type of visualization, keep in mind that it has no axis. It's all relative—similar queries are near one another, and dissimilar queries are far apart. Each circle represents a query. Some of these circles are labeled with the query terms. Both *the size of the circle and the size of the label are based on the number of times the query occurs in the log*. That way, frequent queries jump out at the viewer.

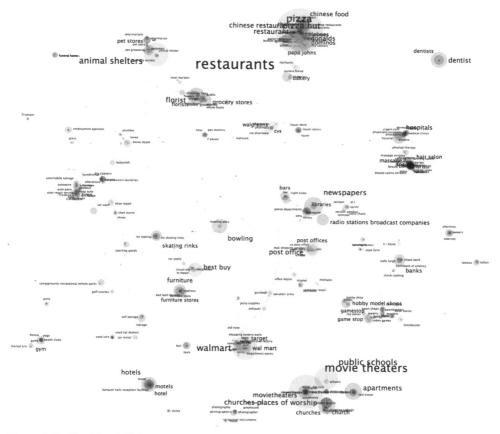

Figure 9-3. *The Top 4,600 queries made on YELLOWPAGES.COM*

Looking at Figure 9-3, it's easy to identify the regions where the system is most often used. "Restaurants" stand out, as do retail stores such as "Walmart" and "Best Buy." That queries for restaurants and retail stores are frequent may not be surprising, given that this is a business search engine. Perhaps less predictable is the large region toward the bottom containing community-related queries, including searches for "public schools," "churches," and "apartments."

This type of visualization is large. It doesn't fit well onto a single printed page; the best way to display it is either to print it as a large poster or to display it as a zoomable version on a computer screen. To make it zoomable, it can be loaded into an application such as Google Maps, Gigapan, or Microsoft's Seadragon.

Since this visualization *is* being published in a book, we'll examine it and the insights it offers by enlarging and discussing a few specific sections.

Figure 9-4 enlarges the cluster of queries that seem to reference community-related businesses. Seeing a depiction of actual user behavior such as this one might leave an impression on a search engineer, perhaps validating his beliefs about the system's usage, or causing surprise and even inspiring design changes.

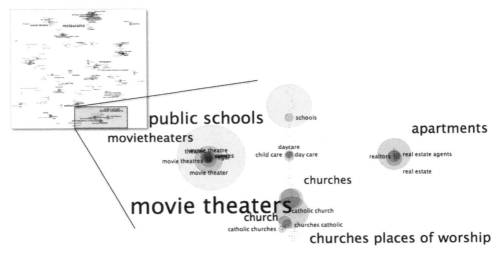

Figure 9-4. *A closeup of one cluster in Figure 9-3*

The cluster shown in Figure 9-5 seems fairly straightforward to characterize, but there are a couple of things worth pointing out. Notice the common but different spellings of GameStop; it is perhaps to be expected that users would behave the same way with the search results regardless of the spelling, so it should also be expected for those queries to appear near one another in the visualization. Perhaps most interesting is the proximity of pawnshop-related queries to bookstore- and game store–related queries. What user querying and clicking behaviors might generate this pattern?

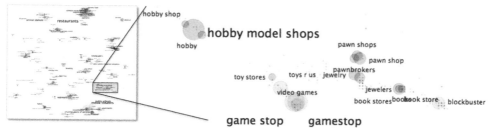

Figure 9-5. *Cluster of largely hobby-related businesses*

This visualization technique is powerful in that it's not just proximity within a single cluster that provides insight, but also proximity of clusters to one another. In Figure 9-6, there are two clusters, one dealing with pharmacies and one with liquor stores, that have been placed relatively close to each other. This indicates that users tend to click on similar business whether they are searching for pharmacies or liquor stores. Whereas in a printed phone book, these two classes of businesses would be found only under their separate categories, a search engine can consider these behavioral associations in producing search results.

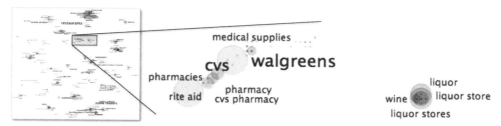

Figure 9-6. *Two nearby clusters: drug and liquor stores*

Advantages and Disadvantages of the Technique

Having looked at one of these "big-picture" visualizations, it's worth discussing the advantages and disadvantages of this technique.

The biggest benefit is that it's scalable and totally algorithmic. The visualization in Figure 9-3 shows 4,600 items, but the algorithms can scale to handle millions. (Obviously, to usefully view millions of items, an interface that allows panning and zooming would be required.)

Another benefit of this technique is that it works nicely as a stable, global substrate on which to display other analytics. For example, we used green and black to differentiate between search and browse queries. We could easily overlay any number of other analytics. Perhaps it would be interesting to show the average ages of the users making specific queries, assuming we had such data, or a prediction of the likelihood of a user using the system again given the query entered. Overlaying such a prediction might give us a picture of where the system performs well and poorly.

The biggest disadvantage (and criticism) of this technique is that it does not allow precise comparisons. It is difficult to quantify and explain the relationships between particular pairs of items in this visualization; other visualization techniques are more effective for such narrow analytics. This is more a technique to inspire new questions about the dataset, or to hint at what the answers to certain questions may be, rather than a source of specific answers.

Another obvious disadvantage is that people are not already educated as to how to interpret such views. Scatterplots, bar charts, pie charts—sure, but not large-scale graph drawings.

A technical issue, illustrated by the otherwise interesting clusters in Figure 9-7, is the difficulty of labeling so many items. The visualizations in this chapter all use automatic labeling algorithms that optimize the placement of the labels to minimize overlap. All the same, some overlap is inevitable. Perhaps as the technique continues to develop, creative new solutions will address this issue.

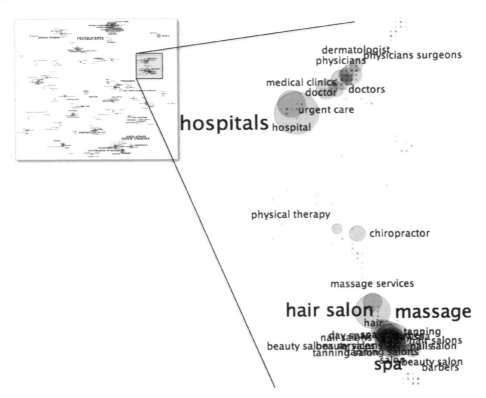

Figure 9-7. *A cluster with labels that are difficult to read*

One final issue with these visualizations is that, as mentioned earlier, they generally involve a reduction from a higher-dimensional dataset to a two- or three-dimensional dataset. Information can be lost in the reduction process, so it is difficult to be certain whether an interesting-looking grouping truly reflects something interesting about the dataset or is merely an artifact of that process.

The Netflix Prize

There have long been visions of enabling individuals to tailor their experience of the Web, and efforts to achieve that goal. Ideally, such personalization will enable services on the Web to understand your tastes well enough to help you discover restaurants, books, music, movies, and other things that will interest you.

Netflix, a company that rents movies by mail and online, has a system that attempts to make appropriate recommendations to its customers. The recommendations are based on the movies that a customer has rated highly, as well as the movies that customers with similar tastes have rated highly. In the fall of 2006, the company started a competition offering a prize of one million dollars to anyone who could improve its recommendation algorithm by 10 percent. As part of this competition, Netflix released a dataset containing 100 million user ratings for 17,700 movies. This dataset can be found online at the UCI Machine Learning Repository (*http://archive.ics.uci.edu/ml/*).

The challenges of building a discovery system from this dataset include the fact that there is both too much data and too little data. There is too much data to use simple techniques to explain it all, or even to browse it. However, from the standpoint of making accurate recommendations, there is less data than we would like. The distribution of ratings is far from uniform—many users have rated few movies, and many movies have few ratings. For those users and those movies, accurate predictions are difficult to make.

Preference Similarity

A well-known measure of similarity used in many recommendation systems is cosine similarity. A practical introduction to this technique can be found in Linden, Smith, and York (2003).

In the case of movies, intuitively, the measure indicates that two movies are similar if users who rated one highly rated the other highly or, conversely, users who rated one poorly rated the other poorly.

We'll use this similarity measure to generate similarity data for all 17,700 movies in the Netflix Prize dataset, then generate coordinates based on that data. If we were interested in building an actual movie recommender system, we might do so simply by recommending the movies that were similar to those a user had rated highly. However, the goal here is just to gain insight into the dynamics of such a recommender system.

Labeling

The YELLOWPAGES.COM visualization was easier to label than this Netflix Prize visualization for a number of reasons, including fewer nodes and shorter labels, but mostly because the nodes were more uniformly distributed. Although the Netflix Prize visualization has a large number of clusters, most of the movies are contained in only a small number of those clusters. This disparity is even more apparent when we look at only the movies with the most ratings.

Two different approaches to labeling were considered:

- Label the top movies, and a random sample of other movies. This will reveal the clusters containing the most popular films, but because of the density of those clusters, it may be difficult to read the labels.

- Divide the page into a grid and label a small sample of nodes in each grid location. This ensures that all clusters will have some labels.

For the visualization in Figure 9-8, the first strategy was used because it illustrates the highly nonuniform distribution both of movies in general and of movies with large numbers of ratings (indicated by larger circles). However, for the enlargements of the visualization in the subsequent figures, the second strategy was used for improved readability.

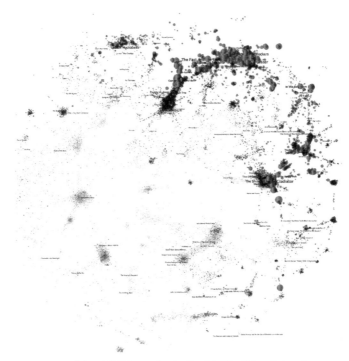

Figure 9-8. *Visualization of the 17,700 movies in the Netflix Prize dataset*

Closer Looks

Other than ratings, the only data in the Netflix Prize dataset is the titles and release dates for the movies. However, competitors in the Netflix Prize have found that latent attributes, such as the amount of violence in a movie or the gender of the user, are important predictors of preference. Not surprisingly, some of the clusters appear to be explainable by these attributes. Why other clusters emerge from user preferences, however, is more difficult to explain.

The first cluster of movies we'll look at (Figure 9-9), containing titles such as *Star Trek*, *X-Files*, and *Dune*, seems to be largely characterized by a genre: science fiction. *Galaxy Quest* is also sci-fi, though satiric sci-fi. *Monk*, a detective comedy, would seem to be the odd member of this collection. However, this is a preference clustering, and preference is by no means defined only by genre. The other possible explanation for this anomaly is that there are very few ratings for *Monk* (note the small size of the node within the cluster), so its placement may be an error; that is, it may not reflect the actual preferences of Netflix users. This is a main source of difficulty not just in creating this visualization, but for the Netflix Prize competition itself; predicting user preferences for movies with few existing ratings is tough.

Figure 9-9. *Cluster of sci-fi movies*

Explaining other clusters can be much more challenging. Consider the example in Figure 9-10. It may make intuitive sense that films such as *Margaret Cho*, *The Man Show*, and *The Rocky Horror Picture Show* (all controversial comedies) would be liked by a certain group of users and reviled by others, and thus would appear as a cluster. But if that's the case, why aren't other movies with a similar type of humor in this cluster? Why is the pull between these particular movies so strong that they form a cluster rather than being distributed amongst other clusters?

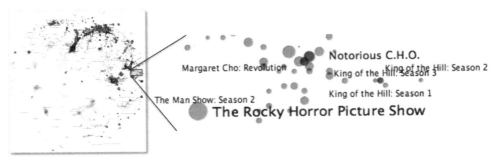

Figure 9-10. *Cluster of movies with similar humor*

Figure 9-11 provides another example of a cluster that intuitively makes sense as a reflection of preference. If we could have access to additional attributes about these movies or the users who rated them highly, which of them might help explain the preferences revealed within this cluster?

Figure 9-11. *Cluster of "family-friendly" movies*

An attempt at explaining the cluster in Figure 9-12 might focus on the fact that most of the films in this cluster are blockbuster action movies. Even if one considers *The Devil's Advocate* something other than an action movie, the leading actor (Keanu Reeves) appears in many such films, so other movies he stars in may be expected to appeal to the same audience.

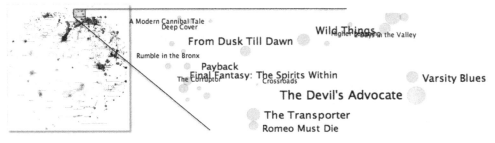

Figure 9-12. *Cluster of action movies*

The cluster in Figure 9-13 is larger and a bit more difficult to characterize, but user preference is well reflected. Most of these films have a certain "feel-good" appeal; the majority are love stories.

Figure 9-13. *Cluster of "feel-good" movies*

An already-mentioned issue is that the movie recommendations might not be as good for users who haven't already rated many movies, because the system doesn't yet know those users' preferences. We call this the *cold start problem*. In fact, we can still have this problem even for users who have rated a lot of movies, if those ratings were spread across a number of contexts. For example, say the user is a guy who doesn't really like the kind of movies in the last cluster but has started renting them for date nights with his girlfriend, and rating the movies based on how well each date goes. If he then starts renting movies for himself, he may not have made enough ratings reflecting his own preferences to be able to discover movies that he will actually like. More broadly, we can describe this issue as context amplifying the issue of data sparsity.

Creating Your Own

You may be interested in creating similar visualizations to the ones shown here for your favorite datasets. There are many tool stacks that can be used to accomplish this. We first used Perl to parse the data and compute the similarities (of course, another language could be substituted for Perl). These similarities were then passed to Shawn Martin's freely available DrL software (*http://www.cs.sandia.gov/~smartin/software.html*). DrL converts the similarities into coordinates for each node using the graph method mentioned earlier. DrL's strength is that it works recursively, so the coordinates reflect a higher-level organization. A good alternative to DrL is GraphViz (*http://www.graphviz.org*).

At this point, we returned to Perl to merge the coordinates with additional information, such as the size, color, and labels of the nodes. Finally, the completed datasets were passed to the commercial graph-drawing library yFiles (*http://www.yworks.com/en/index. html*), which applied a layout to the labels and rendered the whole visualization as a *.png* file. yFiles is an incredibly useful package, but you could bypass this step and, for example, use Perl to directly create an EPS file at the expense of the labels not being laid out.

Conclusion

The two examples shown in this chapter are pretty straightforward applications of this visualization technique. If you are interested in viewing more examples of this type, a number are included in the online Places & Spaces exhibit (*http://www.scimaps. org/maps/browse/*), a collection of large-scale visualizations curated by Katy Borner of Indiana University.

It is worth mentioning that this type of visualization is still an active area of research. Recent developments have focused on expanding this technique to incorporate constraints. A use that would benefit from constraints occurs in the field of systems biology, where one might want to display protein-protein interactions. The similarity measure might be based on the number of interactions between two proteins. The constraints needed might be for some proteins within the nucleus to be given coordinates within a particular circular region and for proteins within the cytoplasm to be given coordinates within a larger circular region, not overlapping with the nucleus region. Likewise, proteins on the membrane might be constrained to be on a circular line, while still grouped by similarity. Like the search and discovery systems visualizations discussed in this chapter, this visualization could provide a big-picture view that helps inspire or validate current intuitions. Thinking up other domains where such visualizations might be useful is left as an exercise for the reader.

References

Linden, Greg, Brent Smith, and Jeremy York. 2003. "Amazon.com recommendations: Item-to-item collaborative filtering." *IEEE Internet Computing* 7, vol. 1: 76–80.

Finding Beautiful Insights in the Chaos of Social Network Visualizations

Adam Perer

> My purpose throughout is to interpret the material by
> juxtaposing and assembling the notations into a unified,
> coherent whole.
>
> —*Mark Lombardi, 2000*

MARK LOMBARDI WAS PERHAPS THE PERFECT NETWORK LAYOUT ALGORITHM. As an
artist intent on communicating complex networks of financial and political scandals, he
diligently drew networks where nodes never overlap, edges rarely cross, and the connections are smooth and curvy (Figure 10-1). This amount of grace and sensitivity is rarely
present in the visualizations of social networks created by computational means. While
advanced computational layout algorithms may be grounded in physical models of springs
and forces, they rarely highlight patterns and trends like Lombardi's drawings do. This
chapter details my attempts to empower users to dig deeper into these chaotic social network visualizations with interactive techniques that integrate visualization and statistics.

Visualizing Social Networks

The increasing amount of digital information in modern society has ushered in a
golden age for data analysis. Ample data encourages users to conduct more frequent
exploratory data analyses to explain scientific, social, cultural, and economic phenomena. However, while access to data is important, it is ultimately insufficient unless
we also have the ability to understand patterns, identify outliers, and discover gaps.
Modern databases are simply too large to examine without computational tools that
allow users to process and interact with the data.

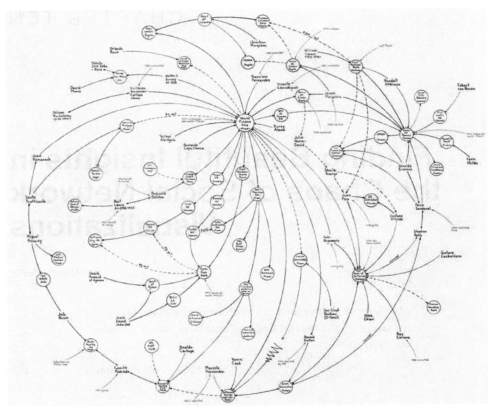

Figure 10-1. *An example of the artist Mark Lombardi's hand-drawn social networks: "World Finance Corporation, Miami, Florida, c. 1970-79 (6th Version)" (1999); image courtesy of PIEROGI Gallery, Brooklyn, NY.*

Our most powerful sensory receptors—our eyes—have far more bandwidth and processing power than our receptors for smell, sound, taste, or touch. Presenting data through information visualizations is therefore an effective way to take full advantage of the strong capabilities of our most powerful human perceptual system. However, choosing an effective presentation is challenging, as not all information visualizations are created equally. Not all information visualizations highlight the patterns, gaps, and outliers important to analysts' tasks, and furthermore, not all information visualizations "force us to notice what we never expected to see" (Tukey 1977).

A growing trend in data analysis is to make sense of linked data as networks. Rather than looking solely at attributes of data, network analysts also focus on the connections between data and the resulting structures. My research focuses on understanding these networks because they are topical, emergent, and inherently challenging for analysts. Networks are difficult to visualize and navigate, and, most problematically, it is difficult to find task-relevant patterns. Despite all of these challenges, the network perspective remains appealing to sociologists, intelligence analysts, biologists, communication theorists, bibliometricians, food-web ecologists, and many other professionals. The growing popularity of social network analysis (SNA) can be seen in, and inspired by, popular bestselling books such as Malcolm Gladwell's *The Tipping Point* (Back Bay Books), Albert-László Barabási's *Linked* (Plume), and Duncan Watts's *Six Degrees* (Norton). Countless analysts wish to analyze their network data, but there are few mature or widely used tools and techniques for doing so.

Network analysts focus on relationships instead of just the individual elements that can explain social, cultural, or economic phenomena; how the elements are connected is just as important as the elements themselves. Prior to the social network analysis perspective, many analysts focused largely on inherent individual attributes and neglected the social facet of behavior—i.e., how individuals interact and the influence they have on one another (Freeman 2004). Using newer techniques from the social network community, analysts can find patterns in the structures, witness the flow of resources or messages through a network, and learn how individuals are influenced by their surroundings.

In practice, social network visualizations can be chaotic, particularly when the network is large. Visualizations are useful in leveraging the powerful perceptual abilities of humans, but cluttered presentations, overlapping edges, and illegible node labels often undermine the benefits of visual exploration. In these situations, interactive techniques are necessary to make sense of such complex static visualizations. *Inherent* attributes are the attributes that exist in the dataset, such as gender, race, salary, or education level. Interactions such as zooming, panning, or filtering by the inherent attributes of nodes and edges can simplify complex visualizations. Unfortunately, such techniques may only get users so far with complex networks and may not tell the whole story, particularly in small-world networks where dense connections will rarely untangle (van Ham 2004). Inherent attributes lack the structural, topological information critical to social network analysts. Our major contribution is to augment information visualizations with *computed* attributes that reflect the tasks of users. Computed attributes can be calculated from relevant statistical importance metrics (e.g., degree or betweenness centrality), clustering algorithms, or data mining strategies.

This approach of leveraging computed attributes is particularly valuable for social network analysts, as they have also come to believe that inherent attributes do not tell the whole story. In fact, an approach taken by many social network analysts is to ignore inherent attributes during exploration to avoid bias, and to only focus on the data's structural properties. For social network analysts, computed attributes can be calculated with a rich set of statistical techniques, from sociology to graph theory, that allow analysts to numerically uncover interesting features within their networks. Analysts might seek a tight-knit community of individuals, or the gatekeepers between them, or the most centrally powerful entities; there are a variety of sophisticated algorithms for finding these traits.

Most visualization tools aim to project complex data into comprehensible views. However, few tools assist users by providing computed attributes that highlight important properties of their data. Users can switch back and forth between statistical and visualization packages, but this can result in an inefficient flow in the analysis process, which inhibits discovery.

SocialAction is the software tool Ben Shneiderman and I created to explore these issues (*http://www.cs.umd.edu/hcil/socialaction*). It provides meaningful, computed attributes on the fly by integrating both statistics and visualizations to enable users to quickly derive the benefits of both. SocialAction embeds statistical algorithms to detect important individuals, relationships, and clusters. Instead of presenting statistical results in typical tabular fashion, the results are integrated in a network visualization that provides meaningful computed attributes of the nodes and edges. With computed attributes, users can easily and dynamically filter nodes and edges to find interesting data points. The visualizations simplify the statistical results, facilitating sensemaking and discovery of features such as distributions, patterns, trends, gaps, and outliers. The statistics simplify the comprehension of sometimes-chaotic visualizations, allowing users to focus on statistically significant nodes and edges. The presence of these rich interactions within one consistent interface provides a fluid, efficient, visual analytic system that allows users to focus on insights and generating hypotheses rather than managing a medley of software packages. I'll walk you through this rich interaction of statistics and visualization later, but let's begin with the motivation for why this is necessary.

Who Wants to Visualize Social Networks?

My fieldwork with social network analysts, both in academia and industry, suggests that pure statistical analysis is the most commonly used technique when attempting to interpret social networks. Although network visualizations are common in research publications and reports, they are typically created for communicative purposes after the analysis is complete and not necessarily visualizations used during the exploratory analysis.

A history of the use of visual images in social networks is described in "Visualizing Social Networks" (Freeman 2000), including one of the earliest known examples of a social network visualization by Jacob Moreno in 1934. In Figure 10-2, the triangle nodes are boys and the circle nodes are girls. Without knowing any details about who the individuals in this classroom are, one quickly learns from the visualization that 1) boys are friends with boys, 2) girls are friends with girls, 3) one brave boy chose a girl as his friend (although this was not reciprocated), and 4) there is an isolated group of two girls. This visualization typifies how a legible and well-positioned network can explain the social structure of individuals.

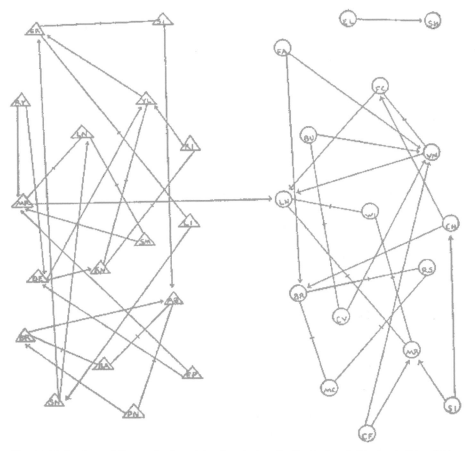

Figure 10-2. *One of the earliest social network visualizations: Jacob Moreno's Friendship Choices Among Fourth Graders (Moreno 1934).*

Social network data is extremely complex, as the dimensionality of the data increases with each relationship. Those familiar with network visualizations might sympathize with these statistically attuned practitioners, as it is very difficult to design a useful network visualization when the number of nodes or edges is large. Large network visualizations are typically a tangled set of nodes and edges, and rarely achieve "NetViz Nirvana" (a phrase coined by Ben Shneiderman to describe the ability to see each node and follow its edges to all other nodes). Network visualizations may offer evidence of clusters and outliers, but in general it is hard to gather deeper insights from these complex visualizations.

My first argument is that it is hard to find patterns and trends using purely statistical methods. My second argument is that network visualizations usually offer little utility beyond a small set of insights. So what should a social network researcher do? Use both—in a tightly integrated way—to arrive at beautiful visualizations. The design of SocialAction centers on this goal.

The Design of SocialAction

Structural analysts have proposed numerous measures for statistically assessing social networks. However, there is no systematic way to interpret such networks, as those measures can have different meanings in different networks. This is problematic, as analysts want to be certain they are not overlooking critical facets of the network. In order to make exploration easier, I interviewed social network analysts and reviewed social network journals to tabulate the most commonly used measurements. I then organized these measures into six user-centered tasks: Overview, Rank Nodes, Rank Edges, Plot Nodes, Find Communities, and Edge Types. In the following sections, I'll describe each of these tasks and their associated features in detail. However, let's first begin with an illustration of the main goals of the process.

Shneiderman's Visual Information-Seeking Mantra—"Overview first, zoom and filter, then details on demand" (Shneiderman 1996)—serves as guidance for organizing the complex tasks of a social network analyst. Analysts begin with an overview of the network, both statistically and visually; see Figure 10-3(a). Measurements of the entire network, such as the density, diameter, and number of components, are computed and presented alongside a force-directed layout of the network. The visualization gives users a sense of the structure, clusters, and depth of a network, while the statistics provide a way to both confirm and quantify the visual findings. If the network is small, or the analysts are interested purely in the topology of the network, this step may be enough.

A more capable analyst will wish to gain a deeper understanding of the individual elements of the network. Users can apply statistical importance metrics common in social network analysis to measure the nodes (also known as vertices) and edges (also known as links). For instance, analysts can rank the nodes by degree (the most connected nodes), betweenness (the gatekeepers), closeness (nodes that are well positioned to receive information), or other metrics. After users select a metric, a table lists the nodes in rank order. SocialAction assigns each node a color, ranging from green (low ranking) to black (average ranking) to red (high ranking). This helps illustrate each node's position among all ranked entities. The network visualization is updated simultaneously, painting each node with the corresponding color. Users now can scan the entire network to see where the important nodes reside; see Figure 10-3(a).

To gain further insights, SocialAction allows users to continue on to step 2 of the Visual Information Seeking Mantra ("filter and zoom"). This is where most other social network analysis packages strand users. Panning and zooming naïvely is not enough to empower users: zooming into sections of the network forces users to lose the global structure, and dense networks may never untangle. SocialAction allows user-controlled statistics to drive the navigation. Users can dismiss portions of the network that do not meet their criteria by using range sliders. Filtering by attributes or importance metrics allows users to focus on the types of nodes they care about, while simultaneously simplifying the visualization; see Figure 10-3(b).

After analysts can make sense of global trends through statistical measurements and visual presentations, but their analyses often are incomplete without an understanding of what the individual nodes represent. Contrary to most other network visualizations, labels are always present in SocialAction. The controls for font size and length allow the analysts to decide their emphasis. In line with step 3 of the Visual Information Seeking Mantra ("details on demand"), users can select a node to see all of its attributes. Hovering over a node also highlights each node's edges and neighbors, achieving NetViz Nirvana for the node of interest; see Figure 10-3(c).

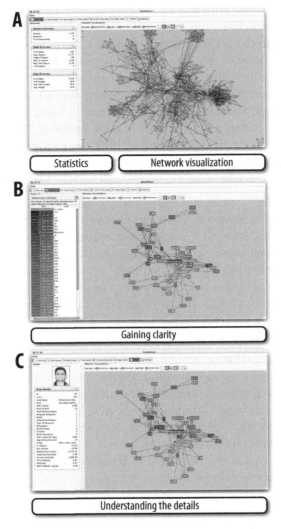

Figure 10-3. *(a) The Statistics side of the interface allows users to choose statistical algorithms to find important nodes, detect clusters, and more. The Visualization side is integrated with the statistics. Nodes are colored according to their ranking, with red nodes being the most statistically important. (b) The gatekeepers are found using a statistical algorithm. Users filter out the unimportant nodes using a dynamic slider that simplifies the visualization while maintaining the node positions and structure of the network. (c) Labels are always given priority so users can understand what the data represents. When a user selects a node, neighbors are highlighted and details appear on the left.*

For another, albeit more lighthearted, example, let's take a look at my personal social network on Facebook. If I visualize the connections using a standard network layout algorithm, I get a Jackson Pollack–like mess; there is something intriguing about the mess, but it certainly lacks the grace of a Lombardi piece. However, if I make use of some statistics (in this case, a clustering algorithm designed to detect communities), I get a much more sensible output. What used to be a bunch of tangled nodes and edges is now my social network grouped into meaningful categories. I can see clusters of my high school friends, my college friends, my graduate school friends, my Microsoft colleagues, and so on (Figure 10-4). An image devoid of meaning becomes beautiful, thanks to our dear algorithmic friends.

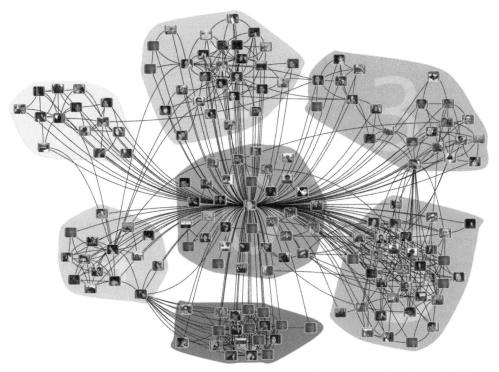

Figure 10-4. *A visualization of my Facebook social network. By running a clustering algorithm on top of the network, seven meaningful communities of friends were found representing different facets of my life. Without clustering, the network was too tangled to provide any meaning.*

In summary, bringing together statistics and visualizations yields an elegant solution for exploratory data analysis. The visualizations simplify the statistical results, improving the comprehension of patterns and global trends. The statistics, in turn, simplify the comprehension of the sometimes-chaotic visualizations, allowing users to focus on statistically significant nodes and edges.

Case Studies: From Chaos to Beauty

Ultimately, what makes network visualization beautiful? An 18th-century Scottish philosopher, David Hume (1742), wrote:

> Beauty is no quality in things themselves. It exists merely in the mind which contemplates them; and each mind perceives a different beauty.

However, Hume's view of beauty was contested. A Scottish associate, Henry Home (Lord Kames), believed that beauty could be broken down to a rational system of rules.

When it comes to visualizations based on underlying data, I side with Lord Kames. Insights offered are the measure of success for a beautiful visualization. Analysts may be seeking to confirm their intuitions, detect anomalies or outliers, or uncover underlying patterns. Chris North, a professor at Virginia Tech, characterizes insights as complex, deep, qualitative, unexpected, and relevant findings. While a helpful characterization, the impression is that measuring insights is perhaps as complicated as measuring beauty. Traditional laboratory-based controlled experiments have proven to be effective for many scientific tests, but do they work for insights? For instance, if I invented new display or input widgets, controlled experiments could compare two or more treatments by measuring learning times, task performance times, or error rates. Typical experiments would involve 20–60 participants each given 10–30 minutes of training, followed by all participants doing the same 2–20 tasks during a 1–3-hour session. Statistical methods such as t-tests and ANOVA would then be applied to check for significant differences in mean values. These summary statistics are effective, especially if there is small variance across users.

However, how does someone break insights into a set of measurable tasks? The first challenge is that analysts often work for days or weeks to carry out exploratory data analyses on substantial problems, and their work processes would be nearly impossible to reconstruct in a laboratory-based controlled experiment (even if large numbers of professionals could be obtained for the requisite time periods). A second difficulty is that exploratory tasks are by their nature poorly defined, so telling the users which tasks to carry out would be incompatible with discovery. Third, each user has unique skills and experience, leading to wide variations in performance that would undermine the utility of the summary statistics. In controlled studies, exceptional performance is seen as an unfortunate outlier, but in case studies, these special events are fruitful critical incidents that provide insight into how discovery happens. Fourth, I wanted more than quantitative analyses of the tool; I also wished to hear about the problems and frustrations users encountered, as well as their thrilling tales of success. For such reasons, I turned to structured and replicated case study research methods to decide if SocialAction could generate beautiful visualizations.

The following sections summarize a few of my case studies of real analysts using SocialAction to visualize their own data. In homage to Mark Lombardi, I have chosen here to report on the covert networks of politicians and terrorists.

The Social Network of Senatorial Voting

Congressional analysts are interested in partisan unity in the United States Senate. For instance, *Congressional Quarterly* calculates such unity by identifying every vote in which a majority of Democrats voted opposite a majority of Republicans, and then counts, for each senator, the percentage of those votes in which that senator voted with his or her party. This metric can be useful for tracking an individual senator's party loyalty from year to year, but it does not reveal much about the overall patterns in the body.

Chris Wilson, then an associate editor for the *US News & World Report*, became interested in voting patterns among United States senators in 2007. Wilson set out to uncover senatorial patterns such as strategic, bipartisan, or geographic alliances in the dataset. He spent significant effort mining voting data from public databases, but was unable to find any distinct patterns through his normal methods of analysis.

Wilson believed social network analysis could yield the answers he sought. His data included voting results for each senator during the first six months of 2007, beginning when the Democratic Party assumed control of the chamber with a one-seat majority. A social network can be inferred from co-occurrences of votes.

Wilson constructed the network such that, when a senator votes with another senator on a resolution, an edge connects them. The strength of each edge is based on how often they vote with each other (e.g., Barack Obama and Hillary Clinton voted together 203 times, whereas Obama and Sam Brownback voted together only 59 times). This led to a very dense network, because there were certain uncontroversial resolutions that all senators voted for (e.g., Resolution RC-20, a bill commending the actions of "the Subway Hero" Wesley Autrey). All the senators were connected, resulting in a visualization resembling a huge, tangled web.

SocialAction allows users to rank edges according to importance metrics. Wilson used this feature to compare network visualizations by dynamically filtering out relationships with low importance rankings. For instance, the 180-vote threshold (about 60 percent voting coincidence) is shown in Figure 10-5. Partisanship is strong even at this fairly low threshold, and the Republican senators who were most likely to vote with Democrats (Collins, Snowe, Specter, and Smith) are evident. This visualization suggests that in this particular Senate, although both parties were partisan, Republicans were less so than Democrats.

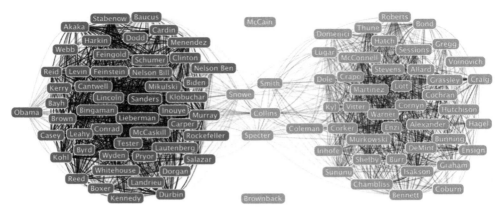

Figure 10-5. *This visualization shows the voting patterns of U. S. senators during 2007. The red Republicans are on the right and the blue Democrats are on the left, with two Independents. Links indicate the similarity of voting records, revealing that Democrats had stronger party loyalty during 2007. Four Republican senators from Northeastern states often voted with Democrats. McCain and Brownback were campaigning for the presidency and did not vote often enough to be connected.*

Another unexpected revelation was that the Democrats appeared to stay more tightly unified than the Republicans as the threshold increased, as evidenced by the much denser and darker connections on the Democrat side. Each edge is slightly transparent, but the constant overlapping of Democrats yields a dark mass, whereas the Republican side is much sparser. Wilson believed this interaction beautifully illustrated the Democratic caucus's success in keeping members in line, an important fact when reviewing legislative tactics. The integration of statistics and visualization made this discovery possible.

To determine the voting patterns of individual politicians, Wilson used SocialAction's statistical importance metrics. The capability to rank all nodes, visualize the outcome of the ranking, and filter out the unimportant nodes led to many discoveries. Wilson stated, for instance, that the *betweenness centrality* statistic turned out to be "a wonderful way to quantitatively measure the centers of gravity in the Senate." SocialAction made it evident that only a few senators centrally link their colleagues to one another. Wilson was also able to use the interactive clustering algorithms of SocialAction to "uncover geographic alliances among Democrats." These findings are just a sample of the sorts of insights that had eluded Wilson prior to his analysis with SocialAction.

Wilson was impressed with the discoveries that SocialAction helped reveal. The tight integration of statistics and visualization allowed him to uncover findings and communicate them to his peers both at the *US News & World Report* and on Capitol Hill. SocialAction received so much attention internally that the magazine hopes to replicate some of its functionality for its online readers. Since completing the case study Wilson has moved to *Slate* magazine, but he still uses SocialAction for investigative reporting. Analysis using

SocialAction has already led to an interactive feature analyzing the social networks of steroids users in Major League Baseball (*http://www.slate.com/id/2180392*), and more stories are planned for the future.

The Social Network of Terrorists

The National Consortium for the Study of Terrorism and Responses to Terror (START) is a U.S. Department of Homeland Security Center of Excellence. START has a worldwide research team that "aims to provide timely guidance on how to disrupt terrorist networks, reduce the incidence of terrorism, and enhance the resilience of U.S. society in the face of the terrorist threat." One member of this team is James Hendrickson, a criminologist PhD candidate who is interested in analyzing the social networks of "Global Jihad."

Previous research has pointed to the importance of radicalization informing and sustaining terrorist organizations. While the radicalization process has been well described from a psychological standpoint, Hendrickson believes theories regarding the group dynamics of terrorism have largely failed to properly measure the size, scope, and other dynamics of group relations. He proposes to systematically compare the density and type of relationships held by members of Global Jihad to evaluate their predictive ability in determining involvement in terrorist attacks. Marc Sageman, a visiting fellow at START, assembled a database of over 350 terrorists involved in jihad when researching his bestselling book, *Understanding Terror Networks* (University of Pennsylvania Press). Hendrickson plans to update and formally apply social network analysis to this data as a part of his PhD dissertation.

The Sageman database has over 30 variables for each suspected terrorist. Among these variables are different types of relationships, including friends, family members, and educational ties. Hendrickson hypothesized that the types of relationships connecting two individuals will hugely affect their participation in terrorist attacks. He began his analysis using UCINET and was able to analyze some of his hypotheses. However, he believed UCINET did not facilitate exploring and generating new hypotheses. Hendrickson initially was skeptical of using visualizations for his analysis. He preferred being able to prove statistical significance quantitatively rather than relying on a human's judgment of an image. However, he says the quick access to the statistical counterparts of SocialAction's visualizations eased his concerns.

In particular, SocialAction's multiplexity feature aided Hendrickson's exploration. SocialAction allows users to analyze different relationship types without forcing users to load new datasets. The visualization shows the selected relationship edges, but keeps node positions stable in order to aid comprehension. The statistical results are also automatically recomputed based on the newly selected structure. For instance, only the "Friend" relationships among jihadists are selected in Figure 10-6(a). (Compare this to the denser Figure 10-3(a), which shows all relationship types.) The nodes here are ranked by degree, so red nodes have the most friends. Jihadists Osama

Bin Laden and Mohamed Atta (known for his role in the 9/11 attacks) are ranked the highest. However, when the religious ties are invoked, a different set of key jihadists emerges; see Figure 10-6(b).

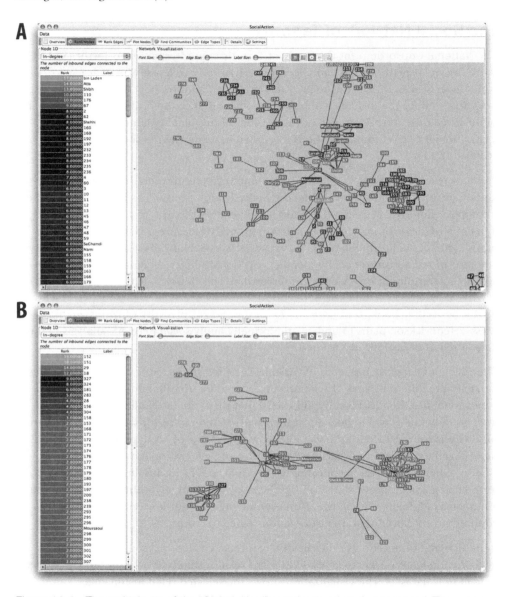

Figure 10-6. *The multiplexity of the "Global Jihad" social network is demonstrated. The upper visualization (a) shows the Friendship network, with bin Laden the most popular individual. The bottom network (b), showing religious ties, offers a much different view of the terrorist organization.*

After analyzing the statistical attributes of nodes, Hendrickson became interested in understanding the individuals' attributes. For example, he was interested in answering questions like, "Does an individual's socioeconomic status or education level impact his position in the terrorist network?" Of course, social network data does not allow users to infer causation, but it may show correlation. Like statistical rankings in SocialAction, users can rank and filter based upon attributes. Hendrickson filtered out individuals without college degrees, religious backgrounds, or engineering expertise, and analyzed the results. The combination of nodal attributes with statistical filtering and plotting streamlined his accustomed workflow, and he commented that he might not have been as free in his thinking if it weren't for the ease of exploration in SocialAction. This analysis inspired Hendrickson to think of new, not-yet-coded attributes to test additional hypotheses. He is currently augmenting Sageman's database with new attributes so he can look for patterns in SocialAction, visually and statistically.

Hendrickson's experience with SocialAction has led to new inspiration for his dissertation thesis. Although he had access to the dataset long before the case study began and had conducted analyses with other SNA software, the integration of statistics and visualization in SocialAction allowed exploration in new, interesting ways. As a result, the START center is interested in making SocialAction the default network analysis tool for internal and external users who wish to access its databases.

One other use of SocialAction by the START center was to look at networks that evolve over time. In their global terrorism network, nodes can be connected based on whether two people committed a terrorist attack in the same area, or used the same weapons, or came from the same region. Edges can also have temporal characteristics; for example, an edge could represent an attack in a certain year. The types of edges used depend on what types of questions the analyst is trying to answer. In tandem with a network diagram, users can see a stacked histogram, as in Figure 10-7. Each node is represented as a line and each column represents an edge type. The node's thickness in each column represents the node's ranking in the network of that edge type. The color is based on the node's overall ranking across all edge types.

In Figure 10-7, two stacked histograms are shown that demonstrate the evolution of a terrorist network over time. This particular network had two types of nodes: terrorist groups and the countries in which they had committed attacks. The country nodes are alphabetized and stacked in Figure 10-7(a), whereas all the terrorist groups appear in Figure 10-7(b). The thickness of the node at each year is based on the node's degree in the network. Nodes are colored based on their degree (red implies high degree, green implies low degree) and are labeled in their peak years (there is a clear peak of attacks in 1992). Various trends can be interpreted from this image, such as that Italy had many different groups attacking in the earlier years, whereas India had peak activity in the later years.

Since there are many more terrorist groups than countries, Figure 10-7(b) is a bit more difficult to interpret. However, these visualizations are interactive, and users can filter them according to name. So, if an analyst typed the word "Armenia," only the nodes with terrorist groups whose names contain the word Armenia (such as the Armenian Secret Army for the Liberation of Armenia, and Justice Commandos for the Armenian Genocide) would be shown.

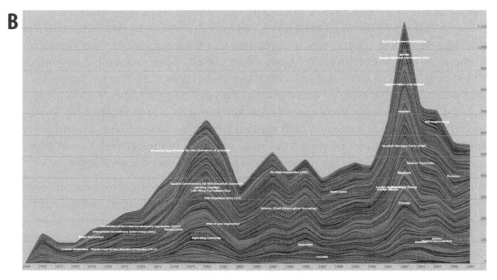

Figure 10-7. *Stacked histograms highlight the temporal trends of two evolving networks. The upper visualization (a) displays the evolution of the country nodes, whereas (b) displays the evolution of the terrorist group nodes.*

In 2007, the temporal visualizations shown in Figure 10-7 were on display at the New York Hall of Science as a part of the Competition on Visualizing Network Dynamics (*http://vw.indiana.edu/07netsci/*). I'll end this chapter with a quote by one of the judges that emphasizes some of the goals of SocialAction and perhaps the essence of creating beautiful visualizations:

> Networks are best read if they are not only "technically accurate" and visually attractive but when they employ a type of rendering that creates a landscape. That creates a bridge for the uninitiated audience to cross into the field of expertise. Dataland travels have now become so enjoyable, they may soon appear as special fare destinations at a travel agency near you. Perer's visuals make that trip into the land of terror networks absurdly attractive. Having intellectual entertainment and visual pleasure with terrorism analysis is perhaps one way to diffuse the very essence of terror—by analyzing it without being terrified. And in the end it leads to a hopefully more rational dealing with it, which is the opposite of what terrorism is trying to instill.
>
> *—Ingo Günther,*
> *Tokyo National University for Fine Arts & Music, Japan*

References

Freeman, Linton. 2000."Visualizing Social Networks." *Journal of Social Structure. http://www.cmu.edu/joss/content/articles/volume1/Freeman.html.*

Freeman, Linton. 2004. *The Development of Social Network Analysis: A Study in the Sociology of Science.* Vancouver, BC, Canada: Empirical Press.

Hume, David. 1742. *Essays: Morale, Political, and Literary.*

Moreno, J.L. 1934. *Who Shall Survive?* Washington, DC: Nervous and Mental Disease Publishing Co.

Shneiderman, Ben. 1996. "The Eyes Have It: A Task by Data Type Taxonomy for Information Visualizations." In *Proceedings of the IEEE Symposium on Visual Languages.* Washington, DC: IEEE Computer Society.

Tukey, John. 1977. *Exploratory Data Analysis.* Boston: Addison-Wesley.

van Ham, Frank. 2004. "Interactive Visualization of Small World Graphs." In *Proceedings of the IEEE Symposium on Information Visualization.* Washington, DC: IEEE Computer Society.

## CHAPTER ELEVEN

Beautiful History: Visualizing Wikipedia

Martin Wattenberg and Fernanda Viégas

IN THE EARLY YEARS OF WIKIPEDIA, we created several visualizations to illuminate the workings of the online encyclopedia. This chapter will take you through our process, from initial sketches to working programs to scientific papers. The messages to take away are the importance of working with real data at all steps; the benefits of starting with rough, preliminary visualizations; and finally, that visualization is just one piece of a larger analysis. The story also illustrates the intuitions that can guide a successful visualization project, from sensing when an area could benefit from visualization to determining when a visualization might be "done."

Depicting Group Editing

Our story begins in 2003. The two of us were working at IBM's Collaborative User Experience Research Lab, which studies how people work together online. We saw that new forms of collaboration were taking place on the Internet and wanted to investigate them. There were many to choose from—this was the time that "Web 2.0" was just beginning to take off—but Wikipedia particularly fascinated us.

In 2003, just two years after the online encyclopedia's birth, the site was still not well known, and among those aware of it there was serious skepticism about its open authorship model. We felt some of this skepticism ourselves, yet many of the articles were interesting and helpful. What was going on? How was such a haphazard process yielding a quality product? Aside from raw curiosity, such a feeling of puzzlement is often a sign of a fertile research area. We decided to investigate. How did the articles on Wikipedia achieve such a high level of quality? Why didn't we see the level of craziness, silliness, and juvenile behavior that touched so many other online communities?

The Data

To answer these questions, we needed to know more. The first step (as in any of our visualization projects) was to find raw data. In the case of Wikipedia, the data wasn't a table of numbers in a database, but a set of document versions and edit histories. One of the initial brilliant decisions by Wikipedia's founders was to keep a full version history of every page available to the public. As we eventually learned, this has critical implications for the resilience of Wikipedia—but as we started the investigation, our main feeling was delight that the data was available.

That feeling of delight soon was mingled with a slight dizziness. Sifting through so much data by hand became confusing. Our database contained an embarrassment of riches, so it was time to bring in visualization technology.

To a casual reader, Wikipedia is just a big collection of articles, much like a traditional encyclopedia. But under the surface, the structure is complex. As most people now know, on each page is a link that lets readers edit the article. Less widely appreciated are two other links labeled *discussion* and *history*. The former goes to a *talk page* where readers and editors can discuss an article. These pages, which hold everything from arguments about page content to requests for homework help, represent the "non-content" pages of Wikipedia. Of immediate interest to us, however, was the link to a page's *edit history*.

The edit history (see Figure 11-1) contains a list of links to the full edit text of all previous versions, along with data on the edit's author, the time at which it was made, and a comment. The comment is optional—a chance for the author to explain the purpose of the edit—but the time and author are automatically logged. When an editor is not signed into the system, that user's IP address is recorded in place of a username.

The edit histories were large in 2003 and are vast today. Of course, different numbers of edits were made in different articles. When we did our initial scrape, the article on "Microsoft" had 198 versions (for a total of 6.3 megabytes of text) while the article on "Cat" had only 54 versions. We began by writing a program to download the histories directly from the site. However, we soon realized this was poor etiquette since it puts a strain on the Wikipedia servers, and instead used a single large file kindly provided by Wikipedia for free. If you'd like to play with visualizing any of this data, the best way is to download the latest version of this snapshot yourself.*

---

* See *http://en.wikipedia.org/wiki/Wikipedia:Snapshots*.

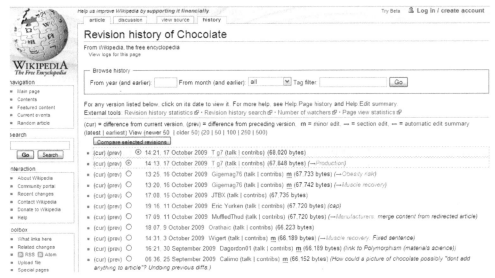

Figure 11-1. *Discussion page for "Chocolate" on Wikipedia: the page lists every change made to the article, including who made the edit, when it was done, etc.*

History Flow: Visualizing Edit Histories

Wikipedia can display *diffs* between pairs of versions, highlighting added and deleted words, but we wanted to be able to see an overview of *all* the article edits that had been made over time. To this end, we set out to create a new visualization technique that we called *history flow*.

Even with our data in hand, we couldn't jump to writing graphics code. We needed to be able to compute the diffs between successive articles ourselves. Determining where and how two files differ seems like a routine operation, used in consumer programs like Microsoft Word as well as in developer tools such as version control software. Yet it is subtler than it appears, and despite (or perhaps because of) the fact that this problem has been studied for so long, it turns out there is no single best way to do this.

The challenge is that there is not a unique way to *describe* the differences between texts. For instance, consider the following two sentences:

- The quick brown fox jumped over the big post.

- The big brown fox jumped over the clay pots.

Most algorithms will tell you that the word "quick" has been deleted and the word "clay" has been inserted. But what about "big"? Was it inserted in one place and deleted in another, or simply moved from the end to the beginning? Similarly, was the word "post" removed and replaced by "pots," or were the letters in "post" rearranged to make "pots"?

The different interpretations are all logically consistent, so the goal is to choose an algorithm that makes sense in a particular context. In our case, we decided that editors might well shift chunks of text—moving a word or sentence from one part of an article to another—but were unlikely to shift letters to anagram individual words. So, we chose an algorithm written by Paul Heckel that would let us track the movement of large passages, but that operated on word-size tokens as atomic units.* The output of the algorithm was a set of correspondences between two sequences, of the form "word #5 in File A corresponds to word #127 in File B."

Heckel's algorithm is straightforward to implement, and we soon had everything in place to begin our analysis. For every article, we had the text of each version, along with a set of "correspondences" between the versions. But how to display this? To start with, since this is time-based data, it made sense to use the x-axis for the sequence, with the first version on the left, the second to its right, and so on. This fit with the way we viewed the history of an article, as a "river" with different "currents" for each section of the document. Initially we used the x-axis for sequence information alone, with an identical number of pixels between each version's position; later we added an option to space the versions by date of edit, so that versions that occurred close in time were also close in space. Both ways of viewing the data turned out to be important later.

Next, we needed to encode the document positions and correspondences between passages. We decided to draw versions as vertical lines whose lengths corresponded to the lengths of each version. In effect, the y-axis encoded the document position within each version. Once we made this decision, it was easy to see how to depict correspondences by drawing lines directly from one version to the next to show matches, much as in Figure 11-2 (an example of the kind of hand-drawn sketch we made on a whiteboard before starting to code).

Our first computed version looked roughly like Figure 11-3, which shows the page for "Abortion" as of 2003. It's crude and a little confusing, but there is a clear structure and even some features that made us wonder if there was a bug in our code. You'll notice a striking gap at version 4, for instance. We checked the data by hand, and this was not an error: we were looking at a version where a malicious user had erased most of the article. Aha! The visualization had already drawn our attention to a critical episode in the article's history.

---

* For the technically minded, the algorithm works by first finding unambiguous matches between tokens found only once in each sequence, and then extending those matches to larger contiguous chunks.

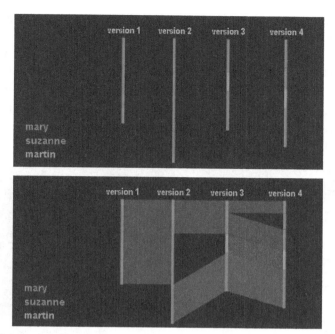

Figure 11-2. *Schematic of history flow's visualization mechanism*

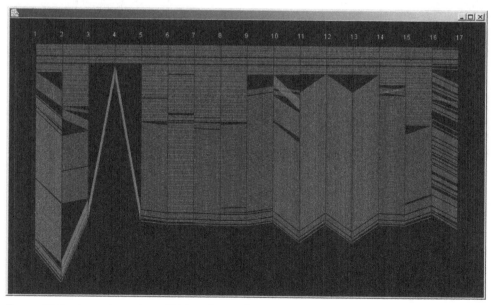

Figure 11-3. *An early version of history flow, with simple lines connecting pieces of text that survive intact over consecutive versions*

Because going back to the original source by hand had been cumbersome, we quickly added the ability to see the original text of each version in a panel at the right. This is typical in visualization development: after getting a prototype visual overview in place, it's often a good idea to make a way to see details. Not only is this a feature that users always want, but it provides an essential way to check the correctness of the overview.

The skeletal visualization was still difficult to read, so we decided to "fill in" the correspondences—i.e., to fill in the interior of each pair of parallel lines. Figure 11-4 shows the result.

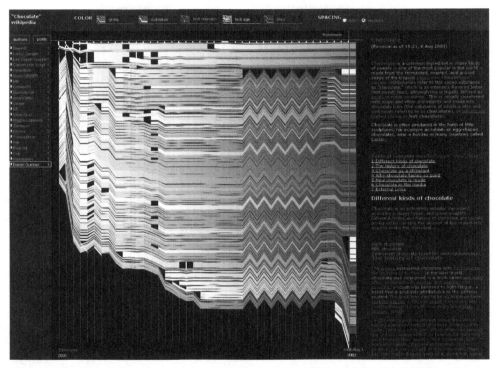

Figure 11-4. *History flow diagram showing text age on the "Chocolate" article in Wikipedia: darker patches represent older passages*

The resulting pictures were easier to read and seemed less complex. In fact, we now felt that we had a natural way to show another variable, through the color of the polygons connecting corresponding passages.

Age of Edit

We were curious whether edits that remained on the site for a long time were of better quality than edits with a short history, or whether they could be distinguished in any other way. Age is a simple numeric variable, and it made sense to portray it using grayscale, as in Figure 11-4. This was the first coloration effect we added, and it had two benefits: not only did it convey the dimension of age, but the varying shades of gray actually made the overall shape of the diagram more legible. This is a counterintuitive but common phenomenon in visualizations: adding extra information can actually help clarify the reading of a complex diagram.

Authorship

Our real goal, however, was to see the human dynamics behind group editing. For this, we needed to portray authorship. We had the necessary data, since each edit came with authorship information (a username for logged-in editors, or an IP address for anonymous contributors). How should we assign colors to individual editors? We wanted a wide range of colors, so that different contributors would be distinguishable, and we wanted any given contributor to have the same color across different pages. At the same time, we wanted to distinguish anonymous from logged-in contributors.*

We settled on an unusual choice of encoding in which our software chose random bright, saturated colors for each user. These weren't genuinely random, but were based on the Java "hashcode" of an author's name. This technique ensured that the colors were consistent across diagrams, and that there was the widest possible range of variation. For anonymous editors, we chose a light shade of gray.

The overall effect was visually dramatic (see Figure 11-5). At a quick glance, a viewer could tell immediately the difference between a page with many anonymous editors (a sea of gray) and a page edited entirely or primarily by logged-in users (fully in color). It was also easy to see when a few editors had dominated the writing of an article. To link author names to their colors, we added a legend at the left of the screen.

---

* Assigning anonymous users distinct colors based on their IP addresses seemed possibly deceptive, since there is no clear correlation between addresses and actual users. Different people logging in through a corporate network at different times may have the same IP address; conversely, it's not uncommon for the same person to edit from different IP addresses.

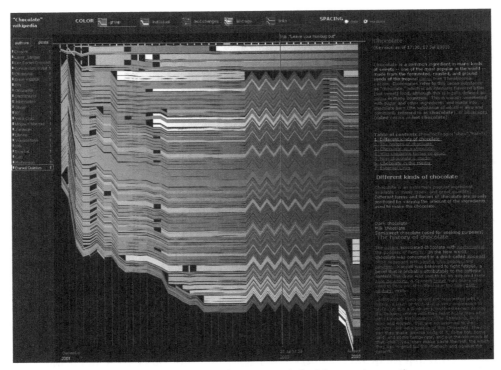

Figure 11-5. *History flow in color: each color represents text from a given author*

Individual Authors

Next, we wanted to make it easier to see just the contributions of individual authors. To this end, we made the author legend clickable: selecting an author recolored the diagram so that the selected author's contributions were highlighted in a bright cream color, while the other areas of the diagram became much darker (see Figure 11-6). We tried several variations before settling on this scheme. The alternative of keeping the selected author's color bright and simply fading the other authors didn't always make the selection stand out, while using white for the selected author became confusing since shades of gray represent anonymous editors in the main view.

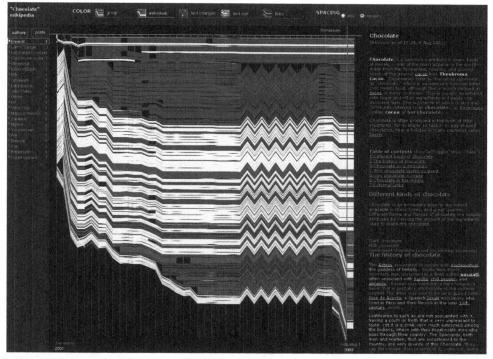

Figure 11-6. *Diagram showing, in cream, the contributions from a single author over time*

We added a few other small features and encodings after this, but the truth is that development slowed because our program had become fun to play with.* In fact, it was possibly too much fun! Instead of coding, we both spent time looking at article after article, fascinated by the variety of patterns. This is a always a good sign in visualization development, and it was reinforced by the fact that people passing by our desks ended up stopping for long conversations, drawn in by the pictures on our screens.

Our visualization allowed us to quickly get a sense of the group of editors involved in each article, the kinds of changes each person made, and even the eventual disagreements on how to proceed. Rather than fight the urge to visualize an endless number of articles, we decided that the visualization technique was, at least for the moment, done. Clearly, it satisfied our initial goal of pointing to patterns of collaboration that seemed to warrant investigation. Next, we turned our attention to using it to obtain scientific results.

---

* There still were plenty of alternatives we had not explored. We saw a glimpse of one such parallel visualization universe when Ben Fry independently created a version history diagram, *revisionist*, to show the evolution of the Processing environment. Instead of adding color and interactivity, he worked with the overall shape, using elegant curves and varying the placement of documents on the *y*-axis to make it easy to follow changes over time.

History Flow in Action

As we examined articles, we began in exploratory mode. As we looked at diagram after diagram, we slowly began to get a sense of what was normal and what was strange. We also began to see several distinct classes of behavior, such as "edit wars" in which authors repeatedly reverted one another's changes, showing up in the visualization as striking zigzags. More importantly, we began to follow up on some of the leads that the pictures showed us.

A good example of how we pursued a visual lead and moved from qualitative to quantitative research was our investigation of often-vandalized articles such as "Abortion." It became clear from the pictures that the vandalism often remained on the site for only a few minutes. When we looked at a history flow diagram in which the versions were equally spaced (Figure 11-7), we saw characteristic black gashes indicating malicious deletions; when we spaced the versions by date of edit, these often disappeared (Figure 11-8).

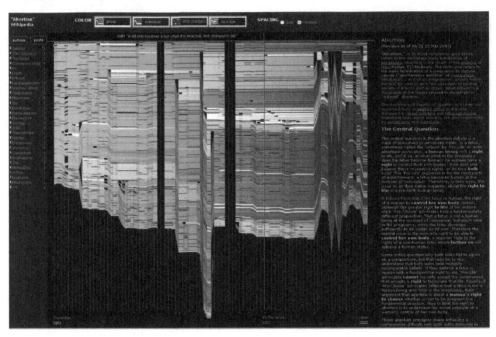

Figure 11-7. Editing history for "Abortion" showing versions equally spaced—black gutters represent "mass deletions," an act of vandalism whereby a user deletes all content in a given article

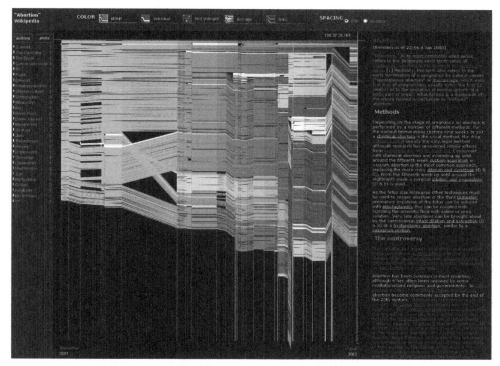

Figure 11-8. Editing history for "Abortion" showing versions spaced by time

Even seeing this pattern many times, however, did not constitute scientific evidence. Perhaps the articles that came to mind happened to be particularly controversial or well policed. To show that vandalism and its quick repair were truly widespread, we would need to take into account many more pages. To do so, we performed a scan of the entire database of Wikipedia edits. With the help of our colleague Kushal Dave, we created a set of criteria that identified particularly egregious vandalism* and wrote a program to examine all the edits that met these criteria. It turned out that the majority of these edits were reverted within minutes, indicating that Wikipedia editors were monitoring the changes closely.

---

* We looked for cases where article length dropped dramatically, as well as for the presence of obscenities on the page. This certainly did not identify all vandalism, but the edits it picked out were indeed largely malicious.

Communicating the Results

The statistical confirmation of our subjective impressions was the final piece of the puzzle, and provided a satisfying resolution to our initial question about Wikipedia. The reason we didn't see evidence of destructive behavior wasn't that this behavior didn't exist, but that it tended to be erased quickly from public view. We wrote up our results and submitted a scientific paper, but we did not stop there.

In addition to helping the scientific case for our argument, there was something about having a few specific numbers that made it easy to explain our results. The visualizations, in turn, gave the numbers credibility by adding depth and detail. We found that there was a great deal of interest in our results outside the academic world. Those unfamiliar with the inner workings of Wikipedia were quickly drawn to the magic and drama of editing an online, public encyclopedia. Scholars, on the other hand, cognizant of the open source style of editing, marveled at the clarity of the images and the wealth of information being presented at once. History flow proved the value of visualizing online communities for both cultural curiosity and scientific research.

Chromogram: Visualizing One Person at a Time

In 2006, we revisited Wikipedia. The encyclopedia was thriving, and we wanted to find out more about the people involved—especially the small core of active users who contributed many edits. What were their strategies for allocating time and energy? We were particularly interested in whether the data matched Yochai Benkler's model of "peer production," which unified activities ranging from Wikipedia to the creation of Linux.

Working with a talented intern, Kate Hollenbach, we decided to analyze the edit histories of the site administrators ("admins"), superusers with special privileges such as the ability to block other users and delete pages. Admins typically have long edit histories on the site and represent a committed core of the Wikipedia community.

Our first attempts to understand this data led to the creation of a series of charts and graphs showing activity levels over time. Creating charts of activity in itself is straightforward. The standard way to display this data is a line chart with time on the x-axis and number of edits on the y-axis. We worked with a series of such charts that were clear but, we felt, uninformative. Unlike the history flow diagrams, we did not see unexpected patterns or obvious leads for future investigation.

One problem seemed to be that simple graphs summarized too much of the data; by compressing tens of thousands of edits into a single numeric time series, we ended up removing important information. We were facing a classic decision in a visualization project: as we traveled through the data, how close to the ground should we fly? There was no way to know *a priori* whether there were interesting small-scale patterns. But since we were not seeing anything of use from 30,000 feet in the air, our only choice was to look more closely.

Showing All the Data

To get closer to the "ground," we decided to look at the individual pages each editor touched. Editing Wikipedia is a repetitive, complex business, and we felt our visualization needed to reflect that. The challenge was that some admins had contributed more than 100,000 edits! (The most active user performed an average of one edit every 10 minutes over the course of two years.) Few visualization techniques can display that number of data points as an understandable picture.

One technique, however, excels at rendering vast datasets. A family of methods known in the academic literature as *pixel-filling visualizations* represent each data point as either a single pixel or, at most, a very small rectangle. Pixel-filling visualizations pack information on the screen to its maximum capacity, and their very density can often lead to an ethereal beauty. Indeed, artist Jason Salavon's beautiful work on displaying an entire movie as a set of pixels is what inspired us to explore them further.[*]

We applied this technique by representing each edit in an admin's history as a small rectangle on the screen. We arranged these rectangles in a block, reading from left to right and top to bottom over time. Then, since spatial position showed sequence information, we had only one variable left to play with: color. This is true, essentially by definition, for all pixel-filling visualizations. Usually, color is defined by a gradient that represents a numeric dimension. Our challenge was that the most important variables—article titles and editor comments—were raw text.

To convert these pieces of text to color, it seemed natural to try the same hashcode technique we had used in history flow. When we applied it, we did begin to see patterns: histories in which an editor tackled the same page many times in a row showed up as long bars of color, while in other cases we could see no repetition at all, indicating editors who tended to float between pages, applying a single change to each and leaving for good.Although we were now seeing more detail than before, we continued to feel that useful information was hidden. For one thing, the names of the articles had structure not captured by the hashcode trick. Often, related articles began with the same phrase (e.g., "List of" or "USS"). We realized that this structure would be preserved by an alphabetical color scheme in which the first letters of each string determined the color. Figure 11-9 provides an explanation of the color scheme, while Figure 11-10 shows how a diagram is constructed.

---

[*] In 2000, Salavon portrayed the movie *Titanic* as a print named "The Top Grossing Film of All Time, 1 × 1." Each frame of the movie was shown as a single dot, whose color was the average of all colors in the frame.

Figure 11-9. *Example colors given to typical words found in Wikipedia edit comments*

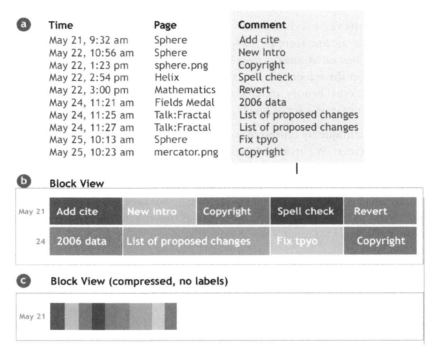

Figure 11-10. *Construction of a Chromogram visualizing user comments per edit*

What We Saw

Once we applied this new color scheme, the pictures snapped into focus. Although the edit histories remained complex and required some squinting, we saw many more types of patterns. The next few images give a sense of what we were looking at.

Figure 11-11 shows an article-title edit history made up of two main colors. These turn out to correspond to the words "births" and "deaths." A typical title is "Births in 1893." What this editor is doing is adding information about the births and deaths of notable people to different year pages.

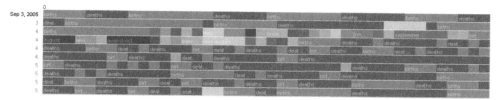

Figure 11-11. *Edits to "birth" and "death" articles*

Some editors found a subject they liked and stuck to it. Figure 11-12 is a sea of purple, a color corresponding to the prefix "USS," or "United States Ship." This editor was working on pages describing specific vessels in the United States Navy.

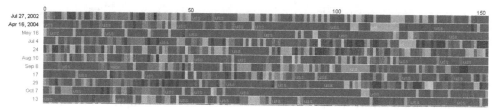

Figure 11-12. *More than 1,000 edits, mostly to articles whose titles begin with "USS"*

After looking through several of these diagrams, we had become accustomed to dense and random-seeming arrays of colors, occasionally interrupted by runs of identical hues. So we were taken aback when we saw Figure 11-13, with several regions where the colors form a kind of rainbow.

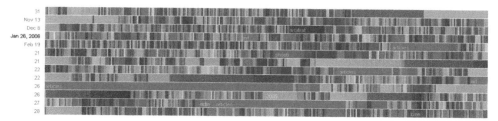

Figure 11-13. *Rainbows*

This visually striking pattern represents sequences of article titles arranged in alphabetical order. While a short alphabetical run could occur by chance, we saw many, some quite long. This was a perfect example of a lead worth investigating. Why did it happen, and what were the effects on Wikipedia?

Some rainbows were subtle. Others were like Figure 11-14. Who could perform such a methodical series of edits? When we checked the user page, we realized that this was the work of a "bot": a software program that was designed to execute automated edits. In this case, the edits included a massive set of routine categorizations of articles on geographic locations.

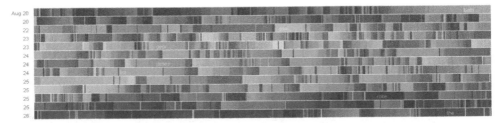

Figure 11-14. *A "bot"*

Analyzing the Data

As with history flow, we decided to verify some of our visual impressions through statistics—for example, the issue of the rainbows representing alphabetically sequenced edits. First, we wrote a program that identified these sequences and calculated their probability of occurring by chance, verifying that this was no random accident. We then went a step further. If many users edit in alphabetical order, might that mean that articles whose titles begin with a letter occurring early in the alphabet receive more attention? It seemed likely that some editors would optimistically begin long projects of editing many pages, only to give up halfway through. After collecting the data to test this hypothesis, we found an inverse correlation between alphabetical position of article title and number of edits, confirming our intuition that articles whose titles start with "a" are edited more frequently than those whose titles start with "z." The relationship wasn't perfect—for instance, the letter L had the most article edits, due to the number of lists it included—but it was strong enough to count as statistically significant.

The rainbows led us to look more closely at how editors used lists to organize their own work as well as the work of others. This phenomenon fit well with Benkler's model of peer production, in which work is divided into small units and people allocate their own time. The visualization had led us to a satisfying resolution of our initial research question.

Conclusion

As our story shows, creating a visualization can entail a path of false starts and dead ends. But while the path is winding, it's not a random walk. Both of our examples follow a consistent process, which we've refined through dozens of past visualizations. Here are three maxims we have found to be essential in all of our visualization projects:

Work with real data

Getting good data is often difficult and annoying. Whether you're negotiating a legal contract for access to a database or writing a program to scrape information from the Web, acquiring the raw material for visualizations is hard. Perhaps for that reason, many people try to multitask, designing visualizations even while they are still working on acquiring data. In our experience, that's almost always a mistake. In the Chromogram project, for instance, it was only after looking at sets of related article titles that we realized an alphabetical coloring scheme might make sense.

Visualize early and often—but know when to say when

As with other types of software development, working iteratively is important. Each of our projects began with a series of sketches. For history flow, these sketches eventually grew to become the final visualizations. For Chromogram, we threw the sketches away and took a look at the data from a different perspective. In each case, we adjusted the level of detail (i.e., the amount of "granularity"). With history flow, adding author colors and edit-age indications snapped our diagrams into focus. For Chromogram, we saw nothing useful until we showed the data at the finest level possible. The iteration did not last forever, though, because we paid attention to signs that we were done. Both history flow and Chromogram could have been polished much further, but each reached a stage where we felt like we were seeing what we had come to see.

Be aware of the larger process

Visualization is just one step in a larger chain of analysis. The chain begins with a question (why does Wikipedia work?) or a vague area of inquiry (how *do* those Wikipedia editors do it?) and ends with analysis, documentation, and presentation of results. A good visualization respects the links in the chain, encoding the right information to drive the initial inquiry and maintaining the right perspective to help lead later analysis and communicate the results.

## CHAPTER TWELVE

Turning a Table into a Tree: Growing Parallel Sets into a Purposeful Project

Robert Kosara

ACADEMIC SOFTWARE PROJECTS TEND TO GROW ORGANICALLY from an initial idea into something complex and unwieldy that is novel enough to publish a paper about. Features often get added at the last minute so they can be included in the paper, without much thought about how to integrate them well or how to adapt the program's underlying architecture to make them fit.

The result is that many of these programs are hacked together, buggy, and frankly embarrassing. Consequently, they do not get released together with the paper, which leads to a fundamental problem in visualization: reproducibility is possible in theory, but in practice rarely happens. Many programs and new techniques are also built from scratch rather than based on existing ones.

The optimal model would be to release the software right away, then come back to it later to refine and rearchitect it so that it reflects the overall design goals of the project. This is seldom done, though, because there is no academic value in a reimplementation (or thorough refactoring). Instead, people move on to the next project.

The original prototype implementation of Parallel Sets (*http://eagereyes.org/parallel-sets*) was no different, but we decided that in order to get the idea out of academia into actual use, we would need a working program. So we set out to rethink and redesign it, based on a better understanding of the necessary internal structures that we had gained over time. In the process, we not only re-engineered the program, but also revised its generated visualization to clarify its underlying idea.

193

Categorical Data

Hundreds of visualization techniques are described in the literature (with more added every year), but only a few specifically work with *categorical data*. Such data consists of only a few values that have special meanings (as opposed to continuous numerical data, where the numbers stand for themselves). Examples include typical census data, like values for sex (male or female), ethnicity, type of building, heating fuel used, etc. In fact, categorical data is crucial for many real-world analysis tasks. The data we originally designed our technique for was a massive customer survey consisting of 99 multiple-choice questions with almost 100,000 respondents. People were asked questions about consumer goods, like detergents and other household items, as well as demographic questions about household income, number of kids, ages of kids, etc. Even in cases where it would have been possible to gather precise information (like age), the survey combined the values into groups that would be useful for later analysis. That made all the dimensions strictly categorical, and almost impossible to visualize using traditional means.

The dataset we will use to illustrate Parallel Sets in this chapter describes the people on board the *Titanic*. As shown in Table 12-1, we know each passenger's travel class (first, second, or third passenger class, or crew), sex, age (adult or child), and whether they survived or not.

Table 12-1. *The Titanic dataset*

Dimension	Values
Class	First, Second, Third, Crew
Sex	Female, Male
Age	Child, Adult
Survived	Yes, No

There are really only three visualization techniques that work particularly well for categorical data: treemaps (Shneiderman 2001), mosaic plots (Theus 2002), and Parallel Sets. The reason for this is that there is a mismatch between the discrete domain of the data and the continuous domain of most visual variables (position, length, etc.). Treating categorical data as if it were numerical is acceptable when all but a few dimensions are continuous, but becomes entirely useless when all of them are categorical (Figure 12-1). While the natural distribution of data in most numerical datasets makes it possible to glean the rough distribution of at least the number of values, this becomes entirely impossible when there are only a few different values that are exactly the same between data points.

Figure 12-1. *Using classical visualization techniques for categorical data: Scatterplot (left) and Parallel Coordinates (right) lead to massive overplotting and do not provide much information even when tricks (such as jittering the data points) are used*

Parallel Sets

Parallel Sets, or ParSets (Bendix 2005, Kosara 2006), is a visualization technique that was designed specifically for interpreting categorical data. When talking to the experts analyzing the customer survey data, we realized that most of the questions they were asking were not based on individual survey responses, but on classes of answers, or sets and set intersections. How many people with more than three children under five years of age buy brand-name detergent? Or, put differently, how many members of Set A are also in Set B? How many first-class passengers on the *Titanic* survived (i.e., how many were in category *first class* on the *class* dimension, and in the *yes* category on *survived*)? How many of them were women (i.e., how many also had the value *female* in the *sex* dimension)?

This approach means that instead of plotting thousands of individual points, we only need to show the possible sets and subsets that exist in the data, as well as their sizes. If the numbers and relative sizes of those sets stayed the same, we reasoned, we could even show that the technique was independent of the actual dataset size.

In addition to the idea of showing the data as sets, ParSets was heavily influenced by Parallel Coordinates (Inselberg 2009), a popular visualization technique for high-dimensional numerical data. The parallel layout of axes makes them easier to read and compare than the nested structures of treemaps and mosaic plots, especially as the number of dimensions increases. It is also easier to design effective interactions for this kind of layout.

The first version of Parallel Sets (see Figure 12-2) was based on the categories first, then on the intersections. For each axis, we showed each category as a box, with its size corresponding to the fraction of all the data points that each category represented. In terms of statistics, this is called the *marginal distribution* (or marginal probability). Each axis is essentially a bar chart, with the bars tipped over rather than standing next to each other.

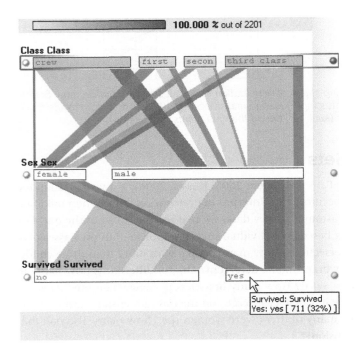

Figure 12-2. *The original Parallel Sets design*

Reading just the bars in Figure 12-2, it is easy to see that the crew was the largest class of people on the *Titanic*, with the third class close behind. The first class was much smaller than the third class, but was actually larger than the second class. It is also quite obvious that there was a majority of men (almost 80%) on the ship, and that only roughly one-third of all people on board survived.

Ribbons connect categories that occur together, showing how often, for example, *first class* and *female* intersect, thus making it possible to tell what proportion of the passengers in first class were women. The ribbons are what makes Parallel Sets more than a bunch of bar charts: being able to see distributions on several axes at the same time allows the user to identify and compare patterns that would otherwise be difficult to spot.

In the case of the *Titanic*, there was clearly an uneven distribution of women among the different classes. While the first class was close to 50% female, the second and third classes had progressively larger majorities of men. The crew consisted of over 95% men.

While the ribbons are clearly useful, they also pose some challenges. They must be sorted and the wider ones drawn first, so that the smaller ones end up on top and are not hidden. Also, when there are many categories there tend to be a lot of ribbons, resulting in a very busy display that is difficult to read and interact with.

Interaction is an important aspect of ParSets. The user can mouse over the display to see actual numbers, and can reorder categories and dimensions and add dimensions to (and remove them from) the display. There are also means of sorting categories on an axis by their size, as well as combining categories into larger ones (e.g., to add up all the passenger classes to better compare them with the crew).

Visual Redesign

One aspect of ParSets that required us to experiment quite a bit was the question of how to order the ribbons going from one axis to the next. We came up with two different orderings that seemed to make good sense, which we called *standard* and *bundled*. Standard mode ordered ribbons only by the category on top, which led to a branching structure but resulted in a rather visually busy display when large numbers of dimensions and categories were included. Bundled mode kept ribbons as parallel as possible by grouping them by both the top and bottom categories, which meant detaching parts of the ribbons from one another vertically.

It was only when we started to reimplement the technique a while later and were looking for a good representation of the visual structures that we realized that we had been looking at a tree structure all along (and that standard mode was the way to go). The entire set of data points is the root node of the tree, and each axis subdivides it into the categories on that axis (Figure 12-3). The ribbons display the tree; the nodes just look different than expected because we collect them on each axis to form the bars.

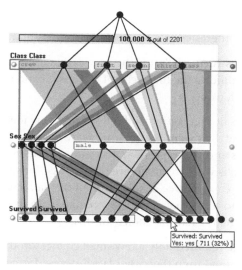

Figure 12-3. *The tree structure in Parallel Sets: nodes on each level are collected into bars, and the ribbons are the connections between the nodes*

We went ahead with our reimplementation without making any major changes to the visual display, but the idea of the tree stuck in my head. So one day, I asked myself: what if we reduced the bars and focused on the ribbons? And lo and behold, I was looking at a much clearer tree structure (Figure 12-4).

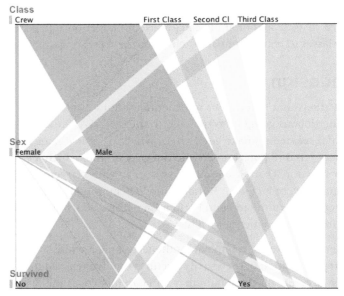

Figure 12-4. *The new Parallel Sets design, showing the tree structure much more clearly*

A simple change had shifted the focus from the category boxes to the ribbon tree. In the new design, the boxes still appear when the user mouses over the lines (to suggest to the user that she can interact with them), but they are only a means to an end. The key information we are interested in is really the decomposition into subsets.

In addition to improved structural clarity, the new design also makes much better use of typography to communicate the hierarchy of dimension and category labels and is much more pleasant to look at.

Looking at data in terms of aggregation and sets is not a new idea. Polaris (Stolte, Tang, and Hanrahan 2002) and, by extension, Tableau* were built on a similar idea: aggregation of individual values and decomposition into subsets. The use of treemaps for non-hierarchical data (which is what treemaps are mostly used for today) is based on the same transformation. Creating a tree of subsets from the data enables one to use any hierarchy visualization to show that data. The treemap, with its emphasis on node size rather than tree structure, is a natural choice for this.

The initial design change required only a few small changes in the program, but it was clear from this point on (and from the rather lackluster performance of our reimplementation) that the perceived need for a visual change had just been a symptom of a fundamental design issue with the program's data model.

* See *http://www.tableausoftware.com*.

A New Data Model

In the original program, the data had been stored the way it came in: as one big table. We later added the ability to create additional dimensions from the data, but the principle did not change. With every change to the display, the program had to work its way through the entire dataset and count the combinations of categories. With larger datasets, this became quite slow and required a lot of memory.

The big advantage of looking at data in terms of sets is that the individual data points are really of no interest; what counts are the subsets. So, the natural next step was to look at all possible aggregations of the data into sets, which could then be used to compute any subsets the user was interested in.

In statistics, this is called a *cross-tabulation* or pivot table. In the case of two dimensions, the result is a table with the categories of one dimension becoming the columns, and the other becoming the rows (Figure 12-5).

Class	Sex		
	female	male	
first	145 44.6% 30.8% 6.6%	180 55.4% 10.4% 8.2%	325 14.8%
second	106 37.2% 22.6% 4.8%	179 62.8% 10.4% 8.1%	285 12.9%
third	196 27.8% 41.7% 8.9%	510 72.2% 29.5% 23.2%	706 32.1%
crew	23 2.6% 4.9% 1.1%	862 97.4% 49.8% 39.1%	885 40.2%
	470 21.4%	1731 78.6%	2201 100%

Figure 12-5. *A cross-tabulation of the class and sex dimensions of the Titanic dataset*

There are two kinds of numbers in this table: counts and percentages. Each cell contains the count of people for its combination of criteria at the top left, and the percentage that number is of the entire dataset at the lower right. That latter percentage is called the *a priori percentage* (or probability). What is generally of more interest, though, are the *conditional percentages* (or probabilities), which tell us the composition of the different classes. In the top-right corner of each cell is the chance of finding the column's criterion given that we know the row (e.g., how many of the passengers in first class were women); at the lower left is the percentage likelihood of finding the row criterion given the column (e.g., what percent of women were in first class).

Because the data is purely categorical, the cross-tabulation contains all the information about it and is all we need to store. If we wanted to recreate the original data from it, we could do that by simply generating as many rows with each combination of categories as are given by the cell. The only case where additional data is needed is when the dataset also contains numerical columns.

A cross-tabulation for more than two dimensions is a bit more involved, but follows basically the same principle. A high-dimensional array is constructed that has as many dimensions as the dataset, with each cell in the array holding the count of how often that combination of values occurred.

Unfortunately, the number of possible combinations gets rather large quite quickly, and is actually much larger than the number of rows in most datasets. In the case of the census data, for example, taking only the dimensions *owned or rented, building size, building type, year built, year moved in, number of rooms, heating fuel, property value, household/family type*, and *household language* (out of over 100 dimensions) would result in 462,000,000 combinations, while the 1% microdata census sample has only 1,236,883 values for the entire U.S.!

The key here is that in the high-dimensional case, most combinations never actually occur in the data. So, it makes sense to only count those that do and store only their information. This is done in our current implementation by simply using an array of integers to hold all the values for each row, and using that as the key for a hash table. In almost all cases, that hash table takes up less space than the original data.

The Database Model

The database is essentially a direct mapping of the hash table that contains the counts for each combination of categories. Each dataset is stored in a separate table, with a column for each dimension in the dataset. Each row contains the values for the categories that describe the cell in the cross-tabulation, as well as the count of how often that combination occurs. There is an additional field, called the *key*, which is unique for each row and is used for joining the table when looking at numerical data.

Aggregating the data is done with a SQL query that simply selects the dimensions the user is interested in plus the total counts, and groups the results by those same dimensions (Table 12-2):

```
select class, sex, survived, sum(count) from titanic_dims
group by class, sex, survived;
```

The database thus aggregates the counts and returns a lower-dimensional cross-tabulation containing only the values needed for the visualization.

Table 12-2. *The result of querying the Titanic dataset to include only the dimensions class, sex, and survived*

Class	Sex	Survived	Count
First	Male	Yes	62
First	Male	No	118
First	Female	Yes	141
First	Female	No	4
Second	Male	Yes	25
Second	Male	No	154
Second	Female	Yes	93
Second	Female	No	13
Third	Male	Yes	88
Third	Male	No	422
Third	Female	Yes	90
Third	Female	No	106
Crew	Male	Yes	192
Crew	Male	No	670
Crew	Female	Yes	20
Crew	Female	No	3

This model is very similar in principle to data warehousing and Online Analytical Processing (OLAP). Most databases have a special *cube* or *rollup* keyword to create an aggregation from a regular table. This has the advantage that no special processing is needed beforehand, but the disadvantage of being slower and requiring more disk space to store all the original values. Structuring the data specifically for fast read and aggregation performance (as is done in data warehouses and our database schema) considerably speeds up the most common operation at the expense of more processing being required when new data is added.

While the ParSets program does not currently show numerical dimensions, it does store them in the database. They are stored in a separate table, containing the key of the row the values correspond to and one column per numerical dimension. Instead of using the count, a simple join query can therefore be used to aggregate any numerical dimension by the cross-tabulation cells. Any standard SQL aggregation (sum, avg, min, max) can be used for this purpose. Eventually, the program will allow the user to select a numerical dimension to use to scale the bars and ribbons, and to also select the aggregation used.

The current version of Parallel Sets stores its data in a local SQLite database. SQLite is a very interesting open source database that operates on a single file. It is used in many embedded applications and is extremely resilient against data corruption (such devices have to expect power failure at any moment). While it does not have all the features of commercial databases, it is small, fast, and does not require any setup. This makes it a perfect data store that has a query language as an added benefit.

Growing the Tree

The cross-tabulation that the database stores and that can be retrieved is only a part of the story, though. To show the user the Parallel Sets display, we need a tree. Whenever the user changes the dimensions or reorders them, the program queries the database to retrieve the new cross-tabulation. It then walks through the resulting data to build the tree. If you look closely, you can actually already see it in Table 12-2. Whenever the same value appears several times in the same column, we're looking at the same node of the tree, and only the nodes to the right of it change, as shown in Table 12-3.

Table 12-3. *The tree structure inherent in the query result in Table 12-2*

Class	Sex	Survived	Count
First	Male	Yes	62
		No	118
	Female	Yes	141
		No	4
Second	Male	Yes	25
		No	154
	Female	Yes	93
		No	13
Third	Male	Yes	88
		No	422
	Female	Yes	90
		No	106
Crew	Male	Yes	192
		No	670
	Female	Yes	20
		No	3

All the program needs to do is go through the result set line by line and build the tree by following the existing nodes from left to right until it encounters a node that does not exist yet. That node is added and its count is taken from the database row.

The database contains only the counts for the tree's leaves, though, not its internal nodes (other databases, such as Oracle, have queries that also return internal nodes when performing cube queries). However, it is easy enough to calculate those by simply summing the values of each node's child nodes recursively, from the leaves to the root node.

The counts themselves are also only the raw material of the fractions, which are calculated in the same step once all counts for a node are known. To actually display the bars and ribbons, percentages are used: the *a priori* percentage of each category becomes the length of the bar, by using it as the fraction of the total width, and the conditional percentages (the lower category on a ribbon given the upper category) are used to determine the width of the ribbon as a fraction of the category bar length (Figure 12-6).

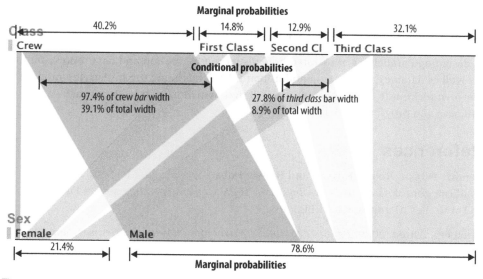

Figure 12-6. *The width of each ribbon represents its marginal probability (proportional fraction) of the total data set, and also its conditional probability within each category*

Parallel Sets in the Real World

Since the program was released in June 2009, it has been downloaded over 750 times (as of January 2010). We have heard from many users who have had success using it with their own data. We even won a prize at VisWeek 2010's Discovery Exhibition (*http://discoveryexhibition.org*) for our entry talking about three case studies using the program. This was written together with Joe Mako (Mako Metrics), Jonathan Miles (Gloucestershire City Council, UK), and Kam Tin Seong (Singapore Management University).

Joe Mako's use of the program was especially interesting, because he used it to show a kind of data flow through many processing stages. Putting the last stage on top meant that the ribbons were colored by final result, which let him easily see where problems occurred. There actually is a visualization technique that is visually (though not conceptually) similar to Parallel Sets that is used for flows, called a Sankey diagram. ParSets can emulate these diagrams for flows that move strictly in one direction and only split up (but never merge). Jonathan Miles and Kam Tin Seong's uses were closer to the original aim of the program, providing interesting insights into survey results and bank customers, respectively.

Conclusion

Academia values novelty, but there is clearly a case to be made for letting ideas develop over time, so they become clearer and more refined. The result is not just a better understanding of the issues and techniques, but better tools that are easier to understand and provide more insights to the user.

Redesigning Parallel Sets illustrated how visual representation and data representation (as well as database design) go hand in hand. Understanding the underlying model of our own technique led to a better visual design, which in turn led to a much-improved database and program model.

References

Bendix, Fabian, Robert Kosara, and Helwig Hauser. 2005. "Parallel Sets: Visual analysis of categorical data." In *Proceedings of the IEEE Symposium on Information Visualization*, 133–140. Los Alamitos, CA: IEEE Press.

Inselberg, Alfred. 2009. *Parallel Coordinates: Visual Multidimensional Geometry and Its Applications*. New York: Springer.

Kosara, Robert, Fabian Bendix, and Helwig Hauser. 2006. "Parallel Sets: Interactive exploration and visual analysis of categorical data." *IEEE Transactions on Visualization and Computer Graphics* 12, no. 4: 558–568.

Shneiderman, Ben, and Martin Wattenberg. 2001. "Ordered treemap layouts." In *Proceedings of the IEEE Symposium on Information Visualization*, 73–78. Los Alamitos, CA: IEEE Press.

Stolte, Chris, Diane Tang, and Pat Hanrahan. 2002. "Polaris: A system for query, analysis, and visualization of multidimensional relational databases." *IEEE Transactions on Visualization and Computer Graphics* 8, no. 1: 52–65.

Theus, Martin. 2002. "Interactive data visualization using Mondrian." *Journal of Statistical Software* 7, no. 11: 1–9. *http://www.theusrus.de/Mondrian/*.

## CHAPTER THIRTEEN

The Design of "X by Y"

An Information-Aesthetic Exploration of the Ars Electronica Archives

Moritz Stefaner

THIS CHAPTER PRESENTS THE PROJECT "X BY Y," a visualization of all entries to the Prix Ars Electronica, a well-known media art award, from 1987 to 2009. The final version of the visualization consists of a series of large-scale prints, splitting up the submissions according to different criteria. This chapter describes the process leading up to the final piece, and the rationale for specific design decisions.

Briefing and Conceptual Directions

The Ludwig Boltzmann Institute for media.art.research contacted me in spring 2009 to work on the submission databases for the Prix Ars Electronica. The media art festival Ars Electronica had its 30th anniversary that year, and together, we decided to take on the challenge of trying to visually analyze all the submissions to the Prix over its 22-year history. The databases containing the submission information had never before been analyzed in their entirety.

In the kickoff meeting for the project, we discussed our objectives. The creative lead of the whole visualization project, Dietmar Offenhuber, explained that different visualizations were to be developed in order to study three different angles on the festival's history:

Quantitative analysis

What can we say about the festival by looking at the submissions over the years? How do the various categories differ, where do the submissions come from, and how do the values change over time?

Social networks

Who were the jury members throughout the years? How are they—as well as the awarded artists—connected to one another?

Art historical context

What impact have the awarded projects had? Where have they been referenced, and how have they influenced the field of media arts?

The project I was to work on would belong to the first category. Specifically, I was to investigate what hypotheses and insights we could generate by looking into the submission data, and whether we could find an appropriate visual to convey the characteristics of the "ars world" to visitors of the exhibition.

Together with the art historians working on the Ars Electronica archives, I tried to define some first directions of interest, reflected in the matrix in Figure 13-1. Without looking at the databases in detail, it was assumed that we should be able to work on basic dimensions like the submission's author, country, year, prize category, and keywords, as well as whether it received a prize. The matrix reflects the *a priori* interest in certain combinations of these factors—i.e., where the experts expected interesting findings to emerge. For instance, it was assumed that we might want to split winners by country (and compare this data to the overall submission statistics) and look at the relationships between authors and categories.

	Author	Country	Year	Category	Keywords	Winner?
Author			✖	✖	✖	✖
Country			✖	✖	✖	✖
Year					✖	
Category					✖	
Keywords						✖
Winner?						

Figure 13-1. *Matrix of initial interest in attribute combinations*

Understanding the Data Situation

Next, I began to look into the available data, together with Sandor Herramhof. Over the years, a number of database schemas with different conventions and varying degrees of modeling detail had been used, which made it very difficult to get an early overview of the existing data. For instance, one database featured additional information stored in an XML format inside a text field, but only for some of the submissions. In order to facilitate the process of acquiring an overview of the data, I developed *dbcounter,** a small nodebox script that would enable us to quickly get an overview of large sets of categorical data. *dbcounter* walks over a CSV file, determines all the unique value attributes, counts how often they occur, and plots the output as an area chart. The gray areas (see Figure 13-2) indicate missing or NULL values. Overall, the tool proved useful for understanding the contents of our databases, especially in finding missing values and getting an idea of the data diversity.

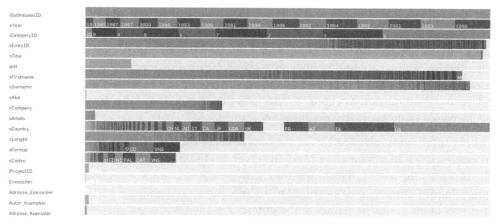

Figure 13-2. First overview of the database contents with dbcounter, a custom nodebox script

From these plots, some facts about the databases quickly became clear:

- There were a number of apparently redundant fields, such as "Land" (German for "country") and "sYear," caused by the merging of database schemas over the years.

- Names, years, and categories were present fairly completely.

- Much less country, company, and web address information was present than expected.

---

* See *http://well-formed-data.net/archives/306/dbcounter-quick-visual-database-stats.*

On the one hand, this quick first analysis allowed us to understand what types of attribute combinations could be expected to be meaningful and to cover at least a large part of the data. As the database migration was an ongoing process, it also provided us with a useful overview of the areas in which we should seek to improve the data, and which fields could be combined or filled up more completely. For instance, the team working on the databases containing the representation country field was in fact trying to complete as much of the information as possible ("It seems like really interesting information, and we are already almost there").

Exploring the Data

After the first quantitative analysis of the individual fields, the next step was to slice and dice a preliminary subset of the data, to investigate correlations and get some hints about the reasons for some of the gaps in the data. For this step we used the commercial software Tableau,* which allowed us to explore the data in the spreadsheets we imported and the databases we connected to using interactive charts in a flexible and expressive workspace. For instance, we used Tableau to characterize the submissions missing country information by year and category (see Figure 13-3), in order to identify the biggest gaps and facilitate the search for the missing information in other media, such as catalog texts. Questions like "How does the number of submissions relate to the submission categories?" and "Has this changed over the years?" can also be answered quite easily in a graphical user interface.

Other explorations included a characterization of companies in terms of the categories in which they had submitted entries. The chart in Figure 13-4, for instance, revealed the potential for some interesting stories. However, it also quickly became clear that a large amount of manual work would be required to clean up all the variations in the spellings of the company names in the different databases if we wanted to be able to make accurate statements.

We also used Tableau to produce an initial world map of the submissions (see Figure 13-5), with the pie charts for each country indicating the category distributions. This early map reveals the European/U.S.-centric nature of the festival. It soon became clear that this simplistic approach to producing a cartogram would be inefficient for this skewed data distribution, motivating the more elaborate approach presented later.

---

* See *http://www.tableausoftware.com*.

sYear	.net	[the next idea]	Computer Animation	Computer Animation / Visual E.	Computer Graphics	Computer Music	cybergeneration - u19 frees..	Digital Communities	Digital Musics	Hybrid Art	Interactive Art	Media.Art. Research Award
						country (group) / prixcategory_en						
							Null, -, NULL					
1987					· 6	· 2						
1988			· 2	· 1	168							
1989			· 2									
1990			· 1		· 8						· 1	
1991					· 1							
1992						● 25					· 3	
1993			● 15		● 30	● 25					● 18	
1994			· 1			● 26					· 5	
1995			· 1			● 15					● 21	
1996			· 2								● 19	
1997	· 5		● 59			· 3					● 15	
1998	· 3			· 6							· 6	
1999	· 5			● 66					● 132		· 2	
2000	· 3			· 8					· 1		· 5	
2001				· 1					· 3			
2002									● 17			
2003									· 7			
2004		● 138		● 126				● 102	● 181		● 141	
2005		· 19		● 43			· 23	· 11	● 51		● 41	
2006		· 6		● 26				· 10	● 33		● 19	
2007		· 12		● 25				· 12	● 56	● 20	● 22	· 8
2008				● 54				● 141	● 62	● 40	● 40	· 7
NULL						· 1						

Figure 13-3. *A plot of submissions with missing country information, split up by year and category*

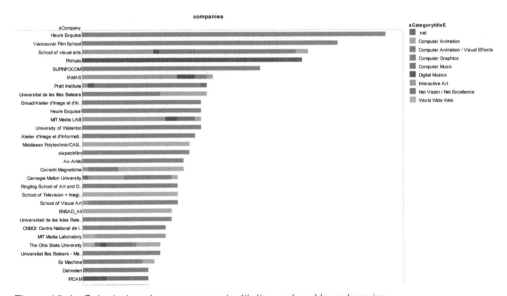

Figure 13-4. *Submissions by company or institution, colored by categories*

Figure 13-5. *World map with submissions per country, split up by category*

I also explored some of the data in Microsoft Excel, as it seemed superior at producing stacked charts we could use for investigating trends over the years or comparing attribute distributions in subsets of the data. For instance, Figure 13-6 shows the relative proportion of submissions and the different types of prizes won by each country. From this chart, it appeared as if the U.S. were responsible for about 30% of all submissions but won over 60% of all Golden Nicas (the highest prize awarded). However, this trend turned out to be much less pronounced in the full and verified set of data analyzed later. We were also aware that the relation of countries to prizes won is a complex and sensitive matter that can only be fully understood by considering various other aspects of the data, such as the number of submissions in each category (for instance, the computer graphics categories in the 1980s had staggering numbers of submissions compared to other categories). So, while there was potential for some interesting insights, we decided that we would present this story only if we were able to provide some context and explanation.

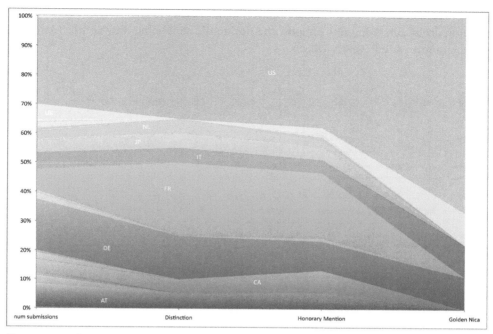

Figure 13-6. *Prizes won by different countries*

First Visual Drafts

The analytic process delivered some initial insights into the data, and gave my collaborators enough opportunities—maybe more than they desired—to correct, clean, and complete the databases. On that basis, borrowing terminology from Tom Armitage's BERG blog post "Toiling in the data-mines: What data exploration feels like,"* I had a good sense of what was *available, significant,* and *interesting,* and of the *scale* of the data. The next step was to work on the visualization principles.

To quickly prototype some different visual options, I switched to Flash ActionScript 3 using the *flare* library,† an advanced general-purpose framework for producing interactive visualizations, and I explored more of the stacked charting options using the Excel charts I started with. One insight I gleaned from these charts was that we should try harder to emphasize the individual data points (e.g., the individual years on the vertical axis in Figure 13-7), rather than producing continuous stacked area charts. In the Ars Electronica case, submissions are made on an annual basis only, so a visual interpolation between years would have been misleading and a distortion of reality.

---

* See *http://berglondon.com/blog/2009/10/23/toiling-in-the-data-mines-what-data-exploration-feels-like/*.
† See *http://flare.prefuse.org*.

These considerations led to the development of more fragile charts, with the interpolation areas toned down to support the notion of them being only connectors between more "solid" yearly events.

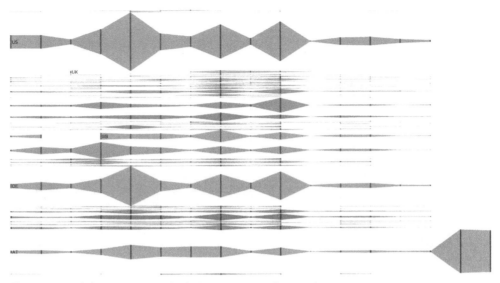

Figure 13-7. *A first attempt at displaying categories by country*

Exploring stacked area charts for categories over the years revealed some additional issues to tackle from a conceptual point of view. The category structure of Ars Electronica underwent a continuous evolution over the years. For instance, the "Computer Music" category was not present in 1991, yet it was in the years before and after. Then, in 1999, it was discontinued and a new category, "Digital Musics," was added. How best to treat this situation is a tricky conceptual question: on the one hand, these are clearly related categories, but on the other hand, it might be too simplistic to unify them and treat them as the same category with a different label. For decisions like these, expert opinions and the designer's view have to be taken into account to formulate an accurate, yet pragmatic and understandable, approach. After some discussions, we resolved the issue by treating these as independent categories but giving them identical colors in the different visualizations (Figure 13-8).

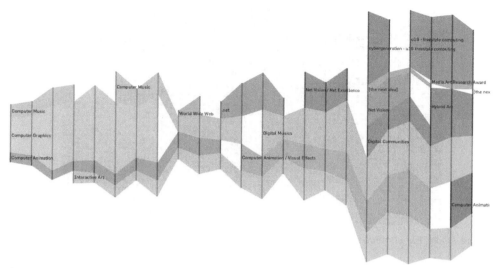

Figure 13-8. *Categories over the years*

I also became more interested in the evocative, implicit communication aspects of the visualization as I explored the existing charts. I felt uncomfortable with their character; from a visual point of view the Flare charts looked appealing, yet a bit too fragile. However, there was also a much bigger concern: while it is interesting to approach a cultural phenomenon like a media art prize in purely quantitative terms, we felt as though we were losing a sense of the scale and diversity of the data and characterizing it in strokes that were too broad. Effective visualization has a strong relation to summarization and prioritization; however, simply creating some rather abstract charts would not have done the topic itself justice. Might not there be a way to display the totals, fractions, and interrelationships without neglecting or even hiding the individual submissions?

The Visual Principle

This motivation led me first to explore dense pixel mosaic displays (Keim 2000), following the idea that I would like to see one visual marker for each individual submission. To get a sense of how many points I could fit on a standard screen, I did some quick tests using random data (see Figure 13-9).

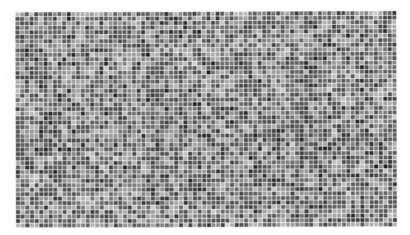

Figure 13-9. *Experimenting with dense pixel displays*

I found the results quite encouraging and decided to investigate further by looking at *QR codes.** Could we actually build QR codes with meaningful URLs that also worked as area- or pixel-based data graphics? Another idea was to do something along the lines of Wattenberg's (2005) colored segments of space-filling curves to produce diagrams similar to treemaps (so-called "jigsaw maps").

The real eureka moment, however, came when I remembered a placement algorithm I had used in an earlier project. Computed on the basis of the *golden angle* (the angle corresponding to a "golden section" of a full circle, or 137.5 degrees), it imitates the arrangement of sunflower seeds—the most efficient and visually mesmerizing way of packing small elements into a large circle. Figure 13-10 shows a first try I produced in a few hours, wherein rings of alternating darkness would indicate years (reminding the viewer of annual age rings in tree trunk cross-sections) and the omitted points would indicate the submissions that were awarded prizes.

* See *http://en.wikipedia.org/wiki/QR_Code.*

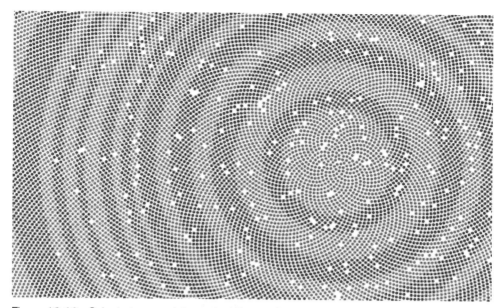

Figure 13-10. *Submissions as dots, packed like sunflower seeds*

Despite its visual complexity, the underlying procedure for creating these types of arrangements can be described by simple rules: for placing the *n*th point, choose a radius of the square root of *n*, multiplied by a constant scaling factor. The angle at which the point is placed is the angle of the preceding point, incremented by the golden angle (2*pi/*phi* = ca. 137.5 degrees).

To distribute the points in a homogenous and uniform manner, it is very important to use precisely this number: if we used, say, 137.4 degrees, the characteristic double spiral would be replaced by spirals in only one direction and the point distances would begin to vary. Using the golden angle, we can add points indefinitely, and each point will be a uniform distance from its neighbors. Why is this the case? Each rational number we pick for dissecting the circle will result in a repetition of angles sooner or later. In the simplest case, if we always move a half-circle ahead, we will only end up with two different angles. It can be shown that for any rational fraction, there will be a repetition and thus a limited set of angles used. Accordingly, if we want to optimize the filling and the distribution of points, we have to use an irrational number—ideally, the most irrational number there is (that is, the one that is the least well approximated by a fraction). This number is *phi*, the number representing the golden section.

The Final Product

Having found a guiding visual principle, many of the open questions and possible combinations were now naturally reduced to what worked within the self-imposed constraints—for instance, the principle dictates circular shapes for all groups of items. As the category distributions were of importance in all the perspectives we discussed, we decided to color-code the categories across all the visualizations to be displayed, with identical colors used for groups of categories that could reasonably be treated as "families" (for instance, the categories in the field of computer animation and film are all shown as orange). In addition, I introduced a shape encoding to indicate whether a submission had received a prize or not (circles for nonwinners, diamonds for winners).

As discussed earlier, on a conceptual level, I became interested in the relation of the totals and sums to the individual submissions. Consequently, I looked for a way to incorporate this information into the final visualization. After some unsuccessful experiments with putting additional labels for the total counts around the circles and overlaying the count numbers on top of the circles, which led to quite cluttered displays, I found a much more satisfying alternative: the numbers could actually be created by the dot pattern itself! As the decision to color-code the categories ruled out all modifications to the points themselves, I decided to skip all positions in the sequence that would occlude the number, if it were overlaid on the circle (see Figure 13-11). That dot would simply go in the next available precalculated position, so the total number of dots would remain the same but the circle size would increase marginally. Obviously, this principle only works for circles with enough dots to create the number; accordingly, the number is only displayed for circles containing a minimum of 100 items.

Figure 13-11. *Numbers created by skipping points in the placement sequence*

All Submissions

Figure 13-12 shows all submissions to the Prix Ars Electronica over the last 22 years. Resembling a tree trunk cross-section, the oldest submissions are located at the center, surrounded by the more recent ones. This constitutes the starting point for all the other graphics, each of which is a split-up version of this one, with data analyzed according to different criteria.

Figure 13-12. *All 37,432 submissions, colored by category and arranged from inside (least recent) to outside (most recent) by submission year*

By Prize

The diagram shown in Figure 13-13 is enough to motivate the whole project: splitting the submissions by the prize received (or not) reveals that only 4% of all submissions have received an honorary mention, a distinction, or a Golden Nica. The remaining 96% of submissions remained invisible—up to now. For this, and all the following, more analytical views, I decided to show the category distribution within the groups of data in a pie chart fashion, in order to avoid the perceptual distortions introduced by the concentric rings in the overview graphic.

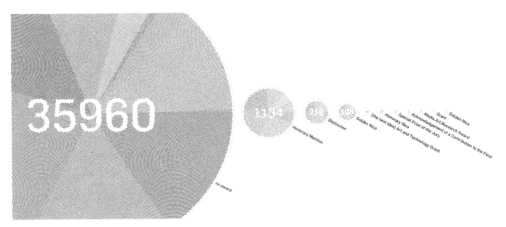

Figure 13-13. *Submissions by prize*

By Category

Figure 13-14 shows a quantitative analysis of the submissions by category. At the same time, it provides a sense of the fraction of awarded projects per category in a fainter section of the pie, composed of diamond shapes in the right part of each circle. It shows, for instance, that the computer graphics category has the highest number of submissions (per single category), but that a low number of prizes has been awarded per submission (a result of the fact that the category has been around for only seven years). Following Wang et al. (2006), the layout of the circles was calculated using Flare's CirclePackingLayout algorithm.

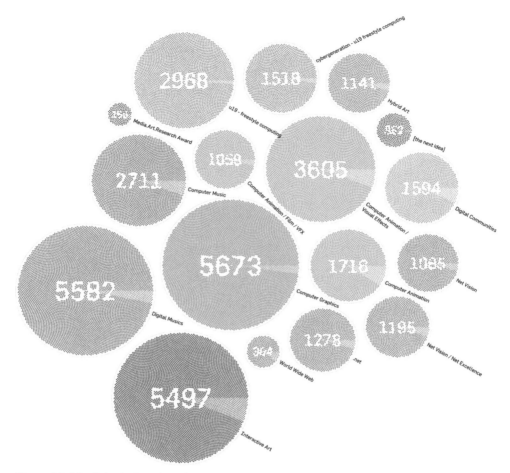

Figure 13-14. *Submissions by category*

By Country

Figure 13-15 shows a map of the submitters' countries of origin. Inspired by the *New York Times*'s map of Olympic medals,* the layout is calculated with a physical rigid body model and attempts to approximate the exact locations, while avoiding circle overlap (see Figure 13-16 for snapshots of the iterative optimization process).

* See *http://www.nytimes.com/interactive/2008/08/04/sports/olympics/20080804_MEDALCOUNT_MAP.html*.

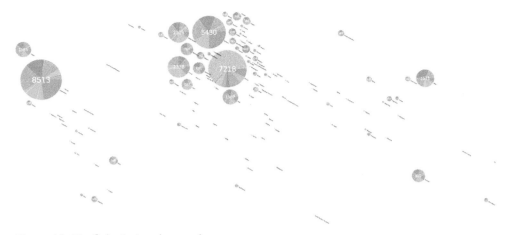

Figure 13-15. *Submissions by country*

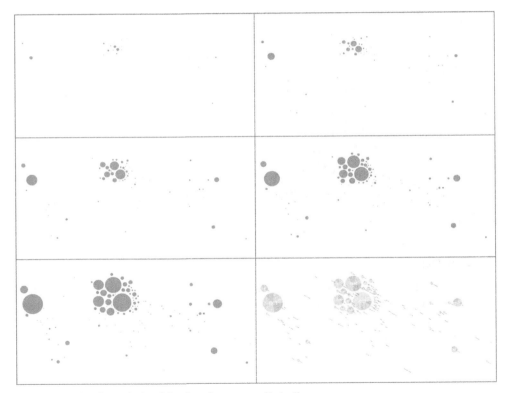

Figure 13-16. *Snapshots of the iterative map optimization*

To get coordinates for the country names I used the online application *mapspread*,[*] which allows users to batch-query tabular data for geocoordinates. However, some manual correction was required, as some of the country names could not be resolved (the Eastern European political landscape, in particular, has changed quite a bit over the last few decades), and others were ambiguous: in fact, even in the final version, the label "Georgia" was mistakenly placed next to the United States instead of over the Eastern European country located between Russia and Turkey.

Inspecting the map in detail reveals the European/U.S.-centric nature of media art, with very few contributions from South America, Africa, Russia, or Asia (with the exception of Japan). Historically, a large number of submissions from France and Spain have been made in the field of computer animation and film (orange). Italy, Sweden, and the UK show a tendency toward music categories (purple), while Japan seems more into interactive art (blue). In contrast, Germany and the U.S. leaned toward computer graphics (red), at least in the early years of the festival. Almost two-thirds of Austria's submissions have been in the (Austrian-only) U19 categories.

By Year

The sequence of pie charts in Figure 13-17 shows a clear division of the prize history in three eras. In 1995 there was a sudden decrease in submissions, coinciding with the discontinuation of the computer graphics category and the introduction of the World Wide Web category. One possible explanation for this drop is that it was more common to submit multiple pieces per year in the computer graphics category. The years after 2004 show a stronger diversification in categories and a sudden increase in submissions, largely due to the introduction of the U19 categories for Austrian artists under 19 years of age.

Figure 13-17. *Submissions by year*

By Year and Category

Figure 13-18 shows a matrix version of the timeline, to allow inspection of the development of individual groups of categories. In both color-coding and row selection, we decided to group corresponding categories even if their titles were changed over the years. (Conversely, it should be noted that some categories whose names did not change had different orientations in different years.) Compared to the single-year chart, this version makes it easier to see how animation/film, music, and later interactive art have become the long-term backbones of the Prix.

* See *http://mapspread.com*.

1987 1988 1989 1990 1991 1992 1993 1994 1995 1996 1997 1998 1999 2000 2001 2002 2003 2004 2005 2006 2007 2008 2009

Figure 13-18. *Submissions by category and year*

Exhibition

"Mapping the Archive" was located at the history lounge exhibition in the Brucknerhaus, and featured six different data visualization perspectives created by Dietmar Offenhuber, Evelyn Münster, Jaume Nualart, Gerhard Dirmoser, and me (Figure 13-19).*

Figure 13-19. *The poster in the exhibition*

To facilitate the discovery of individual stories in the data, we added little annotation arrows to highlight interesting facts (Figure 13-20). Visitors were also encouraged to add their own annotations, resulting in a couple of interesting questions and remarks.

* All visualizations are documented online at *http://vis.mediaartresearch.at.*

Figure 13-20. *Sticky arrow notes with handwritten annotations*

Conclusion

The visualizations presented here were developed over the summer of 2009, through a continuous exchange of ideas and information not only with the technical staff in charge of the archive databases, but also with media art experts commenting on the semantic perspective of the represented information.

I see the work as part of a young tradition of *information aesthetics*.* The scientific discipline of information visualization is usually concerned with characterizing methods of visual mapping in general, and optimizing the readability and understandability of the resulting visualizations. Information aesthetics builds on results from that area; however, being a design discipline, it strives to find a sensory representation of information based on a specific dataset that not only is useable and readable on the explicit data-representation level but, in addition, increases the "propositional density"† of the design piece—in short, the evocative character of a visualization and what can be read "between the lines." This approach places the discipline between the traditional fields of information visualization, user interface design, and art.

I hope this chapter demonstrates some key features of the discipline. First, it is important to look at the process of creating information aesthetic works. In my experience, it is crucial to work with realistic data, already even in the early stages of the design. In principle, many visualization ideas developed by theory early on could work well on

---

* A term first coined by Lev Manovich and explicated in detail in Lau and Vande Moere (2007).
† As defined by William Lidwell (2009).

real-life data structures, but whether they deliver interesting information and are useful for answering the questions in mind—or for provoking new questions—can only be determined when working with the actual data. Developing visualizations has to be a bootstrapping process: you must use them early on to understand which visualizations and data treatments to pursue further. In our case, early visualization experiments with standard tools put us in a position to understand which data fields to use and which combinations of data "smelled" interesting, and provided a good basis for discussing the design features of the future visualization with reference to concrete, realistic examples. If the designer does not allow his own visual explorations to change his mind on the way to the final product, chances are high that the result will only state the obvious, without provoking new questions or revealing interesting stories.

Moreover, it is crucial to be aware of the semantic context of the information displayed, and the semiotic character of the final piece. To give an analogy, in linguistics, the field of semantics is concerned with the study of sentence meaning as it can be constructed from its constituents and their combination. However, it is widely acknowledged that language can only be fully understood by also looking at pragmatics: the study of how language is actually used in a social context. What is the connotation of a word or expression? What associations does it evoke? And what is expressed by not saying anything? What form of expression is expected in a given context, and what goes against the norms?

Much effort has been invested in understanding the syntax and semantics of visual language for information presentation, and now information aesthetics is opening the door for an investigation of the pragmatics of visual language. In the work presented here, for instance, the chosen visual principle was born out of the inherent tension induced by approaching a complex social phenomenon from a purely quantitative angle. What statement were we making in breaking down a tremendously rich and varied dataset, representing 22 years of media art history, in all its facets, into "a couple of numbers"? The form of the visualization tries to capture this tension and resolve parts of it.

Given these considerations, the notion of "aesthetics" in visualization is about much more than "pretty pictures." Surely, joy of use is an important and long-underestimated factor—on many occasions, research on the user experience has shown the importance of interacting in pleasant, stimulating environments. But, as Steve Jobs famously remarked, "Design is not how it looks and feels, but how it works." A truly aesthetic visualization, in addition to being beautiful, "works" by expressing inexplicit features of the phenomenon at hand, and inviting the user/viewer to explore a rich and multifaceted world.

As a final remark, looking at the meaning and context of the information presented in a visualization, one point is often neglected (even in the work presented here): how can we characterize that information in the larger scheme of things? Could we find explanations for some of the patterns observed by connecting to external databases? In the Ars Electronica example, it might have been informative to compare, for instance, submission statistics per country with more information about each country. Is the number of submissions correlated to economic power? Or digital literacy? Or other, less obvious factors? As more and more open data sources for these types of information become available, it is increasingly important to provide the proper context and baselines for actually understanding the significance of patterns arising in the datasets we analyze and present.

Acknowledgments

Thanks go to the Ludwig Boltzmann Institute for media.art.research (Linz), and especially to Dieter Daniels and Katja Kwastek for providing the opportunity and expert input, Sandor Herramhof for the extensive data collecting and processing, Dietmar Offenhuber for creative coordination of the visualization activities, and Ule Münster for the exhibition poster design and the color palette used for the categories.

References

Keim, D.A. 2000. "Designing pixel-oriented visualization techniques: Theory and applications." *IEEE Transactions on Visualization and Computer Graphics* 6, no. 1: 59–78.

Lau, Andrea, and Andrew Vande Moere (2007). "Towards a model of information aesthetic visualization." In *Proceedings of the International Conference on Information Visualisation*. Washington, DC: IEEE Computer Society.

Lidwell, William. 2009. "More with less." *ACM interactions* 16, no. 6: 72–75.

Wang, Weixin, Hui Wang, Guozhong Dai, and Hongan Wang. 2006. "Visualization of large hierarchical data by circle packing." In *Proceedings of the SIGCHI Conference on Human Factors in Computing Systems*. New York: ACM Press.

Wattenberg, Martin. 2005. "A note on space-filling visualizations and space-filling curves." In *Proceedings of the 2005 IEEE Symposium on Information Visualization*. Washington, DC: IEEE Computer Society.

## CHAPTER FOURTEEN

Revealing Matrices

Maximilian Schich

THIS CHAPTER UNCOVERS SOME NONINTUITIVE STRUCTURES in curated databases arising from local activity by the curators as well as from the heterogeneity of the source data. Our example is taken from the fields of art history and archaeology, as these are my trained areas of expertise. However, the findings I present here—namely, that it is possible to visualize the complex structures of databases—can also be demonstrated for many other structured data collections, including biological research databases and massive collaborative efforts such as DBpedia, Freebase, or the Semantic Web. All these data collections share a number of properties, which are not straightforward but are important if we want to make use of the recorded data or if we have to decide where and how our energies and funds should be spent in improving them.

Curated databases in art history and archaeology come in a number of flavors, such as library catalogs and bibliographies, image archives, museum inventories, and more general research databases. All of them can be built on extremely complicated data models, and given enough data, even the most boring examples—however simple they may appear on the surface—can be confusingly complex in any single link relation. The thematic coverage potentially includes all man-made objects: the Library of Congress Classification System, for example, deals with everything from artists and cookbooks to treatises in physics.

As our example, I have picked a dataset that is large enough to be complex, but small enough to examine efficiently. We are going to visualize the so-called Census of Antique Works of Art and Architecture Known in the Renaissance (*http://www.census.de*), which was initiated in 1947 by Richard Krautheimer, Fritz Saxl, and Karl

Lehmann-Hartleben. The CENSUS collects information about ancient monuments—such as Roman sculptures and architecture—appearing in Western Renaissance documents such as sketchbooks, drawings, and guidebooks. We will look at the state of the database at the point just before it was transferred from a graph-based database system (CENSUS 2005) to a more traditional relational database format (CENSUS BBAW) in 2006, allowing for comparison of the historic state with current and future achievements.

The More, the Better?

Having worked with art research databases for over a decade, one of the most intriguing questions for me has always been how to measure the quality of these projects. Databases in the humanities are rarely cited like scholarly articles, so the usual evaluation criteria for publications do not apply. Instead, evaluations mostly focus on a number of superficial criteria such as the adherence to standards, quality of user interfaces, fancy project titles, and use of recent buzzwords in the project description. Regarding content, evaluators are often satisfied with a few basic measures such as looking at the number of records in the database and asking a few questions concerning the subtleties of a handful of particular entries.

The problem with standard definitions such as the CIDOC Conceptual Reference Model (CIDOC-CRM) for data models or the Open Archives Initiative Protocol for Metadata Harvesting (OAI-PMH) for data exchange is that they are usually applied *a priori*, providing no information about the quality of the data collected and processed within their frameworks. The same is true of the user interfaces, which give as much indication of the quality of the content as does the aspect ratio of a printed sheet of paper. Furthermore, both data standards and user interfaces change over time, which makes their significance as evaluation criteria even more difficult to judge. As any programmer knows, an algorithm written in the old Fortran language can be just as elegant as and even faster than a modern Python script. As a consequence, we should avoid any form of system patriotism in project evaluation—that is, the users of a particular standard should not have to be afraid of being evaluated by the fans of another.

Even the application of standards we all consider desirable, such as Open Access, is of questionable value: while Open Access provides a positive spin to many current projects, its meaning within the realm of curated databases is not entirely clear. Should we really be satisfied with a complicated but free user interface (cf. Bartsch 2008, fig. 10), or should we prefer a sophisticated API and periodical dumps of the full database (cf. Freebase), which would allow for serious analysis and more advanced scholarly reuse of the data? And if there is Open Access, who is going to pay the salary of a private enterprise data curator?

Ultimately, we must look at the actual content of any given project. As this chapter will demonstrate, when evaluating a database it makes only limited sense to focus on the subtleties of a few particular entries, as usually there is no average information against which to measure any particular database entry. The omnipresent phenomenon of long tails (Anderson 2006; Newman 2005; Schich et al. 2009, note 5), which we will encounter in almost all the figures in this chapter, suggests that it would be unwise to extrapolate from a few data-rich entries to the whole database—i.e., in the CENSUS, we cannot make inferences about all the other ancient monuments based solely on the Pantheon.

The most neutral of the commonly applied measures remaining for evaluation is the number of records in the database. It is given in almost all project specifications: encyclopedias list the number of articles they contain (cf. Wikipedia); biomedical databases publish the number of compounds, genes, or proteins they contain (cf. Phosphosite 2003–2007 or Flybase 2008); and even search engines traditionally (but ever more reluctantly) provide the number of pages in their indexes (Sullivan 2005). It is therefore no wonder that the CENSUS project also provides some numbers:

> More than 200.000 entries contain pictorial and written documents, locations, persons, concepts of times and styles, events, research literature and illustrations. The monuments registered amount to about 6.500, the entries of monuments to about 12.000 and the entries of documents to 28.000.*

Although these numbers are surely impressive from the point of view of art history, where large exhibition catalogs usually contain a couple of hundred entries, it is easy to disprove the significance of the number of records as a good measure of database quality, if taken in isolation. Just as search engines struggle with near duplicates (cf. Chakrabarti 2003, p. 71), research databases such as the CENSUS aim to normalize data by eliminating apparent redundancies arising from uncertainties in the raw data and the ever-present multiplicity of opinion. Figure 14-1 gives a striking example of this phenomenon. Note that the total number of links remains stable before and after the normalization, pointing to a more meaningful first approximation of quality, using the ratio of the number of links relative to the number of entries: 3/6 vs. 3/4 in this example.

Figure 14-1. *Growing dataset quality by shrinking number of records*

Clearly, more sophisticated measures are required in order to evaluate the quality of a given database. If we really want to know the value of a dataset, we have to look at the global emerging structure, which the commonly used indicators do not reveal. The only thing we can expect in any dataset is that the global structure can be characterized as a nontrivial, complex system. The complexity emerges from local activity (Chua 2005), as the availability of and attention to the source data are highly hetereogeneous

* From *http://www.census.de*, retrieved 9/14/2009.

by nature. Furthermore, every curator has a different idea about the *a priori* data model definitions. As the resulting structural complexity is difficult to predict, we have to measure and visualize it in a meaningful way.

Databases As Networks

Structured data in the fields of art history and archaeology, as in any other field, comes in a variety of formats, such as relational or object-oriented databases, spreadsheets, XML documents, and RDF graphs; semistructured data is found in wikis, PDFs, HTML pages, and (perhaps more than in other fields) on traditional paper. Disregarding the subtleties of all these representational forms, the underlying technical structure usually involves three areas:

- A data model convention, ranging from simple index card separators in a wooden box to complicated ontologies in your favorite representational language

- Data-formatting rules, including display templates such as lenses (Pietriga et al. 2006) or predefined query instructions

- Data-processing rules that act according to the data-formatting instructions

Here, we are interested first and foremost in how the chosen data model convention interrelates with the available data.

As Toby Segaran (2009) pointed out in *Beautiful Data*, there are two ends of the spectrum regarding data model conventions. On one end, the database is amended with new tables, new fields in existing tables, new indices, and new connections between tables each time a new kind of information is taken into consideration, complicating the database model ever further. On the other end, one can build a very basic schema (as shown in Figure 14-2) that can support any type of data, essentially representing the data as a graph instead of a set of tables.

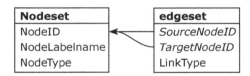

Figure 14-2. *Databases can be mapped to a basic schema of nodes and edges*

Represented in this form, every database can be considered a network. Database entries form the nodes of the network, and database relations figure as the connections between the nodes (the so-called edges or links). If we consider art research databases as networks, a large number of possible node types emerge: the nodes can be the entries representing physical objects such as Monuments and Documents, as well as Persons, Locations, Dates, or Events (cf. Saxl 1947). Any relation between two nodes—such as "Drawing A was created by Person B"—is a link or edge. Thus, there are a large number of possible link types, based on the relations between the various node types.

A priori definitions of node and link types in the network correspond to traditional data model conventions, allowing for the collection of a large amount of data by a large number of curators. In addition, the network representation enables the direct application of computational analytic methods taken from the science of complex networks, allowing for a holistic overview encompassing all available data. As a consequence, we can uncover hidden structures that go far beyond the state of knowledge at the point of time when the database was conceptualized and that are undiscoverable by regular local queries. This in turn enables us to reach beyond the common measures of quality in our evaluations: we can check how well the data actually fits the data model convention, whether the applied standards are appropriate, and whether it makes sense to connect the database with other sources of data.

Data Model Definition Plus Emergence

To get an idea of the basic structure, the first thing we want to see in a database evaluation is the data model—if possible, including some indicators of how the actual data is distributed within the model. If we're starting from a graph representation of the database, as defined in Figure 14-2, this is a simple task. All we need is a nodeset and an edgeset, which can be easily produced from a relational set of tables; it might even come for free if the database is available in the form of an RDF dump (Freebase 2009) or as Linked Data (Bizer, Heath, and Berners-Lee 2009). From there, we can easily produce a node-link diagram using a graph drawing program such as Cytoscape (Shannon et al. 2003)—an open source application that has its roots in the biological networks scientific community. The resulting diagram, shown in Figure 14-3, depicts the given data model in a similar way as a regular Entity-Relationship (E-R) data structure diagram (Chen 1976), enriched with some quantitative information about the actual data.

The CENSUS data model shown in Figure 14-3 is a metanetwork extracted from the graph database schema according to Figure 14-2: every node type is depicted as a metanode, and every link type is depicted as a metalink connecting two metanodes. The metanode size reflects the number of actual nodes and the metalink line width corresponds to the number of actual links, effectively giving us a first idea about the distribution of data within the database model. Note that both node sizes and link line widths are highly heterogeneous across types, spanning four to five orders of magnitude in our example. Frequent node and link types occur way more often in reality than the majority of less frequent types—a fact that is usually not reflected in traditional E-R data structure diagrams, often leading to lengthy discussions about almost irrelevant areas of particular database models.

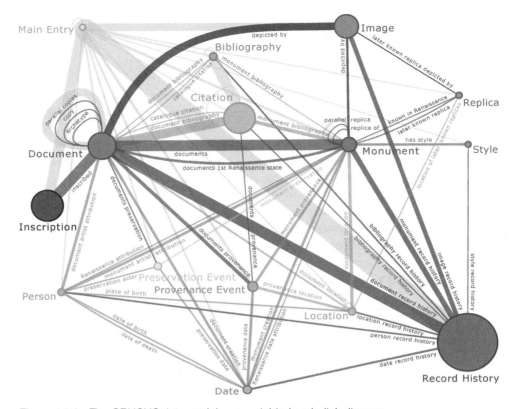

Figure 14-3. *The CENSUS data model as a weighted node-link diagram*

The heterogeneity of node and link type frequency evidenced in Figure 14-3 is not restricted to our example. It is observable in many datasets, including research databases (Schich and Ebert-Schifferer 2009), large bibliographies (Schich et al. 2009), Freebase, and the Linked Data cloud, regardless of whether the number of types is predefined or expandable by the curators. In all cases that I have seen so far, both the number of nodes per node type and the number of links per link type exhibit right-skewed diminishing distributions, which are widely known as *long tails* (Anderson 2006, Newman 2005), and lack a shared average as found in a normal Gaussian distribution. The comparable long-tail structure of hyperlinks in web pages—i.e., of a single link type in only one node type—has been well known for over a decade (*Science* 2009). Figure 14-3 makes clear that the observed heterogeneity is also present at the level of node and link types within more structured data graphs.

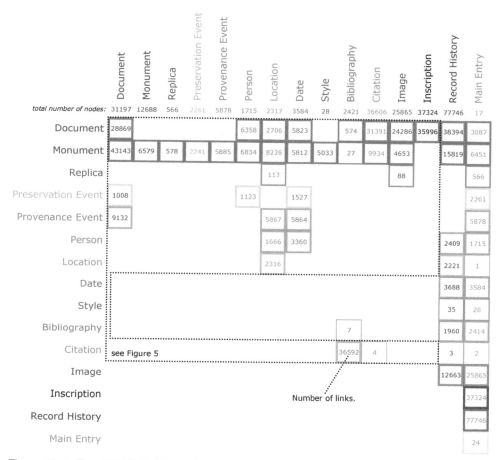

Figure 14-4. *The CENSUS data model as a weighted adjacency matrix*

Network Dimensionality

Looking more closely at Figure 14-3, we can see the central dimensions of the CENSUS database, Monuments and Documents, surrounded by an armature of additional information. Both Monuments and Documents are physical objects, but they differ insofar as the former are the targets and the latter are the sources of the central documentation links. Whereas in general any physical object can function as a Monument or as a Document, the CENSUS divides them into discrete node types because both groups belong to different periods (Classical Antiquity and Western Renaissance): ancient Roman sculptures and architecture as documented by Renaissance drawings, sketchbooks, text, etc.

In addition to these central dimensions, there is another node type representing physical objects called Replica, used for later-known replica Monuments that were discovered only after the defined Renaissance time frame. If the CENSUS is to be generalized to encompass the entire time frame from Antiquity until today, it would make sense to combine Monuments, Documents, and Replicas into a single physical object node type, as all functions are defined by the presence of certain links pointing into or out of a particular node. In the early 1980s, when the data model was initially conceived, its design was influenced by certain functionality constraints regarding relational databases. These constraints no longer apply, so such a change is now possible.

Distributed around the physical objects in Figure 14-3, we find Persons, Locations, and time ranges (such as Date and Style). Relations between all these dimensions are mostly modeled using direct links. For example, each Person is connected directly to a place of birth and a date of birth, making it impossible to disambiguate two alleged Birth Events (such as Venice 1573 and Bologna 1568) in a single Person without further comment.

Other example shortcuts include the document artist attribution and the 1st Renaissance state documentation. Again disambiguation is impossible without further comment. Regarding artist attribution, the CENSUS curators are guided to make a decision instead of recording multiple opinions. In the case of 1st Renaissance state documentation, there is only a single instance by definition. Further states are documented as Preservation Events—an obvious opportunity to simplify the data model.

Preservation and Provenance Events are a notable exception to the aforementioned shortcuts. They state that a particular Monument was altered by a Person or present at a particular Location, at a particular Date, as documented by a particular Document. Both Preservation and Provenance Events allow for easy disambiguation.

Differing opinions across Documents can be reflected by multiple Events, gluing together the respective Monuments, Persons, Locations, and Dates. As with physical objects, the nature of the Events is defined by the presence of certain links. As a consequence, the data model could be generalized further, as was done in projects inspired by the CENSUS such as the Winckelmann Corpus (2000). In general, Events boil down to so-called star motifs (cf. Milo et al. 2002) with a particular combination of link types. Today, Event-like constructions are a standard feature of many database models, such as Freebase, where they are called *compound value types*. In principle, we could also look for such Events in other networks with typed links, where they are not consciously explicit but rather inherent as emergent star motifs (as in the Linked Data graph).

The CENSUS becomes an authoritative—i.e., citable—source of information by providing a variety of metadimensions, such as the (modern) Bibliography. The Bibliography is subdivided into Citations, which are in turn represented as a separate node type. Another source dimension is the Image node type, which contains photographs taken from major photo libraries. Again, both the Bibliography and the Images represent functions of physical objects, which are defined by their adjacent links.

The remaining node types include the Record History, where curators log their actions on other nodes, and the Main Entry dimension, which was probably dissolved during the conversion of the CENSUS to a relational database. In the former graph-based system, due to the lack of tables the Main Entries figured as database chapters, facilitating navigation by bundling together all Persons, Locations, etc.

The Matrix Macroscope

The node-link diagram in Figure 14-3 is only one possibility for depicting the CENSUS data model. As with any network consisting of nodes and links, we can also depict it in the form of a so-called *adjacency matrix* (cf. Garner 1963; Bertin 1981; Bertin 2001; Henry 2008), as shown in Figure 14-4. Here, the node types are represented as the vertical columns and horizontal rows of a table, with link information appearing in the cells. Regarding the place of birth, for example, you can imagine the link pointing from the Person row into the Location column across the respective cell.

As in the node-link diagram, it is also possible to depict the total number of links occurring between two node types in the adjacency matrix; in place of the line width in Figure 14-3, now the explicit number appears in the relevant cell. This highlights the main difference in switching the representation to a matrix: our attention now focuses on the links, rather than on the nodes. It is striking that the matrix in Figure 14-4 not only shows the connections between node types, but also makes immediately clear which node types are not directly connected. In other words, the matrix indicates positive as well as negative correlation. One example of this is the absence of links from the Bibliography node type to authors, publication locations, and publication dates; though the CENSUS provides this information, it is only implicit in the node description text and node label abbreviations (e.g., "Nesselrath 1993"). Of course, we can also spot this absence of information in the node-link diagram, but the matrix makes it way more obvious.

Going beyond the total number of links between two node types, we can put a variety of other useful information into the matrix cells. In Figure 14-5, for example, we see a node-link diagram of all the nodes and links occurring between two node types in a cell. We generate such a diagram using a layout algorithm (such as the yFiles organic layout algorithm, part of the Cytoscape application), which is relatively inexpensive from a computational point of view. As a consequence, all of the explicit node-link data in the database appears in the data model matrix.

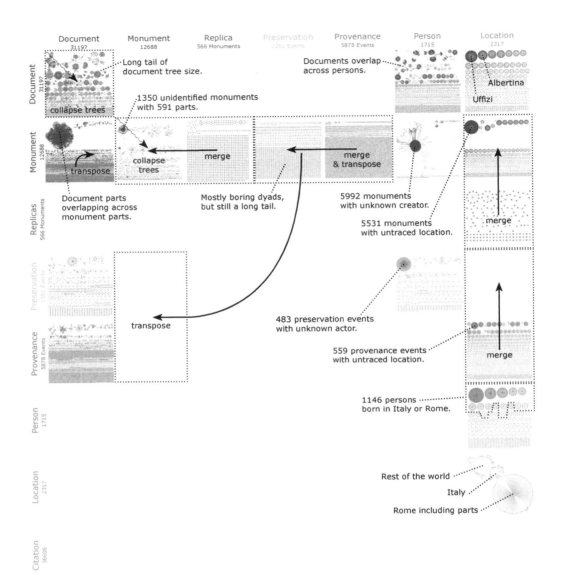

Figure 14-5. *The CENSUS data model as an adjacency matrix, enriched with node-link diagrams, i.e., actual data*

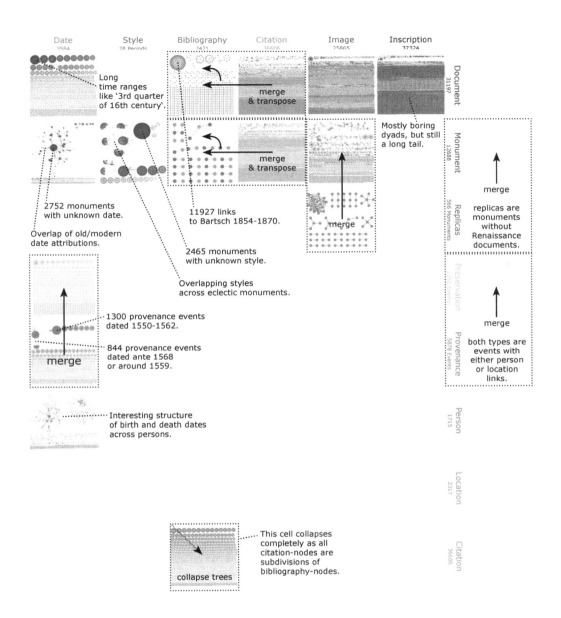

Date
3584

Style
28 Periods

Bibliography
2421

Citation
36606

Image
25865

Inscription
37324

Document
31197

Monument
12688

Replicas
566 Monuments

Preservation

Provenance
5878 Events

Person
1715

Location
2317

Citation
36606

Long time ranges like '3rd quarter of 16th century'.

merge & transpose

merge & transpose

Mostly boring dyads, but still a long tail.

merge

merge

replicas are monuments without Renaissance documents.

merge

both types are events with either person or location links.

2752 monuments with unknown date.

Overlap of old/modern date attributions.

11927 links to Bartsch 1854-1870.

2465 monuments with unknown style.

Overlapping styles across eclectic monuments.

1300 provenance events dated 1550-1562.

844 provenance events dated ante 1568 or around 1559.

merge

Interesting structure of birth and death dates across persons.

This cell collapses completely as all citation-nodes are subdivisions of bibliography-nodes.

collapse trees

Looking at the result in Figure 14-5, we can learn a lot about the database. At first glance, we can see that there are a few cells in which the structure looks more complex, whereas in the majority of cells we find a rather boring collection of stars and some dyads connecting two nodes exclusively. Another thing we can see is that all of the cells contain disconnected networks, in the sense that they are split into discrete components (i.e., groups of connected nodes). It is intriguing that here again we do not find a widespread average for component size. Wherever we look, we see a long tail. A prominent example is the Document-Location cell, wherein we see a clearly diminishing sequence of stars, connecting ever fewer Documents to single Locations; but even in the flattest cases, such as in the Document-Image cell, we find a few larger connected groups, followed by a huge amount of dyads.

A more diluted form of long tail is found in the Location-Location cell. It contains a hierarchy of geographical places rooted in a node representing the world, subdivided into countries, regions, and towns, down to individual collections. The number of subdivisions per Location is again distributed in a heterogeneous way. The majority of subdivisions are found within the country of Italy, almost eclipsing the rest of the world. The most prominent Location is unsurprisingly the city of Rome, which is subdivided into numerous collections. Its prominence reminds me of the oversized space dedicated to the hands in the sensomotory *homunculus* of the human brain (Penfield and Rasmussen 1950; Dawkins 2005, pp. 243–244)—the CENSUS seems to have a *romunculus*. Just as an overly large area of our brain's motor cortex is dedicated to hand–eye coordination and the sense of touch in our hands, the CENSUS Location hierarchy seems to be biased toward sculpture collections in Rome. Like a master pianist, whose centers for dexterity and manual control occupy even more space in the cortex than they would in a regular person, the CENSUS seems to be defined by specialization—such as the addition of Ulisse Aldroandi's famous books (1556 and 1562), which list thousands of sculptures in Roman collections (cf. Schich 2009, pp. 124–125).

Another interesting feature of Figure 14-5 is the disproportionally large stars found in a number of cells. Some of the stars are natural properties of the data, as in the case of the 11,927 Document nodes linked to the Bibliographic node Bartsch 1854–1870, or the 1,146 Persons born in Italy or Rome. However, most of the giant stars are artifacts related to unknown entries, such as an unidentified Monument, unknown Person, untraced Location, unknown Date, or unknown Style; all of these single nodes connect confirmed gaps of information in order to facilitate their further curation. There are 1,350 unidentified Monuments, 5,992 Monuments with unknown creators, 5,531

Monuments with untraced Locations, 2,752 Monuments with unknown Dates, 2,465 Monuments with unknown Styles, 483 Preservation Events with unknown actors, and 559 Provenance Events with untraced Locations in our dataset. To be sure, the presence of all these unknown entries is not an error; the attribution of an unknown Date could, for example, refute an incorrect Renaissance date attribution. However, the numbers provide a feeling of how incomplete our knowledge is. Another consideration is that, if we want to analyze the network structure of each cell, we have to break (or *denormalize*) the unknown nodes; otherwise, the untraced Location shortcut node would, for example, connect many unrelated nodes located at many different unknown places.

Reducing for Complexity

If we look back at Figure 14-3 for a moment, we can see that there are 31,197 Document records in the CENSUS database, of which only 3,087 are connected to the document authority under Main Entry. This points to an important fact: large Documents in the database are represented as trees of nodes. There are in fact only 3,087 Documents, including 28,110 subordinate nodes representing pages, figures, and quadrants within those figures or paragraphs of text—a fact until now rarely communicated about this database. The same is true for Monuments: here again, a small percentage of the records—in particular, the Architecture category—is subdivided into trees of nodes including building parts, rooms, and even tiny individual features of architectural decoration. A third example is the Bibliography, which is subdivided into Citations, such as paragraphs of text in modern scholarly books.

The consequence of all these subdivisions in Figure 14-5 is that particular links point from and to particular subnodes: from Monument parts to Document parts instead of from entire Monuments to entire Documents, or from a feature of a decorated column base to a particular quadrant in a sketchbook figure. The function of all these subdivisions is to enable data storage without a significant loss of information. However, the questions we can resolve in this configuration are often too specific. In order to uncover more interesting global properties of the data and answer questions such as how many sketchbooks a group of Monuments appears in (not how many figures there are in general), or how often they are cited in books (not how many citations there are in general), we have to refine the matrix. A solution for this problem is to collapse the subdivided Documents, Monuments, and Bibliographic Citation nodes as shown in Figure 14-6 and redraw the entire matrix as in Figure 14-7(a).

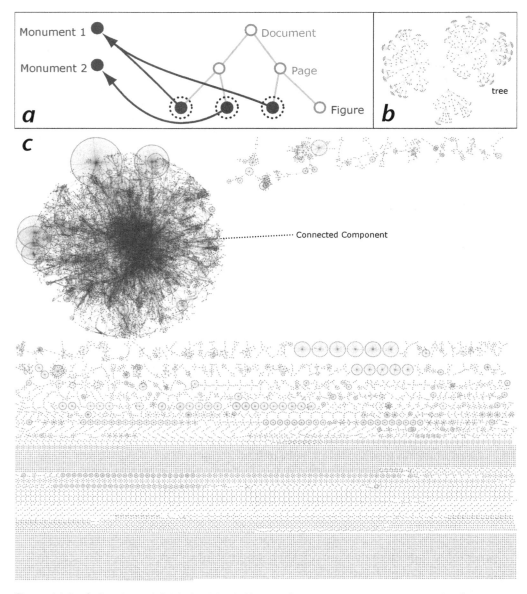

Figure 14-6. *Collapsing subdivided entries in the raw data uncovers interesting complex features*

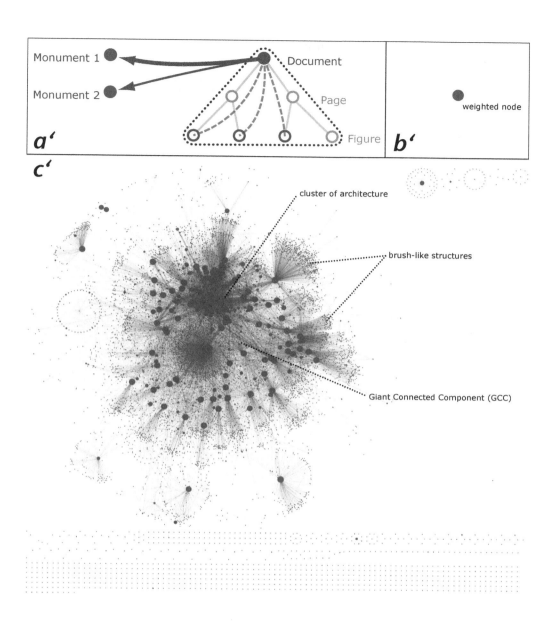

a'

Monument 1

Monument 2

Document

Page

Figure

b'

weighted node

c'

cluster of architecture

brush-like structures

Giant Connected Component (GCC)

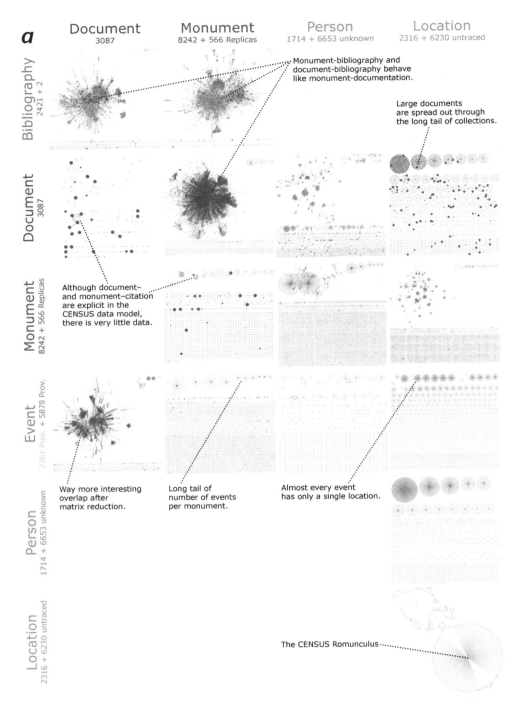

a

Document 3087 **Monument** 8242 + 566 Replicas **Person** 1714 + 6653 unknown **Location** 2316 + 6230 untraced

Bibliography 2421 + 2

Monument-bibliography and document-bibliography behave like monument-documentation.

Large documents are spread out through the long tail of collections.

Document 3087

Monument 8242 + 566 Replicas

Although document– and monument–citation are explicit in the CENSUS data model, there is very little data.

Event 2261 Pres. + 5878 Prov.

Way more interesting overlap after matrix reduction.

Long tail of number of events per monument.

Almost every event has only a single location.

Person 1714 + 6653 unknown

Location 2316 + 6230 untraced

The CENSUS Romunculus····

Figure 14-7. *The refined CENSUS data model matrix, enriched with node-link diagrams (a), and in the basic weighted form (b)*

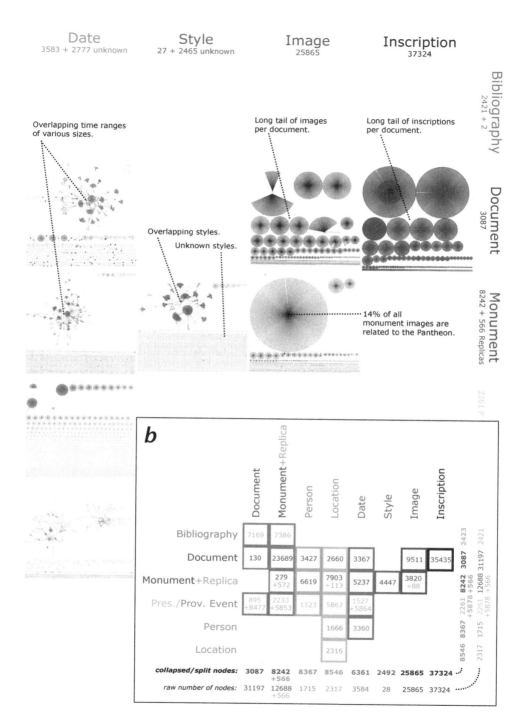

Date
3583 + 2777 unknown

Style
27 + 2465 unknown

Image
25865

Inscription
37324

Bibliography
2421 + 2

Document
3087

Monument
8242 + 566 Replicas

Overlapping time ranges of various sizes.

Long tail of images per document.

Long tail of inscriptions per document.

Overlapping styles.

Unknown styles.

14% of all monument images are related to the Pantheon.

b

	Document	Monument+Replica	Person	Location	Date	Style	Image	Inscription
Bibliography	7169	7386						
Document	130	23689	3427	2660	3367		9511	35435
Monument+Replica		279 +572	6619	7903 +113	5237	4447	3820 +88	
Pres./Prov. Event	895 +8477	2233 +5853	1123	5867	1527 +5864			
Person				1666	3360			
Location				2316				
collapsed/split nodes:	3087	8242 +566	8367	8546	6361	2492	25865	37324
raw number of nodes:	31197	12688 +566	1715	2317	3584	28	25865	37324

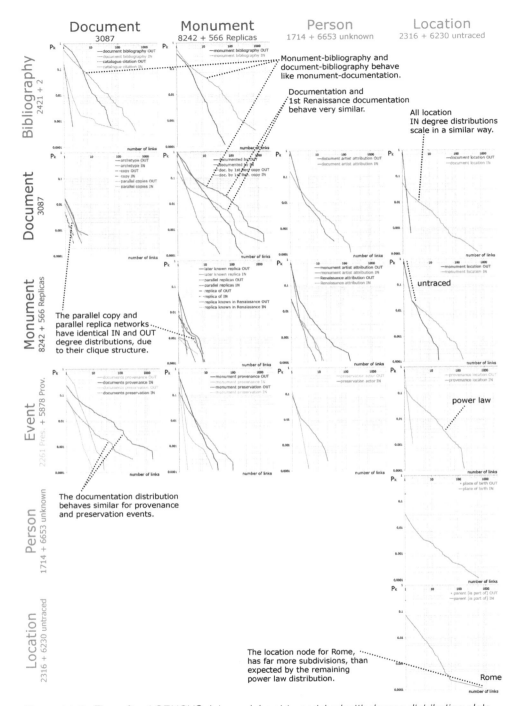

Figure 14-8. *The refined CENSUS data model matrix, enriched with degree distribution plots*

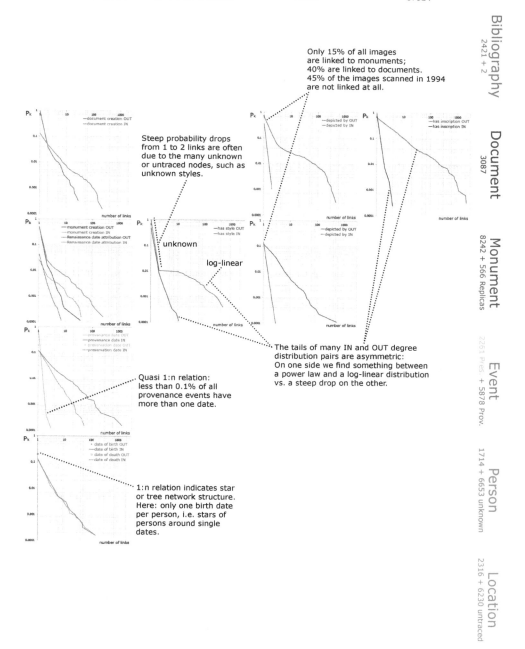

Date
3583 + 2777 unknown

Style
27 + 2465 unknown

Image
25865

Inscription
37324

Bibliography
2421 + 2

Document
3087

Monument
8242 + 566 Replicas

Event
2261 Pres. + 5878 Prov.

Person
1714 + 6653 unknown

Location
2316 + 6230 untraced

Only 15% of all images
are linked to monuments;
40% are linked to documents.
45% of the images scanned in 1994
are not linked at all.

Steep probability drops
from 1 to 2 links are often
due to the many unknown
or untraced nodes, such as
unknown styles.

unknown

log-linear

The tails of many IN and OUT degree
distribution pairs are asymmetric:
On one side we find something between
a power law and a log-linear distribution
vs. a steep drop on the other.

Quasi 1:n relation:
less than 0.1% of all
provenance events have
more than one date.

1:n relation indicates star
or tree network structure.
Here: only one birth date
per person, i.e. stars of
persons around single
dates.

Collapsing the Documents, Monuments, and Bibliographic Citation trees to single nodes works as follows (cf. Schich 2009, p. 28–37). In Figure 14-6(a), we see a raw Document tree: a book, with pages, which in turn are subdivided into figures. Single links point to multiple Monuments or Monument parts. In order to collapse the tree, we represent the book as a single node and combine all the links adjacent to the subdivisions, as shown in Figure 14-6(a'). To preserve as much information as possible, we assign a weight to the new node reflecting the number of collapsed subdivisions and another weight to the links, signifying the number of occurrences in the book. Graphically, our weights now correspond to the node size and the line width: the larger the node of a book is, the more subnodes it contains in its collapsed tree; the broader a line is, the more links it represents. Exemplified in real data, every Document tree in the Document-Document cell of the raw matrix will be reduced to a single node, as shown in Figures 14-6(b)/(b'). Matrix cells that look boring or simple in the raw state become more complex and interesting after the collapse, as in the case of the Document-Monument cell enlarged in Figures 14-6(c)/(c').

The most striking feature of the refined cell in Figure 14-6(c') is the emergence of a so-called Giant Connected Component (GCC), which connects almost 90% of all Monuments and Documents in the CENSUS—a phase transition phenomenon known from many other complex networks and bearing many important implications regarding the propagation of information (Newman, Barabási, and Watts 2006, pp. 415–417; Schich 2009, pp. 171–172). In the core of the GCC, we can see a cluster of large architectural Monuments, which are connected to large overview Documents, such as guidebooks, sketchbooks, and city maps. A surprising feature in the periphery of the GCC is the dominance of brushlike structures connected to large Document nodes: obviously a large percentage of all Monuments in the CENSUS are connected to only one single Document, either because the Documents lack sufficient information or because (for whatever reason) the curators did not identify and normalize them.

As the Document, Monument, and Bibliography trees are collapsed, the consequences affect the whole matrix. Effectively, the diagonal Document-Document and Monument-Monument cells are thinned out, leaving only a few interesting links, such as archetype citation and parallel copy relations. The Citation-Bibliography cell collapses completely.

Further Matrix Operations

Beyond breaking unknown nodes and collapsing the trees of subdivisions, we can do a number of other operations on the raw matrix in Figure 14-5. As with any adjacency matrix, we can sort (or *permutate*) the columns and lines along the horizontal and vertical axes, without losing any information (Bertin 1981; Bertin 2001). We can also transpose cells such as Monument-Event to Event-Monument, or even the whole Bibliography column to a Bibliography line, effectively reversing the direction of the links. Finally, we can merge equivalent node types—such as Provenance and Preservation Events, Monuments and Replicas, or Bibliography and Citation—by creating node supertypes, such as Event, Monument, and Bibliography. The merge reduces the number of columns and lines in the matrix and allows each cell to occupy more space in the visualization. Beyond that, the literature on matrix visualization contains many more possible operations (cf. Henry 2008).

The Refined Matrix

Figures 14-7(a) and (b) show the final result of all refining operations discussed so far. The whole matrix is now more concise, clear, and informative. We can easily see how the CENSUS data is distributed within the data model: Monument- and Document-Bibliography obviously behave like Monument-Documentation, exhibiting a wealth of data. For Document-Document and Monument-Monument dependency relations (such as citations), on the other hand, there is hardly any data, even though the respective links are explicit in the data model. Apparently the data curation workflow was not set up in the right way to collect this kind of information systematically.

As in the raw matrix, we find a long tail of component sizes in every refined cell. Some of the cells still contain mostly stars, as is true for the number of Events per Monument, Images per Document/Monument, Inscriptions per Document, or Events per Location. An interesting case involves the Document-Location cell, where we can see that large Documents are spread throughout all sizes of collections, from the Uffizi in Florence to individual private collections owning a single sketchbook.

Other cells show more overlapping structures, as is the case with overlapping Dates (or time ranges) across Documents and Monuments, or Styles across a few eclectic Monuments such as the Arch of Constantine, which brings together reliefs from different periods of the Roman Empire. Unsurprisingly, Monument-Documentation and the related Bibliography contain the most complex overlap, as this is the central focus of the CENSUS project.

Scaling Up

Readers involved in the network field may point out that the use of node-link diagrams in the matrix, as seen in Figure 14-7(a), is not feasible for datasets an order of magnitude larger than the CENSUS, let alone as large as the entire Semantic Web. Indeed this is a problem, so the question is how to scale the presented approach to really large databases. One solution is to use degree distribution plots or even more sophisticated numerical network measures to get an idea about the actual data within the data model.

In Figure 14-8, we plot a cumulative IN- and OUT-degree distribution (Broder et al. 2000; Newman 2005) for every link type occurring in a matrix cell. As every link points OUT of the source node type and IN to a target node type, there are two distributions for every link type in each cell. The x-axis of each plot indicates the number of links, k; the y-axis provides the cumulative probability, $P(k)$, that a node has at least k links. Note that the distributions are plotted on a log-log scale, meaning that the tick marks indicate a rapid decay from 100% to 0.01% on the y-axis and a rapid increase from 1 to 3,000 on the x-axis. (In a regular linear projection, the slope of each distribution would be so steep that we would not see anything interesting.) It is striking that there is not a single Gaussian bell curve in the plots, as we would expect for, say, the average heights of people. Instead, we find a whole zoology of long tails ranging from beautiful power-laws to log-linear curves, with less clean, bumpier distributions in between.

Nearly all IN and OUT distribution pairs appear to be asymmetric. Birth Dates, for example, are connected to Persons in a 1:n manner, where n is highly heterogeneous. This is no surprise, as this area of information is not subject to the multiplicity of opinion, as we would expect in a prosopographic database, which would focus on people instead of objects. Other areas, such as the occurrence of Locations in Provenance Events, exhibit a quasi 1:n constraint, as it is highly improbable but not impossible for an event to involve more than one location. The most interesting asymmetry is found in true n:n relations, such as the central Monument-Documentation link, where we find distributions with different slopes on both sides of the link. Right now, it is not entirely clear how this asymmetry can be fully explained; however, by comparing a number of data sources, it becomes apparent that the different shapes of these distributions are caused by a variety of factors, such as physical restrictions and accessibility of the source data, as well as attention and other cognitive limits on the side of the curators.

The only symmetric link relationship in the CENSUS can be found in the parallel copy and parallel replica links in the Document-Document and Monument-Monument cells, respectively. Ideally, the IN- and OUT-degree distributions should be identical, as the relevant nodes are fully connected to so-called "cliques." In reality, both link types become more asymmetric the further down we go into the tail of the distributions, as large cliques are hard to maintain. As I recommended to the CENSUS project in 2003, it makes more sense to connect to an unknown archetype Document with n links than to manually connect n parallel copies with $n * (n-1)$ links amongst each other.

Similarly, the behavior of certain relationships that we spotted in Figure 14-7, such as the equivalence of Monument-Bibliography and Monument-Documentation, is confirmed in Figure 14-8 (cf. Schich and Barabási 2009). Not only is there an obvious similarity between these cells, but the same functional equivalence is found in different link types in a single cell. A convincing example are the almost parallel distribution slopes of general documentation and 1st Renaissance documentation in the Document-Monument cell; the same is true for provenance and preservation documentation in the Event-Documentation cell. The Location IN degree scales in a very similar way across all relevant cells in the Location column. Two exceptions to this observed regularity are the steep drop of probability from one to two Monuments per Location (due to the many untraced Monuments) and the accelerating tail in the Location-Location cell (caused by the *romunculus* phenomenon).

One last thing we can observe in all the plots is the fraction of nodes per node type, which are inherent in the individual networks constituted by each individual link type. Looking at the value where the respective curve crosses the *y*-axis shows us, for example, that less than 15% of all Images are connected to Monuments, and less than 40% to Documents. Inversely, we can conclude that at least 45% of the 24,000 images scanned by the CENSUS project's publishing partner in 1994 were still not linked in the database in 2005.

Further Applications

The visualizations presented here can serve as a starting point for a variety of activities. Besides the evaluation of particular project goals by funders and project leaders, further areas of study include the identification of interesting research topics: every single cell in the matrix could be the subject of an extensive investigation, as illustrated in my PhD dissertation, which deals with monument documentation and visual document citation (Schich 2009). Multiple cells that promise an interesting interplay could also be combined within such a study—for example, in order to build trajectories of objects and persons involved in a variety of events across time and space (cf. González, Hidalgo, and Barabási 2008), or to study the effects of network interaction (Leicht and D'Souza 2009). Finally, a number of equivalent visualizations could be used to compare entire databases that already use similar data models, such as the Winckelmann Corpus and the CENSUS, or databases that can be mapped to the same standard, such as the CIDOC CRM.

Instead of dissecting the databases in the way discussed here, it might also be interesting to combine separate networks in a similar visualization. Candidates for such a combination can easily be found in the multipartite universe of conceivable networks (for example, citation, coauthorship, and image-tagging databases in the social sciences, or gene-transcription, protein-protein interaction, and gene-disease databases in biology).

The coarse graining we obtained by collapsing the Document, Monument, and Bibliography trees can also be achieved in many other ways; for example, by concentrating on particular subtrees, or with more sophisticated methods such as block-modelling (cf. Wassermann and Faust 1999, pp. 394–424) or community finding (cf. Lancichinetti and Fortunato 2009; Ahn, Bagrow, and Lehmann 2009), practically addressing the question of how nodes and links in a network are actually defined (cf. Butts 2009).

Finally, the presented combination of matrix and node-link diagrams can be expanded; for example, by placing node-link/matrix combinations (Henry, Fekete, and McGuffin 2007) or scalable image matrices (Schich, Lehmann, and Park 2008) in relevant cells of the data model matrix.

Conclusion

As this chapter has illustrated, enriched and refined data model matrices are very useful for database project evaluation, exposing many nonintuitive data properties that are hard to uncover by simply using the database or looking at the commonly used indicators of quality. As data becomes more accessible in the form of Linked Data, RDF graphs, or open dumps of relational tables, the presented methods can be applied by funders or the projects themselves, within a very short time frame in a mostly automated process.

The visualizations shown here present the first comprehensive big picture of the entire CENSUS database, where we can see the initial data model definition as well as the emerging complex structure in the collected data. By looking at the visualizations, we found out that many of the numbers given in the project description were incomplete or even misleading. Some of the new numbers may be smaller than the initially presented ones, but as we have learned from our analysis, sometimes a little less is more—and more is different (Anderson 1972).

Acknowledgments

For their useful feedback, I would like to thank my audiences at NetSci09 in Venice and SciFoo09 in Mountain View, as well as my colleagues at the BarabásiLab at Northeastern University in Boston. Further thanks go to Ralf Biering and Vinzenz Brinkmann of Stiftung Archäologie in Munich for providing the data and the German Research Foundation (DFG) for funding my research. For a comprehensive bibliography regarding the CENSUS database see Schich 2009, p. 13, notes 20–25.

References

The presented visualizations are available online in large resolution at *http://revealingmatrices.schich.info*.

Ahn, Yong-Yeol, James P. Bagrow, and Sune Lehmann. 2009. "Link communities reveal multi-scale complexity in networks." *http://arxiv.org/abs/0903.3178v2*.

Aldroandi, Ulisse. 1556/1562. "Appresso tutte le statue antiche, che in Roma in diversi luoghi, e case particolari si veggono, raccolte e descritte (…) in questa quarta impressione ricorretta." *Le antichità della città di Roma*. Ed. Lucio Mauro. Venice.

Anderson, Chris. 2006. *The Long Tail*. New York: Hyperion. *http://www.thelongtail.com*.

Anderson, P.W. 1972. "More is different." *Science* 177, no. 4047: 393–396.

Bartsch, Adam. 1854–1870. *Le Peintre-Graveur, nouvelle edition.* v. 1–21. Leipzig: Barth.

Bartsch, Tatjana. 2008. "Distinctae per locos schedulae non agglutinatae" – Das Census-Datenmodell und seine Vorgänger. *Pegasus* 10: 223–260.

Bertin, Jaques. 1981. *Graphics and Graphic Information Processing.* Berlin: de Gruyter.

Bertin, Jacques. 2001. "Matrix theory of graphics." *Information Design Journal* 10, no. 1: 5–19. doi: 10.1075/idj.10.1.04ber.

Bizer, Christian, Tom Heath, and Tim Berners-Lee. 2009. "Linked data—The story so Far." *International Journal on Semantic Web & Information Systems* 5, no. 3: 1–22.

Broder, Andrei, Ravi Kumar, Farzin Maghoul, Prabhakar Raghavan, Sridhar Rajagopalan, Raymie Stata, Andrew Tomkins, and Janet Wiener. 2000. "Graph structure in the Web." *Computer Networks* 33, no. 1–6: 309–319. doi:10.1016/j.physletb.2003.10.071.

Butts, Carter. 2009. "Revisiting the foundations of network analysis." *Science* 325, no. 5939: 414–416. doi: 10.1126/science.1171022.

CENSUS. 1997–2005. *Census of Antique Works of Art and Architecture Known in the Renaissance.* Ed. A. Nesselrath. Munich: Verlag Biering & Brinkmann/Stiftung Archäologie. *http://www.dyabola.de.*

CENSUS BBAW. 2006. *Census of Antique Works of Art and Architecture Known in the Renaissance.* Ed. Berlin-Brandenburgische Akademie der Wissenschaften and Humboldt-Universität zu Berlin. *http://www.census.de.*

Chakrabarti, Suomen. 2003. *Mining the Web: Discovering Knowledge from Hypertext Data.* San Francisco, CA: Morgan Kaufmann.

Chen, Peter P.S. 1976. "The entity-relationship model—Toward a unified view of data." *ACM Transactions on Database Systems* 1, no.1: 1–36. doi: 10.1145/320434.320440.

Chua, Leon O. 2005. "Local activity is the origin of complexity." *International Journal of Bifurcation and Chaos* 15: 3435–3456. doi: 10.1142/S0218127405014337.

Crofts, Nick, Martin Doerr, Tony Gill, Stephen Stead, and Matthew Stiff, eds. 2006. *Definition of the CIDOC Conceptual Reference Model (CIDOC-CRM), Version 4.2.1. http:// www.cidoc-crm.org/docs/cidoc_crm_version_4.2.1.pdf.*

Dawkins, Richard. 2005. *The Ancestor's Tale. A Pilgrimage to the Dawn of Life.* London: Phoenix.

DBpedia. 2009. *DBpedia.* Sören Auer, Christian Bizer, and Kingsley Idehen, admins. Leipzig: Universität Leipzig; Berlin: Freie Universität Berlin; Burlington, MA: OpenLink Software. *http://dbpedia.org.*

Doreian, P., V. Batagelj, and A. Ferligoj. 2005. *Generalized Blockmodeling (Structural Analysis in the Social Sciences)*. Cambridge: Cambridge University Press.

Flybase. 2008. Rachel Drysdale and the FlyBase Consortium. FlyBase. *Drosophila*: 45–59. doi: 10.1007/978-1-59745-583-1_3. See also *http://flybase.org/static_pages/docs/release_notes.html*.

Freebase. 2009. *Freebase*. San Francisco, CA: Metaweb Technologies. *http://www.freebase.com*. For data dumps, see *http://download.freebase.com/datadumps/*.

Garner, Ralph. 1963. "A computer-oriented graph theoretic analysis of citation index structures." In *Three Drexel Information Science Research Studies*, ed. Barbara Flood. Philadelphia, PA: Drexel Press.

González, Marta C., César A. Hidalgo, and Albert-László Barabási. 2008. "Understanding individual human mobility patterns." *Nature* 453: 779–782. doi: 10.1038/nature06958.

Henry, Nathalie, J-D. Fekete, and M. McGuffin. 2007. "NodeTrix: A hybrid visualization of social networks." *IEEE Transactions on Visualization and Computer Graphics* 13, no. 6: 1302–1309.

Henry, Nathalie. 2008. "Exploring large social networks with matrix-based representations." PhD diss., Cotutelle Université Paris-Sud and University of Sydney. *http://research.microsoft.com/en-us/um/people/nath/docs/Henry_thesis_oct08.pdf*.

Lagoze, Carl, Herbert Van de Sompel, Michael Nelson, and Siemeon Warner. 2008. The Open Archives Initiative Protocol for Metadata Harvesting. Protocol Version 2.0 of 2002-06-14. *http://www.openarchives.org/OAI/2.0/openarchivesprotocol.htm*.

Lancichinetti, A., and S. Fortunato. 2009. "Community detection algorithms: A comparative analysis." *Physical Review E* 80, no. 5, id. 056117. doi: 10.1103/PhysRevE.80.056117.

Leicht, E.A., and Raissa M. D'Souza. 2009. "Percolation on interacting networks." *arXiv* 0907.0894v1, *http://arxiv.org/abs/0907.0894v1*.

Milo, R., S. Shen-Orr, S. Itzkovitz, N. Kashtan, D. Chklovskii, and U. Alon. 2002. "Network motifs: Simple building blocks of complex networks." *Science* 298, no. 5594: 824–827.

Nesselrath, Arnold. 1993. "Die Erstellung einer wissenschaftlichen Datenbank zum Nachleben der Antike: Der Census of Ancient Works of Art Known to the Renaissance." Habilitation thesis, Universität Mainz. Available at the CENSUS office at HU-Berlin.

Newman, Mark E.J. 2005. "Power laws, Pareto distributions and Zipf's law." *Contemporary Physics* 46: 323–351. doi:10.1080/00107510500052444.

Newman, Mark E.J., Albert-László Barabási, and Duncan J. Watts, eds. 2006. *The Structure and Dynamics of Networks*. Princeton, NJ: Princeton University Press.

Penfield, W., and T. Rasmussen. 1950. *The Cerebral Cortex of Man: A Clinical Study of Localization of Function*. New York: Macmillan.

Phosphosite. 2003–2007. *PhosphoSitePlus™, A Protein Modification Resource*. Danvers, MA: Cell Signaling Technology. *http://www.phosphosite.org*.

Pietriga, Emmanuel, Christian Bizer, David Karger, and Ryan Lee. 2006. "Fresnel—A browser-independent presentation vocabulary for RDF." In *The Semantic Web—ISWC 2006*, vol. 4273, Chapter 12. Eds. I. Cruz, S. Decker, D. Allemang, C. Preist, D. Schwabe, P. Mika, M. Uschold, and L. M. Aroyo. Berlin, Heidelberg: Springer Berlin Heidelberg.

Saxl, Fritz. 1957. "Continuity and variation in the meaning of images." Lecture at Reading University, October 1947. In Lectures. London: Warburg Institute.

Schich, Maximilian. 2009. "Rezeption und Tradierung als komplexes Netzwerk. Der CENSUS und visuelle Dokumente zu den Thermen in Rom." Ph.D. diss., Humboldt-Universität zu Berlin. Munich: Verlag Biering & Brinkmann. urn:nbn:de:bsz:16-artdok-7002.

Schich, Maximilian, and Albert-László Barabási. 2009. "Human activity—from the Renaissance to the 21st century." In *Cultures of Change. Social Atoms and Electronic Lives. Exhibition Catalogue: Arts Santa Mònica, Barcelona, 11 December 2009 to 28 February 2010*. Gennaro Ascione, Cinta Massip, and Josep Perelló eds. Barcelona: Arts Santa Monica. urn:nbn:de:bsz:16-artdok-9582.

Schich, Maximilian, and Sybille Ebert-Schifferer. 2009. "Bildkonstruktionen bei Annibale Carracci und Caravaggio: Analyse von kunstwissenschaftlichen Datenbanken mit Hilfe skalierbarer Bildmatrizen." Project report. Rome: Bibliotheca Hertziana (Max-Planck-Institute for Art History). urn:nbn:de:bsz:16-artdok-7121.

Schich, Maximilian, César Hidalgo, Sune Lehmann, and Juyong Park. 2009. "The network of subject co-popularity in classical archaeology." urn:nbn:de:bsz:16-artdok-7151.

Schich, Maximilian, Sune Lehmann, and Juyong Park. 2008. "Dissecting the canon: Visual subject co-popularity networks in art research." 5th European Conference on Complex Systems, Jerusalem (online material). urn:nbn:de:bsz:16-artdok-7111.

Science. 2009. Special Issue on Complex Systems and Networks. *Science* 325, no. 5939: 357–504. *http://www.sciencemag.org/content/vol325/issue5939/#special-issue*.

Segaran, Toby. 2009. "Connecting data." In *Beautiful Data*. Sebastopol, CA: O'Reilly Media.

Shannon, Paul, Andrew Markiel, Owen Ozier, Nitin S. Baliga, Jonathan T. Wang, Daniel Ramage, Nada Amin, Benno Schwikowski, and Trey Ideker. 2003. "Cytoscape: A software environment for integrated models of biomolecular interaction networks." *Genome Research* 13, no. 11: 2498–2504. doi: 10.1101/gr.1239303. See also *http://www.cytoscape.org*.

Sullivan, Danny. 2005. "Search engine sizes." *Search Engine Watch*. *http://searchengine-watch.com/2156481*.

Wassermann, Stanley, and Katherine Faust. 1999. *Social Network Analysis: Methods and Applications, Fourth Edition*. Cambridge: Cambridge University Press.

Wikipedia. "Wikipedia: Size comparisons." *http://en.wikipedia.org/wiki/Wikipedia:Size_comparisons*.

Winckelmann Corpus. 2000. *Corpus der antiken Denkmäler, die J.J. Winckelmann und seine Zeit kannten*. Winckelmann-Gesellschaft Stendal, ed. DVD and online database. Munich: Verlag Biering & Brinkmann/Stiftung Archäologie.

CHAPTER FIFTEEN

This Was 1994: Data Exploration with the NYTimes Article Search API

Jer Thorp

IN FEBRUARY OF LAST YEAR, the *New York Times* announced that it was giving away the keys to 28 years of data—news stories, movie reviews, obituaries, and political statistics, all for free. Staring at such a huge pile of information—about 2.6 million articles— we're faced with three important questions. How do we get the data we need? What can we do with that data? And, perhaps most importantly, why should we bother in the first place? In this chapter, I'll try to answer those questions. We'll see how to access information from the NYTimes Article Search API (*http://developer.nytimes.com/ docs/article_search_api*), look at some practical visualization examples, and discuss how the new era of open data is opening doors for artists, entrepreneurs, designers, and social scientists.

Getting Data: The Article Search API

"API" is one of those three-letter acronyms that means very little as a collection of three letters, and even less once you find out what it stands for: application programming interface. While this rather generic term can be applied to all kinds of things within the world of software development, an API typically exists to allow one piece of software to talk to another. If we imagine a database as a physical warehouse that stores information, an API is the shipping and receiving department, and it's open to the public.

In general, interaction with an API is fairly straightforward. We send the API a request (which can be quite simple or very complex), and the API sends us back a formatted set of information. The syntax that we use to communicate with an API and the format the API uses to hand the requested information back to us varies from API to API. Some APIs are quite limited, whereas others unlock all kinds of useful functions. Luckily for us, the NYTimes Article Search API is one of the most robust and well-constructed APIs around.

So what can we ask it? With a few simple requests, the API can answer any of the following questions, and a nearly infinite number more:

- How many articles were published in 1982?

- What organization is mentioned most in articles about fraud?

- How many times was the word "hypercolor" used in fashion articles in 1991?

Let's start with an easy question: how many articles in 1994 mentioned O.J. Simpson?

There are a few different ways to send our question to the API, but all of them involve sending an HTTP request to a specific URL, with some parameters added to the mix. Here's the simplest request:

http://api.nytimes.com/svc/search/v1/article?query=O.J.+Simpson

This request will give us all of the articles in the database (articles are stored from 1981 to the present) that contain the string "O.J. Simpson". To restrict it to 1994, we can add a couple of "extras" to the query:

http://api.nytimes.com/svc/search/v1/article?query=O.J.+Simpson&beg in_date=19940101&end_date=19950101

Finally, the API needs to keep track of who is accessing the information and to ensure that no users are overrunning the published limits. Consequently, every time we access the API we must pass along our *API key*, a string of characters assigned by the NYTimes that is unique to each individual user:[*]

http://api.nytimes.com/svc/search/v1/article?query=O.J.+Simps one&begin_date=19940101&end_date=19950101&api-key=1af 81d####################.##.########

If you go ahead and paste this request into your browser's address bar (inserting your own API key in place of the # signs), you'll get some results; view the source to see the actual data returned by the API. The data is returned to us packaged in a format called JSON, which we will discuss in more detail later in this chapter.

At the bottom of this chunk of data, we can find the answer to our question: 2,218.

---

[*] Log into your *nytimes.com* account, go to *http://developer.nytimes.com*, and click "Request an API key" under the "Getting Started" heading.

We're going to wrap all of this up in some fancy packaging, but these requests are the root of everything we're going to do in this chapter. Any request to the Article Search API is constructed the same general way (see Figure 15-1):

URL Base + Query + Facets + Extras + API Key

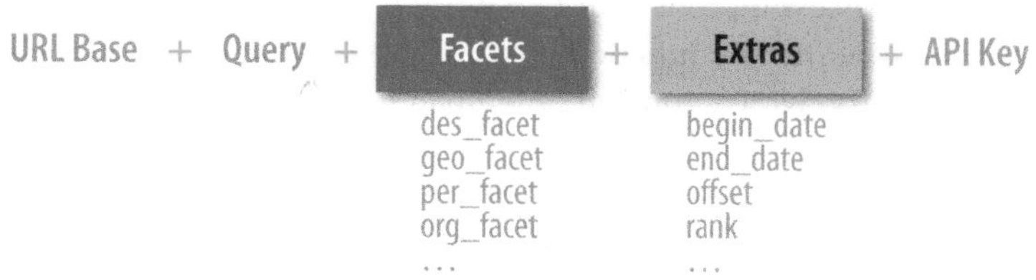

Figure 15-1. *Requests to the New York Times Article Search API are always structured from the same key parts*

Some of these elements are required (Query, API Key), and some are optional (Extras, Facets). However, the basic structure never changes, and neither does the basic approach: ask the API a question, and get an answer. What we really want to do, though, is ask the API lots of questions and get lots of answers. To do that, we need to have a better system than copying and pasting into a web browser.

Managing Data: Using Processing

In the 1990s, American artist Mark Lombardi created a series of hugely complex drawings (which he called *narrative structures*) exposing connections between people and corporations involved in political and financial frauds. Lombardi would meticulously comb through newspaper articles and magazines, recording his findings by hand. He had neither an API to pose his questions to, nor any kind of database or software to store his answers in. Instead, Lombardi amassed a collection of more than 14,000 index cards, on which all of his questions and answers were written and from which he drew his historical diagrams (see Figure 10-1 in Chapter 10).

Unless you happen to have a few thousand index cards and a few weeks of spare time handy, we're going to need to think of a faster way to manage all of our questions and answers. There are a number of different ways we could approach this on a computer, and a variety of different software tools and programming languages that would be up to the task. I use a language called Processing to work with data, so that's what we'll be using in our examples. Processing is a free download, and it's relatively easy to use. I'm going to assume in this chapter that you have already downloaded and installed Processing (if you need help with this, visit *http://www.processing.org*).

In the last section I showed how we can make requests to the Article Search API and get answers back in JSON format. We're going to use Processing to manage our requests, parse and store our answers, and display the results onscreen. The most complicated part of this process involves dealing with the JSON return. Rather than dedicating a few thousand words to showing you how to build your own engine to handle this, we'll use some Processing code that I've written to make the process a lot easier. I've wrapped up a lot of the key functionality that we'll need to deal with the Article Search API into a library, which you can download from *http://www.blprnt.com/libraries/ nytimes*.

Installing libraries in Processing is straightforward—simply drag the unzipped folder into the *libraries* directory in your sketchbook (again, if you need help with this, check out *http://www.processing.org*). If you are interested in the guts of these libraries, the project is open source—a bit of Googling will point you in the right direction. For now, though, all you need to know is that you can take advantage of their functionality to do some useful things. To get started, let's take a look at how we can ask our O.J. question using the new libraries.

First, we import the NYTArticleSearch libraries from the Sketch®Import Library drop-down menu. Then we set the size of our stage and give it a nice clean white background:

```
import blprnt.nytimes.*;
size(800,350);
background(255);
```

Now we're ready to initialize the libraries with our API key:

```
TimesEngine.init(this, "YOUR-API-KEY-GOES-HERE");
```

Next, we'll create a TimesArticleSearch object to manage our questions (queries) and answers (responses):

```
TimesArticleSearch mySearch = new TimesArticleSearch();
```

This simple little object allows us to do pretty much anything we need to do with the Article Search API. Let's get a response for a similar query to our 1994 example, this time asking for results from both 1994 and 1995:

```
mySearch.addQueries("O.J.+Simpson");
mySearch.addExtra("begin_date","19940101");
mySearch.addExtra("end_date","19960101");

TimesArticleSearchResult r = mySearch.doSearch();
println("RESULTS ABOUT O.J.:" + r.total);
```

This may seem more complex than our first example, in which we sent a single *http* request, but here we don't have to deal with the JSON, and we also have a lot of freedom in how we can customize our search. The Article Search API gives us a wealth of options for structuring search requests, allowing us to make both very specific and very general requests.

Let's consider our search for a moment. We are asking the API to find any articles published in 1994 and 1995 that contain the string of characters "O.J. Simpson". What about articles that talk about Orenthal James Simpson? Or just O.J.? Or "The Juice"? One of the most powerful things about the Article Search API is that it ties into the editorial structure of the *New York Times*. When an article is published by the *Times*, it is indexed with a set of editorial information. This information, added by humans and standardized, is available to the API and makes searching a lot more effective. In our case, rather than looking for the phrase "O.J. Simpson", we can instead look for articles labeled with the proper person facet for O.J. Simpson (which is "SIMPSON, O J"). The editorial staff will have added this facet to any article that mentions or references O.J., no matter what name is used in the article body. Our search, then, looks like this:

```
import blprnt.nytimes.*;
size(800,350);
background(255);

TimesEngine.init(this, "YOUR-API-KEY-GOES-HERE");

TimesArticleSearch mySearch = new TimesArticleSearch();

mySearch.addFacetQueries("per_facet","SIMPSON, O J");
mySearch.addExtra("begin_date","19940101");
mySearch.addExtra("end_date","19960101");

TimesArticleSearchResult r = mySearch.doSearch();
println("RESULTS ABOUT O.J.:" + r.total);
```

The only tricky part in using facets is finding out which facets are available and what their standard "names" are. An easy way to access this information is to use the NYTimes API Request Tool, located at *http://prototype.nytimes.com/gst/apitool/index.html*. This tool lets you test out search queries and see the results, all without any fussy code or the need for an API key. To get the proper per_facet for O.J., we can enter "O.J Simpson" into the Search Query field and "per_facet" in the Facet Query field, as shown in Figure 15-2.

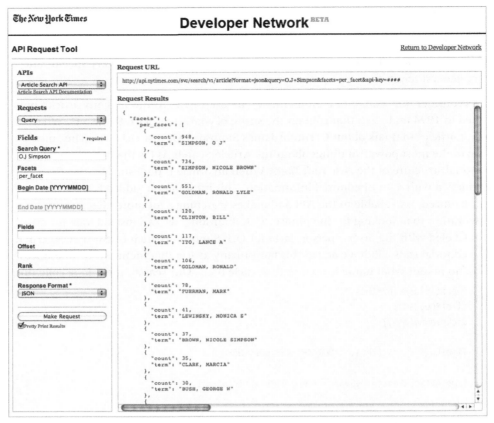

Figure 15-2. *The API Request Tool can be used to find official Times facets for people, topics, and places*

Of course, there was more going on in 1994 and 1995 than white Ford Broncos and ill-fitting gloves. Using the API Tool, we can gather the correct facets for some other events in that time period, like the end of apartheid in South Africa (geo_facet=SOUTH AFRICA) and the genocide in Rwanda (geo_facet=RWANDA). We can construct a new TimesArticleSearch object for each of those searches, or reuse the same one by clearing the facet queries each time. This second option makes the most sense, so let's give it a try:

```
import blprnt.nytimes.*;
size(800,350);
background(255);
```

```
TimesEngine.init(this, "YOUR-API-KEY-GOES-HERE");
TimesArticleSearch mySearch = new TimesArticleSearch();

// OJ search
mySearch.addFacetQuery("per_facet","SIMPSON, O J");
mySearch.addExtra("begin_date","19940101");
mySearch.addExtra("end_date","19960101");
TimesArticleSearchResult r1 = mySearch.doSearch();
println("OJ:" + r1.total

// South Africa search
mySearch.clearFacetQueries();
mySearch.addFacetQuery("geo_facet","SOUTH  AFRICA");
TimesArticleSearchResult r2 = mySearch.doSearch();

println("South Africa:" + r2.total);

// Rwanda search
mySearch.clearFacetQueries();
mySearch.addFacetQuery("geo_facet","RWANDA");
TimesArticleSearchResult r3 = mySearch.doSearch();
println("Rwanda:" + r3.total);
```

This leaves us with three TimesArticleSearchResult objects, which contain the total number of articles returned for each result (we'll see later that these objects can also hold other useful information). It seems like the right time to do some (very) simple visualization with this data. Bar graph, anyone? (See Figure 15-3.)

```
// O.J. bar
fill(255,0,0);
rect(0,50,r1.total,50);

// South Africa bar
fill(0,255,0);
rect(0,150,r2.total,50);

// Rwanda bar
fill(0,0,255);
rect(0,250,r3.total,50);
```

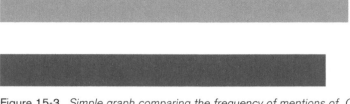

Figure 15-3. *Simple graph comparing the frequency of mentions of O.J. (in red), South Africa (in green), and Rwanda (blue) in the New York Times in 1994 and 1995*

OK. I'll admit it. This isn't the most exciting visualization ever. However, it embodies almost all of the concepts that we'll need to learn to start making visual exploration forays into the huge and treasure-filled NYTimes Article Search database. It also provides a very, very simple model for the three-step process that I follow when making even the most complex data visualizations.

Three Easy Steps

Let's take a short break from tutorializing and think about the basic process involved in a visualization project:

1. Get some data.

2. Convert the data into useful structures.

3. Visualize the data.

Often, this simple procedure is repeated twice during a project: once during discovery and once during production. In the research phase, where the challenge is to dig through a set of data and find something useful or interesting, the "getting data" stage might be repeated many times, while the visualization stage might be kept as simple as possible. In contrast, a production cycle typically occurs once the data has been identified. This means we spend very little time getting data (since we already have it) and much more time in the visualization stage.

Shared in both research and production cycles is step 2: converting the data into useful structures. What are these structures? What makes them useful? For me, this process usually means packaging up individual pieces of data into *objects* (programming structures that let me store related information together). It also typically involves filing these objects into some kind of collection—i.e., a list or a grouping that makes sorting and retrieving the data easy.

In our O.J. example, a lot of this process was handled by the NYTimes Processing libraries that we imported at the very beginning of our sketch. We can see objects being created every time we perform a search. We make a TimesArticleSearch object to manage the request to the API:

```
TimesArticleSearch mySearch = new TimesArticleSearch();
```

and a TimesArticleSearchResult object to store the response from the API:

```
TimesArticleSearchResult r1 = mySearch.doSearch();
```

These unassuming TimesArticleSearchResult (TASR) objects hold a pile of related information about each search result. So far all we've done is to access the total number of results received, a property stored in each result object as an integer called total:

```
println("RESULTS ABOUT O.J.:" + r.total);
```

The TASR object holds much more than that, though! Indeed, for each of the 713 articles marked with the O.J. facet published by the *New York Times* in 1994/1995, we can access the headlines, authors, URLs, excerpts, and more—all from our little TASR. These individual pieces of data are stored inside each TASR as TimesArticleObjects, neatly lined up in an array called articles. By default, the TASR holds the first 10 search results. If we wanted to get the author of the first article in the list, we could do this:

```
println("FIRST HEADLINE:" + r.articles[0].title);
```

Or, to get the web URL for the 10th article:

```
println("10th ARTICLE URL: " + r.articles[9].url);
```

Or for a list of headlines for each article:

```
for (int i = 0; i < r.articles.length; i++) {
    println("AUTHOR #" + i + ": " + r.articles[i].author);
};
```

Here, we are starting to see the tip of the data iceberg that the Article Search API puts at our fingertips. So far, we've done three fairly rudimentary searches and ended up with about 2,000 article results, packaged in a few handy TASRs. Now that we know how to access (at least part of) the results of a search, let's look at some ways to make the searches and results a bit smarter.

Faceted Searching

In our examples so far, we've seen how we can search with facets to make sure that we are getting the results we want. What I haven't mentioned up to now is that facets can also be included in the results of our searches. With facet results, we can find out much more from individual searches, and we can also uncover relationships between facets (people, countries, topics) that are contained within the article database.

Let's start with a simple but very useful example of how we can use facet results to optimize our searching. We found out in an earlier example that there were 488 article results labeled with the Rwanda geo_facet in 1994 and 1995. What if we wanted to break this down further and find out how many articles were published in each individual month of 1994? It would be possible, using the same method that we have already demonstrated, to do 12 individual searches: one for each month. For each of these searches, we could use different values for our begin_date and end_date extras to make sure they return the results for the appropriate months. But that seems like a lot of work, doesn't it?

As you may have suspected by now, a better version of this search can be executed using facet results. In fact, we can do just one search and get the results we want. We start by building the search in the same way we did in our previous example:

```
TimesArticleSearch mySearch = new TimesArticleSearch();
mySearch.addFacetQuery("geo_facet","RWANDA");
```

Rather than using the begin/end_date extras to constrain the search to 1994, though, this time we'll use the publication_year facet:

```
mySearch.addFacetQuery("publication_year","1994");
```

And now, the magic bit. Along with the usual search return (a giant list of articles), we'll ask the API to return us some facets—in this case, publication_year facets:

```
mySearch.addFacets("publication_month");
```

When we run our search, the facet results will be packaged up along with all of our other data into our TASR:

```
TimesArticleSearchResult r = mySearch.doSearch();
```

To access the publication_month results from the TASR, we ask it for an array of TimesFacetObjects related to the particular facet we're interested in (TASRs can contain any number of different facet results):

```
TimesFacetObject[] months = r.getFacetList("publication_month");
```

Now we can find out how many results were from, say, January (1994):

```
println("January results: " + months[0].count);
```

We can also graph the whole year's worth of results (Figure 15-4):

```
for (int i = 0; i < 12; i++) {
    fill(random(150,255),0,0);
    float w = width/12;
    rect(i * w, height, w, -months[i].count * 3);
};
```

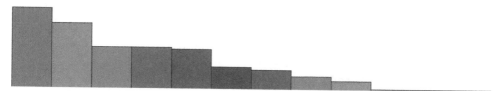

Figure 15-4. *Monthly frequency of mentions of Rwanda in the New York Times in 1994*

On the face of it, we have a really simple program to find mentions of Rwanda during a single year. But this little sketch is actually far more expandable than that. It can graph mentions of any faceted term in any year from 1981 to the present. It wouldn't be much of a stretch to make a more robust graphing tool from this simple code. While I'd love to go over this process in detail here, I've saved us all a bit of time and a lot of pages by building the sketch for you. You can find a link to download the NYTimes GraphMaker at *http://www.blprnt.com/examples/nytimes*.

As useful as this kind of exploration can be, we have so far limited ourselves to discrete searches within the article database. Things get even more interesting when we start to use the API to explore connections among people, places, and subjects.

Making Connections

When we make any search request to the Article Search API, we can ask it to return us a list of facets that were mentioned alongside our search term in the articles that the API has found. For example, we could find out which countries were mentioned alongside Rwanda, or which people were talked about in articles about O.J., or which topics were most often associated with writing about the end of apartheid in South Africa.

We can also make more general requests. By omitting a search term altogether but specifying a time frame, we can request all articles for that time period. If we ask for lists of facets along with these articles, we can find out what the top facets were for a given month, year, or decade. For example, let's find out who were the top personalities mentioned in 1994. First, we'll create a search object and give it an empty query (we use a + sign in place of an empty space):

```
TimesArticleSearch mySearch = new TimesArticleSearch();
mySearch.addQueries("+");
```

Now, let's restrict the search to 1994 and ask the search object to include the per_facet in its results:

```
mySearch.addFacetQuery("publication_year", "1994");
mySearch.addFacets("per_facet");
```

and perform the search:

```
TimesArticleSearchResult r = mySearch.doSearch();
```

If we wanted to list the top personalities mentioned in 1994, we could now do it like this:

```
TimesFacetObject[] stars = r.getFacetList("per_facet");
for (int i = 0; i < stars.length; i++) {
    println(stars[i].term);
};
```

which outputs this rather mixed group of names:

```
CLINTON, BILL
GIULIANI, RUDOLPH W
CUOMO, MARIO M
CLINTON, HILLARY RODHAM
PATAKI, GEORGE E
SIMPSON, O J
SIMPSON, NICOLE BROWN
KERRIGAN, NANCY
GINGRICH, NEWT
RABIN, YITZHAK
CORTINES, RAMON C
ARAFAT, YASIR
RENO, JANET
WHITMAN, CHRISTINE TODD
BERLUSCONI, SILVIO
```

This list reminds us of something about the *New York Times*: it is at the same time a city paper, a national paper, and an international paper. With this in mind, it may be less strange that we see then–Prime Minister of Israel Yitzhak Rabin (who won the Nobel Peace Prize in 1994) mentioned just slightly more often than Ramon Cortines, the Schools Chancellor of New York City. While we may be happy with this broad reach, we might also want to restrict our searches to a certain "version" of the paper. We can do this by again using a facet—this time we'll ask for articles only published from the Foreign Desk by using the desk_facet:

```
mySearch.addQueries("+");
mySearch.addFacetQuery("publication_year", "1994");
mySearch.addFacetQuery("desk_facet","Foreign Desk");
mySearch.addFacets("per_facet");
TimesArticleSearchResult r = mySearch.doSearch();

TimesFacetObject[] stars = r.getFacetList("per_facet");

for (int i = 0; i < stars.length; i++) {
    println(stars[i].term);
};
```

This query results in a more worldly cohort:

```
CLINTON, BILL
ARISTIDE, JEAN-BERTRAND
```

```
YELTSIN, BORIS N
ARAFAT, YASIR
RABIN, YITZHAK
CHRISTOPHER, WARREN M
BERLUSCONI, SILVIO
MANDELA, NELSON
GOLDSTEIN, BARUCH
BOUTROS-GHALI, BOUTROS
CEDRAS, RAOUL
CARTER, JIMMY
POPE
KIM IL SUNG
MAJOR, JOHN
```

This list was generated by a query without a specific keyword or facet search; we could take any or each of these names and ask for a list of the top personalities related to *that* personality. Here, we'll ask for a list of the personalities connected in 1994 to Yitzhak Rabin:

```
mySearch.addQueries("+");

mySearch.addFacetQuery("per_facet","RABIN, YITZHAK");
mySearch.addFacetQuery("publication_year", "1994");
mySearch.addFacetQuery("desk_facet","Foreign Desk");
mySearch.addFacets("per_facet");
TimesArticleSearchResult r = mySearch.doSearch();

TimesFacetObject[] stars = r.getFacetList("per_facet");

for (int i = 0; i < stars.length; i++) {
    println(stars[i].term);
};
```

This query gives us this list:

```
ARAFAT, YASIR
HUSSEIN I
CLINTON, BILL
PERES, SHIMON
GOLDSTEIN, BARUCH
ASSAD, HAFEZ AL-
CHRISTOPHER, WARREN M
CHRISTOPHER, WARREN
WAXMAN, NAHSHON
MUBARAK, HOSNI
SHARON, ARIEL
ABDELSHAFI, HAIDAR
BHUTTO, BENAZIR
BOUTROS-GHALI, BOUTROS
```

We are starting now to get not just simple results with our searches, but also connections between the results. If we were to repeat the process that we used for Rabin with the remaining personalities in our first list, we'd end up with 225 personalities in our "super list." This super list, though, would have repeats: as we can see in the Rabin list, some of the personalities have already appeared, in our first list (Arafat, Clinton, Goldstein, and Boutros-Ghali).

These relationships are a fascinating part of the data that is available to us from the NYTimes database. By examining them, we can uncover both obvious and hidden relationships among people, places, and topics. In Figure 15-5, the same list of 255 names that we mentioned previously is illustrated as a network diagram, with lines showing connections between the personalities mentioned.

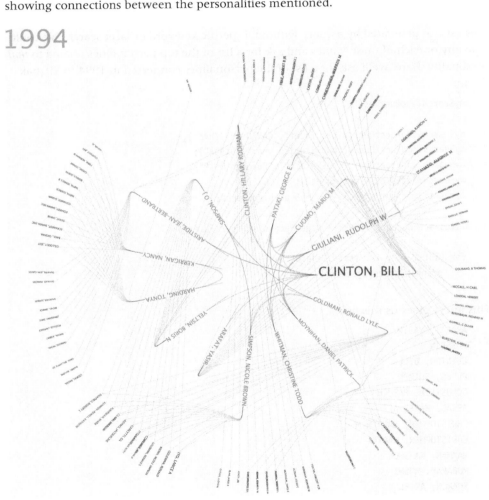

Figure 15-5. *A network diagram showing the most newsworthy personalities of 1994*

This image distills a huge amount of news information into a single graphic. With a typical data retrieval system, this kind of diagram would be extremely time-consuming to produce. As we've seen, the NYTimes Article Search API makes this process considerably easier for us.

Let's take the preceding example and make it a little bit more interesting by combining both personalities and organizations. With just 31 queries to the API, we can create a single image showing how hundreds of people, corporations, and nations were interrelated in the 1994 news year (full source code for this example is available at *http://www.blprnt.com/examples/nytimes*). The result is shown in Figure 15-6.

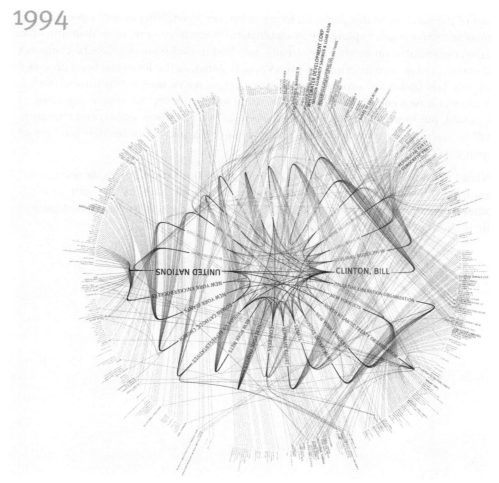

Figure 15-6. *This graphic shows the most frequently mentioned people and organizations in the New York Times in 1994*

Conclusion

The NYTimes APIs present a wealth of information for researchers of any stripe. The database is at the same time a historical record and a live feed—new content is being created every minute of every day. And of course, however vast the NYTimes database might be, it is but a small part of the huge catalog of open data that is available—a catalog that is growing by leaps and bounds with every passing week. Indeed, it seems that we may be sweeping past the first problem of open data—how to make data available—and right into a second, bigger problem: how can we possibly utilize such mammoth amounts of information?

Part of the solution to this problem, in my mind, lies in enabling as many people as possible to access and explore the available data. Many large-scale open data initiatives have concentrated on serving the already data-literate: software developers, computer scientists, and trained information professionals. Much of the focus has been on making this data useful on corporate scales. However, as we've seen in this tutorial, we can explore at least some of these datasets by using simple tools to ask simple questions. This skill, put in the hands of journalists, sociologists, historians, artists, and scientists, will be essential if we want to make really valuable discoveries in this new territory of open data.

What I'm asking of you, then, is to explore. Dig into the Article Search database, ask some questions of your own, and share the answers. And that's just the start. Many other APIs can be explored using the skills you've learned in this chapter, and there are millions of answers to be found. Good luck!

## CHAPTER SIXTEEN

A Day in the Life of the New York Times

Michael Young and Nick Bilton

HAVE YOU EVER WONDERED who the readers of the *New York Times* website are? We have. We also wonder what time of day they tend to visit the site, what devices they use to consume our content, and where they come from. New York, Paris, Boise? We think about all of these questions, from the who and the when to the how and the why.

In the New York Times Research and Development Labs, a simple lunchtime conversation on this very topic led to the development of the research visualization described in this chapter. As you'll see, we started with a very simple collection of location-based data and quickly became engrossed by the amount of data and the potential for visualizations. We eventually created a visualization showing a day's worth of traffic to *nytimes.com* and *mobile.nytimes.com* on a world and a U.S. map.

The first phase of our exploration began with data collection. The *New York Times* website can garner hundreds of millions of page views a month, with the number of unique visitors fluctuating between 17 and 21 million. Plus, there are a number of other gateways to our content, including the mobile website, the Times Reader AIR application, the iPhone application, APIs, and much more.

For this particular experiment, we chose to stick with the standard *nytimes.com* and the mobile version of the website (*mobile.nytimes.com*). We chose to use two sources for simplicity's sake, but even limiting ourselves to these two datasets, there was a vast amount of information for us to sift through and visualize.

The second phase of our exploration led to the creation of a map-based visualization. The visualization showed the traffic patterns and fluctuations of the readers on our web and mobile sites over a 24-hour period.

As we moved through the stages of the visualization, we were not only surprised by the vast numbers of readers coming to the site, but also by the times of day at which they arrived. As you can see from the videos at *http://bit.ly/nytdayinlife*, the *nytimes.com* site is relatively active throughout the evening and has a constant heartbeat of users from around midnight to 5 a.m. As the site's readers begin to wake on the East Coast of the U.S., traffic balloons and the visualization expands; a similar swell takes place around lunchtime as people presumably take a break at work to check in on the daily news. It's fascinating to look at the number of readers accessing the mobile site versus the website (*nytimes.com*); as later visualizations revealed, at different times of the day, there tends to be more mobile than web traffic, and vice versa.

As we gain more opportunities to look at this data, there are some interesting next steps we'd like to take. As time permits, we'd like to automate the process to render the videos on a daily basis, or even at the moments at which traffic spikes, possibly signaling breaking news events. There's also plenty of optimization to be done to the data collection and visualization code (as always). And finally, we've talked about visualizing more specific data: for example, showing a day's worth of traffic coming from a single device such as the iPhone, or taking the users in California and geocoding the stories they are reading to see if they are reading about New York or tend to focus on locations closer to themselves. Other possibilities include looking for patterns in big news days or important stories to try to understand how news spreads throughout the Web, social networks, and geospecific locations.

The opportunities are endless. We believe that although a single picture can tell a thousand words, a single dataset can tell a thousand stories.

Collecting Some Data

Before jumping into the visualization itself, let's first discuss the data behind it. To visualize 24 hours of traffic to *nytimes.com* and *mobile.nytimes.com*, we had to come up with a process to extract and "massage" the data that we needed from the *nytimes* access logs. Since we knew we wanted to create a geographically based visualization showing visits to the site over the period of a day, the data we needed was:

- The timestamp of each visit to the web and mobile sites, for a 24-hour period

- The latitude and longitude of each user/visit

The raw access logs contain a lot of useful information about people visiting the web and mobile sites (such as which browser each visitor is using); however, there is a lot of information unnecessary for our purposes that needs to be filtered out from the logs. Also, the logs don't contain the latitude and longitude for each user/visit, so this was something we needed to add as part of the "massaging" process.

The *New York Times* website, a top-five news site in terms of traffic (according to Nielsen[*]), has roughly 20 million monthly unique visitors. For any single day, that amounts to many millions of page views (or *hits*) on both the web and mobile sites; this is the data that we are looking to collect for our visualization.

Let's Clean 'Em First

The first step in processing the raw access logs is to "clean" them up. This a common process for anyone dealing with web logs of any type. For the visualization, and for other analyses we may do on the log data, we are only interested in hits to the web and mobile sites from humans—not from spiders, bots, or scrapers. To remove the irrelevant data, we run some Java code that identifies nonhuman visitors and strips their hits out of the logs. The original raw access log data for a day amounts to roughly 500–700 MB (compressed) for the website and 80–100 MB (compressed) for the mobile site. While the data is being cleaned, we also do an IP-to-latitude/longitude conversion so we can get the exact location of each user visit. The raw access logs contain the users' IP addresses, which we convert using a commercial database. There are many companies that provide GeoIP databases that enable this sort of translation— MaxMind, for example, provides a commercial database, as well as a free version with a variety of client libraries that can access the database.

Once the data was cleaned and properly geocoded, we had to do one last round of processing on the data. Because of the way the raw access logs were gathered, stored, and then cleaned, the newly cleaned data was located in multiple files and needed to be sorted into a single file containing the day's worth of data that we needed for the visualization. One day's worth of "cleaned" *nytimes.com* log data is stored in 360 files, each of which is approximately 30–40 MB (compressed). The "cleaned" logfiles are larger than the original files due to additional fields in each line, such as GeoIP information. For the mobile site, since the dataset is much smaller, the cleaned data is stored in a single file, which is about 70 MB (compressed). We needed to comb through each of the cleaned logfiles for the day and create a single file (one for the website and one for the mobile site) that contained a time-sorted list of each hit to the web and mobile sites and the latitude and longitude of each visitor. The resulting file would look something like this (line by line):

```
00:00:00,-18.006,-070.248
00:00:00,-22.917,-047.080
00:00:00,-33.983,0151.100
00:00:00,014.567,0121.033
...
```

* See *http://blog.nielsen.com/nielsenwire/online_mobile/msnbc-and-cnn-top-global-news-sites-in-march/*.

Python, Map/Reduce, and Hadoop

For this final step, we created a simple map/reduce script in Python that filtered out all of the unneeded data from the cleaned logfiles, output the data we wanted to keep in a comma-delimited format, and then sorted the data for us. (In the R&D group, we typically use Python for our data collection, processing, and parsing. When visualizing large datasets, we do all of the heavy lifting in Python and create files that are easy to read and parse within the visualization apps.) We ran the map/reduce code using Amazon's Elastic MapReduce web service, which allowed us to run a Python map/reduce job across multiple EC2 instances using Hadoop. Amazon EC2 instances come in different "sizes" (such as small, medium, and large) that offer differing amounts of RAM, CPU cores, and memory, so we experimented with running the map/reduce code on a variety of EC2 instances to find the "sweet spot" of processing time versus cost. The processing took roughly 10–20 minutes (and cost a few dollars), depending on the number of machines (we tried anywhere from 4 to 10) and the size of the EC2 instance (we tried both small and medium).

The resulting output from the map/reduce (Hadoop) job came in multiple, sorted files that were saved to Amazon S3 buckets. To get the data into a single file for use in the visualization (again, one file for web and one for mobile), we downloaded the output files from S3 to a local machine and did a good old-fashioned sort -m on the files to merge them. Now that we had our data in the form we wanted, we were ready to dive into producing the visualization.

The First Pass at the Visualization

Again, the goal of the project was to visualize a day's worth of traffic to *nytimes.com* and *mobile.nytimes.com*, to see how the visits to our sites played out over the day. We wanted to see if there were any interesting patterns occurring in specific geographic regions, or even across the globe. Where and when did mobile traffic spike in the U.S. during the day? Would we see more access to our mobile site in countries like China and India, where mobile penetration is higher than in places like the U.S.? How did visits to our web and mobile sites look during certain parts of the day, like early morning, commuting time, the lunch hour, and the commute home? Some of these questions can be answered with basic site traffic reports, but we wanted to put a new visual spin on the usual reports and allow people to see how the site traffic looked geographically over the course of a day.

In our first stab at the visualization, we created a simple global map and plotted a small yellow circle for each hit to *nytimes.com* and a small blue circle for each visit to *mobile.nytimes.com* as they were happening, second-by-second, throughout the day. Besides the global view, though, we also wanted to create a view that was focused on (or zoomed in on) the U.S.

The first build of our visualization, as we'll describe in gory detail, was a major learning experience for us—there were plenty of challenges involved in trying to visualize and make sense of such a large dataset, and we found this out firsthand. We reworked the code a few times before we settled on the current version, and we are still refining the data gathering and visualization processes as we have time.

Processing

Processing (a design-oriented and open source programming language and IDE) was the visualization tool of choice, for a couple of reasons. First, a few of us in the NYTimes R&D group already had experience using Processing for small data visualization projects, and to explore using devices with sensors as data collection devices. Additionally, we are big fans of the work Ben Fry and Casey Reas (the creators of Processing) and Aaron Koblin have done with this tool, so we thought it would be perfect for visualizing our large datasets.

The first thing we needed for our visualization was some code that would allow us to map the latitude/longitude pairs representing the users who visited our sites onto the 2D map visualization in Processing. Aaron Koblin was kind enough to provide us with some code he has used in a previous project to do this—a nice, compact Java class that converts latitude/longitude pairs to x, y coordinates. All we had to do was pass the lat/long pairs in our data files in to the library, and it would give us the x, y coordinates. We could then feed those through Processing's drawing APIs to draw the points on the map indicating the locations of each *nytimes.com* and *mobile.nytimes.com* visitor.

The Underlay Map

Creating the underlay map—just drawing the world map—took more time than you might expect. First we had to find accurate representations of the U.S. and the world. After numerous data explorations, we ended up using a dataset from UCLA's CENS group that plots the lat/long coordinates of every city throughout the world.

The initial experiments with this dataset rendered it directly in Processing when the application started up, but this took more time than we wanted just for the underlay; since we knew this data wouldn't change, we eventually created a JPEG of the maps and loaded a very small file into the background (see Figures 16-1 and 16-2). This saved us minutes of rendering time (which can add up when parsing large datasets) and processing power, and became the background of all the subsequent data outputs and videos.

Figure 16-1. *U.S. population map*

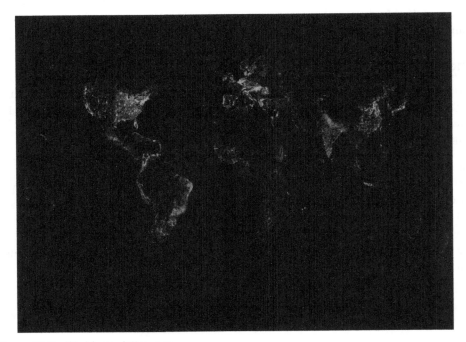

Figure 16-2. *World population map*

Now, Where's That Data We Just Processed?

Now that we had our latitude/longitude projection code and our map outlines, we were ready to start plotting the traffic data onto the map. For the first try at the visualization, we used data from a random day (February 15, 2009) that had no particular breaking news element. The day had average traffic/visits across both the web and mobile sites.

Remember our cleaned up, sorted, and geocoded data files, containing a timestamp and latitude/longitude pair for every view/hit on the web and mobile sites for a given day? The idea now was to create a Processing application that would rip through both the web and mobile logfiles and, for each view/hit, draw a point on the map indicating where the user was based during that visit.

Scene 1, Take 1

Processing apps, for the most part, are made up of two parts: the setup and the draw loop. In the setup() function in your Processing app, you can do any type of setup work that your app will need, like initializing variables, opening input files, loading fonts, etc. The draw loop is where the meat of the Processing code lives. The draw() function in a Processing app is typically called 30 to 60 times per second (this is the frame rate).

Our first attempt looked like this (illustrated in rough pseudocode):

```
void setup()
    - open up both the mobile and web log files
    - load the data for the world map
void draw()
    - draw the world map
    - read a second's worth of log data from the web and mobile log files
    - draw a yellow point for each visit/hit to nytimes mobile site (during that
    second in the log file)
    - draw a blue point for each visit/hit to nytimes.com website (during that second
    in the log file)
```

The code, while it had its problems, gave us something to look at on the screen. We were able to run the app and view the points drawn on the map over time, as the day's web and mobile site traffic played out. It was incredible to watch the traffic patterns emerge over time—the map looked like it had come alive, with blinking lights scattered across the globe (Figure 16-3).

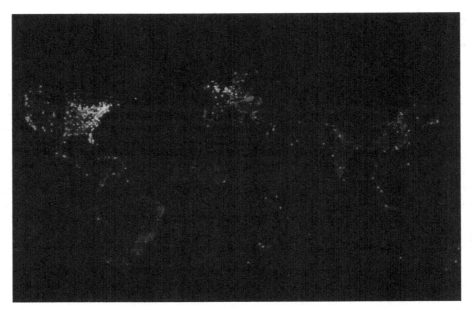

Figure 16-3. *Original visualization showing traffic from around the world to nytimes.com and mobile.nytimes.com—the yellow circles represent traffic to the website, while the blue circles represent traffic to the mobile site*

This was a great first step, but we had some things to fix both in our code and our approach. The following sections describe the three major areas we needed to work on.

No Scale

First, the visualization didn't display any sense of scale for the volume of web and mobile site traffic originating at each user location. At any one time during the day, there might be multiple users coming to the web and mobile sites from the same location (New York, for example, sees very high traffic flows). At times, thousands of people might be on our website, all coming from the same location. Again, think New York!

In the initial version of the app, we were drawing the same size point on the map for each location (lat/long pair) found in the input logfile. To give some indication of scale, we needed to adjust the visual representations of the traffic coming from each location (our blue and yellow points on the map) based on the number of users connecting from that location.

Second, since the yellow (web) and blue (mobile) points were the same size and we drew the web points before the mobile points (in the draw loop), when both types of hit came from the same location, the blue mobile points obscured the yellow web points.

Not good for a visualization.

No Sense of Time

In our first pass at the visualization, we weren't taking into consideration how much time people spent on the web or mobile site for each visit or page view; we simply drew a point on the map for each site visit and left it there for the entire duration of the visualization. Now, no one would have noticed this for some of the larger cities in the world where we have a continuous stream of traffic, but for some small, remote locations, where we get only a few views a day, this gave the impression that we had traffic from those spots throughout the day.

We needed to fix this, in combination with the scale problem—that is, we needed to come up with a way to accurately portray how many people were visiting the site from any one location, and how long they were staying on a specific article, or the site as a whole.

Most importantly, this had to be done for every second of the day!

Time-Lapse

Finally, we wanted to create a time-lapse video for the entire day's traffic, allowing us to easily share the visualization around the New York Times Company. To solve this problem, we decided to use a built-in video library for Processing that saves frames from the draw loop to a video file and creates a clean output movie.

Scene 1, Take 2

Working off the code from the first version of our project, we added the ability to capture the visualization to a file via the Processing MovieMaker library.

We also added support to the app so that each hit to the web or mobile site was properly represented in terms of the lifespan of the visit to the site. On average, a visit to either site lasts three to four minutes. So in this iteration, instead of drawing a point on the map and leaving it there for the entire 24-hour period, we tried slowly fading each point away over the course of three minutes. Of course, not every hit to the web or mobile site is from a unique user making a three-minute visit—many of the hits in our logfiles are from repeat users or users who are browsing multiple pages of the site over a longer period of time. But to keep the initial version of the visualization from getting too complex, we made the blanket statement that each hit would be a "three-minute visit" to the site.

For this slightly simplified representation, we needed to keep track of every view/hit over the course of a day and fade each one out over the course of three minutes. This meant storing a lot of objects in memory. For each hit to the web and mobile site that occurred every second, we created an object in our Processing app whose task was to keep track of that hit's "lifetime"—i.e., how long the point should be on the screen (three minutes)—and we used these objects to help fade the points out over the course of this lifespan.

So, back to our Processing draw loop. We still read in each second of data from the web and mobile logfiles, but now for each hit that occurred we created a Hit object with an initial lifetime value of three minutes and an initial opacity of 100% (these values decreased over every draw loop iteration). After reading in the log data, we iterated through the collection of Hit objects in memory. For each Hit, we redrew the point for the hit with an opacity based on the lifetime left for the hit, fading it out over the course of the three-minute lifetime. As each Hit reached the end of its lifespan, we removed it from memory and removed the corresponding point from the map (i.e., did not redraw it).

Since we were visualizing roughly 400–500 hits/second, this approach meant storing a lot of objects in memory at any moment in time to keep track of all of the hits (or users). We knew this would be problematic and we had some optimization ideas, but we wanted to take baby steps and decided to first see if this approach would work.

Let's Run This Thing and See What Happens!

Adding the support for fading each hit out over the three-minute period got us closer to visually representing the traffic to the site, but more work was needed. For one thing, at this point we still didn't have any sense of scale for the traffic originating from each location worked into the visualization. Speed was another issue—running this version, we were able to produce only about 45 seconds of time-lapse video in 25 minutes! A memory and processor hog, this baby was slow to run and to render. We tried running it on a few different machines in the lab (Mac Minis with 1 GB of RAM, MacBook Pros with 4 GB of RAM, and a Mac Pro), but the app was slow to render on each machine. The visualization was one step closer to what we were looking for, but it needed a new round of optimizations—we needed to produce a day's worth of time-lapse video, and at this point the best we had was about an hour's worth!

The first version of the visualization can be viewed at *http://nytlabs.com/dataviz*.

The Second Pass at the Visualization

Now that we had a taste for the visualization, we needed to get it fully working. Besides adding support to give a sense of scale for the amount of traffic coming from each location, we needed to optimize the app, which required rethinking how we collected the data.

Back to That Scale Problem

Showing each hit per second didn't work without any sense of scale. In the first version of the app, a handful of hits coming from rural Canada had the same visual weight as the thousands coming from New York. Also, showing every hit per second was too expensive in terms of the memory and processing power needed to render the visualization.

After thinking this through, we decided the answer was to visualize the number of hits from each location per minute, instead of per second. For every minute of data in the access logfiles, we'd add up the total number of hits per location. This would give us a sense of the scale of traffic for each location, and would greatly reduce the amount of raw data input to the Processing app. However, this approach meant a change to our data processing and map/reduce jobs.

Massaging the Data Some More

Our Python map/reduce scripts, which originally parsed out the data we needed from the raw access logs and then sorted the data based on time, needed some updates. Now, the script needed to count each hit per location (latitude/longitude pair) per minute and then output that data, sorted by the access time.

If you aren't familiar with how map/reduce works, we recommend doing some basic reading through some of the tutorials available online. Basically, map/reduce is a programming model that allows you to process large amounts of data. The processing is split up into two tasks: mapping and reducing. The Mapper typically takes some input (logfiles in our case), does some minor processing on the data, and then outputs the data in key/value pairs. The Reducer's job is to take the data output from the Mapper and merge or reduce the data into what is usually a smaller dataset.

Our Mapper script read the raw access logfiles and, for each line, output a key/value pair in the following format:

```
Timestamp of the access (in HH:MM format),latitude,longitude        1
```

In this case, the "key" was a comma-delimited string containing the timestamp and latitude and longitude for each hit in the logfile, and the "value" was 1 (a single hit count).

Our Reducer then read in each line from the Mapper and kept track of the number of hits per location per minute. To do this, it stored each "key" output from the Mapper in a Python dictionary and incremented a counter each time it saw the same "key" in the Mapper output. Here's an example of what the Python dictionary looked like:

```
{
    "12:00,40.7308,-73.9970": 128,
    "12:00,37.7791,-122.4200": 33,
    "12:00,32.7781, -96.7954": 17,
    # cut off for brevity...
```

```
    "12:01,40.7308,-73.9970": 119,
    "12:01,37.7791,-122.4200": 45,
    "12:01,32.7781, -96.7954": 27,
    # ...
}
```

Once our Reducer had collected all of the input data from the Mapper, it sorted the data (based on the key) and output it in sorted order.

The code for our early versions of the Mapper and Reducer is reproduced here:

```
Mapper
#!/usr/bin/env python

import sys

# input comes from STDIN (standard input)
for line in sys.stdin:
    # remove leading and trailing whitespace
    line = line.strip()
    # split the line into words
    words = line.split('\t')

    try:
        # output the following:
        # time(HH:MM),latitude,longitude       1
        time = words[1]
        hours,mins,secs = time.split(":")
        t = hours+":"+mins

        print '%s,%s,%s\t%s' % (t, words[44], words[45], 1)
    except Exception:
        pass



    Reducer

    #!/usr/bin/env python

    from operator import itemgetter
    import sys

    locations = {}

    # input comes from STDIN
    for line in sys.stdin:
```

```
# remove leading and trailing whitespace
line = line.strip()

# parse the input we got from mapper.py
key, count = line.split('\t')

try:
    # update the count for each location (lat/lng pair)
    # per minute of the day
    count = int(count)
    locations[key] = locations.get(key, 0) + count

except Exception:
    # count was not a number or some other error,
    # so silently ignore/discard this line
    pass

# sort the data and then output
sorted_locations = sorted(locations.items(), key=itemgetter(0))
for key, count in sorted_locations:
    try:
        time,lat,lng = key.split(',')
        print '%s,%s,%s,%s'% (time, lat, lng, count)
    except Exception:
        pass
```

The New Data Format

After running our new map/reduce scripts on raw access data, we had a more precise dataset to work with. Not only did this process reduce the overall data (from
roughly 30 million lines to 3 million lines for the web access data), but it also gave us
a hit count for each location. Now we had the scale factor we were looking for. Here
is a small sample of the new data—notice the timestamp, latitude, longitude, and hit
counts (per minute):

```
12:00,039.948,-074.905,128
12:00,039.949,-082.057,1
12:00,039.951,-105.045,3
12:00,039.952,-074.995,1
12:00,039.952,-075.164,398
12:00,039.960,-075.270,1
12:00,039.963,-076.728,4
12:00,039.970,-075.832,2
12:00,039.970,-086.160,4
12:00,039.975,-075.048,23
```

Visual Scale and Other Visualization Optimizations

With the data in its new form, instead of plotting a small point for each hit per second, we could now plot a circle for each location per minute and use the hit count as a basis for the size of the circle. This would provide the desired sense of scale, enabling viewers of the visualization to easily tell the difference between the amount of traffic coming from rural Canada and from New York.

This approach also greatly reduced the amount of memory needed by the app. We still needed to keep track of all hits to the web and mobile sites in memory (so that we could fade out the hits over a three-minute period), but now that we were keeping track of locations per minute, the number of Hit objects we needed to store was greatly reduced. For any given minute, we typically have traffic coming from roughly 2,000 to 3,500 different locations around the world. Hit objects for each location must be stored in memory; each persists for three minutes, so at any given time there may be between 6,000 and 12,000 objects in memory—still a lot, but nowhere near the number we had in the previous version.

At this point, the Processing app logic needed to be updated to keep track of the number of hits per location for any point in time, and to scale the size of the circle given the number of hits. Let's look at a quick example to explain this.

Let's assume we are talking about access to our website from a specific latitude/longitude in New York (there are many in the dataset). Looking at a small period during a day, suppose we have the following number of hits beginning at each given time:

```
12:00 - 100 hits
12:01 - 110 hits
12:02 - 90 hits
12:03 - 80 hits
12:04 - 100 hits
```

When we draw the circle on the map for this location, we want the size of the circle to reflect the hit count, which gives us the sense of scale. However, we cannot simply base the size on the number of hits/views initiated during the current one-minute period. Why not? Remember that a typical visit to the site results in a three-minute stay, so we decided to keep track of the number of hits per location for three minutes and drop them from the count only after the three-minute period has passed.

Using the hit counts above, our total hit count per minute would therefore be:

```
12:00 - 100 hits (assuming no previous hits)
12:01 - 210 hits (100 + 110)
12:02 - 300 hits (100 + 110 + 90)
12:03 - 280 hits (110 + 90  + 80)
12:04 - 270 hits (90  + 80  + 100)
```

Notice how, for any given minute, we keep track of new hits during that minute plus the previous two minutes' hit counts.

Updating the Processing app with code to handle keeping track of total hits per location per minute produced the result in Figure 16-4. This new version allowed us to show the scale of hits from different locations on the map at any given minute, as well as showing how that scale expanded and contracted over the day based on the increase or decrease of traffic from each location.

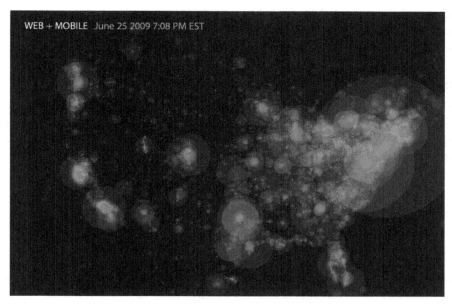

Figure 16-4. *The updated visualization showing traffic from around the U.S. to nytimes.com and mobile.nytimes.com on June 25, 2009—the yellow circles represent traffic to the website, while the red circles represent traffic to the mobile site*

Getting the Time Lapse Working

After updating the Processing app to handle the new data input format and method, we created a full 24-hour time-lapse video. We had been able to run our new code for a few hours at a time without the memory and overall machine latency problems that we were seeing before, but now it was time to generate the full time-lapse video. Instead of trying to render both the web and mobile data on the map for the first attempt at our 24-hour time lapse, we used the mobile data only (which is about 10% the size of the web data); this way, we'd see results, or possibly problems, sooner than if we tried to render both the web and mobile data.

Not knowing how far we should shrink the 24-hour time lapse (should we show the full 24 hours in a 1-minute video, a 10-minute video, or somewhere in between?), we settled on 10 minutes as a test. One of the most exciting moments of the project was pushing Processing's "Run" button when we first attempted to render 24 hours of mobile data. Rendering this data into a 10-minute time-lapse video took about two hours on a MacBook Pro. We had results!

After a few fist bumps and congratulations were thrown around, we watched the video. About two minutes in, we realized it was much too long—the video felt too slow! Time to reload and create something closer to a 1.5-minute time-lapse video.

After a few more attempts and some tweaking to the code and frame rates, we had our video. Once we had the app working for rendering the smaller mobile dataset, we cut it loose on the combined web and mobile data. Being a much larger dataset, it took much longer to render—instead of 2 hours, this one took between 24 and 36 hours, depending on the machine it was running on.

Semiautomating

Ultimately, we want to automate the entire process so that we can easily render the time lapse for any day on command. The process is semiautomated now, and we can fairly easily render multiple time-lapse videos for the same day. For example, we can render any of the following:

- Web and mobile data on a global map
- Web and mobile data on a U.S. map
- Web-only data on global and U.S. maps
- Mobile-only data on global and U.S. maps

How long does it take to render each? Well, it depends on the date and if it was a big news day (i.e., if there was a lot of traffic). For an average day, here is the approximate amount of input data for our visualization and how long it takes to render:

Mobile only

> Data file is approximately 7 MB and 300,000 lines

> Rendering takes roughly 2 hours

Web only

> Data file is approximately 70 MB and 3 million lines

> Rendering takes roughly 1 to 2 days

Web + mobile

> Data file is approximately 77 MB and 3.3 million lines

> Rendering takes roughly 1 to 2 days

Math for Rendering Time-Lapse Video

Within our Processing app, we captured video at 15 frames per second. For each frame, we drew one minute's worth of log data on the screen and then captured it to file. For 24 hours' worth of data, we are capturing 1,440 minutes of data. With 15 minutes' worth of data rendered every second, rendering 1,440 minutes gives us 96 seconds of video (roughly a minute and a half).

So, What Do We Do with This Thing?

As this book is going to press, we have just finishing rendering videos for a few days' worth of data. Outside our offices on the 28th floor of the New York Times Building, we have 10 monitors in the hallway where we display some of our visualizations, including these traffic maps. On six of the monitors, we autoplay the time-lapse videos; on the remaining screens, we display four static screenshots of the overall traffic for the day for our web and mobile sites (in the U.S. and globally). We are starting to share the videos around the company and are exploring more visualizations to see what kinds of patterns we can observe throughout the day. We are also looking at the differences in usage patterns between days that have large breaking news stories and "average" news days.

Conclusion

We've seen a few interesting patterns from the visualizations we have created so far, most of which are illustrated in Figures 16-5 through 16-8.

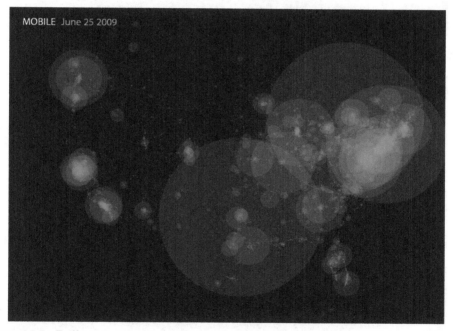

Figure 16-5. *Traffic to mobile.nytimes.com for the entire day of June 25, 2009*

* The two large circles are over Dallas, Texas, and Waterloo, Ontario. Both of these cities are mobile hubs (e.g., Waterloo is BlackBerry/RIM headquarters) and a lot of mobile traffic is proxied through Dallas and Waterloo before arriving at our servers.

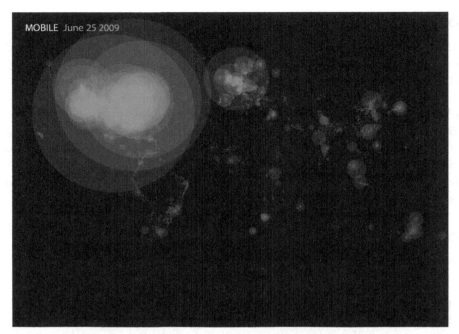

Figure 16-6. *Traffic to mobile.nytimes.com for the entire day of June 25, 2009*

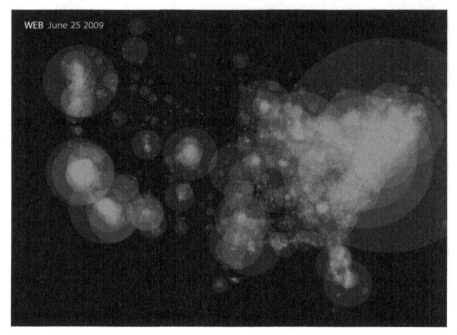

Figure 16-7. *Traffic to nytimes.com for the entire day of June 25, 2009*

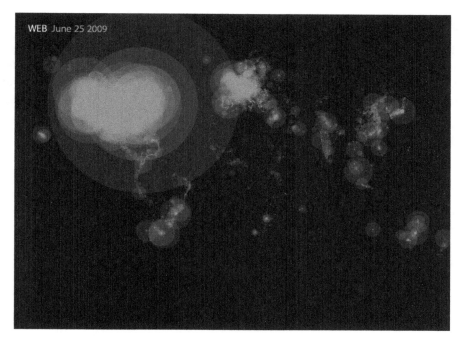

Figure 16-8. *Traffic to nytimes.com for the entire day of June 25, 2009*

First, the mobile site traffic bursts first thing in the morning in the U.S., at around 5:00 or 6:00 a.m., when people are waking up and commuting to work (especially on the East Coast). It continues to hold strong until people get into the office at around 8:30 or 9:00 a.m.; at this time, the traffic on the website surges for the first time in the day. The web traffic, which is strong throughout the day (especially around lunchtime), dips slightly during the afternoon, probably around commuting hours, when the mobile traffic pops up again. This was the behavior that we expected before beginning our research, but the visualization helped confirm our hypothesis.

Another interesting pattern to look at is the strong international traffic to both the web and mobile sites, as well as the mobile traffic coming from parts of Africa, China, India, and Japan.

We think there will be other interesting observations to make from the international and U.S. traffic patterns, and we'll explore them as we're able to render more videos from our traffic data. We invite you to watch for yourself and let us know what you see! You can view samples of the visualizations at *http://nytlabs.com/dataviz/*.

Acknowledgments

Noriaki Okada (an intern at the NYTimes R&D Lab) contributed a large part of the visualization code and research for this chapter. His work can be found at *http://okada. imrf.or.jp*. We would also like to thank Michael Kramer, Ted "Chevy's" Roden, and Dick Lipton for their unwavering support on this project.

## CHAPTER SEVENTEEN

Immersed in Unfolding Complex Systems

Lance Putnam, Graham Wakefield, Haru Ji, Basak Alper, Dennis Adderton, and Professor JoAnn Kuchera-Morin

*Media Arts and Technology,
University of California, Santa Barbara*

Our Multimodal Arena

What would it be like to walk into a real-life "Holodeck" or "Cerebro" and experience a stunning new world unlike anything seen before? Beyond this, what if we were able to experience hitherto unobservable aspects of nature, as environments into which the body cannot actually venture? In fact, these questions are on the minds of scientists and artists working together, right now, in the AlloSphere located in the California NanoSystems Institute at the University of California, Santa Barbara. We have in our hands an instrument that allows us to explore and interact with complex, high-dimensional data and systems—whether they be subatomic particles, the human brain, or entire synthetic ecosystems—as if they were fully immersive worlds.

The AlloSphere is one of the largest scientific/artistic instruments/laboratories in the world for immersive visualization, sonification, and multimodal data manipulation. It is a three-story sphere finely tuned for perceptual experiences with a 360-degree, super-black, nonreflective screen surrounded by a multichannel loudspeaker array, all housed in an echo-free chamber (see Figure 17-1). Multiple users standing on the central bridge (Figure 17-2) can interact through myriad multimodal devices as they experience stereographic projections and spatial audio.

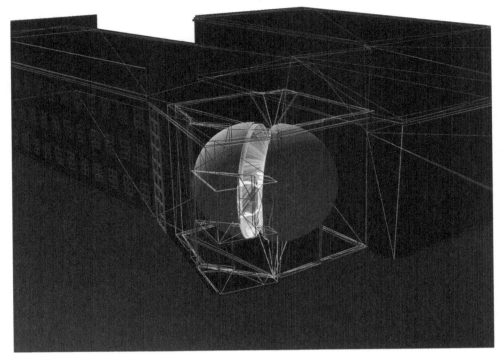

Figure 17-1. *A virtual real-scale model of the AlloSphere*

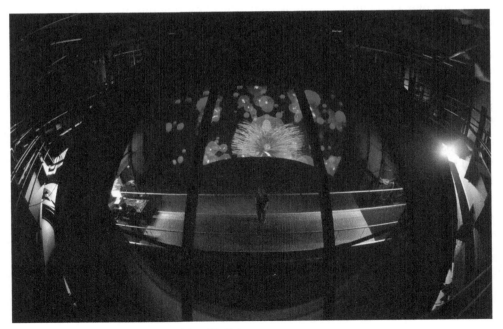

Figure 17-2. *A full-scale photo of the AlloSphere*

The AlloSphere was conceived by composer JoAnn Kuchera-Morin as a general-purpose eye- and ear-limiting multimedia instrument for both new modes of artistic expression and scientific discovery. Her intention was to provide a common meeting ground where diverse researchers can share insights and pursue similar fundamental questions about symmetry, beauty, pattern formation, and emergence. Our attitude to this unique opportunity is to establish a frontier of research that is grounded in both art and science, but not constrained to either one. This has required a holistic rethinking of the fundamental aspects of our creative medium: computation, data, process, perception, interaction, immersion, and evaluation.

With artists, scientists, and engineers working together in the AlloSphere to uncover new worlds through unique and compelling simulations and visualizations, we are implementing our concept of beauty as truth. We help researchers find this truth through the visualization and sonification of intriguing equations. These visualizations offer elegant solutions in their unfolding, allowing us to discover symmetry—and broken symmetry—as it unfolds in these equations.

Our Roadmap to Creative Thinking

The AlloSphere indeed provides a compelling interactive, multimodal environment for a new type of interdisciplinary research that, from the start, tightly integrates quantitative and qualitative approaches to problem solving and discovery. It also offers a unique opportunity for experiencing—using all of our senses—how complex systems unfold over time. We have begun to uncover common themes in how these systems are described in terms of computational constructs and how they can be represented in terms of beauty and symmetry. Our challenge and opportunity in composing beautiful visualizations is thus to strike a balance of both mathematical truth and perceptual expression, and to introduce a new form of art and research as epistemological experiment.

Beauty and Symmetry

Beauty no doubt plays a central role in our perceptual engagement, as it is closely related to symmetry. In fact, beauty and symmetry have shared an intimate relationship since the time of the ancient Pythagoreans, who stated that the key to beauty lies in the proportions of parts and their interrelationships, and that symmetry and harmony are the interrelationships in the domains of sight and hearing, respectively (Tatarkiewicz 1972). This theory has been one of the most enduring throughout our cultural history.

Indeed, symmetry—and its more formal definition as "invariance to transformation" (Weyl 1952)—is the basis of some of the most profound scientific theories of nature, including special relativity, the laws of conservation, and string theory. Symmetry has also played a less acknowledged but vital role in computational simulation. In ancient times, we could observe only the patterns in nature around us; today, through the control over proportion afforded by computation, we can compose systems that generate complex natural patterns with precision and autonomy. At the heart of these complex patterns, we do indeed find symmetries. In fact, symmetry often helps guide our search for significant patterns in the data.

The Computational Medium

Computation and mathematics provide an alluring common language between scientific models and aesthetic practice. Computation is a vital tool for scientific simulation and also an open-ended material for art. By designing and instantiating complex autonomous systems, we open the door to a new kind of knowledge based on synthesis of parts.[*]

Regardless of the questions we want to ask, computation necessitates a formal and discrete description of the basic components of the data and a consideration of the limits of real-time processing. We have found, particularly for physically based models, that the data we work with consists primarily of values associated with positions in space and/or time. Values represent particular internal intensities, such as velocity, flux, frequency, or complex phase, and are typically correlated to positions in space and/or time. Many of the visualization techniques we apply involve filtering out values at a certain position (such as a cross-section) or positions at a certain value (such as a contour line).

How the values and positions are instantiated during a program's execution varies. The values can be explicit (given at regular sampling points or as position/value pairs) or implicit (computed on the fly using an equation or algorithm). Likewise, the positions can be explicit (as position/value pairs) or implicit (determined from the dimensions of a regular lattice).

In working with various computational models, we have observed three general paradigms in how data is represented for storage and processing:

- As a regular lattice of sampled values

- As a collection of position/value pairs

- As a function of position

The difference between the first two is the same as the two general ways images can be represented on a computer: raster-based (as a matrix of pixels) or vector-based (as a set of points connected with curves). The third paradigm is more like a black box that takes in a position and outputs a corresponding value.

With each paradigm, there are specific trade-offs. A lattice permits models consisting of unexpected signals and local interactions, but it requires sampling, leading to aliasing and the need for potentially large amounts of memory to model systems at

---

[*] The field of Artificial Life, for example, attempts to better understand life by attempting to reconstruct its processes *in digito*, but has brought with it a fascinating discussion of creativity itself.

an appropriate level of resolution. In contrast, the position/value and function paradigms allow fine or arbitrary spatial resolution, but make it computationally difficult to model interactions between entities.

A conceptual division that follows naturally from these paradigms is between spatiotemporal fields and sets of free agents. *Fields* are a type of regular lattice in space (possibly time-varying) and serve as the substrata of complex systems. They provide the underlying architecture of structure and dynamics within a system. Fields represent things like density distributions, fluids, and waves. The concept of a field exists in many disciplines: developmental biology has the morphogenetic field and epigenetic landscape, evolutionary biology has the fitness landscape, and physics has quantum fields and wavefunctions. *Agents* are collections of position/value pairs and serve as the superstrata of complex systems. Agents represent actual discrete entities, possibly mobile, in continuous space. They allow us to observe fields more clearly by focusing finely on parts of the entire system and filtering it to see its patterns of invariance. In addition, agents often interact with one another by reading and writing values in a field.

Interpretation As a Filter

Our work involves not only the design and instantiation of complex systems, but also—and just as importantly—the composition of a filter that reduces the overwhelming vastness of the computational/mathematical spaces into forms that we can perceive and draw meaning from. In other words, visualization and sonification involve both the organization of materials (composition) and the presentation of the patterns we are trying to reveal (interpretation).

We often ask ourselves the question "what are we looking for in the data or system?" To begin answering this question, we can say that we are looking for the interesting patterns that reveal essential aspects of the system as it unfolds. Furthermore, we find that utilizing symmetry helps guide our search for significant patterns. The visualization techniques we commonly apply, such as isosurfaces, contours, streamlines, and particle flows, show aspects of a system where its values (or a derived quantity of them) are equivalent or invariant. These "pockets of symmetry" show the similarities in the system and tend to provide a good starting point for more deeply understanding its behaviors and patterns. We know that too much symmetry reduces significance, while too little symmetry is overwhelming; the filter must fall between these extremes of order and disorder. This also applies to time: patterns of interest must maintain identity long enough to be recognized, but also change sufficiently to capture attention.

Composing a filter is an adaptive process that occurs within a modality just as much as across modalities. We find that multimodal representation is important for revealing otherwise hidden or nonobvious symmetries and asymmetries in data. Sometimes, the most natural sensory modality of a dataset or process will not fully depict important aspects of its structure. For example, we find that symmetries of waveforms are better seen and that slightly broken symmetries in spatial data are better heard. We use the transformational capacities of computation to map amongst and between modalities, searching for a balance that will give a more complete mental picture of the phenomena at hand. In fact, there is evidence that the brain's memory system consists of an "episodic buffer" that integrates visual and aural sensory information into a multi-dimensional code that interfaces with long-term memory and can subsequently affect long-term learning (Baddeley 2000).

The agent-based model has played a dominant role in our filtering and presentation of data and systems. Agents are appealing from both a visual and an aural sense since they can have smoother and more continuous movements, versus being restricted to moving on a discrete lattice. In return, they allow us to observe dominant patterns in systems through coherent structures, thus reducing noise. One example is using agents to show flux across a coarsely sampled field using smooth and continuous curves.

Project Discussion

In this section, six research projects will be discussed that span areas ranging from artistic/scientific mathematical abstraction to precise multimodal representation of computational models based on real scientific data and theories. We'll move from real biological data through bio-inspired evolutionary developmental algorithms, to the world of atoms; then, moving from the atomic level down to the electron level in one single hydrogen atom, we will finally arrive at a project that represents the coherent precession of an electron spin.

Allobrain

By Graham Wakefield, John Thompson, Lance Putnam, Wesley Smith, and Charlie Roberts (Media Arts and Technology)

Faculty Directors: Professor JoAnn Kuchera-Morin and Professor Marcos Novak (Media Arts and Technology)

In the Allobrain, we fly through the cortex of the human brain (Figure 17-3). Structural components of functional magnetic resonance imaging (fMRI) data are used to create a space that can be experienced as a "world" through which we can navigate. The raw data maps density values of cerebral metabolic activity across a lattice of spatial coordinates throughout the brain; the visualization contains two isosurfaces through this dataset, selected by the intensity of brain tissue response to the fMRI scan. (An *isosurface* is a 3D contour representing points of a constant value.) Inside this world are "search agents" that navigate autonomously to mine the data, indicating their presence spatially and visually, clustering in regions of interest and reporting back to us through musical sound. "Wanderer agents," color-coded to specific brain regions, take a random walk through the data looking for high blood-density levels. They alert large packs of "cluster agents" to do finer-detailed analysis and visualization in these regions of interest. The wanderer agents can also be commanded to report back to the center of the screen and sing blood-density levels, where higher pitches correlate to higher levels.

Figure 17-3. *Inside the Allobrain*

One can imagine applications not only for medical diagnostics but also for psychological studies in cognition and perception: by revealing many dimensions of information in a single viewing, Allobrain facilitates early discovery of cellular disorder and understanding of how the brain functions. In fact, visual artist and trans-architect Marcos Novak—the creator of this world, and whose brain it is—conceived the project to engage with the neurological bases of aesthetic appreciation. He describes his work as follows:

> When we say that something is "beautiful," what parts of the brain are involved in that assessment, and how? Since there is such great variation among people in aesthetic matters, a better approach to the question of beauty may be to study one or few instances as closed systems, learn as much as possible about them, and then [determine] if what has been learned can be generalized to others.
>
> In particular, this work aims to construct a situation in which most of the elements that pertain to the making of something beautiful are accessible to investigation. Specifically:
>
> - the work to be appraised as beautiful or not
>
> - the method and mechanism of its generation
>
> - the creator, appraiser, and investigator of the work

Furthermore, the aim (scientifically and artistically) is to create a feedback loop in which the art affects the brain and the brain generates new data that creates new art, that in turn affects the brain, that generates new data, and so on.

To seed the process, I wrote a generative algorithm that produced stimuli that I could not anticipate in detail, and that triggered in me the reaction of beauty (in terms of visual and spatial composition). The stimuli consisted of either a) an interactive/generative moving/changing image, [or] b) video recordings of this so that they could be used in the fMRI machine. While in the fMRI machine, I was presented with this video (which I had not seen previously). Whenever I felt that the visual compositions were beautiful to me, I pressed a button. The pressing of the button was timed, so that it could be correlated with the activity of the brain at that instant. The fMRI data was converted into an immersive environment, or "world." This step allows two parallel possibilities: from a scientific viewpoint, it permits the structural and functional data to be perceived from within in ways that conventional visualization techniques do not allow. From an artistic viewpoint, it proposes a novel art form in which the brain (and subsequent mind) produces the world, and the world alters the mind, which in turn produces another world, and so on. In both cases, a feedback loop can be constructed in which the user's response itself helps generate the stimuli that trigger that response, thus amplifying the effect.

Presently, the Allobrain reveals one static snapshot of a thought. As we move the project forward, real-time interactive fMRI data will allow researchers to be immersed in their own thoughts and watch them transform and change, as in Novak's description. The brain will perceive the world and then transform the world through its perception.

Artificial Nature

By Haru Ji and Graham Wakefield (Media Arts and Technology)

http://artificialnature.mat.ucsb.edu

We move now from raw biological data to the processes and systems at the roots of life. Artificial Nature is a transdisciplinary research project and bio-inspired immersive art installation based on generative models drawn from systems biology, artificial life, and complexity sciences rather than empirical data. The computational world of Artificial Nature is an ecosystem consisting of populations of organisms interacting within a dynamic environment, with which spectators interact.

The environment is a spatial field based upon equations of fluid dynamics. Simple particles flowing within it represent different nutrient types (hue) and energy levels (brightness), and interact kinetically with one another. These particles provide the metabolic fuel for the organisms, which are modeled as autonomous agents. Both ingestion of nutrients and disposal of waste products are necessary for organisms to survive and reproduce.

The appearance and autonomous activity of organisms is determined through the interpretation of their genetic descriptions according to local (spatial and historical) conditions. For example, sufficient accumulation of energy triggers some organisms to generate children by asexual reproduction, with small chances of mutation. The shape of these organisms is based upon the Boy surface equation (Boy 1901) and is gradually varied over their lifetimes to indicate gradual growth and development, while health is represented by opacity.

Activities such as ingestion, reproduction, and detection of neighbors are accompanied by different varieties of chirp-like songs, which are fully spatialized in the AlloSphere. These sounds are bright, transient-rich, and tightly clustered, making them easier to distinguish from one another, localize, and connect to visual events.

Spectators can explore this world freely and endlessly using a six-degrees-of-freedom navigator device and can influence it indirectly, creating turbulence just as they might have by playing in a stream or sandpit in their childhood. Sensory data collected through a camera-eye and microphone-ear, and sometimes through touch, become the environmental conditions to which the organisms must adapt. The turbulence of the fluid also feeds back to influence the navigation of the spectators. The entire ecosystem, including the spectators themselves, generates continuous patterns of emergent beauty (Figures 17-4 and 17-5).

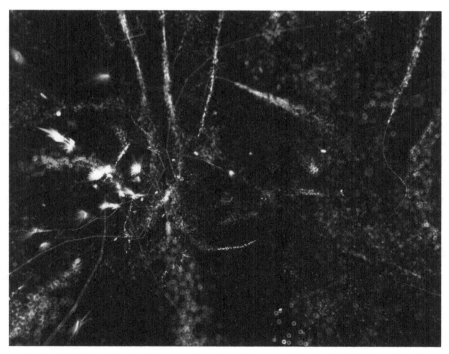

Figure 17-4. *Artificial nutrients being produced and dispersed in the fluid fields of Artificial Nature (version 1: Infinite Game)*

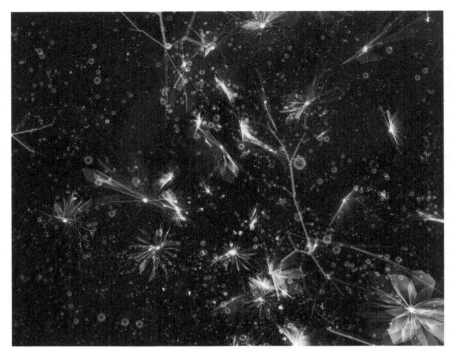

Figure 17-5. *Artificial organisms growing and interacting in Artificial Nature (version 2: Fluid Space)*

We asked what form of art could evolve in the space of the AlloSphere. Artificial Nature responds consciously to this challenge as an immersive artwork, a new kind of experience within an alternative environment—an infinitely unfolding possible world. The open-ended nature of Artificial Nature is grounded in the embodiment of complex adaptive systems drawn from artificial life. These agent-based techniques lend themselves to real-time simulations, and multimodal interaction embeds spectators into the ecosystemic network.

Artificial Nature is itself a project within a larger evolution. As we embed more dimensions and relations into it, new potentials for pattern, structure, meaning, and beauty emerge.

Hydrogen Bond

By Basak Alper, Wesley Smith, Lance Putnam, and Charlie Roberts (Media Arts and Technology), and Anderson Janotti (Materials Research Laboratory)

Faculty Directors: Professor JoAnn Kuchera-Morin (Media Arts and Technology) and Professor Chris G. Van de Walle (Materials Research Laboratory)

As we move from the biological and macroscopic world, we enter the world of atoms and a new materials compound for clean technology, the multicenter hydrogen bond. This is a very important step for the fabrication of transparent solar cells and low-cost display devices. Normally, hydrogen forms a *covalent bond* with other elements (meaning that it bonds by sharing a pair of electrons—since hydrogen has only one electron, it can form only one covalent bond at a time), but in a zinc-oxide lattice it bonds anomalously to four zinc atoms, forming a tetrahedral bond structure.

Our materials science colleagues in the Solid State Lighting and Energy Center at UCSB discovered this unique type of bond structure and requested that we represent their simulation data visually and sonically in ways that their existing tools would not permit. The data we received was a three-dimensional lattice of electrostatic charge density at the site of the hydrogen bond. Visualizing this kind of volumetric data poses a significant challenge as there is no natural way to see inside a solid shape.

A common way of visualizing volumetric data is to draw isosurfaces to reveal internal curvature. By applying isosurfaces to the charge density, we made the shape of the bond structure more clearly visible in a way similar to how contour lines are used on a map to reveal changes in height. Locating local maxima/minima in the data field was also an important goal for the scientists, as it would help them identify critical regions in the bond. We solved this problem by interpreting the gradient as a volumetric data field. Initially we couldn't get any results, because the sampling distance of the data was much larger than the regions we were looking for. We explained how the visualization algorithm worked and convinced the scientists to generate higher-resolution data. Once we got the high-resolution data, drawing zero-value isosurfaces in the gradient field successfully showed the local maxima/minima regions.

To reveal more of the field's shape, we used a visualization technique called *streamlines* that produces curves that run along the flow of a vector field. We started the streamlines near the center of the hydrogen atom and allowed them to flow outward "down" the gradient, where hue indicated fast (red) and slow (green) movement. Although our science partners initially regarded the streamlines as strange, they proved themselves effective by converging upon critical locations in the bond structure.

We extended the standard visualization tools by adding the ability to choose between different visualization modes and overlay selected visualizations in a single view (see Figure 17-6). Conveying different layers of information in one view requires drawing a picture where clutter and ambiguity is minimized. To this end, we utilized a custom lighting algorithm that is less diffused and therefore highlights the curvature of the isosurfaces. We composited both transparent and wireframe renderings to ease perception of multiple transparent surfaces. We found that streamlines and isosurfaces were natural visual complements as they had the ability to show information in perpendicular directions. Showing streamlines and isosurfaces together was not perceived as being as problematic as showing multiple layers of isosurfaces, since they were easier to visually differentiate.

Figure 17-6. *Closeup view of hydrogen in a tetrahedral bond with four zinc atoms (blue)*

In addition to visuals, we used spatial audio for localizing the bond location and the user's position in the lattice (Figure 17-7). In order to give a sonic identity to the atoms, we sonified the *emission spectra* (the relative electromagnetic radiation) of hydrogen, zinc, and oxygen by pitch-shifting their respective emission frequencies down 10 octaves to the audible range.

Figure 17-7. *Researchers immersed in the hydrogen bond*

Given the time-invariant and three-dimensional nature of the data, deciding how to sonify it was a challenge. One solution we came up with was to scan through the density field along a parametric curve. We used a Lissajous curve, since it exhibits a high degree of spatial symmetry and smoothness, minimizing sonic distortion. While this technique had no visual complement, it produced characteristic sounds and helped localize the bond, producing a more complete multimodal experience.

Hydrogen Atom

By Lance Putnam and Charlie Roberts (Media Arts and Technology)

Faculty Directors: Professor Luca Peliti (Kavli Institute of Theoretical Physics) and Professor JoAnn Kuchera-Morin (Media Arts and Technology)

We now move from a lattice of atoms down to the electron cloud of a single hydrogen atom. Much is known about the shapes of single hydrogen atom orbitals, and physicists have little trouble picturing them in their minds. However, when two or more time-varying orbitals are mixed together in superposition, the resulting electron cloud is complex and not readily apparent from the individual equations. Furthermore, mathematical equations and static images do not capture the dynamics of its complex temporal evolution.

Our aim with this work was to create a multimodal experience of a "hydrogen-like" atom through interactive visualization and sonification of its electron wavefunction. We modeled the atomic orbitals as solutions to the time-dependent Schrödinger equation with a spherically symmetric potential given by Coulomb's law of electrostatic force. In this model, the relationship between the nucleus and electron is akin to a bowl (the nucleus) filled with liquid (the electron), with the difference that the liquid can have many different resting shapes and extend outside of the bowl. For computation, the time-invariant structures of the single orbitals were precomputed and stored in a 3D lattice; then, during the simulation, they evolved individually and were mixed together spatially. We programmed several preset orbital superpositions to observe dynamic behaviors such as photon emission and absorption.

The first visualization technique we tried was to render the electron cloud as a 3D volume. This made it easy to see the global, outer shape of the wavefunction, but it was difficult to see its inner and more local structure. To address this, we superimposed collections of agents on the volume rendering that moved along different flows in the wavefunction. This way, we could simultaneously get a sense of the global and local structure of the cloud. We found that using colored lines provided a reasonable compromise among number of mapping dimensions, visual complexity, and computational efficiency (Figure 17-8). Colored line agents gave us three internal dimensions of color and four spatial dimensions of orientation and length that we could use for mapping purposes. We used hue to distinguish different types of flow and orientation to show direction. In addition, the brightness and length of the lines were varied to smoothly fade agents into and out of the scene.

Figure 17-8. *Light emitting configuration of a hydrogen atom*

We also wanted to use sound as a way of notifying us of certain types of events—such as the emergence or dissipation of certain types of shapes—occurring within the cloud. To do this, we used a slight variation on a synthesis technique called *scanned synthesis*. We scanned along the agents like a read head on an audio tape loop and listened to the wavefunction amplitude at their locations. By changing the scan rate, we could change the pitch of the sound. Lower pitches worked best at revealing the local variations in shape, while higher pitches worked best at indicating global characteristics. We also found it effective to assign different pitch classes (pitches a whole number of octaves apart) to the different types of agents so that they could be sonically distinguished from one another. This scanning method was successful in alerting us when and where a cluster of agents formed at a singularity or attractor basin, but did not work so well at informing us about the particular shape formed. Our solution to representing the system more holistically was not to augment single modalities, but to take a multimodal approach, leaving overall shape to visuals and emergence of local structures over time to sound.

An unexpected outcome of doing this representation was seeing a drastic change in the complexity and richness of the wavefunction patterns going from single orbitals to mixtures (Figure 17-9). The composite patterns that emerged had no obvious relation to the parts and were not at all evident from the mathematical equations. We found that interference of waves, a simple and well-known physical mechanism, can serve as a powerful construct when thinking about the creation of complex patterns and emergent behavior.

Figure 17-9. *Higher-order orbital mixture of a hydrogen atom*

Hydrogen Atom with Spin

By Lance Putnam (Media Arts and Technology)

Faculty Directors: Professor Luca Peliti (Kavli Institute of Theoretical Physics) and Professor JoAnn Kuchera-Morin (Media Arts and Technology)

With this project, we desired to expand on the previous hydrogen atom project by using a more complete physical model that included the spin quantum number. We also wanted to move away from the regular sampling in space of the wavefunction toward something with finer spatial resolution. We decided it would be best to not precompute and store the orbitals ahead of time, but instead to compute everything on the fly so that we could get the exact values of the wavefunction at all points in space. In this sense, the computational representation of the wavefunction changed from a lattice of values to a function of position. This new approach also gave us a new perspective on agents as a *general-purpose* visualization and sonification tool. The agents could not only show the derived flows of the wavefunction through their individual movements, but also represent something about its state, such as its oscillation phases. Furthermore, the agents could be programmed to act in an ensemble-like manner to create smoother and more connected shapes.

We started by positioning the line agents on a grid and then modifying their orientation and length based on the underlying wavefunction amplitude. While this gave us a good sense of global characteristics, we found the spatial artifacts (Moiré patterns), due to their regular positioning in space, to be visually disturbing and misleading. To avoid these artifacts, we next tried to randomly position the agents within a cube. This succeeded in eliminating the artifacts, but uncovered two more serious and fundamental problems. First of all, we found it difficult to visually fuse all the individual agents into a coherent form from their individual line shapes. Second, we found that distributing the agents uniformly in 3D space does not lend itself to a natural method of sonification. While we could use separate spatial structures for visualization and sonification, we had found in previous projects—namely, the hydrogen bond project—that an underlying connectedness between aural and visual representation is important for comprehending the scene.

Our solution to these connectivity problems was to arrange the line agents into a loop and keep the agents connected to one another by putting springs between them. This gave us an elastic ribbon that would remain smooth and connected, but still have enough freedom to move through the space and show local properties of the measured field. The width of the loop was mapped to the probability density so that sharp spikes would indicate a high probability of finding the electron at that position (Figure 17-10). The loop also worked well for showing wavefunction states that were more distributed throughout space (Figure 17-11).

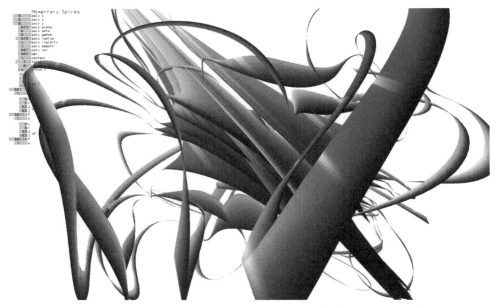

Figure 17-10. *Constructive interference between orbitals of a hydrogen atom with spin*

Figure 17-11. *Outer shell mixture of a hydrogen atom with spin*

The loop, being smooth, also permitted a desirable shape for scanning through the agents for sonification, as was done with the spinless atom. Visually, the loop provided a good compromise between transparency, coherency of shape, and depiction of global and local attributes.

Coherent Precession of Electron Spin

By Dennis Adderton and Lance Putnam (Media Arts and Technology), and Jesse Berezovsky (Center for Spintronics and Quantum Computing)

Faculty Directors: Professor JoAnn Kuchera-Morin (Media Arts and Technology) and Professor David Awschalom (Center for Spintronics and Quantum Computing)

The goal of this project was to represent the *coherent precession*, or change in rotation, of an electron spin within a quantum dot. Seeking out the most capable apparatus for measuring the result of quantum coherence in just such a nanoscale device, we visited the spintronics lab in the UCSB Physics department to learn about Kerr rotation microscopy. This is an optical experiment wherein a very fast laser pulse is focused onto a semiconductor quantum device. The polarization of the pulse induces coherent precession of a single electron spin in the quantum dot. A subsequent pulse measures the rotating polarization of the quantum dot to capture a picture of the precessing spin. From this measurement, it is possible to quantify a characteristic decay time for quantum coherence in the device. Decoherence of the quantum state marks the transition from the quantum to the classical world.

To represent the phenomena of the experiment through sonification, we slowed it down one million times. This allowed us to hear the tone of the electron and the buzz of the pulsing laser. To visualize the phenomena of spin precession, we plotted phase angle on the Bloch sphere, a standard graphical tool for physicists. At this point, we relied on a simple equation from a published experiment (Berezovsky 2008) to give the three-dimensional dynamics (Figure 17-12).

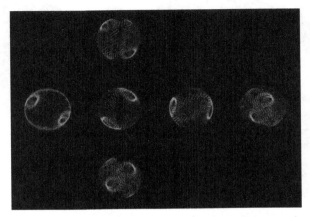

Figure 17-12. *Multiple perspectives on Bloch sphere showing spin precession*

This rudimentary test stimulated our senses but immediately revealed an overly simple aspect of the model that was not obvious from the outset. Although the precession made interesting spherical patterns visually, its temporal components were predominantly sinusoidal and quickly became boring to listen to. It became clear that a more complex system was required to immerse us in a quantum reality.

To engage our senses, we require a more complete quantum mechanical model of nature, rather than a simplified model of the experiment. Representing a theoretical model requires interpretation. Aural and visual analogies are made. As an artist, there is a need to construct an artifact so that something tangible can be discussed. The artwork becomes a philosophical apparatus in the discourse of truth—a truth connected directly to the mathematics that is being visualized and sonified.

These works serve as a basis for our philosophical premise that beautiful visualization is connected to the visualization and sonification of complex mathematical systems that make and break symmetry.

Conclusion

In the AlloSphere, visualization transforms into beautiful immersive multimodal representation, transformation, and creation, resulting in the evolution of a unique field. This new field merges the different criteria and metrics of art and science—art as speculation, generation, and transformation, and science as model/theory building and validation. As we move forward with our research, a new, yet "classical," style of thought is unfolding that integrates science and art into a new environment: a place where new art and new technology emerge in mutual adaptation. As this emerging field and its computation-driven medium develop, the distinction among artists, scientists, and engineers begins to disappear and we realize that we are all engineers, scientists, and artists—we all design, analyze, and create.

References

Baddeley, Alan. 2000. "A new component of working memory?" *Trends in Cognitive Sciences* 4, no. 11: 417–423.

Berezovsky, J., M.H. Mikkelsen, N.G. Stoltz, L.A. Coldren, and D.D. Awschalom. 2008. "Picosecond coherent optical manipulation of a single electron spin in a quantum dot." *Science* 320, no. 5874: 349–352.

Boy, Werner. 1901. "Über die curvatura integra und die topologie der geschlossener flachen." PhD diss., Universität Göttingen, Göttingen.

Tatarkiewicz, Wladyslaw. 1972. "The great theory of beauty and its decline." *Journal of Aesthetics and Art Criticism* 31, no. 2: 165–180.

Weyl, Hermann. 1952. *Symmetry*. Princeton, NJ: Princeton University Press.

## CHAPTER EIGHTEEN

Postmortem Visualization: The Real Gold Standard

Anders Persson

THIS CHAPTER'S TOPIC IS EXTREMELY IMPORTANT to those who work in the field of medical information visualization. Emerging technologies are enabling visual representations and interaction techniques that take advantage of the human eye's broad-bandwidth pathway into the mind, allowing users to see, explore, understand, and validate large amounts of complex information at once.

A striking feature of both clinical routine and medical research today is the overwhelming amount of information—particularly, information represented as images. Practitioners are dealing with ever-larger numbers of images (hundreds or thousands rather than dozens) and more complex, higher-dimensional information (vectors or tensors rather than scalar values, arranged in image volumes directly corresponding to the anatomy rather than flat images). However, they typically still use simple two-dimensional devices such as conventional monitors to review this overflow of images, one by one. As the bottleneck is no longer the acquisition of data, future progress will depend on the development of appropriate methods for handling and analyzing the information, as well as making it comprehensible to users. One of the most important issues for the future is the workflow. The entire chain from the acquisition of data until the point at which the clinician receives the diagnostic information must be optimized, and new methods must be validated.

Normally, performing this validation process on living patients has its limitations. It can in some cases be impossible to know if the acquired diagnostic information is correct as long as the patient is alive; the real gold standard is missing. Postmortem imaging has the potential to solve this problem.

The methodology of autopsy has not undergone any major transformation since its introduction in the middle of the 19th century. However, new radiological digital imaging methods, such as multidetector computed tomography (MDCT) and magnetic resonance imaging (MRI), have the potential to become the main diagnostic tools in clinical and forensic pathology in the future. Postmortem visualization may prove to be a crucial tool in shaping tomorrow's healthcare, by validating new imaging technology and for quality assurance issues.

Background

The importance of autopsy procedures leading to the establishment of the cause of death is well known. In forensic cases, the autopsy can provide key information and guide the criminal investigation. The decreasing trend in the frequency of autopsies over the past years has become a serious issue.

A recent addition to the autopsy workflow is the possibility of conducting postmortem imaging—in its 3D version, also called *virtual autopsy* (VA)—using MDCT or MRI data from scans of cadavers and with direct volume rendering (DVR) 3D techniques. At the foundation of the VA development are the modern imaging modalities that can generate large, high-quality datasets with submillimeter precision. Interactive visualization of these 3D datasets can provide valuable insight into the corpses and enables noninvasive diagnostic procedures. Efficient handling and analysis of the datasets is, however, problematic. For instance, in postmortem CT imaging, not being limited by a certain radiation dose per patient means the datasets can be generated with such a high resolution that they become difficult to handle in today's archive retrieval and interactive visualization systems, specifically in the case of full body scans.

Several studies have shown the great potential of virtual autopsy in forensic investigations. This chapter will investigate several of the reasons for the rising interest in VA.

Impact on Forensic Work

The main questions to be assessed in examinations of the deceased are the cause and manner of death and the severity of injuries suffered, as well as the possibility of forensic reconstructions based on the obtained findings. Forensic documentation of postmortem findings is predominantly based on the same autopsy techniques and protocols that have been used for centuries. The main tools used are scalpels, verbal descriptions, and photographs. A major disadvantage of this approach is that the documentation happens in a haphazard, subjective, and observer-dependent manner. Any findings that have not been documented are irreparably destroyed when the cadaver is sent to the crematory. Modern cross-sectional imaging techniques can overcome these shortcomings, as they provide datasets of cadavers that contain the findings in real dimensions and are storable for the future (Figures 18-1 and 18-2). The digitally acquired data can be referred to at any time as new questions arise, or may be sent to additional experts for a second opinion.

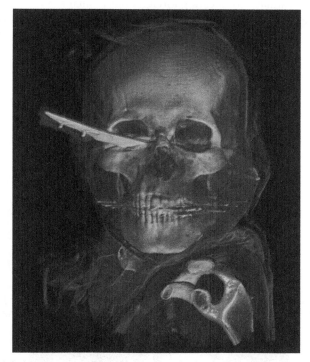

Figure 18-1. *Metal objects can easily be located in the body with computed tomography. In this murder case, there is a knife that penetrates the face, but CT proved that this was not the cause of death.*

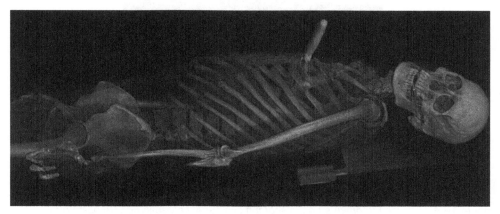

Figure 18-2. *This image shows the cause of death in another case, where the victim was stabbed through the heart with a kitchen knife.*

Some findings that are difficult to visualize in a conventional autopsy can easily be seen in a full body CT, such as air distribution within the body—e.g., in the pneumothorax, pneumopericardium, bloodstream (air embolism), and wound channels (Figure 18-3). A CT can also be invaluable for locating foreign objects such as metal fragments and bullets, which are of great importance for the forensic pathologist (Figure 18-4).

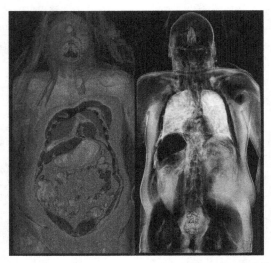

Figure 18-3. *The acquired CT data can be visualized interactively with different parameter settings: in this case, soft tissue to the left and air distribution in the body to the right.*

Figure 18-4. *Tiny lead fragments from a shotgun can easily be visualized with postmortem CT. In a conventional autopsy, these fragments can be difficult or even impossible to find.*

The Virtual Autopsy Procedure

The Center for Medical Image Science and Visualization (CMIV) at Linköping University Hospital in Sweden, in collaboration with the Swedish National Board of Forensic Medicine, has developed a procedure for virtual autopsy that is now used routinely for forensic work. This method has been in use since 2003 and has been applied to over 300 cases so far (mostly homicides). Our experience with VA has shown that full-body, high-resolution DVR visualizations are of great value in criminal investigations and for the validation of new technologies on living patients. Our work has focused on the total workflow for postmortem MDCT and on developing a new type of software that can visualize full-body datasets that could previously only be viewed in separate parts and with limited interactivity (Figures 18-5 to 18-7).

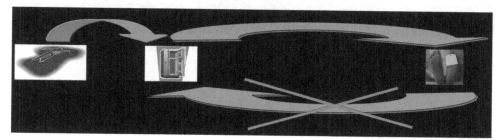

Figure 18-5. *After a conventional autopsy, it is impossible to go back. Findings that have not been documented are irreparably destroyed when the cadaver is sent to the crematory.*

Figure 18-6. *With CT and/or MRI added to the pipeline, it is always possible to go back and redo the virtual autopsy. The digitally acquired data can be referred to at any time when new questions arise, and may be sent to experts for a second opinion.*

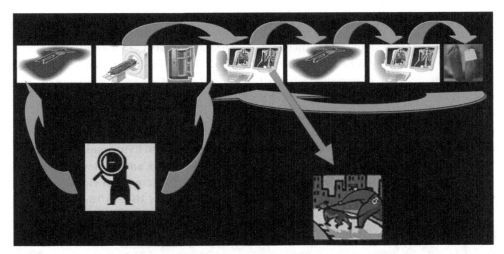

Figure 18-7. *There is a turf battle between the CSI guys and the police regarding keeping the body in the cold storage room. The police are keen on having the autopsy done as soon as possible. The CSI guys try to close the crime scene investigation before the autopsy takes place. Postmortem imaging solves this problem. A preliminary report from the postmortem CT examination makes it possible to preserve the body in the cold storage room.*

Data Acquisition

The traditional physical autopsy at CMIV is extended by adding the CT and MRI as VA activities. In most cases, the forensic pathologist comes to the crime scene and oversees the handling of the human cadaver, which is placed in a sealed body bag before being transported to the forensic department and put in cold storage. The following morning, a full-body dual source CT (DSCT) scan is performed at CMIV with a state-of-the-art SOMATOM Definition Flash scanner (from Siemens Medical Solutions in Germany). Currently, both single- and dual-energy modes are used for virtual autopsy cases; see Figure 18-8(a) and (b). In selected cases, an MRI examination is also performed (using an Achieva 1.5T scanner, from Philips Medical Systems in The Netherlands). All children are routinely examined with MRI, because it offers superior visualization of the brain compared to DSCT (Figure 18-9 and 18-11). The cadaver remains in the body bag throughout the virtual autopsy procedure to ensure the security of technical evidence of forensic value, such as fibers and body fluids, and to avoid contamination.

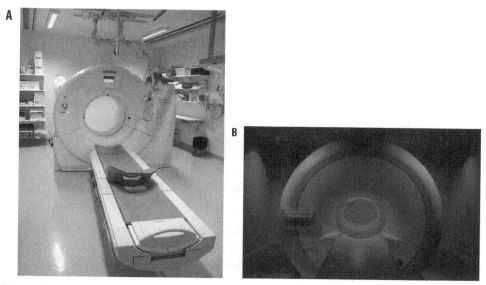

Figure 18-8. *(a) A state-of-the-art dual source computed tomography scanner with dual energy possibilities. (b) A magnetic resonance scanner. Both scanners are used for virtual autopsies at CMIV.*

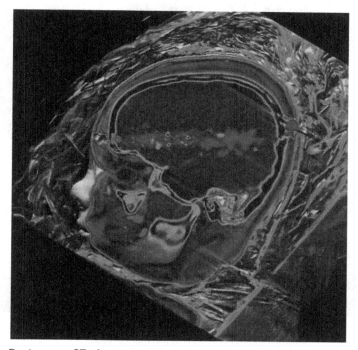

Figure 18-9. *Dual energy CT of a small child who has been shot. Note the excellent visualization of the bullet and the bullet track. Easy to present in the courtroom.*

Computed tomography: Use of dual energy CT

Dual energy CT (DECT) with two x-ray sources running simultaneously at different energies can acquire two datasets showing different attenuation levels. DECT allows additional information about the elementary chemical composition of CT-scanned material to be obtained. Compton scattering can be determined by using two different average photo energies, which correspond to two different tube voltages (80 and 140 kV). In other words, x-ray absorption is energy-dependent—e.g., scanning an object with 80 kV results in a different attenuation than scanning it with 140 kV. This physics phenomenon can help to discriminate between materials with similar atomic numbers, such as calcium and iodine contrast. Colors can then be assigned according to changes in the CT numbers between the two energy settings, and the resulting color-mapped, dual-energy image can differentiate between calcifications and iodine contrast.

This technique can also be used to better visualize postmortem blood clots in vessels, and possibly bleeding in soft tissue. The material-specific difference in attenuation shown in the resulting image could facilitate classifications of different tissue types such as blood, soft tissue, tendons, and cartilage (Figure 18-10).

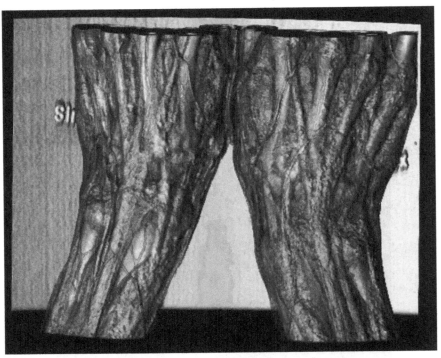

Figure 18-10. *Tendons examined with dual energy CT. Tendons and small vessels can be visualized without IV contrast. Ligaments between the carpal bones are visualized.*

DECT has the potential to be an important diagnostic tool in the healthcare of tomorrow. However, further research needs to be done to explore this new technique. VA can speed up this research.

MRI: Use of synthetic magnetic resonance imaging

It is difficult to generate good contrast MRI images on dead, cold bodies—body temperature influences the MR relaxation times of all tissues, and hence clinically established protocols need to be adjusted for optimal image quality at any given temperature. This problem can be solved by measurement of the absolute MR tissue parameters for tissue characterization, T1, T2, and proton density (PD).

Since this can be difficult to implement on a clinical MRI scanner, a new approach has been invented at CMIV called *synthetic MRI*. In this approach, the three absolute parameters are translated into ordinary MR contrast images (Figures 18-11 and 18-12). A color scale can be used such that each tissue acquires a specific color composition depending on its MR tissue parameters, independent of body temperature. Since the MR parameters are absolute, an identical color transformation will lead to a specific color-to-tissue relation, and a visual segmentation of tissue. Especially for postmortem imaging, this is important, since the image contrast may vary dramatically with temperature (Figure 18-12).

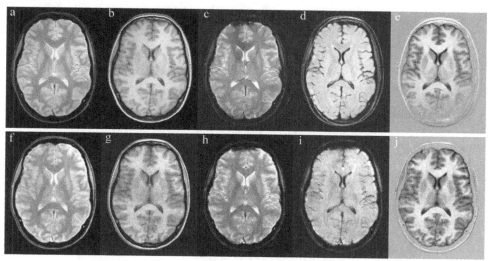

Figure 18-11. *Example of synthetic MRI on a living patient: the upper row are conventional images and the lower row are the synthetic counterpart based on a single dataset.*

Figure 18-12. *Full-body synthetic MRI scan. The contrast can be synthesized, the tissue can be segmented, and based on the MR parameters even temperature can be established.*

Postmortem examinations do not suffer from motion artifacts, and high-resolution images can be obtained with a long scan time. An example is shown in Figure 18-13, which shows a head shot wound in 1.2 mm isotropic resolution. Since synthetic MRI is based on absolute values, it can be used to render 3D images with CT postprocessing software, resulting in the volume renderings displayed in Figures 18-13 and 18-14.

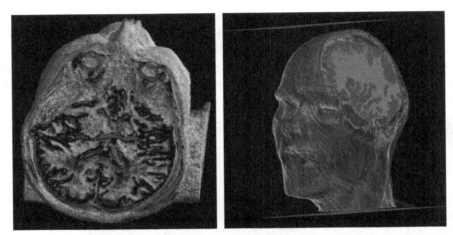

Figure 18-13. *Postmortem synthetic MRI examination of a gunshot wound in high isotropic resolution. Red color in the lefthand image represents blood.*

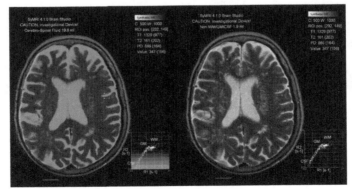

Figure 18-14. *Automatic segmentation of cerebrospinal fluid (19.8 ml for this slice) and pathology (1.9 ml for this slice) with synthetic MRI.*

Visualization: Image Analysis

In preparation for the physical autopsy, the pathologist and the radiologist conduct a collaborative DVR session. They can obtain a clear survey of the entire body quickly, and localize fractures and air pockets. The full-body procedure permits fast localization of foreign objects such as metal fragments or bullets. Another important aspect is the high resolution of the data, which, in a seamless visualization, allows details such as dental information to be extracted for identification purposes (Figure 18-15). This can provide essential information in the early part of a police investigation. After scanning, the forensic personnel leave CMIV and start the conventional autopsy. Data from the collaborative DVR session is transferred to the forensic institute for them to use, and if more information is needed later, new contact with the radiologist is made.

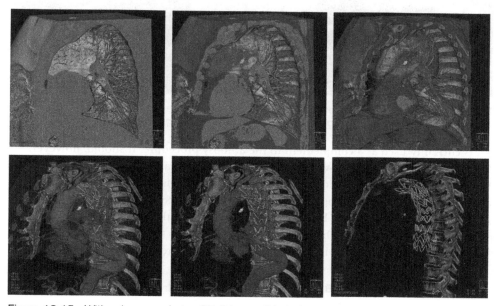

Figure 18-15. *With volume rendering 3D, it is possible to interactively change settings so that the body can be visualized seamlessly, from skin to skeleton.*

Objective Documentation

An important added value of the virtual autopsy procedure is that the captured DSCT data is stored, which enables the procedure to be iterated. Often, findings during the physical autopsy lead to new questions that the VA can answer. The pathologist and the crime investigators can also—at any point during the investigation—re-examine the cadaver and search for additional information (Figure 18-16). Moreover, in crime scene investigations, new findings may require other hypotheses to be scrutinized by postmortal imaging.

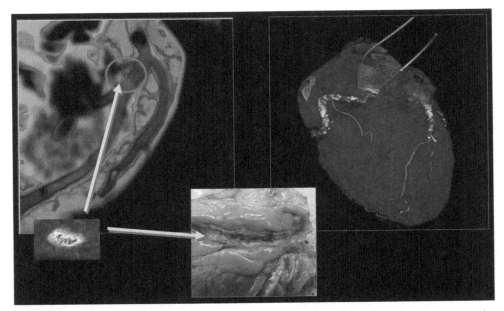

Figure 18-16. *Dual energy CT of the heart and the coronary arteries. More plaque components can be visualized with dual energy compared to conventional single energy images (red circle).*

VA is currently used as a complement to the autopsy procedure. It should, however, be noted that the workflow overhead introduced is minimal, as the time needed for the DSCT scan and visualization session is short in comparison to the physical autopsy, and that it can make the autopsy more efficient because the pathologist will have prior knowledge of the case before beginning the autopsy. That the cadaver remains in a sealed body bag throughout the VA procedure also secures technical evidence, such as fibers and body fluids, which in forensic cases may be of great importance.

Advantages and Disadvantages of Virtual Autopsy

Let's take a look at the advantages of VA compared with conventional autopsies:

- It is time-saving. The VA can be a complement to standard autopsies, enabling broad, systematic examinations of the whole body that are normally difficult and time consuming; for example, an examination of the entire bone structure or searching for the presence of air in the body (Figures 18-3 and 18-4).

- It is noninvasive. Once an invasive traditional autopsy has taken place, the body cannot be reassembled in its original state, thus precluding other forensic pathologists from conducting a fresh analysis on the same body (Figures 18-5 through 18-7).

- A traditional autopsy may be rejected by family members, perhaps due to religious beliefs that prohibit the desecration of the remains of a deceased person. For example, Orthodox Judaism prohibits disturbing dead bodies except when such action may save others, and decrees that practices such as organ removal should be avoided. Islam is likewise opposed to desecrating or even exposing the body of a deceased believer.

- Autopsy protocols and photographs used as evidence in criminal cases can be difficult for jurors to understand. VA visualizations are typically clearer (Figures 18-4 and 18-9).

- Storage of VA data poses few problems, whereas autopsy records such as tissue sections are difficult to store indefinitely (Figure 18-16).

- With potential global pandemics such as bird flu (avian influenza A) and swine flu (the H1N1 virus) posing an increasing threat, the practice of eviscerating the victims can pose serious health risks to coroners, pathologists, and medical examiners. With a VA, these risks are minimized.

However, virtual autopsies also have several shortcomings:

- For MDCT, soft tissue discrimination is low. Energy-resolved CT (DECT) has the potential to resolve this problem (Figure 18-10).

- The large amount of data produced is a problem to analyze, but better and faster postprocessing programs should solve this.

- MRI is a time-consuming investigation and not optimal on a cold body. Synthetic MRI is a promising alternative (Figure 18-14).

- Postmortem imaging with MDCT and MRI does not give any color documentation of the body. It may be possible to solve this issue with new volume-rendering 3D methods and body surface scanning (Figure 18-15).

- Macro morphology is absent (no histology and chemistry). This can be solved to a certain extent with MDCT guided biopsies or magnetic resonance spectroscopy (Figure 18-16).

- Circulation and possible bleeding points are difficult to visualize, although promising results have been achieved with postmortem angiography. As has been shown, postmortem CT angiography can be a feasible way to obtain more information from the VA (Figure 18-17).

- Postmortal gas can be difficult to distinguish from other types of gas (bowel gas, gas in wound channels, etc.). Therefore, it is important to execute the postmortem imaging examination soon after death has occurred (Figure 18-18).

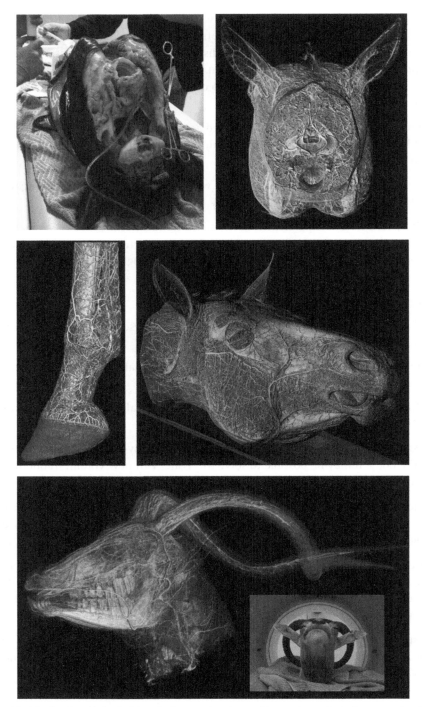

Figure 18-17. *Contrast injected in arteries postmortem with good results in horse and antelope. Data has been acquired with dual energy CT.*

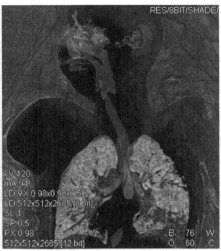

Figure 18-18. *With conventional autopsies, different kinds of body gases are difficult to examine.*

The Future for Virtual Autopsies

Both MDCT and MRI can be used for postmortem imaging. In principle, it is easy to visualize bone, gas, and metal with MDCT. However, it is important to be aware of not only the capabilities, but also the limitations of these technologies.

Visualization research in the future must include the overall aim of implementing a virtual autopsy workstation that includes everything needed to perform state-of-the-art virtual autopsies. Visualization tools to increase the quality and efficiency of virtual autopsy procedures need to be developed. Research and development efforts focusing on novel rendering and classification techniques are also needed to improve usability and to specifically address forensic questions. Another important goal is to establish designated protocols for the main forensic case categories.

The data analysis research includes the implementation of computer-aided diagnostic tools that can, once applied to the postmortem data, help search for and characterize relevant forensic findings. These tools can also deliver general information about the deceased individual such as height, body weight, sex, major injuries, foreign bodies (e.g., projectiles), and likely causes of death in an automatically generated preliminary, written virtual autopsy protocol.

When all of these tasks have been successfully addressed, the technology involved within all processes of a virtual autopsy can be improved to enable automation of the entire workflow. This will allow for virtual autopsies to be performed in large numbers within a reasonable time frame. This would be invaluable in handling incidents with significant numbers of victims such as those created by the tsunami catastrophe in Asia in 2004, where no autopsies were performed at all.

As terrorists improve their applied technologies day by day, it is unthinkable that forensic pathologists should not also be able to make use of emerging technologies in order to gather as much information as possible from their victims (Figure 18-19). In times where no one can really feel safe, we should not only focus on the prevention of catastrophe, but also prepare ourselves to handle disasters adequately when they do occur.

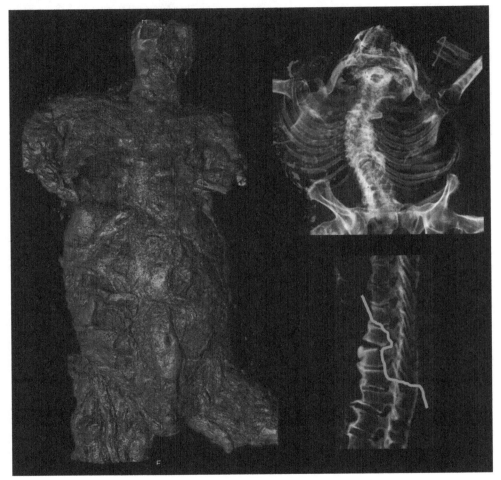

Figure 18-19. *Postmortem CT of a burned person. Metal in the body makes it impossible to use MRI. Before the CT examination, there was no suspicion of murder, but several fractures that could not be explained pointed the investigators in the right direction—murder!*

For a new era of digital autopsies to truly emerge, several forces must work in unison. Medical professionals and legal authorities must determine standard protocols for scanning and storing data. Legal systems around the world must accept the admissibility of imaging evidence in determining the cause and manner of death. Also, specialists in new fields such as postmortem radiology will need to be trained. Radiologists are typically trained to interpret images of living patients, but the dead often look different; severe trauma or the effects of decomposition can displace organs. Understanding these differences will require knowledge and expertise that does not exist on a widespread basis today.

Invasive autopsies will likely remain the norm for at least the next few years. However, in some cases, we may begin to see traditional autopsies being replaced by noninvasive virtual autopsies, with minimally invasive, image-guided tissue sampling conducted when necessary. Postmortem VA has the potential to gain high acceptance in the population compared with the traditional autopsy, making it possible to maintain high levels of quality control in forensic and traditional medicine.

Conclusion

The virtual autopsy is a newly developed procedure that will enhance the classic autopsy, giving it the capacity to achieve more reliable results. In some cases, the virtual autopsy could also replace the normal autopsy. Research on the unique aspects of postmortem radiology must, however, be undertaken to identify cases in which its use is most beneficial and to validate the new procedures. Clearly, the introduction of this new autopsy method is likely to have a major impact on forensic medicine, the judicial system, the police, and general medicine in the future.

References and Suggested Reading

Donchin, Y., A.I. Rivkind, J. Bar-Ziv, J. Hiss, J. Almog, and M. Drescher. 1994. "Utility of postmortem computed tomography in trauma victims." *Journal of Trauma* 37, no. 4: 552–555.

Etlik, Ö., O. Temizöz, A. Dogan, M. Kayan, H. Arslan, and Ö. Unal. 2004. "Three-dimensional volume rendering imaging in detection of bone fractures." *European Journal of General Medicine* 1, no. 4: 48–52.

Jackowski, C. 2003. "Macroscopical and histological findings in comparison with CT- and MRI- examinations of isolated autopsy hearts." Thesis, Institute of Forensic Medicine. O.-v.-G.-University of Magdeburg.

Jackowski, C., A. Persson, and M. Thali. 2008. "Whole body postmortem angiography with a high viscosity contrast agent solution using poly ethylene glycol (PEG) as contrast agent dissolver." *Journal of Forensic Sciences* 53, no. 2: 465–468.

Jackowski, C., W. Schweitzer, M. Thali, K. Yen, E. Aghayev, M. Sonnenschein, P. Vock, and R. Dirnhofer. 2005. "Virtopsy: Postmortem imaging of the human heart in situ using MSCT and MRI." *Forensic Science International* 149, no. 1: 11–23.

Jackowski, C., M. Sonnenschein, M. Thali, E. Aghayev, G. von Allmen, K. Yen, R. Dirnhofer, and P. Vock. 2005. "Virtopsy: Postmortem minimally invasive angiography using cross section techniques—Implementation and preliminary results." *Journal of Forensic Sciences* 50, no. 5: 1175–1186.

Kerner, T., G. Fritz, A. Unterberg, and K. Falke. 2003. "Pulmonary air embolism in severe head injury." *Resuscitation* 56, no. 1: 111–115.

Ljung, P., C. Winskog, A. Persson, C. Lundstrom, and A. Ynnerman. 2006. "Full-body virtual autopsies using a state-of-the-art volume rendering pipeline." *IEEE Transactions on Visualization and Computer Graphics* 12, no. 5: 869–876.

Oliver, W.R., A.S. Chancellor, M. Soltys, J. Symon, T. Cullip, J. Rosenman, R. Hellman, A. Boxwala, and W. Gormley. 1995. "Three-dimensional reconstruction of a bullet path: Validation by computed radiography." *Journal of Forensic Sciences*, 40, no. 2: 321–324.

Ros, P.R., K.C. Li, P. Vo, H. Baer, and E.V. Staab. 1990. "Preautopsy magnetic resonance imaging: Initial experience." *Magnetic Resonance Imaging* 8: 303–308.

Thali, M., W. Schweitzer, K. Yen, P. Vock, C. Ozdoba, E. Spielvogel, and R. Dirnhofer. 2003. "New horizons in forensic radiology: The 60-second digital autopsy-full-body examination of a gunshot victim by multislice computed tomography." *The American Journal of Forensic Medicine and Pathology* 24: 22–27.

Thali, M., U. Taubenreuther, M. Karolczak, M. Braun, W. Brueschweiler, W. Kalender, and R. Dirnhofer. 2003. "Forensic microradiology: Micro-computed tomography (Micro-CT) and analysis of patterned injuries inside of bone." *Journal of Forensic Sciences* 48, no. 6: 1336–1342.

Thali, M., K. Yen, W. Schweitzer, P. Vock, C. Boesch, C. Ozdoba, G. Schroth, M. Ith, M. Sonnenschein, T. Doernhoefer, E. Scheurer, T. Plattner, and R. Dirnhofer. 2003. "Virtopsy, a new imaging horizon in forensic pathology: Virtual autopsy by postmortem multislice computed tomography (MSCT) and magnetic resonance imaging (MRI)—a feasibility study." *Journal of Forensic Sciences* 48, no. 2: 386–403.

Yen, K., P. Vock, B. Tiefenthaler, G. Ranner, E. Scheurer, M. Thali, K. Zwygart, M. Sonnenschein, M. Wiltgen, and R. Dirnhofer. 2004. "Virtopsy: Forensic traumatology of the subcutaneous fatty tissue; Multislice Computed Tomography (MSCT) and Magnetic Resonance Imaging (MRI) as diagnostic tools." *Journal of Forensic Sciences* 49, no. 4: 799–806.

## CHAPTER NINETEEN

Animation for Visualization: Opportunities and Drawbacks

Danyel Fisher

DOES ANIMATION HELP build richer, more vivid, and more understandable visualizations, or simply confuse things?

The use of Java, Flash, Silverlight, and JavaScript on the Web has made it easier to distribute animated, interactive visualizations. Many visualizers are beginning to think about how to make their visualizations more compelling with animation. There are many good guides on how to make static visualizations more effective, and many applications support interactivity well. But animated visualization is still a new area; there is little consensus on what makes for a good animation.

The intuition behind animation seems clear enough: if a two-dimensional image is good, then a moving image should be better. Movement is familiar: we are accustomed to both moving through the real world and seeing things in it move smoothly. All around us, items move, grow, and change color in ways that we understand deeply and richly.

In a visualization, animation might help a viewer work through the logic behind an idea by showing the intermediate steps and transitions, or show how data collected over time changes. A moving image might offer a fresh perspective, or invite users to look deeper into the data presented. An animation might also smooth the change between two views, even if there is no temporal component to the data.

As an example, let's take a look at Jonathan Harris and Sep Kamvar's We Feel Fine animated visualization (*http://wefeelfine.org*). In this visualization, blog entries mentioning feelings are represented as bubbles. As users move between views, the bubbles are reorganized into histograms and other patterns. For example, one screen shows the relative distribution of blog entries from men and women, while another shows the relative distribution of moods in the blog entries. While the bubbles fly around the screen freely, there are always a constant number on the screen. This constancy helps reinforce the idea of a sample population being organized in different ways. Animation is also used to evoke emotion: the bubbles quiver with energy, with those that represent "happy" moving differently than bubbles that represent "sad."

Not all animations are successful, though. Far too many applications simply borrow the worst of PowerPoint, flying data points across the screen with no clear purpose; elements sweep and grow and rotate through meaningless spaces, and generally only cause confusion.

I have had several occasions to build animated visualizations. In 2000, I worked with fellow grad students building GnuTellaVision, which visualized the growing Gnutella peer-to-peer network. Since then, I have been involved in a variety of projects that have shed light on animated visualization: for example, I worked on a project that explored animated scatterplots, and I was a close bystander on the DynaVis project, which looked at transitions between different visualizations. In this chapter, I will talk through some of these experiences and to try to develop some principles for animating visualizations.

Animation can be a powerful technique when used appropriately, but it can be very bad when used poorly. Some animations can enhance the visual appeal of the visualization being presented, but may make exploration of the dataset more difficult; other animated visualizations facilitate exploration. This chapter attempts to work out a framework for designing effective animated visualizations. We'll begin by looking at some background material, and then move on to a discussion of one of the most well-known animated visualizations, Hans Rosling's GapMinder. One of the projects I worked on explored animated scatterplots like GapMinder; this makes a fine launching point to discuss both successes and failures with animation. As we'll see, successful animations can display a variety of types of transformations. The DynaVis project helps illustrate how some of these transitions and transformations can work out. The chapter concludes by laying out a number of design principles for visualizations.

Principles of Animation

At its core, any animation entails showing a viewer a series of images in rapid succession. The viewer assembles these images, trying to build a coherent idea of what occurred between them. The perceptual system notes the changes between frames, so an animation can be understood as a series of visual changes between frames. When there are a small number of changes, it is quite simple to understand what has happened, and the viewer can trace the changes easily. When there are a large number of changes, it gets more complex.

The Gestalt perceptual principle of *common fate* states that viewers will group large numbers of objects together, labeling them all as a group, if they are traveling in the same direction and at the same speed. Individual objects that take their own trajectories will be seen as isolates, and will visually stand out. If all the items move in different directions, however, observers have far more difficulty following them. Perception researchers have shown that viewers have difficulty tracking more than four or five objects independently—the eye gives up, tracking only a few objects and labeling other movement as noise (Cavanagh and Alvarez 2005).

Animation in Scientific Visualization

Attendees at the annual IEEE VisWeek conference—the research summit for visualization—are divided into two groups: information visualizers and scientific visualizers. The two groups give different talks, sit in different rooms, and sometimes sit at different tables at meals. Watching the talks, one quickly notices that roughly half of the papers in the scientific visualization room feature animation, while almost no papers in the information visualization room do. You could say that the difference between the groups is that scientific visualizers are people who understand what the *x*-, *y*-, and *z*-axes actually mean: they are very good at picturing the dimensions of an image and understand the meaning of depths and distances. The dynamic processes they often represent—wind blowing over an airplane wing, hurricanes sweeping across maps, blood flowing through veins—also involve an additional dimension: that of time. As it would be difficult to squeeze its representation into any of the other three dimensions, animating is an attractive method for displaying such processes.

In contrast, data visualization is less straightforward. Information visualizers usually work with abstract data spaces, where the axes do not correspond to the real world (if they mean anything at all). Viewers need to get acclimated to the dimensions they can see, and learn how to interpret them. Consequently, there are comparatively few examples of animation published in the information visualization community. (We will discuss some of these later.)

Learning from Cartooning

Animation, of course, appears popularly in places outside of visualizations. Movies and cartoons depend on some of the same physical principles as computer animation, so several people have asked whether cartooning techniques might bring useful insights to the creation of animated visualizations. As early as 1946, the Belgian psychologist Albert Michotte noted the "perception of causality" (Michotte 1963). It is easy to believe that the movement in an animation shows intent: that this point is *chasing* another across the screen (rather than moving in an equivalent trajectory one second behind it), that this ball *hit* another (rather than "this dot stopped at point A, and this other dot moved from A to B"), and so on. Thus, we can ascribe agency and causality where none really exists.

In cartoons, of course, we wish to communicate causality. Traditional cartoonists have described how they endow drawn shapes with the "illusion of life" (Johnston and Thomas 1987) in order to convey emotion, and several rounds of research papers (Lasseter 1987; Chang and Ungar 1993) have tried to see how to distill those ideas for computer animation and visualization.

Traditional cartoonists use a barrage of techniques that are not completely true to life. *Squash and stretch*, for instance, distorts objects during movement to draw the eye toward the direction of motion: objects might stretch when they fly at their fastest, and squashing them conveys a notion of stopping, gathering energy, or changing direction. Moving items along *arcs* implies a more natural motion; motion along a straight line seems to have intent. Before objects begin moving, they *anticipate* their upcoming motion; they conclude with a *follow-through*. *Ease-in, ease-out* is a technique of timing animations: animations start slowly to emphasize direction, accelerate through the middle, and slow down again at the end. Complex acts are *staged* to draw attention to individual parts one at a time.

Visualization researchers have adapted these techniques with differing degrees of enthusiasm and success—for example, the Information Visualizer framework (Card, Robertson, and Mackinlay 1991), an early 3D animated framework, integrated several of these principles, including anticipation, arcs, and follow-through. On the other hand, some elements of this list seem distinctly inappropriate. For instance, squashing or stretching a data point distorts it, changing the nature of the visualization; thus, we can no longer describe the visualization as maintaining the consistent rule "height maps to *this*, width maps to *that*" at each frame of the animation. In their research on slideshows, Zongker and Salesin (2003) warn that many animation techniques can be distracting or deceptive, suggesting causality where none might exist. Also, they are often meant to give an illusion of emotion, which may be quite inappropriate for data visualization. (An exception would be We Feel Fine, in which the motion is supposed to convey emotion and uses these techniques effectively to do so.)

The Downsides of Animation

Animation has been less successful for data visualization than for scientific visualization. Two metastudies have looked at different types of animations—process animations and algorithm visualizations—and found that both classes have spotty track records when it comes to helping students learn more about complex processes.

The psychologist Barbara Tversky found, somewhat to her dismay, that animation did not seem to be helpful for process visualization (i.e., visualizations that show how to use a tool or how a technique works). Her article, "Animation: Can It Facilitate?" (Tversky, Morrison, and Bétrancourt 2002), reviews nearly 100 studies of animation and visualization. In no study was animation found to outperform rich static diagrams. It did beat out textual representations, though, and simple representations that simply showed start and end state without transitions.

Algorithm animation is in many ways similar to process visualization: an algorithm can be illustrated by showing the steps that it takes. Some sort algorithms, for example, are very amenable to animation: an array of values can be drawn as a sequence of bars, so the sort operations move bars around. These animations can easily show the differences between, say, a bubble sort and an insertion sort. Christopher Hundhausen, Sarah Douglas, and John Stasko (2002) tried to understand the effectiveness of algorithm visualization in the classroom, but half of the controlled studies they examined found that animation did not help students understand algorithms. Interestingly, the strongest factor predicting success was the *theory* behind the animation. Visualization was most helpful when accompanied by constructivist theories—that is, when students manipulated code or algorithms and watched a visualization that illustrated their own work, or when students were asked questions and tried to use the visualization to answer them. In contrast, animations were ineffective at transferring knowledge; passively watching an animation was not more effective than other forms of teaching.

GapMinder and Animated Scatterplots

One recent example of successful animated visualization comes from Hans Rosling's GapMinder (*http://www.gapminder.org*). Rosling is a professor of Global Health from Sweden, and his talk at the February 2006 Technology, Entertainment, Design (TED) conference* riveted first a live audience, then many more online. He collected public health statistics from international sources and, in his brief talk, plotted them on a scatterplot. In the visualization, individual points represent countries, with x and y values representing statistics such as life expectancy and average number of children and each point's area being proportionate to the population of the country it represents. Rosling first shows single frames—the statistics of the countries in a single year—before starting to trace their progress through time, animating between the images with yearly steps in between.

Figure 19-1 shows three frames of a GapMinder-like animation. On the x-axis is the life expectancy at birth; on the y-axis is the infant mortality rate. The size of bubbles is proportionate to the population. Color-coding is per continent; the largest two dots are China and India.

Rosling's animations are compelling: he narrates the dots' movement, describing their relative progress. China puts public health programs in place and its dot floats upward, followed by other countries trying the same strategy. Another country's economy booms, and its dot starts to move rapidly rightward. Rosling uses this animation to make powerful points about both our preconceptions about public health problems and the differences between the first and third world, and the animation helps viewers follow the points he is making.

---

* Available online at *http://www.ted.com/talks/hans_rosling_shows_the_best_stats_you_ve_ever_seen.html*. Rosling presented similar discussions at TED 2007 and TED 2009.

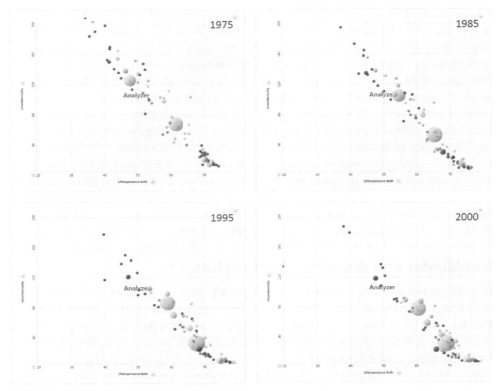

Figure 19-1. *A GapMinder-like visualization showing information about a set of 75 countries in 1975, 1985, 1995, and 2000; this chart plots life expectancy (x axis) against infant mortality (y axis)—countries at the top-left have a high infant mortality and a short life expectancy*

Too many dots?

The perceptual psychology research mentioned earlier showed that people have trouble tracking more than four moving points at a time. In his presentation, Rosling is able to guide the audience, showing them where to look, and his narration helps them see which points to focus on. He describes the progress that a nation is making with the assistance of a long pointer stick; it is quite clear where to look. This reduces confusion.

It also helps that many of the two-dimensional scatterplots he uses have unambiguously "good" and "bad" directions: it is good for a country to move toward a higher GDP and a longer life expectancy (i.e., to go up and to the right), and bad to move in the opposite direction (down and to the left).

With Rosling's sure hand guiding the watcher's gaze, the visualization is very effective. But if a temporal scatterplot were incorporated into a standard spreadsheet, would it be useful for people who were trying to learn about the data?

Testing Animated Scatterplots

At Microsoft Research, we became curious about whether these techniques could work for people who were not familiar with the data. We reimplemented a GapMinder-like animation as a base case, plotting points at appropriate (*x, y*) locations and interpolating them smoothly by year. We then considered three alternative static visualizations that contained the same amount of information as the animation. First, of course, we could simply take individual frames (as in Figure 19-1). Even in our earliest sketches, however, we realized this was a bad idea: it was too difficult to trace the movement of points between frames. The ability to follow the general trajectories of the various countries and to compare them is a critical part of GapMinder; we wanted users to have a notion of continuity, of points moving from one place to another, and the individual frames simply were not helpful.

We therefore implemented two additional views, using the same set of countries and the same axes as Figure 19-1, for the years 1975–2000. The first is a *tracks* view, which shows all the paths overlaid on one another (Figure 19-2). The second is a *small multiples* view, which draws each path independently on separate axes (Figure 19-3). In the tracks view, we cue time with translucency; in the small multiples view, we instead show time by changing the sizes of the dots.

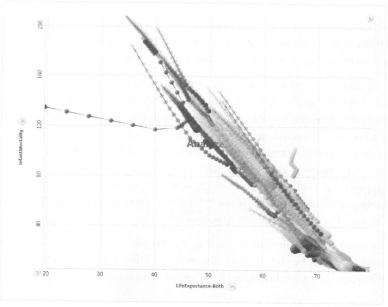

Figure 19-2. *Tracks view in which each country is represented as a series of dots that become more opaque over time; years are connected with faded streaks*

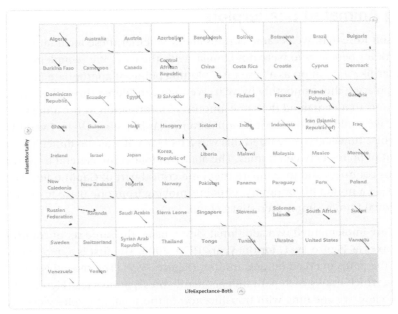

Figure 19-3. *Small multiples view in which each country is in its own tiny coordinate system: dots grow larger to indicate the progression of time*

We wanted to understand how well users performed with the animation, as compared with these static representations. Users can set up their own scatterplots at the GapMinder website, but would they be able to learn anything new from their data?

We chose 30 different combinations of (*x*, *y*) values based on public health and demographic data from the United Nations, and presented users with fairly simple questions such as "In this scatterplot, which country rises the most in GDP?" and "In this scatterplot, which continent has the most countries with diminishing marriage rates?" We recruited users who were familiar with scatterplots, and who dealt with data in their daily work. Some subjects got to "explore" the data, and sat in front of a computer answering questions on their own. Others got a "presentation," in which a narrator showed them the visualization or played the animation. We measured both time and accuracy as they then answered the questions.

The study's numerical results are detailed in Robertson et al. (2008). The major conclusions, however, can be stated quite simply: animation is both slower and less accurate at conveying the information than the other modalities.

Exploration with animation is slower

We found that when users explored the data on their own, they would often play through the animation dozens of times, checking to see which country would be the correct answer to the question. In contrast, those who viewed a presentation and could not control the animation on their own answered far more rapidly: they were forced to choose an answer and go with it. Thus, animation in exploration was the slowest of the conditions, while animation in presentation was the fastest.

Interestingly, this might shed light on why the process animations by Tversky et al. found so little success. In our tests, users clearly wanted to be able to move both forward and backward through time; perhaps this is true of process animations, too. More effort may be required to get the same information from an animation as opposed to a series of static images, because you have to replay the entire thing rather than just jumping directly to the parts you want to see.

Animation is less accurate

Despite the extra time the users spent with the animation, the users who were shown the static visualizations were always more accurate at answering the questions. That is, the animation appeared to detract from the users' ability to correctly answer questions. Their accuracy was not correlated with speed: the extra time they spent in exploration did not seem to drive better outcomes.

This seems like bad news for animation: it was slower and less accurate at communicating the information. On the other hand, we found the animation to be more engaging and emotionally powerful: one pilot subject saw life expectancy in a war-torn country plummet by 30 years and gasped audibly. Generally, users preferred to work with the animation, finding it more enjoyable and exciting than the other modes. They also found it more frustrating, though: "Where did that dot go?" asked one angrily, as a data point that had been steadily rising suddenly dropped.

These findings suggest that Rosling's talk is doing something different from what our users experienced. Critically, Rosling knows what the answer is: he has worked through the data, knows the rhetorical point he wishes to make, and is bringing the viewers along. He runs much of his presentation on the same set of axes, so the viewers don't get disoriented. His data is reasonably simple: few of the countries he highlights make major reversals in their trends, and when he animates many countries at once, they stay in a fairly close pack, traveling in the same direction. He chooses his axes so the countries move in consistent directions, allowing users to track origins and goals easily. He takes advantage of the Gestalt principle of common fate to group them, and he narrates their transitions for maximum clarity.

In contrast, our users had to contend with short sessions, had to track countries that suffered abrupt reversals, and did not have a narrator to explain what they were about to see; rather than learning the answer from the narrator, they had to discover it themselves. This suggests to us that what we were asking our users to do was very different from what Rosling is doing—so different, in fact, that it deserves its own section.

Presentation Is Not Exploration

An analyst sitting before a spreadsheet does not know what the data will show, and needs to play with it from a couple of different angles, looking for correlations, connections, and ideas that might be concealed in the data. The process is one of foraging—it rewards rapidly reviewing a given chart or view to see whether there is something interesting to investigate, followed by moving on with a new filter or a different image.

In contrast, presenters are experts in their own data. They have already cleaned errors from the dataset, perhaps removing a couple of outliers or highlighting data points that support the core ideas they want to communicate. They have picked axes and a time range that illustrate their point well, and they can guide the viewers' perception of the data. Most importantly, they are less likely to need to scrub back and forth, as we saw users doing with our animation, in order to check whether they have overlooked a previous point. In these conditions, animation makes a lot of sense: it allows the presenter to explain a point vividly and dramatically.

The experience of exploration is different from the experience of presentation. It is easy to forget this, because many of our tools mix the two together. That is, many packages offer ways to make a chart look glossy and ready for presentation, and those tools are not clearly separated from the tools for making the chart legible and ready for analysis. In Microsoft Excel, for example, the same menu that controls whether my axis has a log scale also helps me decide whether to finish my bar chart with a glossy color. The former of these choices is critical to exploration; the latter is primarily useful for presentation. After I finish analyzing data in Excel, I can copy the chart directly into PowerPoint and show the result. As a result of this seamlessness, few people who use this popular software have seriously discussed the important distinctions between presentation and exploration.

Table 19-1 summarizes major differences between the needs of exploration and presentation.

Table 19-1. *Differentiating exploration from presentation*

	Exploration	**Presentation**
Characteristics	Data is surprising. Data may have outliers. Data is likely to move unpredictably. Viewer controls interaction.	Data is well known to the presenter. Data has been cleaned. Viewer is passive.

Table 19-1. *Differentiating exploration from presentation*

	Exploration	Presentation
Goals/procedures	Analyze multiple dimensions at once. Change mappings many times. Look for trends and holes.	Present fewer dimensions to make a point. Walk through dimensions clearly. Highlight critical points. Group points together to show trends and motion.

These two perspectives are not completely disjoint, of course. Many interactive web applications allow users to explore a few dimensions, while still not exposing raw data. The tension between presentation and exploration suggests that designers need to consider the purpose of their visualizations. There are design trade-offs, not only for animation, but more generally.

Types of Animation

Some forms of animation are most suited to presentation, while others work well for exploration. In this section, we'll discuss a hierarchy of different types of transformations, ranging from changing the view on a visualization to changing the axes on which the visualization is plotted to changing the data of the visualization. Let's begin with an example of a system that needs to manage two different types of changes.

Dynamic Data, Animated Recentering

In 2001, peer-to-peer file sharing was becoming an exciting topic. The Gnutella system was one of the first large-scale networks, and I was in a group of students who thought it would make a good subject of study. Gnutella was a little different from other peer-to-peer systems. The earlier Napster had kept a detailed index of everything on the network; BitTorrent would later skip indexing entirely. Gnutella passed search requests between peers, bouncing around the questions and waiting for replies. When I used a peer-to-peer search to track down a song, how many machines were really getting checked? How large a network could my own client see?

We instrumented a Gnutella client for visualization, and then started representing the network. We rapidly realized a couple of things: first, that new nodes were constantly appearing on the network; and second, that knowing where they were located was really interesting. The appearance of new nodes meant that we wanted to be able to change the visualization *stably*. There would always be new data pouring into the system, and it was important that users not be disoriented by changes taking place in the visualization as new data came in. On the other hand, we did not want to pause, add data, and redraw: we wanted a system where new data would simply add itself to the diagram unobtrusively.

Because the Gnutella network used a peer-to-peer discovery protocol, it was often interesting to focus on a single node and its neighbors. Is this node connected to a central "supernode"? Is it conveying many requests? We wanted to be able to focus on any single node and its neighbors, and to be able to easily estimate the number of hops between nodes. This called for changing the *viewpoint* without changing the remainder of the layout.

Our tool was entitled GnuTellaVision, or GTV (Yee et al. 2001). We addressed these two needs with two different animation techniques. We based the visualization on a radial layout, both to reflect the way that data was changing—growing outward as we discovered more connections—and in order to facilitate estimation of the number of hops between the central node and others. A radial layout has the virtues of a well-defined center point and a series of layers that grow outward. As we discovered new nodes, we added them to rings corresponding to the number of hops from the starting node. When a new node arrived, we would simply move its neighbors over by a small amount (most nodes in the visualization do not move much). As the visualization ran, it updated with new data, animating constantly (Figure 19-4).

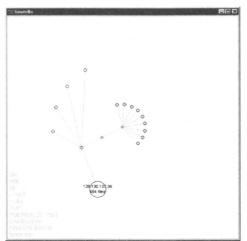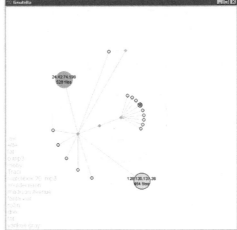

Figure 19-4. *GTV before (left) and after (right) several new nodes are discovered on the network—as nodes yield more information, their size and color can also change*

When a user wanted to examine a node, GTV recentered on the selection. In our first design, it did so in the most straightforward way possible: we computed a new radial layout and then moved nodes linearly from their previous locations to the new ones. This was very confusing, because nodes would cross trajectories getting from their old locations to the new ones. The first fix was to have nodes travel along polar coordinate paths, and always clockwise. Thus, the nodes remained in the same space as the visualization was drawn, and moved smoothly to their new locations (Figure 19-5). Because GTV is oriented toward examining nodes that may be new to the user, and is constantly discovering novel information, it was important that this animation facilitate exploration by helping users track the node paths.

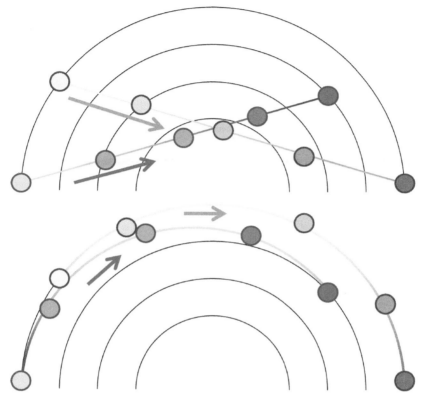

Figure 19-5. *Interpolation in rectangular coordinates (top) causes nodes to cross through each others' paths; interpolation in polar coordinates (bottom) makes for smooth motion*

A radial layout has several degrees of freedom: nodes can appear in any order around the radius, and any node can be at the top. When we did not constrain these degrees of freedom, nodes would sometimes travel from the bottom of the screen to the top. We wanted to ensure that nodes moved as little as possible, so we added a pair of constraints: nodes maintained, as much as they could, both the same relative *orientation* and *order*. Maintaining relative orientation means that the relative position of the edge from the old center to the new center is maintained. Maintaining relative order means that nodes' neighbors will remain in the same order around the rings. Both of these are illustrated in Figure 19-6.

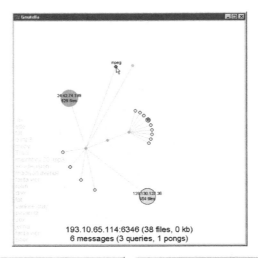

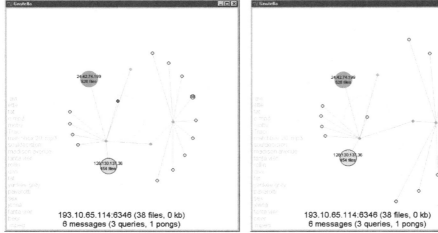

Figure 19-6. *Animated recentering: the purple highlighted node becomes the center, and other sets of nodes maintain their relative positions and orders (the large blue node stays below, and the set of small yellow nodes spreads along an outer ring)*

Last, we adapted the *ease-in, ease-out* motion from cartooning in order to help users see how the motion was about to happen.

This section demonstrated some useful principles that are worth articulating:

Compatibility

Choose a visualization that is compatible with animation. In GTV, the radial layout can be modified easily; new nodes can be located on the graph to minimize changes, and—like many tree representations—it is possible to recenter on different nodes.

Coordinate motion

Motion should occur in a meaningful coordinate space of the visualization. We want to help the users stay oriented within the visualization during the animation, so they can better predict and follow motion. In GTV, for instance, transforming through rectangular coordinates would be unpredictable and confusing; the radial coordinates, in contrast, mean that users can track the transition and the visualization retains its meaning.

Meaningful motion

Although animation is about moving items, unnecessary motion can be very confusing. In general, it is better to have fewer things move than more in a given transition. Constraining the degrees of freedom of the GTV animation allows the visualization to change as little as possible by keeping things in roughly the same position.

A Taxonomy of Animations

There are many sorts of change that might occur within a visualization. In the discussion of GapMinder, we talked about changes to data; in the example of GTV, we examined changes to both the data and the view. There are more types of transitions that one might wish to make in a visualization, though. The following is a list adapted from one assembled by Heer and Robertson (2007). Each type of transition is independent; it should be possible to change just the one element without changing any of the others. Many of these are applicable to both presentation and exploration of data:

Change the view

Pan over or zoom in on a fixed image, such as a map or a large data space.

Change the charting surface

On a plot, change the axes (e.g., change from linear to log scale). On a map, change from, for example, a Mercator projection to a globe.

Filter the data

Remove data points from the current view following a particular selection criterion.

Reorder the data

Change the order of points (e.g., alphabetize a series of columns).

Change the representation

Change from a bar chart to a pie chart; change the layout of a graph; change the colors of nodes.

Change the data

Move data forward through a time step, modify the data, or change the values portrayed (e.g., a bar chart might change from Profits to Losses). As discussed earlier, moving data through a time step is likely to be more useful for presentations.

These six types of transitions can describe most animations that might be made with data visualizations. Process visualizations would have a somewhat different taxonomy, as would scientific visualizations that convey flow (such as air over wings). Next, given this set of transitions, we will discuss some examples of how these animations might be managed.

Staging Animations with DynaVis

Two people exploring a dataset together on a single computer have a fundamental problem: only one of them gets the mouse. While it is perfectly intuitive for one of them to click "filter," the other user might not be able to track what has just happened. This sits at an interesting place between exploration and presentation: one of the major goals of the animation is to enable the second user to follow the leader by knowing what change the leader has just invoked; however, the leader may not know specifically what point he is about to make. Animation is plausibly a way to transition between multiple visualizations, allowing a second person—or an audience—to keep up. For the last several years, we have been experimenting with ways to show transitions of data and representations of well-known charts, such as scatterplots, bar charts, and even pie charts.

DynaVis, a framework for animated visualization, was our starting point. A summer internship visit by Jeff Heer, now a professor at Stanford, gave us a chance to work through a long list of possibilities. This discussion is outlined in more detail in his paper (Heer and Robertson 2007).

In DynaVis, each bar, dot, or line is represented as an object in 3D space, so we can move smoothly through all the transitions described in the preceding section. Many transformations are fairly clear: to filter a point from a scatterplot, for instance, the point just needs to fade away. There are several cases that are much more interesting to work through, though: those in which the type of representation needs to change, and those in which more than one change needs to happen at a time. When the representation is being changed, we try to follow several basic principles. Here are the first two:

Do one thing at a time

Ensure that the visualization does not entail making multiple simultaneous changes. This might mean *staging* the visualization, to ensure that each successive step is completed before the next one is started.

Preserve valid mappings

At any given time during a step, ensure that the visualization is a meaningful one that represents a mapping from data to visualization. It would be invalid, for example, to rename the bars of a bar chart: the fundamental mapping is that each bar represents one *x*-axis value.

Figure 19-7 shows a first attempt at a transition from bar chart to pie chart. There are some positive aspects to the transition. For example, the bars do not move all at once, so the eye can follow movement fairly easily, and the bars maintain their identities and their values across the animation. While there are some issues with occlusion as the bars fly past each other, they move through a smooth trajectory so that it is reasonable to predict where they will end up. Finally, the animation is well staged: all the wedges are placed before they grow together into a full pie.

This visualization has a critical flaw, though. The length of the bar becomes the length of the pie wedge, so longer bars became longer wedges. However, longer bars will ultimately have to become fatter wedges in the final pie chart. That means that bars are becoming both fat and long, or both skinny and short. This, in turn, means that the visualization does not employ a constant rule (such as "number of pixels is proportionate to data value").

That leads us to the next principle:

Maintain the invariant

While the previous rule referred to the relationship between data elements and the marks on the display, this rule refers to the relationship of the data values to the visualization. If the data values are not changing, the system should maintain those invariant values throughout the visualization. For example, if each bar's height is proportionate to the respective data point's value, the bars should remain the same height during the animation.

Figure 19-8 illustrates both of these principles in a more successful bar chart to pie chart animation. This chart shows a 1:1 correspondence between the drawn entity— the bar, the curved line, or the pie slice—and the underlying data. This assignment never changes: the bar furthest on the left ("A") becomes the leftmost pie slice (also "A"). The invariant is maintained by the lengths of the bars, which remain proportionate to the data values. While we do not illustrate it here, we follow similar principles in changing a bar chart into a line chart: the top-left corner of the bar represents the value, so as the bar shrinks into a line, that data point will remain rooted at the top-left corner of the bar.

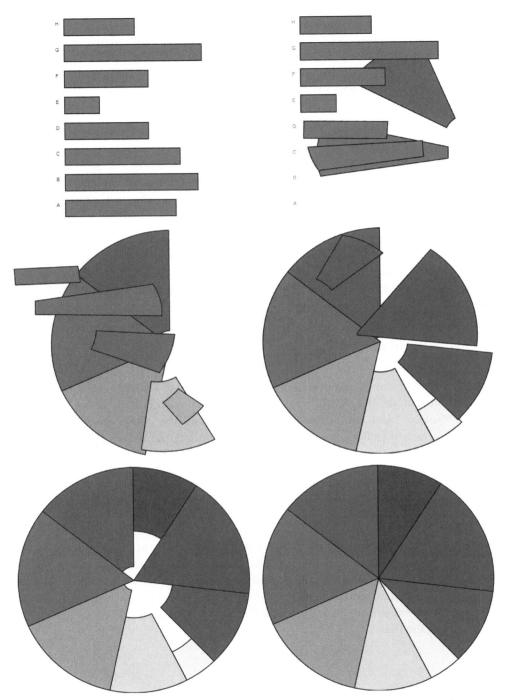

Figure 19-7. *Less successful bar chart to pie chart animation: long bars become long, fat wedges on the pie; short bars become short, skinny wedges; then all wedges grow to full length*

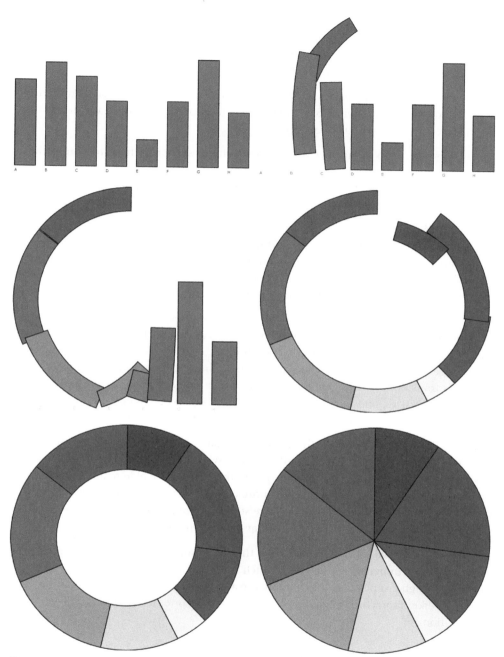

Figure 19-8. *Better bar chart to pie chart animation: the lengths of the bars are maintained as they are brought into the ring; the ring then fills to become a pie*

Another interesting case brings back the cartoon notion of *staging*. In GnuTellaVision we were able to recenter in a single motion, but in DynaVis it often makes more sense to break a transformation into two steps. For instance, in each of these examples, we ensure that we change only one thing at a time:

- To filter a dataset in a bar chart, we first remove bars we will not use, and then close ranks around them. To unfilter, we open space for the bars that will be added, and then grow the bars up.

- To grow or shrink a bar, such as when data changes, we may need to change the axes. Imagine growing a bar chart from the values $(1,2,3,4,5)$ to $(1,2,10,4,5)$—the y-axis should certainly grow to accommodate the new value. If we grow the bar first, it will extend off the screen; therefore, we must change the axis before changing the bar.

- When sorting a selection of bars, sorting them at once could cause all bars to pass through the center at once. This is confusing: it is hard to figure out which bar is which. By staggering the bars slightly, so that they start moving a small amount of time apart, we found that the sort operation was much clearer.

Staging is not always appropriate, though. In Heer and Robertson's report on the project (2007), they found that some staged animations are more challenging to follow. In particular, when resizing segments of a donut or pie chart, it was difficult to monitor the changes as the pie turned to accommodate the new sizes. DynaVis attempted to stage this transition by extracting segments to either an external or an internal ring, adjusting their sizes, and then collapsing them back into place. While this made the changes much more visible, it also added a layer of potentially confusing action.

Heer and Robertson collected both qualitative results—how much users liked the animations—and quantitative ones—finding out which animations allowed users to answer questions most accurately. They found that users were able to answer questions about changes in values over time more easily with the animations than without; furthermore, the animations that were staged but required only one transition did substantially better than the animations that required many transitions.

Even with these caveats, though, it is clear that these sorts of dynamics could potentially help users understand transitions much more easily: compared to a presenter flipping through a series of charts, forcing the audience to reorient after each slide, a DynaVis-like framework might allow users to remain oriented thoughout the presentation.

Principles of Animation

There have been several attempts to formulate principles for animation. Tversky, Morrison, and Bétrancourt (2002) offer two general guidelines at the end of their article: that visualizations should maintain *congruence* and *apprehension*. The former suggests that the marks on the screen must relate to the underlying data at all times. The latter suggests that the visualization should be easy to understand. The principles we have articulated fit into these categories. (Other, related guidelines have been suggested in Heer and Robertson's [2007] discussion of the DynaVis research, by Zongker and Salesin [2003] in their discussion of animation for slideshow presentations, and, with regard to graph drawing, by Freidrich and Eades [2002].)

The principles that we have discussed in this chapter are:

Staging

> It is disorienting to have too many things happen at once. If it is possible to change just one thing, do so. On the other hand, sometimes multiple changes need to happen at once; if so, they can be staged.

Compatibility

> A visualization that will be disrupted by animation will be difficult for users to track. For example, it is not disruptive to add another bar to a bar chart (the whole set can slide over), and it may not be disruptive to add another series to a bar chart. However, a squarified treemap is laid out greedily by size; growing a single rectangle will require every rectangle to move to a new location and will look confusing.

Necessary motion

> In particular, avoid unnecessary motion. This implies that we want to ensure that motion is significant—i.e., we should animate only what changes. In general, the image should always be understandable. As the DynaVis user tests showed, excess motion—even significant motion—can be confusing.

Meaningful motion

> The coordinate spaces and types of motion should remain meaningful. This also entails two points discussed earlier: *preserve valid mappings* and *maintain the invariant.*

Verifying that you've adhered to these principles can help you figure out whether an animation is headed in the right direction.

Conclusion: Animate or Not?

In this chapter, we have discussed the difference between presentation and exploration of data. We have also discussed the various layers of a visualization that might be altered, and some principles for making a visualization-safe animation.

So now you're staring at a visualization you're working on, and trying to decide whether to animate it or not. The question that this chapter has repeatedly asked is: what function does the animation serve? If it is meant to allow a user to smoothly transition between views, then it is likely to be helpful. On the other hand, if the user is meant to compare the "before" to the "after," the animation is less likely to be of use.

Users want to understand why a change is happening, and what is changing. If everything on the screen is going to move around, perhaps it would be better to simply switch atomically to a new image; this might spare the user the difficulty of trying to track the differences. Finally, animations mean that it can be more difficult to print out visualizations. Individual frames should be meaningful, so that users can capture and share those images. Animation imposes a burden of complexity on the user, and that complexity should pay off.

Further Reading

Here are a few animated data visualization projects that have some relevance to this discussion, which you may want to explore further:

- Many researchers begin playing with zooming and panning as basic operations in a visualization with Pad++, a zoomable architecture for laying out data in large spaces (Bederson and Hollan 1994).

- Scatterdice (Elmqvist, Dragicevic, and Fekete 2008) explores a way to transition between scatterplots by rotating through the third dimension.

- Visualizations of tree data structures include ConeTrees (Card, Robertson, and Mackinlay 1991), CandidTree (Lee et al. 2007), and Polyarchy (Robertson et al. 2002). Researchers have explored animation with treemaps by zooming (distorting) the treemap (Blanch and Lecolinet 2007) and moving through 3D space (Bladh, Carr, and Kljun 2005).

- Graph layout is often animated as the layout progresses; in the last 10 years, the graph-drawing community has turned to considering ways to update graphs in response to underlying data. In addition to the work cited earlier (Friedrich and Eades 2002), we note GraphAEL (Erten et al. 2003).

Acknowledgments

I am grateful to Professor Jeffrey Heer of Stanford University, both for his valuable conversations on these topics when we shared an office and for his predigested versions of these concepts, produced in his 2007 Infovis paper (Heer and Robertson 2007) and his Stanford course notes. Jeff also contributed a chapter to *Beautiful Data*, the sister volume to this book, discussing his work with *sense.us*. My thanks also for feedback and ideas for this paper from my colleagues, Steven Drucker, Roland Fernandez, Petra Isenberg, and George Robertson.

References

Bederson, B.B., and J.D. Hollan. 1994. "Pad++: A zooming graphical interface for exploring alternate interface physics." In *Proceedings of the 7th Annual ACM Symposium on User Interface Software and Technology*. New York: ACM Press.

Bladh, Thomas, David A. Carr, and Matjaz Kljun. 2005. "The effect of animated transitions on user navigation in 3D tree-maps." In *Proceedings of the Ninth International Conference on Information Visualization*. Washington, DC: IEEE Computer Society.

Blanch, Renaud, and Eric Lecolinet. 2007. "Browsing zoomable treemaps: Structure-aware multi-scale navigation techniques." *IEEE Transactions on Visualization and Computer Graphics* 13, no. 6: 1248–1253.

Card, Stuart K., George G. Robertson, and Jock D. Mackinlay. 1991. "The information visualizer, an information workspace." In *Proceedings of the SIGCHI Conference on Human Factors in Computing Systems*. New York: ACM Press.

Cavanagh, Patrick, and George Alvarez. 2005. "Tracking multiple targets with multifocal attention." *TICS* 9: 349–354.

Chang, Bay-Wei, and David Ungar. 1993. "Animation: From cartoons to the user interface." In *Proceedings of the 6th Annual ACM Symposium on User Interface Software and Technology*. New York: ACM Press.

Elmqvist, N., P. Dragicevic, and J.-D. Fekete. 2008. "Rolling the dice: Multidimensional visual exploration using scatterplot matrix navigation." *IEEE Transactions on Visualization and Computer Graphics* 14, no. 6: 1141–1148.

Erten, C., P.J. Harding, S.G. Kobourov, K. Wampler, and G. Yee. 2003. "GraphAEL: Graph animations with evolving layouts." In *Proceedings of the 11th International Symposium on Graph Drawing*. Springer-Verlag.

Fisher, Danyel A. 2007. "Hotmap: Looking at geographic attention." *IEEE Transactions on Visualization and Computer Graphics* 13, no. 6: 1184–1191.

Friedrich, C., and P. Eades. 2002. "Graph drawing in motion." *Journal of Graph Algorithms and Applications* 6, no. 3: 353–370.

Heer, Jeffrey, and George G. Robertson. 2007. "Animated transitions in statistical data graphics." *IEEE Transactions on Visualization and Computer Graphics* 13, no. 6: 1240–1247.

Hundhausen, Christopher D., Sarah A. Douglas, and John T. Stasko. 2002. "A meta-study of algorithm visualization effectiveness." *Journal of Visual Languages & Computing* 13, no. 3: 259–290.

Johnson, Ollie, and Frank Thomas. 1987. *The Illusion of Life*. New York: Disney Editions.

Lasseter, John. 1987. "Principles of traditional animation applied to 3D computer animation." In *Proceedings of the 14th Annual Conference on Computer Graphics and Interactive Techniques*. New York: ACM Press.

Lee, Bongshin, George G. Robertson, Mary Czerwinski, and Cynthia Sims Parr. 2007. "CandidTree: Visualizing structural uncertainty in similar hierarchies." *Information Visualization* 6: 233–246.

Michotte, A. 1963. *The Perception of Causality*. Oxford: Basic Books.

Robertson, George, Kim Cameron, Mary Czerwinski, and Daniel Robbins. 2002. "Polyarchy visualization: Visualizing multiple intersecting hierarchies." In *Proceedings of the SIGCHI Conference on Human Factors in Computing Systems*. New York: ACM Press.

Robertson, George, Roland Fernandez, Danyel Fisher, Bongshin Lee, and John Stasko. 2008. "Effectiveness of animation in trend visualization." *IEEE Transactions on Visualization and Computer Graphics* 14, no. 6: 1325–1332.

Tversky, Barbara, Julie B. Morrison, and Mireille Bétrancourt. 2002. "Animation: Can it facilitate?" *International Journal of Human-Computer Studies* 57: 247–262.

Yee, Ka-Ping, Danyel Fisher, Rachna Dhamija, and Marti A. Hearst. 2001. "Animated exploration of dynamic graphs with radial layout." In *Proceedings of the IEEE Symposium on Information Visualization*. Washington, DC: IEEE Computer Society.

Zongker, Douglas E., and David H. Salesin. 2003. "On creating animated presentations." In *Proceedings of the 2003 ACM SIGGRAPH/Eurographics Symposium on Computer Animation*. New York: ACM Press.

## CHAPTER TWENTY

Visualization: Indexed.

Jessica Hagy

Visualization: It's an Elephant.

VISUALIZATION. To one person, it's charts and graphs and ROI. To another, it's illustration and colorful metaphor and gallery openings. To a third, it's that wonderfully redundant compound word: infographics. *Visualization.* It's a term that's been pulled and yanked like so much conceptual taffy. It's like that old tale of three blindfolded men who are asked to describe an elephant. One touches the elephant's tail and says, "An elephant is like a rope." Another touches the elephant's leg and says, "An elephant is like a tree trunk." The third man touches the elephant's trunk and says, "An elephant is like a snake." None of them is completely wrong, but none is completely right, because none of them can see the entire animal (Figure 20-1).

Visualization is only something (and everything) you can see. It's both the entire mosaic and a single, sparkling tessera. It's not just graphs. It's not just visual metaphors. It's not just graphic design in service instead of bullet points. It's not just sketching out ideas. It's not just data analysis. Those are just slivers of the larger concept.

Really good, beautiful, powerful visualization—visualization that touches both the mind and the heart—isn't just about an image, a snapshot, or a glance through a windowpane (Figure 20-2). Powerful visualization passes the elephant test: it's practically impossible to describe, but instantly recognizable. This chapter will describe various aspects of that elephant. Together, they'll help to paint a clear picture of what visualization really is, from tusk to toe.

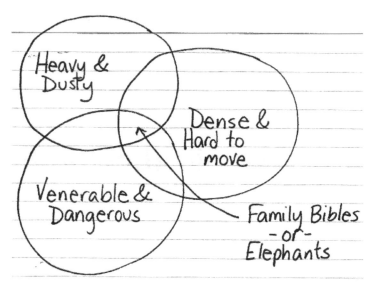

Figure 20-1. *There's always more to it*

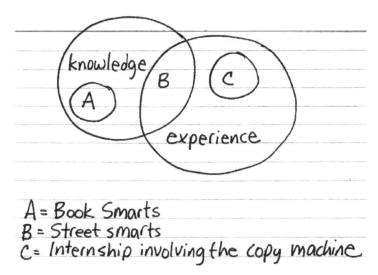

A = Book Smarts
B = Street smarts
C = Internship involving the copy machine

Figure 20-2. *Knowing and doing go hand in hand*

Visualization: It's Art.

There's an image, a message in it. People stare at it and debate it. Framers are employed for another day because of it. Quality can be subjective, and aesthetics are always debatable—but the intrinsic artistry is evident. Like pornography, art is something you know when you see it, and no sooner (Figure 20-3). And visualization is widely perceived to be an art.

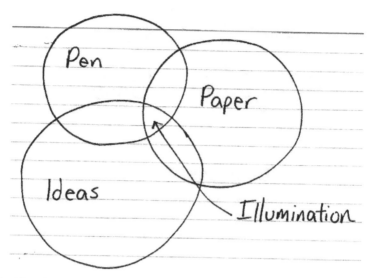

Figure 20-3. *Visualizing aha moments*

Visualization practitioners often have an air of creativity about them: they draw or paint or wear glasses with thick, black frames. Of course, as soon as something is branded as an artistic endeavor, the barriers to entry rise up around it. Those who believe they can't draw and those who would never assign themselves the label of "creative" shy away from visualization for this reason. And that's too bad—because you don't have to be a Rembrandt to have an idea that can be understood by scrawling a stick figure or two.

The beauty inherent in visualization (it can be argued) is the idea behind the image: the concept conveyed by the lines and shapes that your rods and cones observe. Just as anyone with a lump of clay can technically sculpt, anyone with an idea that can be conveyed visually can technically create a visualization (Figure 20-4). The quality of the sketch or the visualization will always be debatable. The quality of any piece of art, and of any image, will always be debatable.

Visualization, eye of the beholder—you get the idea.

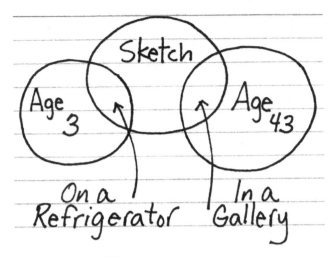

Figure 20-4. *Don't outgrow your skills*

Visualization: It's Business.

There's this little program out there—you may have heard about it. It's cheap, it's pretty much universal, and it has turned the idea of the visual aid into a tool of khaki-loving middle managers. It's called PowerPoint, and it, single-handedly, has transported visualization into the land of business (Figure 20-5).

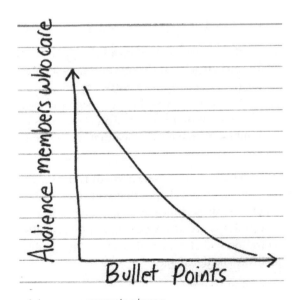

Figure 20-5. *Power point = an oxymoronic phrase*

There's no denying it: visuals are compelling. Want someone to ignore your prose? Make sure to include a lot of pictures, or graphs if you took math in college. When making a presentation to a board of directors, a prospective client, or for a midterm grade in an MBA class, going without PowerPoint is seen as quaint at best and ill-prepared at worst (Figure 20-6). Why? Because visualization is an excellent tool of persuasion. And persuasion is just another word for sales.

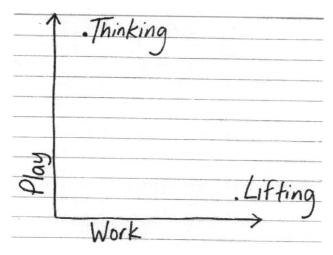

Figure 20-6. *Ideas can work for you*

Mergers. Acquisitions. Negotiations. Advertising. Propaganda. Business communication is being conveyed visually every day. Here's the back of my napkin. Here's my whiteboard. Here's the doodle of my exit strategy that I drew in that last four-hour meeting.

Seeing is believing. And believing—well, when people believe in something, they buy into it. How do you think corporate headquarters, political dynasties, and mega-churches get built?

Visualization: It's Timeless.

Those famous cave paintings in France weren't to-do lists, sentences, words, or even letter forms. They were images. Thousands of years ago, hieroglyphics held images in each character. Written Chinese does the same today. We understand smiles before we understand words. As powerful as language is, it's not as instinctive or primal as visualization (Figure 20-7).

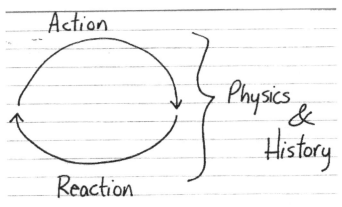

Figure 20-7. *Same old story, different authors*

When we see a photograph or a painting, or the map on the weatherman's green screen, we learn a lot more a lot faster than we would if such an image were described in words. We can listen to an hour-long description of abject poverty, or we can look at an image of a vulture hovering near an emaciated child for a fraction of a second. No matter how compelling the verbal argument is, the image shares its story faster. While we may have advanced as societies to employ complex vocabularies and languages packed with idioms and metaphors and grammars that vicious nuns teach us as children, we are still able to communicate without our languages—with only images (Figure 20-8).

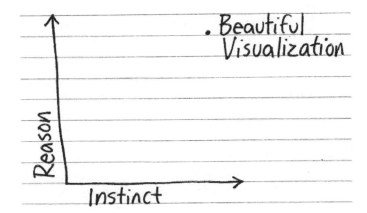

Figure 20-8. *To see is to know*

Just imagine: cave paintings and shapes scratched in ancient dirt. Before punditry. Before poetry. Before PowerPoint.

Visualization: It's Right Now.

What says more: a name or a logo? How do people recognize you: your avatar or your resume? What's the more precious piece of real estate: a famous URL or a lot in a famous zip code? Today, logos tell epic stories. Screen names equal human identities. Web addresses fund mansion renovations and the purchase of ranches, islands, and city blocks.

More than ever, we are swimming in information. We are pickling in data. More information than any human world has ever seen before or could ever hope to comprehend is generated every day (Figure 20-9). And so we turn to visualization as a means to collect, condense, and convey this information.

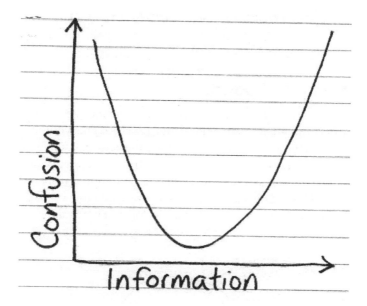

Figure 20-9. *Water, water, everywhere*

Visuals crunch data. They take reams of chunky, unwieldy, black and white spreadsheets and compact them into sleek, colorful charts. Visuals reveal patterns in vast amounts of data; they take complex and difficult-to-understand theories and elegantly explain them (Figure 20-10). Imagine data points as molecules of ice. Visualizations are the resulting snowflakes: gorgeous and organic arrangements of many smaller pieces of information.

When we want to make sense of the sea of information around us, we make visualizations. It's the age of information. And thus, one could argue that it's the age of visualization, too.

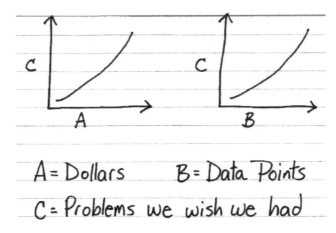

$A = Dollars \quad B = Data \, Points$
$C = Problems \; we \; wish \; we \; had$

Figure 20-10. *Use either to get what you need*

Visualization: It's Coded.

Letters represent sounds. Words represent ideas. We combine and weave our sentences to tell stories. The hood ornament on your car represents your tax bracket. Your wrinkles speak to your age. We communicate in codes—aural, visual, tactile, and social. Even our DNA is a code—we are built from the ground up to communicate with representational bits of data (Figure 20-11). Visualization is just another form of coded communication, with the axes of graphs as shorthand for correlation, and with characters in editorial cartoons standing in for ideologies. Photographs and paintings represent history.

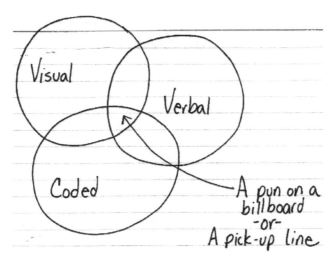

Figure 20-11. *Wink wink, nudge nudge*

As visualization becomes a larger area of inquiry—in ivory towers, in art studios, and on message boards—the idea of semiotics will be raised more frequently. As we look closer at signs and symbols, we'll see that we communicate with visualizations almost as much as we speak in words. From a single finger raised to the driver who just ran that red light to hearts drawn on love notes to the use of increasingly trite emoticons, we use symbols to express ourselves.

Metaphors. Idioms. Inside jokes (or literary allusions, if you're an English major). Our communications involve many layers of symbolism, many codes that we interpret in every conversation. Visualizations are another way to represent ideas; another not-so-secret code. The clearer the visualization is, the more people there are who can crack that code.

Gang tattoos, Rorschach tests, pieces of art with multiple interpretations—these are just a few of the many visualizations that hold hidden (and sometimes, profound) meanings (Figure 20-12).

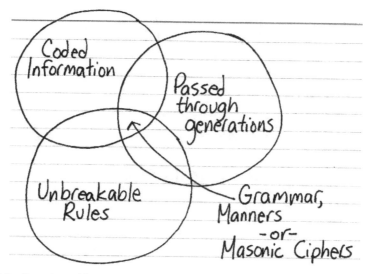

Figure 20-12. *Secrets and/or societies*

Visualization: It's Clear.

One of the beauties often attributed to visualization is simplicity. Pure clarity! Marvelous obviousness! Splendid simplicity! An image can set the tone for a presentation, a feature article, an annual report. We look. We see. We understand. Between first glance and "Oh, I get it," just a fraction of a second passes.

We don't always have time to dissect meanings or read a 10-page summary. We want to look at a chart, see year-over-year results, and move on. Images are incredibly good at conveying information quickly. Clarity allows us to understand and carry on. Ambiguity takes time to ponder—time that we just don't have.

We learn more about a person in the first 10 seconds of meeting him than hours of Google-stalking could have ever told us. We judge books by covers and real estate by curb appeal. We see a picture of the Statue of Liberty with a noose around her neck and we understand that injustice is occurring. We see devil horns drawn on a poster of the jock running for class president and we understand that someone dislikes him. It's clear what visuals convey (Figure 20-13). But just because the message is clear, it might not always be true.

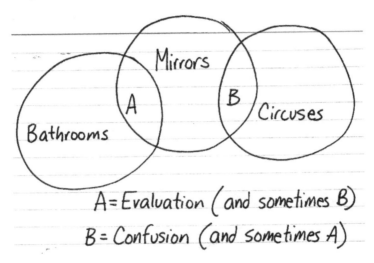

Figure 20-13. *It's all context*

We don't trust news from biased sources. When an offer sounds amazing, we know that the fine print will be dense and long and written against us. Truth in advertising is a myth. Remember this when gazing upon a beautiful visual. Its message may be clear and obvious, but the motivations behind it may take more time to see (Figure 20-14).

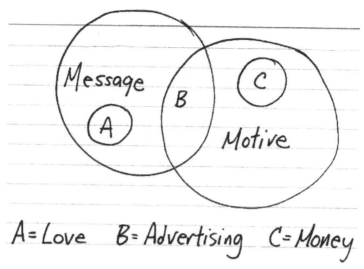

Figure 20-14. *Ask why you are seeing what's in front of you*

Visualization: It's Learnable.

The display of information, in any and all forms, is open to everyone to both create and consume. From the way you wear your hair to the color of your coat, you are sending visual signals and conveying visual information. Anyone can pick up a pen and draw a line on the wall or a sheet of paper. Pixels can likewise be rearranged to express the thoughts of anyone with access to a computer.

You don't have to speak Italian to appreciate the art of Michelangelo. Anyone can visit the Louvre and leave inspired. Likewise, an infant can recognize human faces and expressions without knowing so much as a word.

And just like learning to read and to communicate with words, it's possible through practice to become a skilled visual communicator. *Drawing* is the ability to translate scenes onto paper—making a direct translation. *Visualization* is the ability to put ideas onto paper—taking data and distilling it into a concept. Don't confuse the two. The thinking process is different, even if a pen and paper unite the two skills. Ideas (concepts, theories, equations, opinions, processes) behave differently than a still life painting of a bowl of fruit (Figure 20-15).

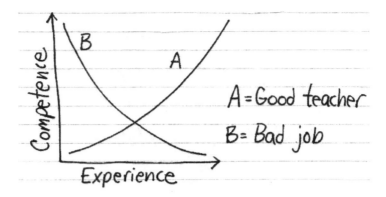

Figure 20-15. *Know more, do more*

Sketching symbols and metaphors can be done in a sloppy, messy fashion, and still be powerful and clear. Remember that the next time you trace a heart in the steam on a windowpane (Figure 20-16).

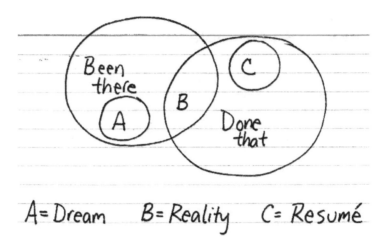

Figure 20-16. *You are what you do*

Visualization: It's a Buzzword.

So, is this a meme (Figure 20-17)? Is visualization merely the latest turn of phrase that's sweeping the feature pages of business magazines, RFPs, and course syllabi? Is it another word that marketers are batting around to sound smart? Or is it less of a fad, and more of a response to our current data-saturated environment?

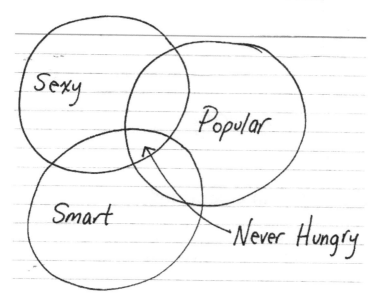

Figure 20-17. *Welcome to the Internet*

Visualization is getting a lot of attention: it helps us cope with information overload, saves us time, and reaches us on an innate level. Well-crafted visualizations are compelling and beautiful to look at and to intellectually enjoy. And with software at the disposal of so many, there has never been an easier time to turn ideas into images. And so it seems that the popularity of visualization is a function of necessity: the more data we have to sift through, the easier it is to convert that data to images, the easier it is to juxtapose images with text, the more we want to persuade others and promote ourselves, the more visualizations we'll see all around us.

The word is popular. The idea is popular. The applications are popular. Visualization helps us communicate. It enables and fosters connections. And as long as those last two statements are true, we can but hope that visualization is popular like the Beatles, and not the Monkees (Figure 20-18).

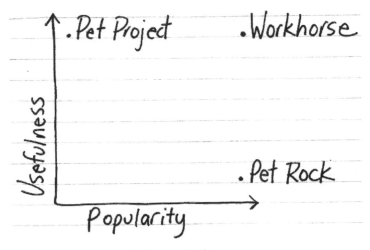

Figure 20-18. *Are you joining a revolution or a fad?*

Visualization: It's an Opportunity.

If you want to connect, compel, and communicate, you need to use visuals. You can combine art and business. You can reach people quickly, powerfully, and emotionally with visuals. Even if you don't think of yourself as creative, or as an artist, you can be a visualizer (Figure 20-19).

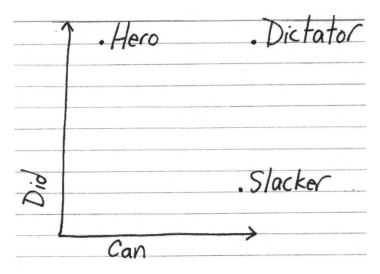

Figure 20-19. *Your excuses aren't valid*

Just as writers read to sculpt their skill, visualizers look. They stare with intensity and peer into places others would rather ignore. They look not only at images, but also at events. They gawk at causes and effects and motives and means. And sometimes, they close their eyes and wonder how to illustrate the universe in a Word document, or the depth of their feelings in an email, or the scope of their business in a single slide (Figure 20-20).

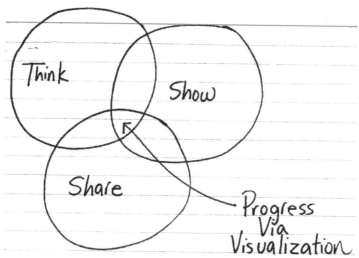

Figure 20-20. *Look closer and go further*

Observation is the first step toward visualization, and you are doing it at this very minute. If you can think it, you can visualize it. If you can visualize it, you can share it. And if you can share it, you can change the world.

But first: look around you. You're looking at opportunity.

Contributors

Dennis Adderton is an electrical engineer with a background in the design of instrumentation for scientific research. He is currently employed as research engineer on the AlloSphere project for the University of California, Santa Barbara, and studies media arts under Dr. JoAnn Kuchera-Morin.

Basak Alper is a PhD candidate in the Media Arts and Technology program at the University of California, Santa Barbara. She has been working on computer graphics and visualization for the past five years. Her recent research efforts are in human-centered aspects of multimodal visualizations in virtual reality environments.

Nick Bilton is the lead technology writer for the *New York Times* Bits Blog. He has a background in design, user interfaces, journalism, hardware hacking, documentary film, and programming. He previously worked as a researcher in the Times Research & Development Labs, looking at the media landscape 2–10 years out. In addition to working at the *Times*, Nick helped co-found NYCResistor, a hardware hacker space in Brooklyn, New York. He is also an adjunct professor at NYU in the Interactive Telecommunications program.

Michael Driscoll fell in love with with data visualization over a decade ago as a software engineer for the Human Genome Project. He is the founder and principal data scientist at Dataspora, an analytics consultancy in San Francisco.

Jonathan Feinberg is a computer programmer who lives in Medford, Massachusetts, with his wife and two sons. Please write to him at *jdf@pobox.com*, especially if you know of any Boston-area Pad Thai that can go up against the Thai Café in Greenpoint, Brooklyn.

Danyel Fisher is a researcher at Microsoft Research's VIBE (Visualization and Interaction) team. His research interests center on information visualization and online collaboration, and the ways that visualizations can be used together. Danyel received his PhD from the University of California, Irvine, in 2004. His past research has reflected social computing activity, visualized email messages and traffic, and colored in maps and geographical software. He is a co-author of the JUNG graph-drawing package; his current projects can be found at *http://research.microsoft.com/~danyelf*.

Jessica Hagy is a writer, speaker, and consultant who boils soupy, complex ideas into tasty visual sauces for companies in need of clarity. She's the author of acclaimed site *thisisindexed.com*, and her work has appeared in the *New York Times*, the BBC Magazine Online, *Paste*, *Golf Digest*, *Redbook*, *New York Magazine*, the *National Post* of Canada, the *Guardian*, *Time*, and many other old and new media outlets.

Todd Holloway can't get enough of information visualization, information retrieval, machine learning, data mining, the science of networks, and artificial intelligence. He is a Grinnell College and Indiana University alumnus.

Noah Iliinsky has spent the last several years thinking about effective approaches to creating diagrams and other types of information visualization. He also works in interface and interaction design, all from a functional and user-centered perspective. Before becoming a designer, he was a programmer for several years. He has a master's in technical communication from the University of Washington, and a bachelor's in physics from Reed College. He blogs at *http://ComplexDiagrams.com*.

Eddie Jabbour is co-founder and creative director of KICK Design in New York City. For over 20 years, KICK Design has partnered with the world's most prestigious brand owners to create excitement and innovation through visual impact.

Haru Ji is a sculptor, trans-artist, and researcher exploring the subject of life in art through artificial life world-making as computational art. She is currently a PhD candidate in media arts and technology at the University of California, Santa Barbara, and a researcher in the AlloSphere Group at the California NanoSystems Institute. She has exhibited computational installations, digital sculptures, virtual architecture, video installations, sculptural objects, and 3D animations at exhibitions and art festivals worldwide including ISEA, EvoWorkshops, and SIGGRAPH, with corresponding publications. She forms one-half of the collaborative research project and immersive ecosystem "Artificial Nature," exploring the expansion of media art toward art-as-it-could-be. URL: *http://haru.name*.

Valdean Klump lives in San Francisco, California, and is a writer at Google Creative Lab.

Aaron Koblin is an artist from San Francisco, California, who is well known for such data visualization projects as the Sheep Market, Ten Thousand Cents, and Radiohead's "House of Cards" music video. He is currently technology lead at Google Creative Lab.

Robert Kosara is an assistant professor of computer science at the University of North Carolina, Charlotte. His research interests include the visualization of categorical data, the visual communication of data, and theoretical foundations of visualization. Robert runs the website *http://EagerEyes.org.*

Valdis Krebs is chief scientist at Orgnet.com in Cleveland, Ohio. Orgnet.com provides social network analysis software and services for organizations, communities, and their consultants.

Dr. JoAnn Kuchera-Morin is a composer, professor of media arts and technology and music, and a researcher in multimodal media systems, content, and facilities design. As a leader in the field of digital media for over 25 years, she created, designed, and is developing a digital media center within the California Nanosystems Institute at the University of California, Santa Barbara, in which the culmination of her design is the Allosphere Research Laboratory, a three-story metal sphere inside an echo-free cube, designed for immersive, interactive scientific and artistic investigation of multidimensional data sets. She serves as director of the Allosphere Research Facility.

Andrew Odewahn is the director of business development at O'Reilly Media, where he helps companies engage with O'Reilly's passionate audience of alpha geeks. He is author of two books on database development, founder of tagcaster.com, graduate of NYU's Stern School of Business, and Appalachian Trail thru-hiker.

Anders Persson MD, PhD, is an associate professor and director for the Center for Medical Image Science and Visualization (CMIV; *http://www.cmiv.liu.se*) at Linköping University in Sweden. The center conducts focused front-line research within multidisciplinary projects providing solutions to tomorrow's clinical issues. The mission is to develop future methods and tools for image analysis and visualization for applications within health care and medical research.

Adam Perer, PhD, is a research scientist at IBM Research Haifa in Israel. His research interests include designing new visualization techniques to help people make sense of complex data. More information about his work can be found at his web page, *http://perer.org/.*

Lance Putnam is a composer and researcher investigating the relationships between frequency and space in the context of computer-generated sound and graphics. He is currently a PhD candidate in the Media Arts and Technology program at the University of California, Santa Barbara. He holds a BS in electrical and computer engineering from the University of Wisconsin, Madison, and an MA in electronic music and sound design from UCSB. He was selected as one of eight international students to present his research in media signal processing at the 2007 Emerging Leaders in Multimedia

Workshop at the IBM T. J. Watson Research Center in New York. His work, S Phase, has been shown at the 2008 International Computer Music Conference in Belfast, Northern Ireland, and the 2009 Traiettorie Festival in Parma, Italy.

Maximilian Schich is an art historian working as DFG visiting research scientist at BarabásiLab—Center for Complex Network Research at Northeastern University in Boston, where he collaborates with network scientists, studying complex networks in art history and archaeology. Maximilian obtained his PhD in 2007, and has over a decade of consulting experience, working with network data in art research, brokering within the tetrahedron of project partners, users, programmers, and customers. He worked several years with Projekt Dyabola as well as within Bibliotheca Hertziana (Max-Planck Institute for Art History), the Munich Glyptothek, and Zentralinstitut für Kunstgeschichte. You can find more of his work at *http://www.schich.info*.

Matthias Shapiro is a software designer and information visualization hobbyist based out of Salt Lake City, Utah. He creates most of his visualizations in Silverlight and moonlights as an independent evangelist for information visualization, speaking about the importance of visualization to senators, CNN anchors, Microsoft conference attendees, and anyone who is not wise enough to flee from his line of sight.

Julie Steele is an editor at O'Reilly Media interested in connecting people and ideas. She finds beauty in discovering new ways to understand complex systems, and so enjoys topics related to organizing, storing, and visualizing data. She holds a master's degree in political science (international relations) from Rutgers University and is developing Gov 2.0 content for O'Reilly as that space continues to grow. Julie also works with topics related to Python, PHP, and SQL, and is co-founder of a NYC group of not-yet-programmers learning Python.

Moritz Stefaner is a researcher and freelance practitioner on the crossroads of design and information visualization. His main interest is how information visualization and data mining can help us in organizing and discovering information. He holds degrees in cognitive science and interface design. His work has been exhibited at SIGGRAPH and Ars Electronica. Recently, he was nominated for the Design Award of the Federal Republic of Germany 2010. His work can be found at *http://moritz.stefaner.eu* and *http://well-formed-data.net*.

Jer Thorp is an artist and educator from Vancouver, Canada. A former geneticist, his digital art practice explores the many-folded boundaries between science and art. Recently, his work has been featured by the *New York Times*, the *Guardian*, and the Canadian Broacasting Company. Thorp's award-winning software-based work has been exhibited in Europe, Asia, North America, South America, Australia, and all over the Web. Jer is a contributing editor for *Wired UK*.

Fernanda Viégas and Martin Wattenberg are the founders of Flowing Media, Inc., a visualization design studio located in Cambridge, Massachusetts. The two became a team in 2003 when they decided to visualize Wikipedia, leading to the history flow project described in Chapter 11. Before founding Flowing Media, they led IBM's Visual Communication Lab, where they explored the power of visualization as a mass medium and the social forms of data analysis it enables.

Viégas is known for her pioneering work on depicting chat histories and email. Wattenberg's visualizations of the stock market and baby names are considered Internet classics. Viégas and Wattenberg are also known for their visualization-based artwork, which has been exhibited in venues such as the Museum of Modern Art in New York, London Institute of Contemporary Arts, and the Whitney Museum of American Art.

Graham Wakefield is exploring open-ended autonomy in computational art by drawing inspiration from biological systems and bio-inspired philosophy. He is a PhD candidate in media arts and technology at the University of California, Santa Barbara, and holds both a master's of music in composition from Goldsmiths College, University of London, and a BA in philosophy from the University of Warwick. In addition to being a researcher at the CNSI AlloSphere (AlloBrain, Cosm, LuaAV), he is a software developer for Cycling '74 (Max/MSP/Jitter), and a lecturer at the Southern California Institute for Architecture (SCI-Arc). His works and publications have been performed, exhibited, and presented at international events including SIGGRAPH, ICMC, and ISEA.

Martin Wattenberg and Fernanda Viégas are the founders of Flowing Media, Inc. See above.

Michael Young is a creative technologist in the Research & Development group of the New York Times Company. He leads a small team of technologists tasked with proto-typing and exploring the future of content consumption across multiple platforms and devices. More of his work can be found at *http://81nassau.com*.

Index

Numbers

2D graphics, 46
3D animated framework, 332
24-hour time-lapse video, 285–286
    displaying, 287
    math for rendering, 286
    semi-automating, 286
2008 presidential election results map,
    11–13, 17–18

A

Abortion (Wikipedia), 184–185
Abramoff, Jack, 133
Achieva 1.5T scanner, 316
achieving beauty, 6–10
Adderton, Dennis, 369
    Coherent Precession of Electron Spin,
      307–308
    Immersed in Unfolding Complex
      Systems, 291–310
adjacency matrix, 235, 246
Adobe Illustrator, 33

Adobe Photoshop, 26, 33
advanced computational layout
    algorithms, 157
aggregation of individual values, 198, 200
Aircraft Situation Display to Industry
    (ASDI) feed, 94
Akaka, Daniel, 138
Aldroandi, Ulisse, 238
algorithm animation, 333
Allobrain, 296–298
    inside, 297
AlloSphere, 291–293, 299, 300, 309
    full-scale photo, 292
    virtual real-scale model, 292
Alper, Basak, 369
    Hydrogen Bond, 300–303
    Immersed in Unfolding Complex
      Systems, 291–310
alphaWorks website, 58
Amazon.com, 143
    also bought books, 112
    community-of-interest maps, 114
    InFlow 3.1, 116

context
  map mapping, 88
  question, visual data, and context,
    16–18
contributions from a single author over
    time, 183
conventions, using thoughtfully, 10
coordinate motion, 343
Cortines, Ramon, 266
cosine similarity, 151
country maps, 32–33
Cranston, Alan, 138
crime rates map, 22–23
criminal investigations, 312
cross-sectional imaging techniques, 312
cross-tabulation, 199–204
CSI guys, 316
CT scans, 316
  burned person, 326
  child who has been shot, 317
  DSCT (dual source CT), 316
  dual energy CT (DECT), 318–319
  full-body dual source CT (DSCT) scan,
    316
  heart with knife, 313
  knife penetrating face, 313
  lead fragments from a shotgun, 314
  MRI (see MRI)
  SOMATOM Definition Flash scanner,
    316
  visualized interactively, 314
cues, preattentively processed, 61, 63
cumulative IN- and OUT-degree
    distribution, 247–249
curated databases in Art History and
    Archaeology, 227
Cytoscape, 231, 235, 254

D

D'Amato, Alfonse, 138
Daniels, Dieter, 225

data
  changing, 344
  filtering, 343
  gathering, 19–20, 26
  grouping, 29–30
  reordering, 343
  smaller datasets and color, 22
  sorting, 26–28
    technical version, 28–29
database model, 200–202
databases as networks, 230–231
  a priori definitions of node and link
    types, 231
  network representation, 231
  possible node types, 230
  uncovering hidden structures, 231
data-formatting rules, 230
Data.gov, 19
data mining and visualizing social
    patterns, 103–122
  Amazon.com (see Amazon.com)
  categories of outcomes, 119
  deriving network structures, 104
  different data-mining algorithms, 110
  discovery matrix for social network
    analysis, 120
  key to understanding dynamics of
    networks, 112
  Pareto 80/20 rule, 122
  social graphs, 103–111
    Amazon.com purchasing data, 111–
      121
    emergent social graph of women
      based on common attendance at
      social events, 109
    Southern Women dataset, 104–111
data mining strategies, 159
data model
  convention, 230
  definition plus emergence, 231–254
data-processing rules, 230
data sources, 19
Dataspora labs, 67

Replica, 234
Republicans' "Contract with America", 131
research-oriented contexts, 8
research, visuals intended to aid, 8
Resolution RC-20, 167
RGB color space, 65
ribbons, 196–198
Roberts, Charlie
    Allobrain, 296–298
      Hydrogen Atom, 303–305
      Hydrogen Bond, 300–303
Robertson, George, 350
Rocky Horror Picture Show, 153
Roden, Ted "Chevy's", 290
romunculus, 238
Rorschach tests, 361
Rosling, Hans, 330, 333, 334, 337
Roth, William, 138
R programming language, 65–68
Rules for Radicals, 121
Rwanda, 260–265

S

Sageman, Marc, 169
Salavon, Jason, 187
Salomon, George, 70, 75, 83
    1958 New York City subway map, 70
Sankey diagram, 204
Saxl, Fritz, 227
scalability, 149
scalable vector graphics (SVG), 33
scale-free network, 113
Scatterdice, 350
scatterplots, 1
    287 pitches thrown by the major
        league pitcher Oscar Villarreal in
        2008, 59–60
    adding color to data, 62–63
    animated, 333–337
      testing, 335–337
    using small multiples on canvas, 61–62
    varying plotting symbols, 60–61

schematic of history flow's visualization
    mechanism, 179
Schich, Maximilian, 372
    Revealing Matrices, 227–254
science fiction genre, 153
scientific visualization, 331
SciFoo09, 250
Seadragon, 148
search and discovery, 143–156
    creating your own visualizations, 156
    Netflix Prize, 151–155
      cluster of action movies, 155
      cluster of "family-friendly" movies,
        154
      cluster of "feel-good" movies, 155
      cluster of movies with similar
        humor, 154
      cluster of sci-fi movies, 153
      cosine similarity, 151
      labeling, 152
      latent attributes, 153–156
      preference similarity, 151
    Perl, 156
    product recommendations, 143
    visualization technique, 144
      advantages and disadvantages of,
        149–151
    web search engines, 143
    YELLOWPAGES.COM, 143, 145–151
      analyzing queries, 146
      categorical similarity, 146
      clusters of queries, 148, 149
      final visualization, 147–149
      precise comparisons, 150
      query logs, 145–146
      scalability, 149
      Top 4600 queries, 147
search engine indexes, 229
Segaran, Toby, xi, 111, 230, 253
semantic context of information, 224
Semantic Web, 112, 114, 227
    matrices, 247

X

Colophon

The cover fonts are Akzidenz Grotesk and Orator. The text font is Adobe's
Meridien; the heading font is Akzidenz Grotesk; and the code font is LucasFont's
TheSansMonoCondensed.

Get even more for your money.

Join the O'Reilly Community, and register the O'Reilly books you own. It's free, and you'll get:

- $4.99 ebook upgrade offer
- 40% upgrade offer on O'Reilly print books
- Membership discounts on books and events
- Free lifetime updates to ebooks and videos
- Multiple ebook formats, DRM FREE
- Participation in the O'Reilly community
- Newsletters
- Account management
- 100% Satisfaction Guarantee

Signing up is easy:

1. **Go to: oreilly.com/go/register**
2. **Create an O'Reilly login.**
3. **Provide your address.**
4. **Register your books.**

Note: English-language books only

To order books online:
oreilly.com/store

For questions about products or an order:
orders@oreilly.com

To sign up to get topic-specific email announcements and/or news about upcoming books, conferences, special offers, and new technologies:
elists@oreilly.com

For technical questions about book content:
booktech@oreilly.com

To submit new book proposals to our editors:
proposals@oreilly.com

O'Reilly books are available in multiple DRM-free ebook formats. For more information:
oreilly.com/ebooks

O'REILLY®

Spreading the knowledge of innovators | oreilly.com

Have it your way.

Lightning Source UK Ltd.
Milton Keynes UK
UKOW07f1929300315

248760UK00007B/29/P